P9-EMK-684

FROMMER'S EasyGuide to
PARIS 2018

5th Edition

By Anna Brooke
& Margie Rynn

FROMMER'S STAR RATINGS SYSTEM

Every hotel, restaurant, and attraction listed in this guide has been ranked for quality and value. Here's what the stars mean:

★ Recommended
★★ Highly Recommended
★★★ A must! Don't miss!

AN IMPORTANT NOTE

The world is a dynamic place. Hotels change ownership, restaurants hike their prices, museums alter their opening hours, and buses and trains change their routings. And all of this can occur in the several months after our authors have visited, inspected, and written about these hotels, restaurants, museums, and transportation services. Though we have made valiant efforts to keep all our information fresh and up-to-date, some few changes can inevitably occur in the periods before a revised edition of this guidebook is published. So please bear with us if a tiny number of the details in this book have changed. Please also note that we have no responsibility or liability for any inaccuracy or errors or omissions, or for inconvenience, loss, damage, or expenses suffered by anyone as a result of assertions in this guide.

Underground tunnels lead to the Arc de Triomphe (p. 156) so that tourists don't risk their lives crossing the always-clogged traffic circle to get a close-up view.

CONTENTS

1 THE BEST OF PARIS 1

2 PARIS IN CONTEXT 10

The Making of Paris 10
Paris Today 21

3 SUGGESTED ITINERARIES & NEIGHBORHOODS 23

Iconic Paris in 1 Day 23
Iconic Paris in 2 Days 27
Iconic Paris in 3 Days 29
An Itinerary for Families 30
Paris for Romantics 31
City Layout 33
Neighborhoods in Brief 34

4 WHERE TO STAY 43

What to Expect 43
Practical Matters 45
The Right Bank 46
The Left Bank 64
Alternative Lodgings 77

5 WHERE TO DINE 80

Practical Matters 81
The Right Bank 82
The Left Bank 108
The Top Tearooms 125
The Top Cafes 126

6 EXPLORING PARIS 129

The Right Bank 129
The Left Bank 172
Organized Tours & Classes 190
Especially for Kids 193
Active Paris 195

7 WALKING TOURS OF PARIS 200

Walking Tour 1: Montmarte 200
Walking Tour 2: The Marais 206

8 SHOPPING 215

Shopping by Area 215
Department Stores 219
Markets: Food & Flea 221
Recommended Stores 223

9 ENTERTAINMENT & NIGHTLIFE 235

Theater 236
Landmark Multiuse Venues 237
Opera & Classical Music 238
Cabaret 239
Movies 242
Live Rock, Jazz & More 243
The Bar Scene 247
Dance Clubs 250
The Gay & Lesbian Scene 252
Spectator Sports 253

10 DAY TRIPS FROM PARIS 255

Versailles 255
Chartres 263
Giverny 266
Vaux-le-Vicomte 269
Fontainebleau 271
Disneyland Paris 274

11 PLANNING YOUR TRIP TO PARIS 277

12 USEFUL TERMS & PHRASES 295

INDEX 302

MAP LIST 310

ABOUT THE AUTHORS 313

View from the Arc de Triomphe.

A LOOK AT PARIS

Writers and poets have extolled the charms of Paris for centuries, and for good reason: It's one of the most seductively beautiful cities in the world, with leafy boulevards stretching from one grand monument to another, magnificent churches, and graceful squares. The Seine River cuts a fetching swath between the city's Left and Right banks. Gardens like the Tuileries and Luxembourg are meticulously laid out, with spraying fountains and elegant statuary. But Paris is not just a pretty face; it's full of historical landmarks and world-class art. Cafe culture is state of the art here, and the local tribe is famously fashionable. The surrounding countryside is equally beautiful, home to storied chateaux like Versailles and Fontainebleau. It's all a feast for the eyes and senses—so here are a few reasons to visit Paris.

Completed in 1345, the Cathédrale de Notre-Dame (p. 129) sits on the small Ile de la Cité in the middle of the Seine River.

The Louvre (p. 138) is one of the world's largest museums, with some 35,000 works of art and countless priceless masterpieces.

Look up: The Louvre was originally built as a palace, so even its ceilings are works of art.

The iron footbridges along the Canal St-Martin (p. 170) were among the picturesque backdrops for the film *Amelie*. The canal is lined with bohemian cafes and bistros.

Like the Canal St-Martin (above), the banks of the Seine are a major gathering spot for Parisians when the weather turns warm.

The elegant Hôtel de Soubise (p. 211) holds the Museum of French History.

Molière, Chopin, Jim Morrison, and other notables are buried in the Cimitière du Père-Lachaise (p. 167).

Notre-Dame's infamous gargoyles (p. 129) keep watch over the Paris cityscape.

Opened in 1846, the Hôtel Chopin (p. 58) has its entry in one of Paris's "passages"—covered arcades filled with shops.

The Philharmonie de Paris (p. 239) performs in this acoustically and visually rich space by French architect Jean Nouvel.

The stunning Frank Gehry–designed art museum of the Louis Vuitton Foundation opened in 2014 (p. 157).

The grand foyer of the Opéra Garnier (p. 146).

Sunbathing along the Seine on the Paris Plage (p. 196).

Stained glass and the beautiful vaulted ceiling of the Cathedral of Sainte-Chapelle (p. 143).

Jazz clubs abound in Paris, but few are as good as New Morning Theatre (p. 245).

The "inside out" exterior of the Pompidou Centre (p. 148).

The Picasso Paris museum doubled its exhibition space when it reopened in 2014 (p. 154).

The family-owned Brasserie de l'Isle Saint-Louis, founded in 1953, is an excellent place to recharge after touring nearby Notre Dame.

LEFT BANK

Children can rent vintage toy boats at the Luxembourg Gardens and set them sailing for just €3.50. Doing so in front of the Luxembourg Palace makes the experience even grander.

More than four million passengers use the Paris Metro system, with its Art Nouveau–inspired architecture. Pictured is the Saint Michel station.

Many consider Le Bon Marché, opened in 1852, the world's first department store. Even its escalators are elegant.

Ernest Hemingway was a regular at Les Deux Magots (p. 127) in St-Germain-des-Pres.

Napoleon is buried in the church of the monumental building complex known as Hôtel des Invalides, completed in 1678 (p. 184).

Note the ornate hairstyle on this wood-carved statue of St. Mary-Magdalene in the Musée de Cluny (p. 177).

The bones of ex-Parisians line the tunnel walls of the underground cemetery known as Les Catacombes (p. 189).

Coco Chanel was one of the many famous people who sipped tea in the Belle Epoque interior of the Angelina tearoom.

The Musée d'Orsay, in the old Gare d'Orsay train station, holds one of the world's richest collections of Impressionist and Post-Impressionist art (p. 185).

Rodin fountain sculpture in the formal gardens at the Musée Rodin (p. 188).

The nave and magnificent rood screen inside the church of Saint-Etienne-du-Mont (p. 178).

Cheeses at Marché Mouffetard.

SIDE TRIPS

Venetian mirror makers were considered defectors when they came to France to create Versailles' Hall of Mirrors (p. 261). In fact, the Venetian government was so incensed that it hired assassins to try to kill the artisans.

One of three stained-glass rose windows in the Cathedral of Our Lady of Chartres (p. 263).

The most-visited theme park in Europe, Disneyland Paris has been a smash hit since it opened in 1992 (p. 274).

Generations of French Kings, and Napoleon, used the Chateau de Fontainebleau (p. 271) as a residence.

Claude Monet famously painted his gardens at Giverny (p. 266); they look the same today as they did back then.

Louis XIV so loved Chateau de Vaux-le-Vicomte (p. 269) that he jailed its owner (for life) and confiscated the castle.

A FOREWORD TO THIS EASY GUIDE TO PARIS

By
Arthur Frommer

It always happens. Toward the end of every TV, radio, or newspaper interview, I am asked, "If you could vacation in only one place in the world, where would it be?" And I disappoint the questioner by responding not with an exotic or colorful choice—such as New Guinea or Montevideo—but simply with the city of Paris. And while the deflated interviewer changes the subject, I go babbling on about how Paris never fails to enchant.

LET ME COUNT THE WAYS

It's true—I can never get enough of the City of Light. To me, Paris is on the frontier, the leading edge, of every touristic activity. It rules the roost not only in cuisine—who could deny that?—but also in art and museums; in concerts, dance, and opera; in political discourse and intellectual debate (scan the newspaper headlines if you doubt that); in monuments and history (from the Pantheon to the Tomb of Napoleon); in fashion and shopping; in its cafes and bars (where you can spend the entire afternoon sipping a single glass of wine and not be asked to move on); in the availability of its civic services (get sick and a roaming ambulance with a doctor on board will almost instantly be at your side); in its luscious-looking open-air markets; in the excitement of its student life; in literature and economics (its resident novelists, philosophers, scientists, and scholars are legendary); and in every other field and endeavor I can name. Return to it for the second time or even the fiftieth—it still seems new.

So obviously, a guidebook series such as ours must have an important volume devoted to Paris. And this one, by Brit-turned-Parisienne Anna Brooke, is surely among the leading examples.

Anna came to Paris some 16 years ago and fell in love with it during a study abroad year. She moved straight back after her studies, thinking she'd stay a year or two, and here she still is! While enjoying the delights of her adopted city, she proceeded to carve out a career as a distinguished travel journalist, whose writings have appeared in numerous prestigious newspapers and magazines. Anna also composes music and lyrics for film and the stage and writes fiction for children.

Although her *Easy Guide to Paris* devotes more-than-sufficient space to organized commercial tours of Paris (including the fabled Bateaux Mouches riverboats), it's clear from the text that she primarily regards Paris as a walking city, to be explored on your own, often while wandering at random. Here, after all, is a metropolis so built to human scale, so lovely in its architectural design, so lined with small shops with their dynamic proprietors, that there is never an uninteresting block in it. Let me repeat: *You can walk its ancient streets for hours and you will never be uninterested.*

I hope that your decision to carry a light-and-manageable Easy Guide will greatly assist you in your enjoyment of Paris, and that Anna's own special perspectives will make your visit full of joy—and memorable.

Cordially,

Arthur Frommer

THE BEST OF PARIS

P aris is a magnificent city, worthy of all the superlatives that have been heaped upon it for centuries. Its graceful streets, soaked in history, really are as elegant as they say. Its monuments and museums really are extraordinary, and a slightly world-weary fin-de-siècle grandeur really is part of day-to-day existence. But Paris is so much more than a beautiful assemblage of buildings and monuments. It is the pulsing heart of the French nation.

If you look beyond its beautiful facade, you'll see that this is a city where flesh-and-blood people live and work and a place with a palpable urban buzz. Not only is Paris the nation's capital; if you include the suburbs, it is home to 20% of the country's population and the source of most French jobs. For the best in art, culture, and business, all roads lead to Paris.

Not all that long ago, Paris was not only the navel of France but also the shining beacon of Europe. All the continent's greatest minds and talents clamored to come here: The city seduced Nietzsche, Chopin, Picasso, and Wilde, and then in the 1920s it drew Hemingway and the Lost Generation of American writers and artists. After World War II, it became the iconic backdrop of a new form of cinema: La Nouvelle Vague (the French New Wave), with many cineastes engaging with the political and social unrest of the time.

For yes, from since before the French Revolution to the terrorist attacks of 2015–17, Paris has always played center stage to turmoil—much of it romanticized (think *Les Misérables*), some of it too recent to properly put into perspective. But one thing is certain: Upheaval has always been as much a part of its urban makeup as the Seine—which is why Paris's coat of arms features a boat and the motto FLUCTUAT NEC MERGITUR ("She is tossed by the waves but does not sink"), a reminder that no matter what happens, Paris will prevail and protect those within her walls.

And it's true. Despite the heartache of recent events, Paris is still a bastion of the best of French culture. The culinary legacy alone is enough to fill several books. You can eat your way to nirvana in the city's restaurants, gourmet food stores, and bakeries. The architecture ranges from the lavish opulence of **Place Vendôme** (p. 143) to

A view of the Alexandre III bridge and the Place de la Concorde.

the contemporary madness of **Musée du Quai Branly** (p. 187). The city is also home to some of the world's greatest museums, including the legendary **Louvre** (p. 138). And let's not even get into the city's concert halls, nightspots, parks, gardens, and cafes—at least not just yet. Even if you have time to see only a fraction of what you'd like to see, in the long run, it really won't matter. What counts is that you'll have been to Paris, sampled its wonders, and savored the experience—and that counts for a lot.

THE best AUTHENTIC PARIS EXPERIENCES

o **Seeing the city from above:** Whether it's from the top of the **Eiffel Tower** (p. 182), in front of the **Sacré Coeur** (p. 164), or next to a gargoyle on **Notre-Dame** (p. 129), seeing the city from aloft will make your heart sing. Paris's only city-center skyscraper is the **Tour Montparnasse** (p. 42), but even that has a 56th-floor observation deck, from which you can scan the cityscape and see many of the most famous monuments poking out above the elegant Haussmannian buildings.

o **Strolling across the Pont Neuf:** The view from here is dramatic. To one side, you'll see the **Ile de la Cité,** and to the other, the **Eiffel Tower** and the **Louvre.** It's a little like standing in the navel of the Parisian universe, and, in fact, you are: The island upon which this bridge straddles dates back to the city's earliest beginnings.

o **Walking along the Seine at night:** Paris is beautiful in the daytime, but at night, when many of the monuments are lit up, it's positively bewitching. An evening stroll along the banks of the Seine is about as romantic as it gets. A **nighttime** boat cruise (p. 190) is another great way to enjoy the magic.

o **Sipping an apéro at a sidewalk cafe at sunset:** After work or before play, Parisians love to meet up to have an *apéritif,* usually a light alcoholic drink like a glass of wine, a French beer, or—the latest trend—a Spritz (a sparkling wine cocktail made with Italian Campari) on a cafe terrace. Join the locals in this early-evening ritual and feel like a real Parisian.

More and more Parisians are now biking around the city.

o **Soaking up the atmosphere at a farmer's market:** All kinds of Parisians frequent the city's many **covered and open-air markets** (p. 221), which sell fresh fruits, vegetables, meats, cheeses, and other goodies. Don't be afraid to plunge into these noisy places; you'll be participating in a tradition that goes back centuries. Just ask before you touch the merchandise; the vendors do the selecting and the bagging here.

o **Riding a bike:** Ever since the advent of the **Velib'** low-cost bike-rental program (p. 283) in 2007, Paris has been evolving into a two-wheeler city. Sign up online for a day's or a week's worth of bike access and buzz around like a local—the city is small enough and flat enough that riding is a snap. Helmets aren't obligatory yet, but you might choose to wear one, because traffic can be hairy.

PARIS'S best ARCHITECTURAL LANDMARKS

o **Best monuments to La Gloire (the glory of France):** The Arc de Triomphe— the world's largest triumphal arch (p. 156)—is about as grandiose as it gets, at least until you arrive at the magnificent **Place de la Concorde** (p. 163), another flamboyant national gesture. If that's not enough, the church of **La Madeleine** (p. 158) was originally meant to be a temple to military glory, and the **Panthéon** (p. 177) is a church made into a crypt for the nation's intellectual heroes.

o **Best monuments to spiritual glory:** Despite the French obsession with keeping the Republic secular, the capital harbors some of the world's most exquisite churches. No matter what your views are on religion, you'll be bowled over by the soaring arches of the **Cathedral of Notre-Dame** (p. 129), the stained glass of **Sainte-Chapelle** (p. 143), or the superb rood screen at **St-Etienne du Mont** (p. 178).

o **Best monuments to human ingenuity:** Extraordinary engineers and architects have spent time in this city, leaving behind some amazing buildings in their wake. Most famously, the **Eiffel Tower** (p. 182) gracefully reaches for the sky, while exerting minimal pressure on the ground. The land under the Belle Epoque wonder that is the **Palais Garnier** (p. 146) is stabilized by the man-made underground lake that inspired Gaston Leroux's *Phantom of the Opera* story. Modern architects also have made their mark, mostly on the city's museums, be it the inside-out structure of the **Centre Pompidou** (p. 148) or the billowing glass "sails" of the **Fondation Louis Vuitton** (p. 157).

Arc de Triomphe on the Avenue des Champs-Élysées.

PARIS'S best RESTAURANTS

o **Best for romance:** Thinking of popping the question? Think no more, just reserve a table at **La Tour d'Argent** (p. 112) and get it over with once and for all. With its panoramic views over the Seine to Notre-Dame, legendary kitchen, and elegant decor, there's no better setting.

o **Best for families:** At **Rosa Bonheur** (p. 107), which is set inside the Buttes Chaumont park, parents can enjoy tapas on a large, outdoor terrace while their kids play in the grass. French-fry freaks and their meat-eating parents will love **Le Relais de l'Entrecôte** (p. 116), where delicious steak-frites with a special sauce is the only thing on the menu.

o **Best splurge:** If you are planning to pull out all the stops, do it at **Arpège** (p. 119), where elegance meets excellence on the plate and in the decor. Alain Passard deftly creates miracles with vegetables that come from his own gourmet farm as well as other fresh, top-quality ingredients.

o **Best value:** For a taste of bistronomy (as in, modernized, gourmet bistro food) at a reasonable price, look no further than **Mangetout** (p. 117). Affordable and ample, the Breton cooking at **Chez Michel** (p. 105) will satisfy any size appetite.

o **Best classic bistro:** For once, the critics seem to agree on something: **Bistrot Paul Bert** (p. 102) is one of the best in the city, and that's saying a lot in a city with as many great bistros as this one.

- **Best seafood:** Next door to the much-hyped neo-bistro **Septime** (p. 102) is shellfish-centric **Clamato** (p. 102), a seafood lovers' Eldorado that serves plates of oysters, fish rillettes (a sort of pâté), and smoked shrimp (not to mention excellent wine) in a beautifully toned-down dining room.
- **Best for Gluten-Free:** You don't need to suffer from gluten intolerance to appreciate the delicious home-cooked dishes at **Noglu** (p. 99), snuggled in Passage des Panoramas, once of Paris' most atmospheric covered passages.
- **Best for wine enthusiasts:** If what's in your glass is just as important as what's on the plate, saunter over to **Les Papilles** (p. 113), where the walls are covered with shelves of the best bottles, and the knowing staff will guide you in your search for the ultimate elixir.

PARIS'S best HOTELS

- **Best view:** You won't want to get up in the morning at **Hôtel Brighton;** you'll be happy just staying in bed and gazing at the panorama, which, depending on the room you stay in, might include the Louvre, Tuileries gardens, or Eiffel Tower. See p. 46.
- **Best for families:** Right by the Bois de Vincennes (the city's eastern park, an ideal spot for a family picnic; p. 198), **Hôtel de la Porte Dorée** offers pretty rooms at very affordable rates and caters to kids with free crayons, toys, and cots. See p. 63.
- **Best splurge:** It's hard to say whether the decor is modern or period at **Relais St-Germain,** but it doesn't really matter, because it's simply beautiful— dark wood, plush fabrics, and priority seating at the coveted Le Comptoir du Relais downstairs. See p. 71.

The dining room at Lasserre.

Alexandre Dumas Room at the Relais St-Germain.

o **Most charming period piece:** Hôtel **Caron de Beaumarchais** re-creates the ambience of 18th-century Paris, when the hotel's namesake, the author of *The Barber of Seville*, was cavorting in the neighborhood. A bit of Old France right in the middle of the trendy Marais neighborhood. See p. 51.

o **Most eco-friendly:** Off the beaten track in the 11th arr., **Eden Lodge** uses solar panels for all its lighting, has high-tech self-cleaning floor tiles, and serves delicious organic breakfasts. It also overlooks one of the loveliest hidden residential gardens in town. See p. 61.

o **Best for a quirky honeymoon:** A location (quite literally) on the Seine; cool, cabinlike rooms; a hip cocktail bar; and a bijou outdoor pool—**OFF Paris Seine** is the city's first floating hotel and a wacky but romantic spot for couples with a sense of fun. See p. 69.

o **Best value:** Blessed with a terrific location in the Marais next to a lovely and leafy square, **Hôtel Jeanne d'Arc le Marais** is a terrific budget option. See p. 52.

PARIS'S best MUSEUMS

o **Musée d'Orsay:** A breathtaking collection of pre-, post-, and just plain old Impressionists deck the walls of this museum, including Renoir, Van Gogh, Manet, Degas, Gauguin, and a slew of other masters of 19th-century art. Not only is the artwork incredible; the building itself, a transformed Belle Epoque train station, is a delight. See p. 185.

o **Musée du Louvre:** One of the world's largest and best museums, this colossus of culture has its share of masterpieces, including the Mona Lisa, the Venus de Milo, and Winged Victory. But aside from these three famous ladies, there are mountains of other incredible works to see, from ancient Egyptian sculptures to Renaissance masters to stunning gems and jewelry. See p. 138.

- **Musée du Quai Branly:** This ultramodern museum gives center stage to artworks that are often overlooked: those of traditional societies in Africa, Asia, and even North America. You'll find everything from a shaman's cloak from Papua New Guinea to Australian aboriginal art as well as delicate carvings, intricate weavings, and other masterpieces. See p. 187.
- **Musée Jacquemart-André:** Set in a gorgeous 19th-century mansion, this small museum offers a chance to see exquisite art and how the other half lived. Highlights include a beautiful winter garden, a collection of Italian Renaissance masters, and a magnificent tearoom with a Tiepolo on the ceiling. See p. 160.
- **Musée Picasso Paris:** After 5 long years of renovations, this magnificent museum now offers an even better survey of all things Picasso. Housed in a grandiose 17th-century *hôtel particulier,* the collection explores the artist's many periods in a beautiful Marais setting. See p. 154.

THE best FREE & DIRT-CHEAP PARIS

- **Attending a free concert:** Every summer, the **Parc Floral** (in the Bois de Vincennes) hosts a bevy of free concerts: first the Paris Jazz Festival in June and July, and then Classique au Vert in August. See p. 198.
- **Picnicking in the Luxembourg Gardens:** You couldn't get richer surroundings if you were at a three-star restaurant, and yet you only pay a few euros for a sandwich. Sometimes being cheap is the best revenge. See p. 179.

Sculptures at the Louvre.

o **Seeing Paris from a city bus:** Take your own tour of Paris by bus—for the price of a Métro ticket. Some of the municipal bus lines' routes would put a professional tour bus to shame, like route Nos. 63 and 87, which hit many of the city's major sites. Visit www.ratp.fr for route maps.

o **Dawdling over a coffee in a cafe:** Okay, you might pay 2.50€ for a cup of coffee, but that means you can sit for hours watching the world go by in an atmospheric cafe and have an authentically Parisian experience to boot.

o **Enjoying the newly refurbished banks of the Seine, "Les Berges":** What used to be a stretch of noisy roadway between the Musée d'Orsay and the Pont d'Alma is now a place for walking, running, and holding hands, with picnic areas, food and drink, floating gardens, and sports activities as well as lounge chairs for taking an impromptu siesta. See p. 196.

THE best NEIGHBORHOODS FOR GETTING LOST

o **Montmartre:** If you get away from the crowds at the Sacré Coeur, this mythic neighborhood is a great place to wander up and down winding lanes, tilt at windmills, admire the view, and cafe-hop. You could also take our Montmartre walking tour (p. 200).

o **The Latin Quarter:** Once again, the trick here is to ditch the crowds on rue de la Huchette and take off for the less-trampled corners of this historic student quarter, such as near the universities on rue Erasme, at the food shops on **rue Mouffetard,** or down by the delightful **Jardin des Plantes.**

o **The Marais:** Get lost in style in this trendy neighborhood, known as much for its delightful boutiques and hip restaurants as for its magnificent 17th- and 18th-century *hôtels particuliers,* aristocratic mansions, many of which have been turned into terrific museums. See our Marais walking tour on p. 206.

o **Belleville:** You'll see another side of Paris in this diverse working-class district, where a mix of artists and immigrants have made it into one of the city's most vibrant neighborhoods. **Parc de Belleville** offers wonderful views of Paris; around **rue de Menilmontant,** you'll find cool bars and vintage shops. Farther east is the romantic **Père-Lachaise** cemetery (p. 167).

THE best UNEXPECTED PLEASURES IN PARIS

o **Sipping cocktails on a rooftop:** Watch the sun set over Paris's chimney pots and the distant Byzantine **Sacré Coeur** (p. 164) at **Le Perchoir,** a hip rooftop cocktail bar and restaurant in the trendy 11th arr. See p. 248.

o **Sunbathe on the Seine:** Enjoy the sand and sun at **Paris Plage** (p. 196), an annual summer fiesta where the riverbanks become a beach, and concerts, snack bars, tea dances, and other activities are open to one and all.

- Ice-skate in front of the Hôtel de Ville: From December through February, you can rent skates and glide around the rink on the plaza in front of Paris's splendid Renaissance city hall (p. 150).
- Watch weavers make tapestries: At the Manufacture Nationale des Gobelins (p. 173), you can take a tour and see skilled artists at their giant looms creating magnificent woven works.
- Sip mint tea in a Moroccan tearoom: Dream you're in the Kasbah at the tearoom at the Mosquée de Paris (p. 125), which is covered in beautiful mosaic tiles.

Sunbathing on the Seine.

PARIS'S best OF OUTDOORS

- **The best gardens:** It's hard to choose between the grand geometry of the **Tuileries** (p. 135), the relaxed elegance of the **Luxembourg Gardens** (p. 179), or the colorful palette of **Giverny** (p. 266).
- **The best parks:** The **Bois de Boulogne** (p. 197) has lakes, gardens, and even a small amusement park (the **Jardin d'Acclimatation;** p. 195) for your rambling pleasure. There's no amusement park at the Bois de Vincennes, but there is a medieval castle, the **Château de Vincennes,** complete with ramparts and a keep (p. 198), as well as the **Parc Floral** (p. 198) and a smartly refurbished zoo, the **Parc Zoologique de Paris** (p. 167).
- **The best primrose promenade:** The **Promenade Plantée** (p. 166) must be the world's skinniest garden: Because it's set atop a former train viaduct, you can stroll among the flowers and greenery from the place de la Bastille all the way to the Bois de Vincennes.

PARIS IN CONTEXT

2

Before there was Paris, there was the Seine. Much wider than it is today, the river looped and curved through the region, and at one point, split into two branches. One branch dried up, leaving a wide band of marshlands to the north, while the other, sprinkled with islands, remained. This swampy bog offered little indication that it had potential for urban grandeur. Yet one day it would become the lifeline of one of the world's greatest cities.

THE MAKING OF PARIS

Origins

Prehistoric Paris did have two things going for it: a river that led all the way to the Atlantic and those strategically placed islands, which offered both protection and shelter. The largest one, the core of what would one day become the **Ile de la Cité,** attracted the attention of a tribe of Celtic people called the Parisii, who fished and traded along its banks somewhere around the 3rd century B.C. Though they weren't the first Parisians (traces of human habitations have been found dating back to Neolithic times), they were the first to firmly implant themselves in the area, and they made ample use of the river not only as a source of food, but as a trade link. Their island had the good fortune of being on the "Pewter Route," a trade route that stretched from the British Isles to the Mediterranean. As a consequence, the Parisii's wealth was such that by the 1st century B.C., they were minting their own gold coins.

Roman Rule (1st C. B.C.–A.D. 2nd C.)

There is no recorded history of Paris before the Romans showed up in 52 B.C., but when Caesar and his boys marched in, the Parisii numbered several thousand, and the island bustled with activity. Soon thereafter, however, the Parisii's main activity would be trying to get rid of the Romans. Though they fought valiantly, they were massacred by Caesar's troops, and a new Roman town was built both on the island and on the Left Bank, on the slopes of the **Montagne St-Genevieve** (where the Panthéon now stands; p. 177). The new town, for reasons that remain unclear, was baptized Lutécia and ran along a ramrod-straight north-south axis; the linc of this road survives in today's **rue St-Jacques.** (The Parisii would eventually get their due, however, as the city would be renamed Civitas Parisiorum in the 4th c., which eventually was whittled down to Paris.) Though there were only around 8,000 inhabitants, by the 2nd century the town boasted three **Gallo-Roman baths** (you can see the ruins of the largest of these at the corner of blvds. St-Michel and St-Germain in the Musée de Cluny; p. 177) and a vast amphitheater (a piece of which can be seen at the **Arènes de Lutèce,** just off rue Monge in the Latin Quarter).

Barbarian Invasions (3rd–5th C.)

By the 3rd century, the city was subject to waves of barbarian invasions. Most of the population took refuge on the Ile de la Cité, which was then encircled by ramparts. Somewhere around this time, St-Denis was decapitated when he was martyred up on a nearby hill, which in time would be dubbed **Montmartre** (p. 200). Legend has it that the saint picked up his severed head and walked with it for several kilometers, preaching all the while; the **Basilica of St-Denis** (just north of Paris) was built on the place where he finally dropped. The event, which supposedly happened around 250, coincides with Christianity's first appearance on the Parisian scene. Another particularly pious Christian, a young nun named Geneviève, was credited with turning Attila the Hun away from Paris in 451. Alerted that the barbarians were approaching, the citizenry was in a state of panic; Geneviève reassured them, telling them that God was with them. In the end, the Huns didn't march on Paris, but on Orléans; the grateful population, convinced it was Geneviève's doing, made her into the city's patron saint. A church was raised in her honor on the hill that's now known as the **Montagne-Ste-Geneviève;** it was pulled down and replaced by a magnificent new one, commissioned by Louis XV in the 18th century, which was subsequently turned into a national mausoleum after the Revolution and renamed the **Panthéon** (p. 177).

Merovingian & Carolingian Dynasties (6th–10th C.)

At the end of the 5th century, the Franks (a Germanic people) invaded and established the Merovingian dynasty of kings; the first, Clovis, made Paris the capital of his new kingdom in 508. The Merovingians were ardent Catholics; under their rule the city sprouted dozens of churches, convents, and monasteries. Childebert I, the son of Clovis, inaugurated a small basilica that would soon be dubbed **St-Germain-des-Prés** after the saint was buried there in 576. Over time, this church would grow into a powerful abbey and intellectual center that would dominate much of the Left Bank up until the Revolution. Even after the abbey was dismantled, and many of its buildings burned, the church lived on, as did the name of the neighborhood. Though the city enjoyed a certain amount of prosperity during this time, it was short-lived; the Merovingians, known as the "do-nothing" kings, were eventually toppled, and by the 8th century, a new dynasty, the Carolingians, had replaced them.

The most famous member of this clan was Charlemagne, who went on to conquer Italy and was crowned emperor by the Pope in 800. Arts and letters thrived during this period, and the city began to build up on the Right Bank, around the church of **St-Gervais–St-Protais,** and the Port du Grève, where the **Hôtel de Ville** (p. 150) now stands. Starting in the mid–9th century, the city was periodically ravaged by Normans and Vikings, who would sack Paris on their way to plundering Burgundy. The Normans were particularly persistent; after a barricade was erected on the Seine to keep their

Notre-Dame.

boats from passing in 885, they laid siege to the city for an entire year. It was only after King Charles the Simple signed a treaty in 911 giving the Normans Normandy that life returned to normal, but by then Paris was in ruins. The age of the Carolingians was drawing quickly to a close.

The Founding of the Capetian Dynasty (11th C.)

In 987, Hugues Capet, the Count of Paris, was crowned king of France; his direct descendants ruled the country for 3½ centuries, and two branches of the Capetian dynasty, the Valois and Bourbons, would continue to rule (with a brief pause during the Revolution) until 1848. With the Capetians came stability, and Paris rebuilt and grew, particularly on the Ile de la Cité and the Right Bank. The Left Bank, flattened by the Normans, was left as it was; little by little it was covered with fields and vineyards. The 12th century was a period of economic growth; it saw the birth of **Les Halles** (p. 145), the sprawling central market around which a new commercial quarter developed. In 1163, ground was broken on the **Cathédrale de Notre-Dame de Paris** (p. 129). Finished 200 years later, Notre-Dame remains one of the world's most exquisite examples of medieval architecture.

It was around this time that that mushy, marshy strip of land on the Right Bank, known as the **Marais** (or swamp), was partially drained and carpeted with farms. Philippe Auguste, before taking off on a crusade, had a sturdy rampart built around the newly extended city limits; fragments of this wall can still be seen today (see "Walking Tours," p. 200). Philippe's grandson, Louis IX (St-Louis), added another architectural jewel to the cityscape: the **Sainte-Chapelle** (p. 143), a small church whose upper-story walls are almost entirely made of brilliantly colored stained glass. Louis had it built to house a treasure he bought from the debt-ridden Byzantine emperor: Christ's crown of thorns and some fragments of the holy cross (the relics are now in Notre-Dame).

Medieval Glory & Gore (12th–14th C.)

By the 12th century, Paris boasted a population of around 200,000, much larger than other European capitals, as well as a burgeoning reputation as an economic as well as intellectual center. Quality fabrics, leather goods, and metalwork were produced in Paris, as well as art objects. The University of Paris was slowly coming into being, and colleges were popping up all over the Left Bank; in 1257, Robert de Sorbon established the small theological college that became the **Sorbonne** university. The city seemed unstoppable.

But the 14th century would, in fact, put an end to this fruitful period. When the last Capetian king, Charles IV, died in 1328, the succession to the throne was disputed, in part because the closest descendent was Edward III, king of England, who also presided over a chunk of southwestern France. This and many other gripes exploded into the Hundred Years War, which devastated France for over a century. Expansion in Paris came to an abrupt halt, the endless wars and riots wore down the populace, and in 1348 the Black Plague killed tens of thousands. In the early 1400s Paris was hit by famine and a string of extremely cold winters. Between one disaster and another during this period, the city lost about half of its population. In 1420, the English occupied Paris; despite the efforts of Joan of Arc and Charles VII, who laid siege to the city in 1429, troops loyal to the Duke of Bedford (the English Regent) didn't leave until 1437. This same duke was responsible for having Joan burned at the stake in Rouen in 1431.

Sainte-Chapelle.

Renaissance Renewal (16th C.)

Slowly, the city came to life again. The population increased, as did commercial and intellectual activity. The invention of the printing press spread new ideas across Europe. After centuries of rejecting the texts and ideas of classical antiquity, scholars embraced the concept of Humanism, which would find a home in Paris. Great thinkers such as Erasmus and John Calvin were drawn to the city's universities. More colleges emerged from the academic landscape: In 1530, François I established a school that would become the prestigious **College de France,** and in 1570 the **Académie Française** was founded by Charles IX. If the Renaissance made its mark on the intellectual life of the city, it had little impact on its architectural legacy. The Renaissance kings liked Paris but lived and did their building elsewhere. François I, the most construction-happy among them, brought some of the greatest masters of the Italian Renaissance, like Leonardo da Vinci and Benvenuto Cellini, to France, but their genius was mostly displayed in François' châteaux on the Loire and at **Fontainebleau** (p. 271), not in the capital. The king's primary contribution to the cityscape was the remodeling of the **Louvre** (p. 138) and construction of the **Hôtel de Ville** (p. 150), designed by the Italian architect Boccador. The latter building was burned down in 1871 during the fall of the Paris Commune; the existing edifice is a fairly faithful copy erected in 1873. Two glorious churches, **St-Etienne du Mont** (p. 178) and **St-Eustache** (p. 144), also were built during this period; their decoration attests to the jubilant spirit of the times.

War once again interfered with the city's development when the bloody struggle between the country's Protestants and Catholics morphed into the Wars of Religion in 1557. Even the marriage of the future king, Henri of Navarre, a Protestant, to Marguerite de Valois, a Catholic, did not diffuse the conflict: A week after their wedding, August 24, 1572, the bells of **St-Germain l'Auxerrois** (p. 145) signaled the beginning of the St-Bartholomew's Day massacre, which resulted in the deaths of between 2,000 and 4,000 Parisian Protestants. When in 1589, Henri was declared King of France (as Henri IV), Parisians would not let the Protestant monarch enter the city. After 4 months of siege, the starving citizens relented and in the end, to show his goodwill, the king converted, famously declaring that "Paris is worth a mass."

Henri IV lived on to be an enormously popular king, whose structural improvements left a lasting mark on the city. He was the force behind the **Pont Neuf** (p. 151), which straddles the Right and Left banks, as well as the Ile de la Cité. To create the bridge, two small islets off the western tip of the Ile de la Cité were filled in and made part of the larger island; the tranquil **Place Dauphine** was also created during this time. Henri also conceived the strikingly harmonious place Royale (now called **Place des Vosges; p. 155**). The king would not live to see it finished; in 1610, when the royal carriage got stuck in a traffic jam on rue de la Ferronerie, he was stabbed by Ravaillac, a deranged Catholic who was convinced that Henri was waging war against the Pope.

The Age of Louis XIV (17th C.)

The 17th century saw a building frenzy among the aristocracy. Marie de Médicis built the Italian-style **Palais du Luxembourg** in 1615, around the same time that the **Marais** (p. 148) was inundated with splendid palaces and *hôtels particuliers,* or mansions. The new **Ile St-Louis,** made from the joining of two previously uninhabited islets to the east of the Ile de la Cité, was filled with stately mansions that only the rich could afford. After Marguerite de Valois moved in to the neighborhood, the **St-Germain** quarter also became a place to see and be seen. Finally, in 1632 the powerful Cardinal Richelieu built a huge palace, now called the **Palais Royal** (p. 141), near the Louvre, which encouraged yet another new neighborhood to develop.

In 1643, a 5-year-old boy named Louis XIV acceded to the French throne, where he would stay for the next 72 years. One of the most influential figures in French history, Louis XIV spent his early years in Paris, under the protection of his mother, Anne of Austria. It was not a happy time: The city was writhing under a nasty rebellion called La Fronde, instigated by cranky nobles trying to wrest control back from the powerful prime minister, Cardinal Mazarin. The young monarch and his mother were chased from one royal residence to the next. When Louis grew up and things calmed down, he settled into the **Louvre,** commanding his team of architects, led by Le Vau, to complete the **Cour Carrée** and other unfinished parts of the palace. The spectacular colonnade on the eastern facade dates from this period. Louis eventually decided to build his own castle, one that was far enough from the noise and filth of the capital and big enough to house his entire court—the better to keep a close eye on political intrigues. The result was the **Château of Versailles** (p. 258), a testament to the genius of Le Vau and that of master landscape architect André Le Nôtre.

Even if Louis XIV didn't live in the city, he certainly added to its architectural heritage. He was responsible for the construction of **Les Invalides** (p. 184), a massive military hospital, and two squares, **Place des Victoires** and place Louis-le-Grand, today known as **Place Vendôme** (p. 143). Two gigantic entryways, celebrating Louis' military victories, were built at the city gates; the **Porte St-Denis** and the **Porte**

Galeries in Palais Royal.

St-Martin. Both of these triumphal archways still hover over parts of the 10th arrondissement by Métro Strasbourg–St-Denis, looking somewhat out of place in this working-class district.

From Enlightenment to Revolution

Paris continued to grow, and the population density increased. At the turn of the 18th century, some 500,000 Parisians were crammed into a vast network of narrow, mostly unpaved streets. Sewers were nonexistent, and clean drinking water was a luxury. While life in the rarified atmosphere of the aristocratic salons of the **Marais** was brimming with art, literature, and deep thought, down on the ground it was filled with misery. Poverty and want were the constant companions of the vast majority of Parisians. On an intellectual level, the city was soaring—under the reign of Louis XV, Paris became a standard-bearer for the Enlightenment, a school of thought that championed reason and logic and helped construct the intellectual framework of both the American and French Revolutions. Salons—regular meetings of artists and thinkers in aristocratic homes—flourished, as did cafes; drawn in by the wildly popular new drink called coffee, these were the ideal meeting place for philosophers, writers, and artists, as well as a new breed of politicians with some revolutionary ideas. Political debates were particularly passionate in the cafes in the galleries of the **Palais Royal** (p. 141), which had been filled with shops and opened to the public by Duke Louis Philippe d'Orléans.

Meanwhile, back in Versailles, the court of Louis XVI seemed to be utterly oblivious of the mounting discontent in the capital. As the price of bread skyrocketed and more and more Parisians found themselves on the street (there were more than 100,000 homeless people in the city in 1789, out of an overall population of between 600,000 and 700,000), the disconnect between the aristocracy and the common man threatened to rupture into a bloody conflict. Amazingly, Louis XVI and his wife, Marie Antoinette, continued to live their lives as if the civil unrest in the capital didn't concern them. A financial crisis in the royal treasury prompted a meeting of the Estates-General in Versailles in May 1789, a representative body that had not been convened since 1616. The assembly began demanding a more democratic system of taxation, and better representation of the Third Estate (the people). When the King tried to close down the proceedings, the group, which had renamed itself the National Assembly, dug in its heels and wrote a constitution. The royals kept dithering and trying to break up the assembly, until finally, the Revolution erupted on July 14, 1789, when an angry mob stormed the Bastille prison. There were only seven prisoners in the fortress, but no matter—the genie was out of the bottle, and the pent-up anger of the populace was unleashed.

The royal family was imprisoned and beheaded. But after the initial euphoria faded and the high ideals were set down on paper, the leaders of the Revolution began to squabble, and factional skirmishes became increasingly deadly. The events of the Revolution are too many to relate here, but within a few years, not only were aristocrats being sent off to the guillotine, but just about anyone who disagreed with the ruling powers, including many of the leaders who wrote the rules. Finally, Robespierre, who directed the bloodiest phase of the Revolution, known as "the Terror," had his turn at the guillotine, and a new government was set up. Called the Directory, this unsuccessful attempt at representational government met its end when a general named Napoleon Bonaparte staged a coup in 1799.

The Empire

Under Napoleon, Paris slowly put itself back together. The economy restarted, and the Emperor turned his attentions to upgrading the city's infrastructure, building bridges (**Pont St-Louis, Pont des Arts, Pont d'Iéna,** and **Pont d'Austerlitz**), improving access to water (the **Canal de l'Ourcq**), and creating new cemeteries like **Père-Lachaise** (p. 167) because the old ones were so crowded that they had become public health hazards. Napoleon was also responsible for the **rue de Rivoli,** a wide east-west boulevard, the first of several that would be laid down later on in the 19th century. The collection of the **Louvre** was greatly enhanced by all the booty the Emperor acquired during his many military campaigns. Napoleon's love of war would eventually be his undoing; after his defeat by the English at Waterloo he was exiled to the isle of Ste-Helena, where he died in 1821. Paris holds huge monuments to his memory, in particular the **Arc de Triomphe** (p. 156), which honors the Imperial Army. His tomb lies in **Les Invalides** military complex and museum (p. 184).

The Restoration & Urban Renewal

Incredibly, after all the blood that was spilled in the name of the Republic, Louis XVI's brother (Louis XVIII) became King of France in 1814. What's

Place de la Bastille.

more, another brother, Charles X, became king after Louis XVIII's death. What both brothers had in common is that they tried to bring back the old days of absolute monarchy, while the citizenry had become accustomed to the reforms of the Revolution and the relatively benign rule of Napoleon. This, coupled with the continuing poverty of many Parisians, resulted in two serious uprisings, "Les Trois Glorieuses," the 3 "glorious" days in July 1830, and the Revolution of 1848. In fact, it is these two uprisings, and not the Revolution itself, that are honored on the column in the **Place de la Bastille** (p. 167), the site of the infamous prison. After Charles, a republic was declared, and Napoleon's nephew, Louis-Napoleon, ran for and won the presidency. He liked being president so much that he didn't want to give up power at the end of his term, so he staged a coup and declared the birth of the Second Empire, calling himself Napoleon III.

Under Charles X, the unhygienic state of the city center started to cause serious alarm, particularly after a cholera epidemic in 1832 devastated the population. Many residents fled to the outer limits of the city, away from the overcrowded poor quarters where the filthy streets were often completely clogged with traffic. City administrators began to draft plans for new avenues, in particular the prefect, Rambuteau, who went ahead and started laying down wide boulevards, like the one named after him.

But it was Napoleon III who really changed the face of Paris when he gave urban planner Baron Haussmann free rein to "modernize" the city. Not only did Haussmann lay down wide boulevards that eased congestion and opened up vistas, he cleverly arranged them so that if ever there was yet another popular uprising, they would facilitate military maneuvers and make it tough for citizens to set up barricades. Over half of the city was ripped up and rebuilt; Haussmann instituted strict regulations for the height of the new buildings and the style of their facades. The result: the elegant buildings and boulevards you see today. On the plus side, the city finally got a decent sewage system and water access, and the squalid slums were knocked down. Several parks were created, such as **Buttes Chaumont** (p. 172) and the **Bois de Boulogne** (p. 197) as well as grand plazas like the **Place de la République** (p. 166) and **place du Trocadéro.** On the other hand, the character of the city was completely changed, and much of its social fabric was pulled down with the houses. Working-class Paris has been slowly disappearing ever since.

From the Commune to the Belle Epoque

The boulevards were put to the test during the Paris Commune of 1870, a brief but bloody episode that was yet another attempt of the French people to construct a democratic republic—though this time it was in the wake of the Franco-Prussian war. The boulevards did their job: The rebellion was crushed, and at least 20,000 communards were executed. When the smoke cleared, a new government was formed, and to everyone's surprise, it was a republic. The National Assembly had intended to form a constitutional monarchy, but the heir to the throne had no interest in the word "constitutional." As a stopgap measure, a temporary republic was set up—little did anyone know that it would last for 60 years.

There must have been an audible sigh of relief from Parisians, who would finally enjoy a little peace and harmony—or at least enough of a break from war and woe to have a good time. And so they did. During the "Belle Epoque," the years at the end of the 19th century and the beginning of the 20th, the arts bloomed in Paris. Groundbreaking art expositions introducing new

movements like Impressionism (around 1874) and Fau-
vism (around 1905) changed
people's ways of seeing painting. Up in **Montmartre,** an
entire colony of artists and
writers (Picasso, Braque,
Apollonaire, and others) were
filling cafes and cabarets in
their off hours. The Lumière
brothers and Léon Gaumont
showed their newly hatched
films in the city's first movie
theaters. The city hosted a
number of World's Fairs
including that of 1889, which
created the **Eiffel Tower**
(p. 182), and 1900, which left
behind the **Pont Alexandre
III bridge** (p. 151), as well as

Strolling through Montmartre.

the **Grand and Petit Palais** (p. 158 and 163). Another great moment in 1900
was the inauguration of the Paris Métro's first underground line.

The World Wars

The fun came to an abrupt halt in 1914 with the outbreak of World War I,
which killed 8.4 million Frenchmen. Calling all Parisians to arms, General
Gallieni and his troops fought off the approaching German army (the Battle
of the Marne) and saved Paris from occupation. The city did get bombarded,
however; on Good Friday, 1918, the church of **St-Gervais–St-Protais** took a
direct hit and more than 100 people died.

The city rebounded after the war, both economically and culturally, especially during the 1920s, *les années folles* ("the crazy years"). Paris became a
magnet for artists and writers from all over. Americans, in particular, came in
droves—F. Scott Fitzgerald, Henry Miller, Ernest Hemingway, and Gertrude
Stein were some of the better-known names. They and other European expats
like Marc Chagall, James Joyce, and George Orwell gathered in **Montparnasse** cafes like **Le Dôme, Le Select,** and **La Coupole.**

The 1930s brought economic depression and social unrest—a dreary backdrop for the approaching war. The Germans were re-arming, and Hitler was
rising to power; in May 1940 Germany invaded the Netherlands, Luxembourg, and Belgium and broke through France's defensive Maginot line. The
Germans occupied Paris on June 14, and for 4 years the city would know
hunger, curfews, and suspicion. The Vichy government, led by Marchal
Pétain, in theory governed unoccupied France, but in fact, collaborated with
the Germans. One of the darkest moments of the occupation was in July 1942,

when the French police rounded up 13,152 Parisian Jews, including 4,115 children, and parked them in a velodrome before sending them off to Auschwitz; only 30 survived. General Charles de Gaulle became the leader of the Free French and organizer of the Resistance; after the Allies landed in Normandy in 1944, Paris was liberated, and de Gaulle victoriously strode down the **Champs-Élysées** before a wildly cheering crowd. He would later become president of the country (1958–69).

Postwar Paris

Writers and artists filtered back to the cafes once the war was over (some had never left), and the **Café de Flore** (p. 126) and **Les Deux Magots** (p. 127) were headquarters for existential all-stars like Jean-Paul Sartre and Simone de Beauvoir. But the late 1940s was also the beginning of the end of French colonial rule, which was punctuated by violent clashes, including a revolt in Madagascar and a war in Indochina that would eventually entangle the United States. In North Africa, Morocco and Tunisia won their independence relatively peacefully, but France would not let go of Algeria without a long and bloody fight, its repercussions still being felt today. The war in Algeria led to the collapse of the French government; de Gaulle was asked to start a new one in 1958. Thousands of Algerian refugees flooded France, with many settling in the Paris region; Algeria finally gained its independence in 1962.

The writer André Malraux was de Gaulle's minister of cultural affairs from 1958 to 1969 and was responsible for protecting and restoring endangered historic districts like the **Marais.** Elsewhere, modern architects were putting their own questionable stamp on the city, like the doughnut-shaped **Maison de Radio France** in the 16th arrondissement, and the vaguely "Y"-shaped **Maison de UNESCO** in the 15th. The late 1960s also marked Paris in less concrete ways. In May 1968, students, hoping to reform the university system, joined a general workers' strike that was paralyzing the nation. The police invaded **La Sorbonne** to calm the protests, and students and sympathizers took to the streets. The confrontations became violent, with students attacking police with cobblestones—**boulevard St-Michel** was subsequently paved with asphalt. This was a period of profound social change; those who participated still proudly refer to themselves as *soixante-huitards* (68ers).

The 1970s was a period of architectural awkwardness—horrified by the idea of becoming a "museum city," then-president Georges Pompidou decided to modernize. One idea that thankfully never came to fruition was to pave over the Canal St-Martin to make way for a freeway that would cut through the center of the city. The dismal **Tour Montparnasse** dates from this period, as does the destruction of the old Les Halles marketplace, which was replaced with an unpleasant underground shopping mall (**Forum des Halles,** which has been rebuilt and covered over by a massive glass canopy; see box, p. 145). Pompidou's one "success" is the nearby **Centre Pompidou** (p. 148), whose strange, inside-out design provoked howls of outrage when it was built but now has been accepted as part of the Parisian landscape. When François

Musée du Quai Branly.

Mitterrand became president in 1981, he too wanted to leave an architectural legacy, and the list of his *grands projets* ("big projects") is lengthy. Fortunately, most were considerably more palatable than his predecessor's. It is to Mitterrand that we owe the **Musée d'Orsay,** the **pyramid** (and underground shopping complex) at the Louvre, and the ultra-modern **Bibliothèque National François Mitterrand,** as well as the **Institut du Monde Arabe** (p. 176) and the **Opéra Bastille.** President Jacques Chirac was the force behind the excellent **Musée du Quai Branly** (p. 187), which opened in 2006.

PARIS TODAY

Recent decades have brought Paris long periods of relative calm, punctuated by seismic upheavals, like the Métro bombings and paralyzing strikes that both hit the city in 1995. More recently, the city went into a state of shock after the terrorist attacks on the satiric newspaper *Charlie Hebdo* and a kosher supermarket, not to mention the coordinated assaults on restaurant terraces, the Stade de France stadium, and the Bataclan concert hall in November 2015, and the attacking of Police officers on the Champs Elysées in 2017. France has been on red-alert levels ever since, with officials doing everything they can to reassure tourists that they can visit Paris in safety, a crucial issue in a city where tourism is one of the major pillars of the economy. If anything, they have erred on the side of caution; don't be surprised to see soldiers in camouflage on the streets.

Random acts of terror aside, Paris is still Paris, and then some. The city has been looking slicker and cleaner in the last few years. Renovation of historic buildings is ongoing and a vigorous anti-dog-doo campaign has even made some headway on cleaning up the notoriously messy sidewalks. The city has continued to evolve, in large part thanks to mayor Bertrand Delanoë (in office 2001–14), whose dynamic and imaginative leadership gave the city a much-needed shot of energy. Paris feels younger these days, with refreshed public spaces, like the new and improved **Place de la République** (p. 166) and the delightfully pedestrianized **banks of the Seine** (see Les Berges; p. 196), which now include floating gardens, picnic areas, and yoga classes.

The advent of the **Velib' bike program** in 2007 (p. 283) is slowly transforming Paris into a bike-friendly place. Since then, the city has backed a host of other green measures, including bus lanes, pedestrian-friendly riverbanks, and Autolib', a Velib'-like program where you can rent an electric car to toodle around the city. Other innovative initiatives from city hall include the ever-popular **Paris Plage**—an urban beach on the banks of the Seine—and **Nuit Blanche,** an annual all-night cultural party.

In 2014, Delanoë stepped down and his protégé, **Anne Hidalgo,** was elected Paris's first female mayor. One of her top priorities is air pollution, which is an increasing problem in the capital, so much so that on particularly smoggy days, driving is restricted and the Métro is free.

Despite dour economic forecasts (which seems as interminably cloudy as the city's weather forecast), on the surface at least the capital seems to be in the pink of good health. Paris has managed to carefully conserve its architectural heritage and its traditional way of life while making a serious effort to enter the modern world. Paris is, after all, the capital of France and the third-largest economy in the European Union, and a certain dynamism comes with the territory—even if it is framed in Belle Epoque swirls and Mansard roofs. Yet even if the pulse of life in the capital ticks faster than it once did, it still allows for aimless intellectual discussions in cafes, leisurely Sunday strolls through Parisian parks, and relaxed lunches over glasses of wine. And maybe it is exactly that gentle aesthetic that makes the city one of a kind. It is rare in today's turbulent world to find an urban center that so harmoniously mixes tradition and modernity, without enslaving itself to either.

SUGGESTED ITINERARIES & NEIGHBORHOODS

P aris is an embarrassment of riches—there are so many wonderful things to see, it's hard to know where to begin. And while you are standing there thinking about it, the clock is ticking and your precious time is withering away. In this chapter, we offer up detailed itineraries so you can see the city's highlights in a short time without wearing yourself to a frazzle, and provide a couple of custom tours for particular interests. We also give you an overview of the city layout and break down the neighborhoods one by one, so you can design an itinerary of your own.

3

ICONIC PARIS IN 1 DAY

If you have just 1 day in Paris, your biggest challenge will be trying not to spend the whole day wishing you had more time. Here's an itinerary that will give you at least a taste of the city, and give you ideas for your next trip. *Start: The Champs de Mars, 7th arrond, Métro: Ecole Militaire, RER: Champs de Mars–Tour Eiffel.*

---

1 The Eiffel Tower ★★★

Hopefully you've gotten there early on a weekday, and it won't take too long to go up and take a gander at the splendid view of the city from the second floor. If lines are too long, skip the view and cross the bridge (Pont d'Iéna), heading up to the esplanade at the **Palais de Chaillot ★**, where you can admire the Iron Lady in all her splendor. Or if you really want to climb to the top, book your ticket and a time-slot online beforehand. See p. 182.

If you haven't done so already, cross the bridge (Pont d'Iéna) and head up to the Palais de Chaillot and the Place du Trocadéro. Hop on the no. 63 bus (direction Gare de Lyon), which will cruise past Les Invalides, and down boulevard St-Germain. Get off at the church of St-Germain-des-Prés.

Paris Neighborhoods

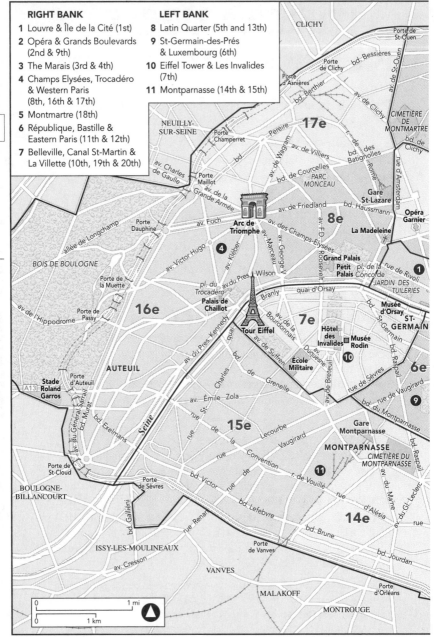

RIGHT BANK

1 Louvre & Île de la Cité (1st)
2 Opéra & Grands Boulevards (2nd & 9th)
3 The Marais (3rd & 4th)
4 Champs Elysées, Trocadéro & Western Paris (8th, 16th & 17th)
5 Montmartre (18th)
6 République, Bastille & Eastern Paris (11th & 12th)
7 Belleville, Canal St-Martin & La Villette (10th, 19th & 20th)

LEFT BANK

8 Latin Quarter (5th and 13th)
9 St-Germain-des-Prés & Luxembourg (6th)
10 Eiffel Tower & Les Invalides (7th)
11 Montparnasse (14th & 15th)

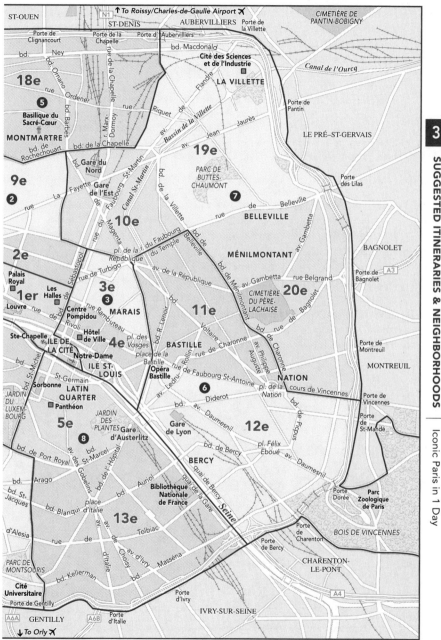

2 St-Germain-des-Prés ★★★

After visiting the church (p. 181), cross the square to at least stroll by **Les Deux Magots** ★ (p. 127) and the **Café de Flore** ★ (p. 126), two legendary cafes that were the home base of Sartre and De Beauvoir and scores of other artists and intellectuals. The cafes are crowded and pricey for lunch, so here's another option:

Lunch at Marché St-Germain ☕

If you wander a little farther down boulevard St-Germain and take a right on rue Mabillon, you'll find yourself at the Marché St-Germain, a covered market that is half shops and half market stalls filled with delectable goodies (closed Mon). Either pick up the fixings for a picnic here, or try one of the dozens of restaurants that surround the market. Our personal favorite is Le P'tit Fernand (p. 116).

Walk back out to boulevard St-Germain and turn right and continue to rue de l'Ancienne Comédie and turn left to Carrefour de Buci; then veer right on rue Dauphine and continue down to the Seine (admiring the galleries and antiques shops as you go). When you reach the river, cross the Pont Neuf.

3 Ile de la Cité ★★

Admire the view from the **Pont Neuf** ★ (p. 151), which straddles the island. Wander around the pretty **Place Dauphine** ★ (you'll find the entrance opposite the statue of King Henri IV on horseback) and stroll along the quays of this island, where some of the first Parisians set up camp. If you opted for a picnic lunch, the tree-shaded park, **Square du Vert Gallant** (at the very tip of the island), is a lovely spot.

The Eiffel Tower.

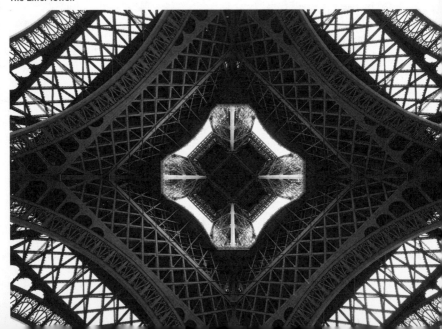

4 Notre-Dame ★★★

Visit the cathedral, and if you have the energy, climb the steps to the tower to take in yet another gorgeous view (and ogle some cute gargoyles). See p. 129.

Cross over the Pont d'Arcole, turn left onto Quai de Gevres and walk to place du Châtelet. If you are tired, you can take the No. 7 Métro from here to Palais-Royal–Musée du Louvre. Otherwise, you can walk another 10 minutes or so down the Quai de la Mégisserie to the Louvre.

Place de la Concorde.

data:image/white;base64,

5 The Louvre ★★★

Spend what's left of the afternoon admiring the outsides of the buildings (save the museum for the next trip) and wandering through the **Tuileries Garden ★★★**. See p. 135.

Stroll west through the gardens until you arrive at the Place de la Concorde.

6 Place de la Concorde ★★★

From this vantage point, you can not only take in the place itself (p. 163) but also peer down the **Champs-Élysées ★★** and see the **Arc de Triomphe ★★★** (p. 156) in the distance.

If you still have energy in the evening, finish your visit with an **evening cruise** along the river (see "Boat Tours," p. 190), from which you can admire just about all of the above gussied up in elegant lighting effects.

ICONIC PARIS IN 2 DAYS

Now you have a little more space to breathe. This itinerary also starts at the Eiffel Tower, but then takes off in another direction. *Start: The Champs de Mars, 7th arrond, Métro: Ecole Militaire, RER: Champs de Mars–Tour Eiffel.*

Day 1

1 The Eiffel Tower ★★★

If the lines for the elevators are too long, climb the stairs to the first floor. But for a better view, you'll have to stand on line for the elevators to the second floor or, for a serious thrill, the third. You can beat the crowds with some forward planning, though, by reserving your ticket and an allocated time-slot on the tower's website. See p. 182.

Take the RER C to St-Michel–Notre-Dame.

2 The Latin Quarter ★★★

Admire the Place St-Michel and the Boul' Mich (boulevard St-Michel) and try to imagine it all filled with long-haired students throwing *pavés* (paving stones) during the heady days of May 1968, when protesters brought the country to a standstill. Then wander up the boulevard and consider stopping in at the **Musée de Cluny** ★★ (p. 177). After, continue up past the dome of **La Sorbonne** (one of France's oldest universities, founded in 1257) to the **Luxembourg Gardens** ★★★ (p. 179). Either picnic here or settle down at a nearby table:

Lunch near the Luxembourg Gardens ☕

If it's a weekday and you are hungry, enjoy a terrific meal at **La Ferrandaise** (p. 116), about a block away. If you just want something light, and/or La Ferrandaise is closed, stop in for a *croque-monsieur* (a French version of a grilled-cheese sandwich) or a salad at **Le Rostand,** a Belle Epoque cafe with a lovely terrace just across the street from the gardens (6 place Edmond Rostand, 6th arrond.; ✆ 01-43-54-61-58; RER: Luxembourg).

Walk up rue Soufflot toward the stunning domed Panthéon at the top of the hill.

3 Le Panthéon ★

Marvel at the neoclassical proportions of this national mausoleum's magnificent interior dome, home to Foucault's Pendulum, the device that first proved the Earth's rotation (p. 178).

Back on rue Soufflot, turn right down rue Saint-Jacques, the city's old Roman road, and cross the Seine to Ile de la Cité.

4 Notre-Dame ★★★

Visit the cathedral, and if the line is not long and you are not too tired, climb the stairs to see the fabulous view from the towers.

Walk across the Pont d'Arcole to the Right Bank and the place de l'Hôtel de Ville.

5 The Marais ★★★

By now you deserve a break from the city's icons and are ready to shop or just sit in a cafe in this trendy—and beautiful—neighborhood. If you are still hungry for culture, you could visit one of the many museums here, but if not, save them for another day/trip. Around sunset, stop by **place des Vosges** ★★★ (p. 155) for a pre-dinner *apéritif* before you hunt down a restaurant.

Day 2

1 The Louvre ★★★

Start your day as early as possible at this mega-museum, which should keep you going until at least lunchtime, when you can either call it quits or simply take a nice long break and eat at one of the restaurants recommended on p. 80–128. If you are in a hurry to get back to the artwork, there are two tasty sandwich counters under the pyramid. After the Louvre, you can recover in the **Tuileries Garden** ★★★.

Le Nemours ☕

If you are in need of refreshment after the Louvre (and who isn't?), this slick cafe on the Place Colette (right next to the Palais Royal) is an excellent choice. Great pastries, too.

Stroll west through the Tuileries gardens until you arrive at the Place de la Concorde.

2 Place de la Concorde ★★★

From this grandiose plaza (p. 163), you can look down the **Champs-Élysées** ★★ and see the **Arc de Triomphe** ★★★ (p. 156) in the distance.

Take the bus no. 84 or 94, or Métro line 12 (direction Mairie d'Issy) to the 6th arrondissement.

3 St-Germain ★★★

End your day in this delightful neighborhood, where you can visit two of the city's loveliest churches (**St-Germain-des-Prés**, p. 181; **St-Sulpice**, p. 181), check out famous literary cafes (**Les Deux Magots**, p. 127, **Café de Flore,** p. 126), or shop 'til you drop. Then find a restaurant (p. 80), after which you can explore the nearby nightlife.

ICONIC PARIS IN 3 DAYS

Now that you've seen all the absolute must-sees, you have time to explore some of the great stuff you've missed. Here is a third day of discovery. *Start: Musée d'Orsay, Métro: Assemblée Nationale, RER: Musée d'Orsay.*

Day 3

1 Musée d'Orsay ★★★

Spend the morning enjoying this incredible collection of Impressionist and 19th-century artworks (p. 185), and then break for lunch at one of the museum's three restaurants (light snacks, chic cafeteria, or full-on Belle Epoque restaurant). If Impressionists aren't your thing, you could start the day at **Musée du Quai Branly** ★★★ (p. 187).

Leave the museum and take the steps down to the banks of the Seine. If you are starting from Musée d'Orsay, turn left (west); if you are coming from Musée du Quai Branly, turn right (east).

2 Les Berges ★★★

Weather willing, enjoy the newly restored riverbanks (see sidebar on p. 196), strolling westward. Once a busy roadway, this embankment is now a delight for pedestrians with floating gardens, running lanes, and gourmet snack bars (May–Oct only).

At the Pont Alexandre III, go up the stairs and admire the winged horses hovering above before going down into the Métro Invalides and taking line 13 (direction Asnières or St-Denis) and changing to line 12 (direction Porte de la Chapelle) at Gare St-Lazare. Get off at place des Abbesses. Take the elevator up (don't get smart and take the stairs; it's a looong way up).

3 Montmartre ★★★

While away the rest of the afternoon on top of this scenic hill ("La Butte"), clambering around the cobbled streets and perhaps taking a walking tour (p. 200). If your feet have had enough, take the **Montmartrobus,** a small bus run by the transit authority that will take you all over the Butte with a regular bus ticket (for a route map, go to www.ratp.fr). Visit the **Musée de Montmartre** (p. 166) to find out

Sacré Coeur Basilica in Montmartre.

more about the artists and poets who made this neighborhood famous. Around sunset, take in the panorama in front of the **Sacré Coeur,** and bid adieu to Paris with a drink at one of the cafes on **place des Abbesses.**

AN ITINERARY FOR FAMILIES

Paris can be a challenge with kids, and parents may be frustrated because there are so many wonderful grown-up things to see. The trick is to admit to yourself that you just won't see as much as you'd like to and schedule lots of playtime. In the end, everyone will be less stressed out and happier, even if you didn't get to see all 14 of those museums you had planned to visit.

Day 1

Spend the morning at the **Luxembourg Gardens,** where your offspring can go wild at the huge **playground, sail boats** in the fountain, **ride a pony,** or just run around and have fun. Depending on your situation, parents can take turns sneaking off to visit nearby attractions, like the **Panthéon** (p. 177), **Musée Zadkine** (p. 180), and **St-Etienne-du-Mont** (p. 178), or find peace and quiet in a **Latin Quarter** cafe. Then walk down to **St-Germain-des-Prés** (p. 181) and peek into the church before lunching at **Le Relais de l'Entrecôte** (p. 116). After lunch, walk back up to **St-Sulpice** (p. 181) and catch the no. 87 bus to the **Champs de Mars,** where you will visit the **Eiffel Tower** (p. 182). After that, everyone will be pooped. Thankfully, the **boat ride on the Seine** leaves just down by the river.

Day 2

Start your day at the **Jardin des Plantes** (p. 172), where you can choose between the **Museum National d'Histoire Naturelle** (p. 176), the **Ménagerie** (a small zoo; p. 173), and the **playground**. There's also a fun boxwood **labyrinth** at the top of a little hill. Lunch at the nearby **Mosquée de Paris** (p. 125), a lovely tearoom attached to the Paris Mosque with an outdoor enclosed patio. If there are science geeks in your crew, head to the **Musée des Arts et Métiers** (p. 154) after lunch. Otherwise spend the afternoon at the **Palais de Tokyo** (p. 162), a contemporary art museum that is so wacky both kids and parents are sure to have a blast.

Day 3

Kids may not appreciate the view at **Sacré Coeur** (p. 164), but they will enjoy the ride in the **funicular** that you take to get there (follow the signs from the Abbesses Métro stop). Once there, you'll find plenty of space to run around on the esplanade and lots of buskers for entertainment. After toodling around Montmartre, grab a bite to eat at **Coquelicot,** a kid-friendly cafe-cum-bakery on rue des Abbesses. After lunch, wander around the **covered passages** off the Grands Boulevards (see "Arcades," p. 218), where you can window shop without worrying about anyone running off into the street and reward everyone's good behavior with a visit to **Grévin,** a fun wax museum just off the Passage Jouffroy. If everyone is still in a jolly mood, take the number 4 Métro (from Strasbourg Saint-Denis) all the way back to Cité and for an early-evening visit to **Notre-Dame,** when the crowds have thinned.

PARIS FOR ROMANTICS

Paris must be the honeymoon capital of the world, and for good reason—it seems like every time you turn a corner you see something (or someone) beautiful. Here is a 2-day itinerary for a romantic getaway, or just for hopeless romantics. *Start: Pont Neuf, in front of the statue of Henri IV.*

Day 1

This itinerary starts in front of a statue of one of France's great romantic kings, Henri IV, who was known for his good humor and love of wine, women, and song (among other things). Walk down the steps to the pretty **Square du Vert Galant,** a quiet garden at the very tip of the island where you can contemplate the fantastic view and/or make out without anyone bothering you (in general, make-out sessions are well tolerated, and even applauded, in public parks here). From here, you can walk to the **Louvre** (p. 138) and take in endless representations of people in love, from all eras. If you can afford it, splurge on lunch at **Le Grand Véfour** (p. 83), a gourmet restaurant in the **Palais Royal** (p. 141) with magnificent

View of an evening cruise from Pont Neuf.

18th-century decor. If you are on a tight budget, a nice picnic in the **Tuileries Garden** (p. 135) should do the trick. After lunch, drift over to the **Place Vendôme** (p. 143) to look at the high-end jewelry displays. Then wander over to the **Place de la Concorde** (p. 163) and stroll up the **Champs-Élysées.** At this point, you'll be in need of refreshment, so you can stop into **Ladurée** (p. 125) for tea and *macarons.* Now it's time to think about dinner. You could opt for elegant tapas at **Pinxo** or more affordable fusion food at **Le Fumoir** (p. 88). As night falls, the obligatory romantic stroll is along the pedestrian-only **Pont des Arts** (p. 151), where you can take in the gorgeously illuminated monuments lining the Seine.

Day 2

After sleeping in, start your day with a late breakfast at **Le Petit Cler** (p. 122), an adorable cafe on, that's right, rue Cler. After, mosey over to the **Musée Rodin** (p. 188), where you can contemplate, and even imitate, Rodin's famous marble sculpture "The Kiss." When you are done inside, amble about the beautiful gardens and enjoy other legendary works, like "The Thinker." If it's nice out, grab a **Velib'** (p. 283) and cycle down to the recently remodeled banks of the Seine, **Les Berges** (p. 196), where you can cycle or stroll free and easy by the river below the Quai d'Orsay. If the weather is bad, take the no. 13 Métro up to Miromesnil and have tea at the beautiful **tearoom** at the **Musée Jacquemart-André** (p. 125). If you are up for it, visit the museum after (p. 160). Otherwise, it's time to start thinking about the evening's activities. A true romantic will have bought tickets to something at the **Palais Garnier** (p. 146), but others will be just fine with **La Bellevilloise** (p. 246) in trendy Ménilmontant, where you can eat, drink, and dance the night away.

CITY LAYOUT

One of the nice things about Paris is that it's relatively small. It's not a sprawling megalopolis like Tokyo or London. Paris *intramuros,* or inside the long-gone city walls, measures about 87 sq. km (34 sq. miles) excluding the large exterior parks of Bois de Vincennes and the Bois de Boulogne and counts a mere 2.2 million habitants. The suburbs, on the other hand, are sprawling.

Getting around is not difficult, provided you have a general sense of where things are. The city is vaguely egg shaped, with the Seine cutting a wide upside-down U-shaped arc through the middle. The northern half is known as the **Right Bank,** and the southern, the **Left Bank.** To the uninitiated, the only way to remember is to face west, or downstream, so that the Right Bank will be to your right, and the Left to your left.

The city is neatly split up into 20 official **arrondissements,** or districts, which spiral out from the center of the city. The lower the number of the arrondissement, the closer you'll be to the center. As the numbers go up, you'll head toward the outer city limits. The lower-numbered arrondissements also correspond to some of the oldest parts of the city, like the Louvre and the Ile de la Cité (1st arrondissement) or the Marais (3rd and 4th arrondissements). Note that the arrondissements don't always correspond to historical neighborhoods.

If you are in the city for more than a few days, and still believe in maps, it's worthwhile to invest in a **purse-size map book** (ask for a "Paris par Arrondissement" at bookstores or larger newsstands), which costs around 8€, and includes public transit and Velib' stands. Modern souls may prefer to download the application created by the city's transit authority, the RATP. Called "Next Stop Paris," this free app (available on www.ratp.fr as well as iTunes), will guide you around town on public transportation. You may also want to download such usable offline apps as CityMaps2Go, MAPS.ME, and Citymapper.

Paris is old, so the logic of its **streets and avenues** is often as contorted as the city's history. That said, some major boulevards function as reference points. On the Left Bank, boulevard St-Michel acts as a more or less north–south axis, with boulevard St-Germain cutting a vaguely east–west semicircle close to the city center and boulevard Montparnasse cutting a larger one farther out. On the Right Bank, boulevard de Sebastopol runs north–south, with rue de Rivoli crossing east–west near the river. As rue de Rivoli heads east, it turns into rue de St-Antoine; to the west, it jogs around the Place de la Concorde and becomes the Champs-Élysées. Farther north, a network of wide boulevards crisscrosses the area, including boulevards Haussmann, Capucines, and Lafayette.

There are also several enormous star-shaped traffic roundabouts, where several large avenues converge: On the Left Bank place Denfert-Rochereau and place d'Italie are major convergence points; on the Right Bank place de la Bastille, place de le Nation, and place de la République reign to the east, and place de Charles de Gaulle (also called Etoile), home of the Arc de Triomphe, commands to the west.

NEIGHBORHOODS IN BRIEF

Paris is a city for walkers. One lovely neighborhood after another unfolds along its sidewalks, punctuated by plazas and monuments that are best experienced at ground-level. At every turn there seems to be an intriguing area that begs to be explored.

The Right Bank
LOUVRE & ILE DE LA CITÉ

Best for: Museums, historic sights, architecture, transportation hubs
What you won't find: Evening entertainment, quiet streets
Parameters of the neighborhood: 1st arrondissement & part of the 4th

This is the heart of the city, and the oldest part of Paris, though you'd never know it to see it now. In the 19th century, Baron Haussmann, Napoleon's energetic urban planner, tore down almost all of the medieval houses that once covered this area. The **Ile de la Cité** is where the city first emerged after Gallic tribes started camping out here in the 3rd century B.C. By the A.D. 1st century, the Romans were building temples, and by the Middle Ages, a mighty fortress sat across the river on the Right Bank. The fortress has long since been incorporated into the majestic buildings of the **Louvre** (p. 138), which along with the **Jardin des Tuileries** (p. 135) takes up a big chunk of the neighborhood (you can see vestiges of it—the old stone foundations—in the **Carousel du Louvre,** an underground shopping mall set below the museum). Today, the Ile is mostly visited for the soaring **Cathedral of Notre-Dame** (p. 129) and the gemlike **St-Chapelle** (p. 143), along with the historic **Conciergerie** (p. 134).

While the major museums and sites are to the west, the people's part of this neighborhood is on its eastern edge, near **Les Halles** (the city's former food market) and **place du Châtelet.** Parisians descend on this area for their shopping needs, particularly along the bustling **rue de Rivoli** and around the newly remodeled **Forum des Halles** mall and park (p. 145). When the covered food market was demolished and relocated to the suburban town of Rungis in the 1970s, Les Halles lost its charm—and unfortunately, despite its multimillion-euro refurbishment, it's still not particularly picturesque, but it is a hotspot for high-street boutiques. During the day the area's very safe—if not a little overcrowded—but avoid its Châtelet-les-Halles RER station late at night when troublemakers sometimes to hang out. The same is true of the seedy rue St-Denis, just to the east, as this is one of Paris's red-light districts.

OPERA & GRANDS BOULEVARDS

Best for: Good restaurants, covered passages, boutiques
What you won't find: Monuments (with the exception of the Opéra Garnier) and museums, green spaces
Parameters of the neighborhood: 2nd & 9th arrondissements

When the Grands Boulevards were plowed through the city in the 19th century (see box above), they created a new opportunity for stylish Parisians to

Neighborhoods in Brief

SUGGESTED ITINERARIES & NEIGHBORHOODS

Rue Montorgueil in Les Halles district.

stroll, see, and be seen, while theaters and cafes flourished. Times changed and so did fashion, and for decades this area was considered a has-been. In recent years, it's undergone a transformation, particularly in the 9th arrondissement, where cafes, boutiques, and restaurants have popped up in between the church of St-Georges and place Clichy, in an area that used to be known as "New Athens." Many artists of the 19th-century Romantic movement, like George Sand and Eugène Delacroix, lived and worked here; the quaint **Musée de la Vie Romantique** (p. 148) is worth an hour's visit, with beautiful trinkets, letters and drawings that once belonged to Sand. Today, those in the know call it SoPi (South of Pigalle), as entrepreneurial Parisians have begun opening trendy bakeries, shops, and restaurants. The 9th is also the home of the **Grand Magasins** (big-name department stores), which are located on boulevard Haussmann near Gare St-Lazare, as well as the grandiose **Palais Garnier,** home of the Opéra de Paris. An important monument in the 2nd arrondissement is the neo-classical **Palais Brogniart** built between 1808 and 1813 on place de la Bourse to house the city's former **Bourse,** the French stock exchange. To the east, the trendy set descends on **rue Montorgueil,** a picturesque, cobbled market street, and the pedestrian area around **rue Etienne Marcel,** which has gained a reputation as a hip fashion district. This also is the arrondissement with the greatest concentration of *passages,* the **19th-century covered shopping arcades** that were the forefathers of today's shopping malls (but much prettier; see "Arcades," p. 218).

THE MARAIS

Best for: *Restaurants, nightlife, window shopping, 17th-century mansions, museums*
What you won't find: *Bargain shopping, iconic sights, open spaces*
Parameters of the neighborhood: *3rd & 4th arrondissements*

What was once marshy farmland (*marais* means "marsh" or "swamp") quickly became a seat of power when the Knights Templar decided to build a fortress here in the Middle Ages. Other religious orders followed suit, and after King Charles V built a royal residence here in the 14th century, the ensuing real-estate boom produced a slew of mansions and palaces. In the 17th century, King Henri IV created a magnificent square bordered by Renaissance-style townhouses, today called the **place des Vosges.** If the Marais was hot before, then it was positively on fire. Nobles and bourgeois pounced on the neighborhood, each one trying to outdo the other by constructing more and more resplendent *hôtels particuliers,* or private mansions.

But by the time the Revolution flushed out all its aristocrats in the 18th century, the overstuffed quarter was already falling out of fashion. The magnificent dwellings were abandoned, pillaged, partitioned, and turned into stores, workshops, and even factories. The new residents were working class, with more immediate concerns than saving historic patrimony. The neighborhood fell into disrepair, and periodic attempts on the part of the city to "clean up" unfortunately resulted in the destruction of many architectural gems.

The area underwent a real renovation in the 1960s, and today several of the most **magnificent mansions** have been restored and are open to the public in the form of museums like the **Carnavalet** (p. 150), **Musée Cognacq-Jay** (p. 152), and the **Musée Picasso** (p. 154). The architecturally odd **Centre Pompidou** (p. 148) is also located here.

Today the area is terribly *branché* (literally, "plugged in"), and you'll see some of the hippest styles in boutique windows here, as well as dozens of happening restaurants and bars lining the narrow streets. The neighborhood remains a mix, though—jewelry and clothing wholesalers bump up against stylish cafes and shops. The vibrant gay scene on rue Vieille du Temple intersects with what's left of the old Jewish Quarter on **rue des Rosiers.**

CHAMPS-ÉLYSÉES, TROCADÉRO & WESTERN PARIS

Best for: *Serious strolling (on the Champs-Élysées), museums, monuments, chic restaurants, and stores*
What you won't find here: *Affordable eateries or hotels, regular folk*
Parameters of the neighborhood: *8th, 16th & 17th arrondissements*

The **Champs-Élysées** cuts through this area like an asphalt river—it's the widest boulevard in Paris. Crossing the street here feels a bit like traversing a raging torrent (be sure to wait for the light). There are fans and foes of this epic roadway. Some find its lights and sparkles good clean fun, while others dismiss it as crass and commercial. However you feel about the street itself, you're bound to be impressed by the **Arc de Triomphe** (p. 156), which lords

Neighborhoods in Brief

SUGGESTED ITINERARIES & NEIGHBORHOODS

Baron Haussmann: A Man with a Plan

The Paris you see before you was radically transformed in the late–19th century by a pugnacious urban planner named Georges-Eugène Haussmann. Before Haussmann got his hands on it, Paris was a mostly medieval city of tiny streets and narrow alleyways—and major sanitation problems. Everyone agreed that something needed to be done to facilitate traffic and clean up the city, but no one managed to come up with a solution. Enter Baron Haussmann. Named prefect of the Seine by Napoleon III, Haussmann pushed through wide boulevards (Malsherbes, Haussmann, and Sebastapol, among others), demolished dozens of old neighborhoods, and encouraged promoters to build new buildings, following, of course, his strict rules on the style of the facades and the height of the structures. The result was the elegant "Haussmannian" architecture that lines most of the city's streets, as well as

the system of central arteries that collect in star-shaped intersections at various points. The boulevards were strategically placed—one of the reasons for their creation was to make it easier to crush rebellions in the worker's quarters, and garrisons were set up at crucial intersections. Streets were also now too wide in most areas to be easily barricaded. Haussmann also accessorized his new neighborhoods and streets; the famous kiosks, benches, and lampposts you see around the city today date from this epoch. While there's no denying that his projects improved traffic, sanitation, and security and gave a pleasing architectural unity to the cityscape, Haussmann's take-no-prisoners approach has been criticized for having neutered the personality of entire neighborhoods (the Ile de la Cité, for example, was almost entirely razed) and destroying important historical buildings.

over the boulevard from its western tip. To the south of the Champs are some of the most expensive stores, restaurants, and homes in the city (particularly around Ave. Montaigne). To the north, a largely residential area extends up to the beautiful **Parc Monceau** (p. 163), which is surrounded by some equally delightful museums, like the **Musée Jacquemart-André** (p. 160) and the **Musée Nissim de Camondo** (p. 162).

To the west, the illustrious Seizième (sez-ee-*em,* 16th), is the most exclusive arrondissement of the city. Lying on the outer western edge of the city, this residential area is packed with magnificent 19th-century residences and apartment houses, as well as many fine parks and gardens. In fact, the arrondissement shares its western border with the **Bois de Boulogne** (p. 197), one of the city's two huge wooded parks. While the 16th is not known for its liveliness, it is graced with a terrific array of museums. The **Palais de Chaillot** shelters the **Cité de l'Architecture** (p. 158), just down the street is the vast **Musée Guimet** (p. 161), and a little farther on there are two modern art museums in the **Palais de Tokyo,** not to mention a half-dozen others, like the **Marmottan** (p. 161), sprinkled around the arrondissement. And a stop at the esplanade on the **place du Trocadéro** is a must. Between the two wings of the Palais de Chaillot is a superb view of the Eiffel Tower, which you can walk to by strolling down the hill through the **Jardins du Trocadéro.**

MONTMARTRE

Best for: *Restaurants, nightlife, atmosphere*
What you won't find here: *Monuments (with the exception of Sacré Coeur), major museums, grand architecture*
Parameters of the neighborhood: *18th arrondissement*

Once a village overlooking the distant city, Montmartre is now as inseparable from Paris as the Eiffel Tower, which means it's a major target for the tour-bus crowd. And crowded it is, especially in the area immediately around the **Basilica of Sacré-Coeur** (p. 164) and the overdone **place du Tertre.** Yet, if you wander around the cobbled streets that surround **place des Abbesses,** you'll find plenty of hip boutiques and cute restaurants frequented by an upwardly arty crowd, who have also staked out territory in the working-class neighborhoods immediately east and north of the basilica.

Farther east is the lively immigrant quarter of **Barbès,** home to large communities from Africa, India, and the Maghreb (North Africa). Here you'll find a jumble of inexpensive stores selling everything from long-necked teapots to pajama-like salwar trousers, as well as tiny restaurants that offer exotic delicacies.

RÉPUBLIQUE, BASTILLE & EASTERN PARIS

Best for: *Nightlife, good restaurants, Revolutionary history, arty boutiques*
What you won't find here: *Major monuments and museums, high-end shops*
Parameters of the neighborhood: *11th & 12th arrondissements*

These two arrondissements were pretty much off the tourist radar until 1989, when the new **Bastille opera house** provoked an explosion of bars and restaurants in the surrounding streets. Though the shine has already worn off the **nightspots** of rue de Lappe and rue de la Roquette (just off the place de la Bastille) the nocturnal life of the 11th arrondissement is far from dull, as new clubs and cafes have opened farther north on rue de Charonne and **rue Oberkampf.** Now even Oberkampf has become thoroughly saturated, and intrepid partyers are staking out new ground in Ménilmontant in the 20th.

North of the **place de la Bastille** is the vast pedestrian-friendly **place de la République.** To the east is the Faubourg St-Antoine, a historic workers' quarter that has been inhabited by woodworkers and furniture makers since the 13th century. After a few centuries, the density of underpaid, overburdened workers made St-Antoine a breeding ground for revolutionaries. The raging mob that stormed the Bastille prison in 1789 originated here, as did those of the subsequent uprisings of 1830, 1848, and the Paris commune.

In recent years, the area has become a magnet for foodies, as young chefs have opened some of the city's most exciting restaurants, like **Septime** (p. 102) on rue de Charonne. While the architecture here is nowhere near as grand as elsewhere in Paris, the neighborhood has retained an authenticity that's rarely found in the more popular parts of the city. There are still a large number of furniture stores and ébénistes (woodworkers) tucked into large interior courtyards accessible by covered passages off rue du Faubourg

St-Antoine. Make a point of wandering down one of these; you'll be rewarded with a look at a way of life that has survived the centuries. This quarter extends all the way past the **Viaduc des Arts** (p. 217) to the **Gare de Lyon** train station, a magnificent example of Belle Epoque architecture. At the western end is the **Bois de Vincennes,** one of the city's two wooded parks.

BELLEVILLE, CANAL ST-MARTIN & NORTHEAST PARIS

Best for: *Nightlife, restaurants, strolling (along the canal), arty boutiques*
What you won't find here: *Major monuments, museums, and architectural wonders*
Parameters of the neighborhood: *10th, 19th & 20th arrondissements*

For a long time, no one seemed to care about these arrondissements. They were too far from the center of the city, too working-class to be of interest to the trendy set, and too monument-less to appeal to tourists. Then, with real estate skyrocketing, young professionals and artists began to move in. Suddenly, the forgotten **Canal St-Martin** was blooming with cafes and restaurants and the streets around it were full of trendy shops. Artists looking for studio space discovered multi-ethnic **Belleville,** a cultural melting pot of immigrants from North Africa (both Jewish and Muslim), Asia (this is Paris's second biggest Chinatown), and other parts of the world. The vast park and cultural venues of **La Villette** (p. 171) have also attracted new interest away from the center. Happily, these areas aren't really gentrified (yet), and parts are infused with a certain youthful energy that's hard to come by in other areas. Relatively tourist-free, these districts offer an opportunity to see a more local side of the city.

Aside from the **Parc de la Villette,** there are two other green havens here: the **Parc des Buttes Chaumont** (p. 172) and the **Père-Lachaise Cemetery** (p. 167), where the likes of Jim Morrison, Edith Piaf, and Chopin are buried. There are also several good bars and music venues around **Ménilmontant** to the north of the cemetery and around **place St-Blaise** to the south.

The Left Bank
LATIN QUARTER

Best for: *Affordable dining, student bars, art-house movie theaters, museums, Jardin des Plantes*
What you won't find here: *Good shopping, quiet (at least not in the environs of place St-Michel)*
Parameters of the neighborhood: *5th arrondissement*

Since the Middle Ages, when the **Sorbonne** and other academic institutions were founded, this has been a student neighborhood. (It earned its name as the "Latin" Quarter because back in the old days, all classes were taught in Latin.) Today the area still harbors the highest number of colleges and universities in the city, and you'll certainly see plenty of students and professors hanging around the restaurants and cafes around here. You'll also see plenty of tourists, who tend to swarm around the warren of tiny streets that lead off of the place

Pantheon.

St-Michel. Avoid rue de la Huchette (except for the great swing-dancing club, **Le Caveau de la Huchette;** p. 244), which is lined with garish restaurants of questionable quality. **Boulevard St-Michel,** a legendary artery that once was lined with smoky cafes filled with thinkers and rabble-rousers, has now fallen prey to chain stores, though a few big bookstores have held on. The boulevard also harbors the **Musée de Cluny** (p. 177), a terrific collection of medieval art and Roman ruins.

For a more authentic taste of this neighborhood, wander east and upward, around the windy streets on the hill that leads to the **Panthéon** (p. 177), the church of **St-Etienne-du-Mont** (p. 178) and around rue Monge, toward the lovely **Jardin des Plantes** (p. 172). Surrounded by the city's **natural history museum,** this botanical garden is a wonderful place to relax. Down by the Seine, the museum of the **Institut du Monde Arabe** is housed in a spectacular building by architect Jean Nouvel.

ST-GERMAIN-DES-PRÉS & LUXEMBOURG

Best for: Fine dining, historic cafes, shopping, parks (the Jardin du Luxembourg)
What you won't find here: Penniless intellectuals and artists, low prices
Parameters of the neighborhood: 6th arrondissement

The church of **St-Germain-des-Prés** (p. 181), the heart of this neighborhood, got its name (St. Germain of the Fields) because when it was built in the 11th century, it was in the middle of the countryside. What a difference a millennium makes. The church became the nucleus of a huge and powerful abbey, which would later constitute an autonomous minicity complete with a hospital and a prison. The Revolution cut the church down to its current size, and an elegant collection of apartment houses, squares, and parks grew up around it, making it one of Paris's most appealing areas to live in (as real-estate prices will attest). If the neighborhood has always had aristocratic airs (it was a favorite haunt of the nobility during the 17th and 18th c.), during the last part of the 19th century up to the mid–20th century it was also a magnet for penniless artists and intellectuals, who hung out in legendary cafes like the **Café de Flore** (p. 126) and **Les Deux Magots** (p. 127).

Today few struggling creative types can afford either the rents or the price of a cup of coffee around here, and young artists and thinkers have moved north and east to cheaper parts of town. Though the ambience is decidedly bourgeois these days, the neighborhood is still dynamic, and the cafes and shops along the boulevard St-Germain are crowded with a mix of politicians, gallery owners, French celebrities and editors. This is also a fun neighborhood for shopping—there's everything here from 500€ pumps on chic rue des St-Pères to 30€ sundresses on the more plebian rue des Rennes. And when you've tired yourself out, you can stroll over to the magnificent **Jardin du Luxembourg** (p. 179) for timeout by the fountain.

EIFFEL TOWER & LES INVALIDES

Best for: Iconic monuments, majestic avenues, grand vistas, museums
What you won't find here: Affordable restaurants or shopping, nightlife
Parameters of the neighborhood: 7th arrondissement

The **Eiffel Tower** (p. 182) reigns over this swanky arrondissement, where the streets that aren't lined with ministries and embassies are filled with elegant apartment buildings and prohibitively expensive stores and restaurants. A large portion of the neighborhood is taken up by the **Champs de Mars,** a park that stretches between the tower and the **Ecole Militaire,** and by the enormous esplanade in front of the **Invalides** (p. 184), which sweeps down to the Seine with much pomp and circumstance. Some of the city's best museums are around here, including the **Musée d'Orsay** (p. 185), the **Musée Rodin** (p. 188), and the **Musée du Quai Branly** (p. 187), whose wacky architecture has added some spice to this very staid area.

Café Les Deux Magots.

While there's certainly a lot to see here, the neighborhood is a little short on human warmth—this is not the place to come to see regular Parisians in their natural habitat. One exception is the area around the pedestrian **rue Cler,** a market street that is home to many delightful small restaurants and food stores. Word is out about this cozy corner, however, so expect to see plenty of tourists when you go into that cute *boulangerie* for a couple of croissants.

MONTPARNASSE

Best for: *Shopping, historic cafes, nightlife*
What you won't find here: *Extraordinary architecture, museums, monuments*
Parameters of the neighborhood: *14th & 15th arrondissements*

In the early 1970s, government officials decided the time had come to make Paris a modern city. Blithely putting aside concerns for historic patrimony and architectural harmony, the old Montparnasse train station and its immediate neighborhood were torn down and a 56-story glass tower and shopping complex was erected in its place. A new train station was constructed behind the tower, as well as a barrage of modern apartment buildings and offices. Fortunately, even ugly contemporary architecture didn't manage to kill the neighborhood—at the foot of the **Tour Montparnasse,** life goes on as it always has. A few steps away from the station, tiny old streets are still lined with stores, cafes, and *créperies* (crêpe restaurants), these last being an outgrowth of the large Breton (that is, from Brittany) community that still inhabits this area. Farther down boulevard Montparnasse, you'll find legendary brasseries like **La Coupole** (p. 127) and **Le Select,** where Picasso, Max Jacob, and Henry Miller used to hang out in the 1920s. For a bit of calm, take a walk around the **Cimetiére du Montparnasse** (p. 189), where artists like Charles Baudelaire and Constantin Brancusi are buried. In the evenings, crowds pour into the many restaurants and movie theaters around the station.

To the south, the arrondissement takes a more residential turn, with the exception of rue Daguerre, a lively market street a block south of the cemetery, and farther south, rue d'Alésia, a discount shopper's mecca. The 14th is also home to **Les Catacombes** (p. 189), former limestone mines lined with the bones of millions of Parisians whose remains were moved here in the 18th century when the city's overcrowded graveyards became unhygienic. It makes for a spooky (and intriguing) visit.

WHERE TO STAY

There are more than 1,500 hotels in Paris, from palaces fit for a pasha to tiny, family-run operations whose best features are their warm welcome and personal touch. In theory, you should be able to find something in line with your budget, your timeframe, and your personal tastes. But if you can't find the hotel of your dreams in the list that follows, don't despair—at the end of this chapter I list alternative lodging options, like bed-and-breakfasts and short-term apartment rentals.

WHAT TO EXPECT

4

Parisian lodgings can be many things: charming, opulent, cozy, homey, and even outrageous. But keep in mind the following: **Parisian hotel rooms tend to be small.** Why do we stress this? Because inevitably, tourists who come from countries where hotel rooms are often staggeringly big (does anyone actually need two king-size beds in a double room?) are shocked when they check in to tiny family hotels in ancient buildings. And its not just budget lodgings—even nifty boutique hotels can have snug rooms.

Don't be too hard on the management, however; most historic Parisian buildings are protected by city regulations that make it difficult, if not impossible, to make structural changes. If you absolutely need room to stretch out, ask for a triple or even a quadruple room (if they're available). Otherwise, consider an international chain hotel, where space and extra amenities are usually not a problem, or an apartment rental with a separate bedroom.

Amenities

Unless you are staying in a hotel in our "expensive" category, you should be prepared for **minimal amenities.** Washcloths are scarce, toiletries are few, and a few of the smaller hotels still don't have elevators (and when they do, they're often closet size). Assume that most guest rooms are large enough to sleep in comfortably, but you'll have to do your yoga workout somewhere else. All of the rooms in the hotels listed below have in-room bathrooms with toilets, unless otherwise mentioned.

Now that we've prepared you for the worst, here's what Parisian hotels *do* have (besides charm and personality, *bien sûr*). Almost all have in-room TVs with cable channels and hair dryers in the

GETTING THE best rate

These days, finding a good room rate is a bit like playing the stock market. You see a great rate on a cute double in the Latin Quarter. Do you buy, or do you wait to see whether the price dips in the morning? Prices on hotel and aggregator websites vary radically from day to day, depending on availability, season, and the vagaries of the market. Variables include date, demand, length of stay, and if you are prepared to pay for a non-refundable booking.

While online travel booking sites like Expedia and Priceline are convenient to use when searching for room rates, often the best place to look is the **hotel's official website,** particularly in the case of smaller, affordable hotels. Why? Those sites charge hotels fees as much as 20%, a percentage that many hotels feel obliged to pass on to the customer. Another low-tech but fruitful method is to simply call the hotel and see what they are offering that day—you might happen on a nonpublished, last-minute discount.

Most hotels are listed on both online travel agency sites and those that aggregate prices from a number of sources. Frommers.com did a study, in the spring of 2017, to determine which sites consistently found the best rates for city center hotels and two websites did far better than the rest of the pack: **Booking.com** and **Agoda.com**. So do search those two, along with contacting hotels directly. A nice boutique hotel that you thought was completely out of your budget might have rates that are not so different from middle- or even low-price lodgings—if you reserve several months in advance or happen on a seasonal promotion. Many hotels offer discounts for stays of over 3 nights; if they don't offer one upfront, it's worth asking.

Perpetually fluctuating prices make it difficult to fix rates in guidebooks; the prices quoted here attempt to offer a realistic range, with the top price reflecting the rack rate (the maximum "official" rate) and the lower figure corresponding to the average discount Internet rate. **Note:** Unless indicated, rates do not include breakfast.

---

bathrooms. Irons and hair dryers (if they are not in the room) can usually be found at the reception desk. Almost all have hotel-wide Wi-Fi.

Most hotel rooms have air-conditioning. That said, since normal Parisian weather is anything but tropical—June and July can be sweater weather—your chances of encountering sweltering heat are relatively low. Still, if you're coming in the summer months, check; you may want to think twice about taking a room on a non-air-conditioned top floor or facing a noisy street that makes it impossible to open the windows at night.

While a continental **breakfast** (juice, coffee, or tea, and a croissant and/or baguette) is still the traditional way to start the day, many hotels now also offer a generous buffet that may include various breads, sweet buns, fruit, yogurt, ham, cereal, juice, and sometimes eggs and bacon. A buffet breakfast might seem pricey at somewhere between 15€–25€, but keep in mind that a bare bones continental version will usually cost at least 9€. If you are a light eater, you'll likely spend less and have more fun at the corner cafe. Romantics will appreciate the fact that at most hotels, you can have your breakfast delivered to your room for no extra charge.

PRACTICAL MATTERS

When to Reserve

Paris is one of the world's top travel destinations, and hotels can book up fast during high season (see below). Even during what should be a slow month, the city might be completely booked up because of a trade show or festival that you are not aware of.

Make sure you understand the cancellation policy—most hotels take at least 1 night's stay as a deposit, which they will keep if you don't show up. What's more, cancellation policies vary depending on the type of rate or package you end up with. Like airlines, some hotels now offer special low prices that must be paid up in advance and are nonrefundable. Some insist that you cancel a week in advance to get a full refund; for others, 24 hours will do. Read the fine print when you reserve.

High & Low Seasons

Parisian hotel rate fluctuations are a little like the weather—it's difficult to distinguish one season from the other. Everyone seems to agree that August is the lowest of low season. That's when most of France heads for the beach, and hotels are desperate for business. December in the run-up to Christmas is also low, but the days around New Year's are high. The rest of the year is a free-for-all, heavily dependent on the scheduling of trade shows. For the nitty-gritty on trade-show dates, visit the **Paris Tourist Office site** (www.parisinfo. com) and click on "Going Out," then "Fairs and Trade Shows in Paris," where you can get a rundown on both trade shows and conventions. In general, September and October are usually high season, while November, the first 2 weeks of December, and January are low season. Once spring arrives, prices tend to rise.

Seeing Stars

French hotels are graded by a government-regulated system that hands out 0 to 5 stars (plus "Palace'" status for upper-end five-starred properties; see p. 57), which the hotels then must post at the entrance to their establishment. Unfortunately, palaces aside, the criteria used often has more to do with quantity than quality. Rooms are rated for size, number of beds, and the presence or absence of items like hair dryers and minibars—overall atmosphere and charm are not necessarily a factor. So it's possible to end up in a darling two-star hotel that's much nicer than a three-star down the street with big rooms and a minibar but all the ambience of a rehab center. What's more, the recent addition of a fifth star prompted everyone to try to jump up a notch, so the most basic hotel might now have three stars. One thing is sure: The more stars it has, the more a hotel is allowed to charge. Our advice: Use the French star system as a rough estimate of quality, then do some homework on your own.

By the way, the stars besides the listings below are our own and have no relation to the French star system. You'll find our criteria at the front of the book.

THE RIGHT BANK
Louvre & Île de la Cité (1st Arrondissement)

It was here that Paris began, and it is here that you will still find a great number of the city's most famous sights—and the highest concentration of tourists. While the central location is tempting, be forewarned that this is not where you will find cute neighborhood stores or a slice of typical Parisian life. What's more, the area is pretty dead at night. Admittedly, if you only are in town for 1 or 2 days, a central locale is key, since time will be of the essence. But if you have a little more time, you'll find much more comfortable lodgings, at lower prices, just a 10-minute walk away.

EXPENSIVE

Hôtel Brighton ★★★   If you pop for a room with a view at this gracious hotel, you will not be disappointed. A splendid vista from the Louvre to the Tuilleries gardens and the Eiffel Tower spreads before you as you loll in your bed. While not every room has the jackpot view, most in the "deluxe" and "executive" categories do, and all have a subdued, sophisticated decor with elegant fabrics draping the windows, and tasteful decorative touches. Top notch-bedding, plush bathrobes and high thread counts are all part of the package. In short, this classy establishment belongs under the arcades of the rue de Rivoli, and if it is not quite as grand as its neighbor the Meurice (where you'll get a 20% discount at the spa), it is also about one-third the price. Rooms are spacious and airy, with a mix of reproduction and real antiques and roomy bathrooms. Understandably, rooms with views book up early.

218 rue de Rivoli, 1st arrond. www.paris-hotel-brighton.com. ℂ **01-47-03-61-61.** 61 units. 239€–400€ double; 290€–680€ suite (sleeps 2–4). Métro: Tuileries. **Amenities:** Bar; concierge; laundry service; room service; tea room; Wi-Fi (free).

MODERATE

Hôtel Britannique ★★   When you step into the salon off the lobby here, you'll be tempted to immediately throw yourself into one of the plush armchairs and order a cup of tea. Decidedly British in decor and atmosphere, these lodgings are located on a remarkably quiet street, considering that it is about a minute away from the busy Place du Châtelet. The immaculate, soundproofed rooms are comfortably and conservatively furnished, with gentle swags of drapery hanging over the bed and windows. Rooms facing the street are the most pleasant, with large windows that offer views of the Théâtre du Châtelet across the way; rooms on the courtyard are larger, though, and can be made into triples. There

> ### Going Solo
>
> Though the listings below show room rates for two people, single rooms are often available for solo travelers at reduced rates. The best tactic is to ask the hotel directly, since they don't always advertise their smallest rooms, even on their own websites. While some singles are comparable to a regular double, others might be tiny, and the toilet facilities may be on the landing.

4

WHERE TO STAY | The Right Bank

price CATEGORIES

Expensive	300€–500€
Moderate	150€–300€
Inexpensive	Under 150€

are adjoining rooms for families and one suite that sleeps four. A good value, considering the quality of the lodgings and the central location.

20 ave. Victoria, 1st arrond. www.hotel-britannique.fr. ℰ **01-42-33-74-59.** 39 units. 208€–299€ double; 350€–518€ suite (sleeping 2–4). Métro: Châtelet. **Amenities:** Wi-Fi (free).

Hôtel Thérèse ★★★ Just a few steps from the Palais Royal and a few more from the Louvre, these beautiful lodgings combine old-fashioned Parisian charm with modern Parisian chic. The decor blends colors, textures and styles in a way that complements the building's history instead of clashing with it. Comfy sofas invite you to relax in the lobby, whose stylish decor includes lots of mirrors, bookcases, and unique lighting fixtures. The stylish yet comfortable decor extends to the rooms, which feature pleasing soft colors, subtle geometric patterns, upholstered headboards, and on the third floor, very high ceilings. Despite its central location, the tiny street is very quiet, and light floods the building from both sides. Rooms are Parisian size, which means the least expensive are small; the rates go up with the dimensions. There is a handicapped-accessible room on the ground floor.

5–7 rue Thérèse, 1st arrond. www.hoteltherese.com. ℰ **01-42-96-10-01.** 40 units. 200€–390€ double; 350€–370€ Family room (up to 4). Métro: Palais-Royal or Pyramides. **Amenities:** Bar; bicycles; concierge; laundry; loaner laptops, room service; Wi-Fi (free).

INEXPENSIVE

Hôtel du Cygne ★ Chock-full of exposed beams and stone walls (not to mention narrow stairways—there is no elevator), this 17th-century building has been carefully restored, and the simple lodgings receive ongoing tender loving care from Isabelle Gouge, the friendly owner. Most of the rooms are predictably small, but are cheerfully decorated with fresh white walls, floral bedspreads, and the owner's personal touches. If you can handle the climb to the top floor, you'll be rewarded with a roomy suite that can sleep three. The hotel is located near Les Halles (a little seedy at night) and the Montorgueil neighborhood (very hip at night).

3–5 rue du Cygne, 1st arrond. www.hotelducygne.fr. ℰ **01-42-60-14-16.** 18 units. 80€–135€ double; 155–185€ suite up to 3 people. Métro: Etienne Marcel. RER: Les Halles. **Amenities:** Wi-Fi (free).

The Marais (3rd & 4th Arrondissements)

Centuries ago, this neighborhood was a swamp (*marais*), but now it's merely swamped with stylish boutiques, restaurants, and people who seem to have

Right Bank West Hotels

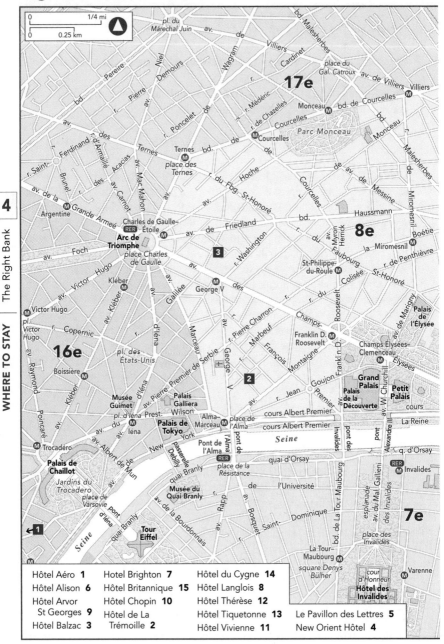

Hôtel Aéro **1**	Hotel Brighton **7**	Hôtel du Cygne **14**	
Hôtel Alison **6**	Hôtel Britannique **15**	Hôtel Langlois **8**	
Hôtel Arvor	Hôtel Chopin **10**	Hôtel Thérèse **12**	
St Georges **9**	Hôtel de La	Hôtel Tiquetonne **13**	Le Pavillon des Lettres **5**
Hôtel Balzac **3**	Trémoille **2**	Hôtel Vivienne **11**	New Orient Hôtel **4**

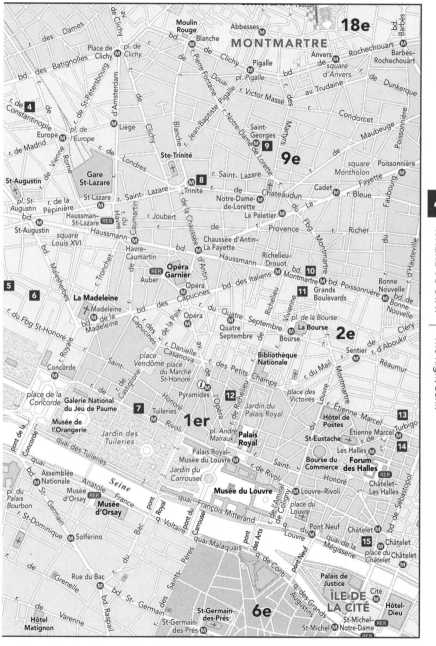

Parisian Hotels & Accessibility

Hotels in centuries-old buildings may be full of charm, but they also often feature narrow staircases and/or tiny elevators, so if accessibility is a concern, be sure to check when you reserve. Parisian hotels are evolving: Most hotels in the moderate and expensive categories now have at least one wheelchair-accessible room.

just stepped out of a hair salon. Stunning 16th- and 17th-century mansions, which had fallen into disrepair, have been scrubbed down and fixed up over the past few decades, and they shine like pearls along the narrow streets of this fashionable area where clothing stores, cool bars, and clubs have invaded Paris's historic Jewish quarter. There are many excellent museums here, including the Musée Picasso and the Musée Carnavalet. In short, this is a great area to stay in, but also a victim of its own success. You might not hear a lot of French in some of those cute cafes on rue Vielle du Temple.

EXPENSIVE

Hôtel du Petit Moulin ★★ Famed designer Christian Lacroix has turned one of the oldest bakeries in Paris into a hip hotel with a artistic soul. While its 19th-century facade hasn't changed since it sold baguettes, the inside now reflects the lovely, if idiosyncratic, world of Mr. Lacroix. Each room has a different constellation of colors, periods, and patterns that somehow blend together in elegant harmony. Some of the artwork on the walls is by the master himself. You can serve yourself in the cozy "honesty bar"; just write down what you consumed on the pad of paper. Guests have access to the spa and bicycles at the Pavillon de la Reine (see below), which is under the same ownership.

29–31 rue du Poitou, 3rd arrond. www.hoteldupetitmoulin.com. ✆ **01-42-74-10-10.** 17 units. 185€–500€ double; 360€–500€ junior suite for up to 3 people. Parking 20€. Métro: St-Sebastien Froissart. **Amenities:** Concierge service; honesty bar; iPads and Mac-Books loaned to guests; laundry service; room service; Wi-Fi (free).

Pavillon de la Reine ★★★ Just off the place des Vosges, this "Queen's Pavilion" harkens back to the days when the magnificent square was the home of royalty. You certainly feel like a noble as you pass through an arcade into a small formal garden, and enter this elegant mansion, which is set back from the hustle and bustle of the Marais. Despite its 54 rooms, the hotel feels small and intimate, like a lord's private hunting lodge in the country. The decor is a suave and subtle combination of modern and antique history: Dark period furniture blends with rich colors on the walls and beds, and choice objects and historic details abound. Several of the deluxe rooms are duplexes with a cozy sleeping loft; two new luxury suites were added in 2017. There is also a full spa for guests, offering sauna and fitness room, as well as massages and treatments.

28 place des Vosges, 3rd arrond. www.pavillon-de-la-reine.com. ✆ **01-40-29-19-19.** 56 units. 340€–550€ double; 600€–2,500€ suite. Métro: Bastille. **Amenities:** Bar; concierge; fitness room; laundry service; room service; sauna; spa; Wi-Fi (free).

Courtyard entrance of Pavillon de la Reine.

MODERATE

Hôtel Caron de Beaumarchais ★★★   In the 18th century, Pierre August Caron de Beaumarchais—author of *The Barber of Seville* and *The Marriage of Figaro*—lived near here, and this small hotel celebrates both the playwright and the magnificent century he lived in. The walls are covered in high-quality reproductions of period fabrics; rooms are furnished with authentic antique writing tables and chandeliers; and period paintings and first-edition pages of *The Barber of Seville* hang on the walls. You half expect Pierre Auguste himself to come prancing through the door. The rooms are smallish, but the high ceilings (with exposed beams) and tall windows let in lots of light, making them feel spacious. Unlike other parts of the Marais, there are food stores, buses and metro stops close by, and it's a short walk to the Seine.

12 rue Vieille-du-Temple, 4th arrond. www.carondebeaumarchais.com. ✆ **01-42-72-34-12.** 19 units. 120€–200€ double. Métro: St-Paul or Hôtel de Ville. **Amenities:** Wi-Fi (free).

Hôtel Saint-Louis en l'Isle ★★   Set on the tiny main drag of the tranquil Île Saint-Louis, this friendly place has a prime location on one of the city's most desirable pieces of real estate. The impeccable rooms are done up in a low-key modern style with historic touches: stone floors, dark wood furniture, and framed etchings of 17th- and 18th-century nobles from days of yore. The street-side rooms are quiet but a little dark; if you want a lot of light ask for a corner room, or splurge on one of the rooms on the top floor. The elevators stop at landings between floors, so you'll have to be able to manage stairs here. There is a handicap-accessible room on the ground floor.

75 rue St-Louis-en-l'Ile, 4th arrond. www.saintlouisenlisle.com. ✆ **01-46-34-04-80.** 20 units. 185€–255€ double; 245€–295€ triple. Métro: Pont Marie. **Amenities:** Wi-Fi (free).

Jules et Jim ★★   The entrance to this gem of a hotel is so discreet you could walk right past it, but find your way inside and you're in for a treat: A cobbled courtyard with an outdoor fireplace merges into a low-key cocktail bar with vintage-inspired furniture, while the rooms—all ultra-comfortable—flaunt hip decor such as white walls with clever back lighting and beautiful wall art. Some have bathrooms with floor-to-ceiling windows; others, on the upper floors, provide panoramic rooftop views. For those needing extra rooms there's the duplex suite, resplendent in dark woods and retro-chic furniture (but its staircase is not child-proof, so this isn't appropriate for families with toddlers).

11 rue des Gravilliers, 3rd arrond. www.hoteljulesetjim.com. ℘ **01-44-54-13-13.** 23 units. 221€–310€ double; 400€ duplex for up to 4 people. Métro: Arts et Métiers. **Amenities:** Cocktail bar; Wi-Fi (free).

INEXPENSIVE

Hôtel Jeanne d'Arc le Marais ★★★   Considering its prime location in the southern Marais, right next to the leafy place du Marché St-Catherine, this cozy hotel is an incredible deal. Not only that, its simple rooms have recently had a tasteful make-over, featuring textured wallpaper and contemporary lighting fixtures. And as ever, everything is impeccable, from the quality bedding to the spotless bathrooms. Families will be interested in the spacious and reasonably priced quads. Rooms book up months in advance, especially for fashion weeks (Feb, Mar, July, and Sept). *Note:* There is another hotel with the same name in the 13th arrondissement—make sure you have the right hotel when you reserve, or you will be in for an unpleasant surprise.

3 rue de Jarente, 4th arrond. www.hoteljeannedarc.com. ℘ **01-48-87-62-11.** 34 units. 110€–215€ double, 180€–290€ quad. Métro: St-Paul. **Amenities:** Computer in lobby; Wi-Fi (free).

MIJE Auberge de Jeunesse ★   Yes, it's a hostel, but one that is housed in three different 17th-century buildings, complete with exposed beams and ancient courtyards. The private rooms and dormitories are basic but spotless, and the location (southern Marais) can't be beat. While it's not as much fun as Generator (p. 64), it's more centrally located and has a higher charm factor. There's a 3€ per person membership fee (per year).

Guest room and balcony at the Hôtel Caron de Beaumarchais.

11 rue du Fauconnier; 6 rue de Fourcy; and 12 rue des Barres, 4th arrond. www.mije.com. ℘ **01-42-74-23-45.** 435 beds. 34€ per person in dormitories; private rooms: 82€ double, 107€ triple, 134€ quad, 168€ quint, 201€ sext. Breakfast and sheets included in room rate. Métro: St-Paul. **Amenities:** Library; restaurant; Wi-Fi (free).

Cosmos Hôtel **10**
Eden Lodge Paris **11**
Generator Paris **8**
Hostel MIJE
 Fauconnier **5**
Hôtel Caron de
 Beaumarchais **4**
Hôtel de la
 Porte Dorée **13**
Hôtel du Petit
 Moulin **3**
Hôtel Jeanne d'Arc
 le Marais **6**
Hôtel Paris Bastille
 Boutet **12**
Hôtel Saint-Louis
 en l'Isle **1**
Jules et Jim **2**
Le Citizen **9**
Pavillon de la Reine **7**

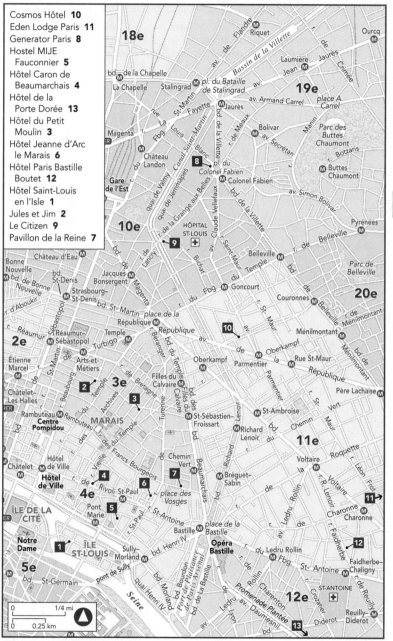

4

WHERE TO STAY | The Right Bank

Even if Paris isn't quite as connected as some other major international cities, free Wi-Fi is available throughout almost all hotels, and there is often a computer or laptop available for guest use in the lobby as well as a printer. Some hotels even loan iPads or laptops to their guests. Wi-Fi is also widely available in restaurants, train stations, and even public gardens.

Champs-Élysées, Trocadéro & Western Paris (8th, 16th & 17th Arrondissements)

Even grander than the 7th arrondissement, the area around the Champs-Élysées is positively mythic. To the south of the boulevard, along avenues Montaigne and George V, are the most exclusive designer shops in the city; to the north, elegant buildings, shops, and restaurants stretch up to lovely Parc Monceau, which has some excellent museum neighbors, including Musée Jacquemart-André. Affordable lodgings are scarce around here, especially near the Champs and the Arc de Triomphe, where the high prices often have more to do with the location than the quality of the accommodations. Ironically, the location is not particularly central; it's a good hike from here to Notre-Dame.

EXPENSIVE

Hôtel Balzac ★★★ Chandeliers and yards of rich fabric await you in the lobby of these luxurious lodgings, which were built for the director of the Paris Opéra in 1853. Just a few steps away from the Champs-Élysées, this classy townhouse features spacious rooms with huge beds, high threadcounts, and swags of chiffon and velour around the bed and windows. The ambience is classic and very French, with reproduction antiques, high ceilings, and subtle colors. Visiting dignitaries can opt for a Presidential Suite with views of the Eiffel Tower; lesser mortals will be happy with the junior and corner suites, which feature separate sitting areas. There's a covered interior courtyard where you can enjoy a drink on a plush sofa. **Pierre Gagnaire,** a gourmet pleasure palace of a restaurant, is in the same building.

6 rue Balzac, 8th arrond. www.hotelbalzac.com. ✆ **01-44-35-18-00.** 69 units. 300€–660€ double; 480€–1,320€ suite and junior suites; 1,440€–2,200€ Royal and Presidential suites. Métro: George V. **Amenities:** Restaurant; babysitting; bar; business center; dry cleaning; room service; concierge; private parking (30€); Wi-Fi (free).

Hôtel de La Trémoille ★★★ Just off the hyper-sophisticated avenue George V and steps away from the Champs-Élysées, this classy hotel is as refined and elegant as its surroundings, and has a lovely young staff to attend to your (almost) every need. The spacious rooms have exceptionally high ceilings (except for those on the sixth floor), tall windows, and a subtly modern decor. The white walls have kept their 19th-century trimmings, while the curtains, bedsteads, and covers are all rich fabrics in subtle shades of grey, purple or green. Rooms on the second and fifth floor have small balconies. The suites are vast, by Paris standards. Guests have access to the hotel's new spa and fitness space, as well as its gourmet restaurant, Louis 2.

14 rue de la Trémoille, 8th arrond. www.tremoille.com. ✆ **01-56-52-14-00.** 93 units. 295€–730€ double; 500€–1,260€ suite. Métro: Alma-Marceau. **Amenities:** Restaurant; bar; concierge; iPod docks, laundry; spa; room service; Wi-Fi (free).

MODERATE

Hotel Aéro ★★   Located in what used to be the village of Passy (before it got gobbled up by the 16th arrondissement), these colorful lodgings lie on a cute pedestrian market street. The soundproofed rooms are just upstairs from the hotel's restaurant, which features a large outdoor terrace that sprawls out onto a leafy square. Despite the decorator's fondness for fuchsia, the room decor is pleasantly subdued, with lots of warm wood colors and arty mosaic tiles in the bathrooms. Everything is in tip-top condition, and double-paned windows keep out most street noise. If you are a light sleeper, ask for a room on the courtyard.

3 place de Passy, 16th arrond. www.parishotelaero.com. ✆ **01-46-47-10-00.** 14 units. 150€–230€ double. Métro: Passy or La Muette. **Amenities:** Restaurant; bar; concierge service; Wi-Fi (free).

Le Pavillon des Lettres ★★★   Just around the corner from the Élysées Palace (headquarters of the French President) and across the street from the powerful Ministry of the Interior, this tastefully chic hotel is located in the navel of the French political universe. The theme here, however, is literature. Each of the 26 exquisite rooms is designated by a different letter of the alphabet and linked to a famous author. If you are in room Z, for example, you

Junior suite at Hôtel de la Trémoille.

might find a copy of Zola's *Nana* on the bedside table and some of the author's text on the wall behind the headboard. The room design is serenely hip: The colors are sober, but the materials are soft and comforting, in handsome shades of grey, olive green, beige, and mauve. While the rooms are a little small, the ceilings are mostly high and bathrooms are spacious. Tapas are served at cocktail hour.

12 rue des Saussaies, 8th arrond. www.pavillondeslettres.com. ✆ **01-49-24-26-26.** 26 units. 200€–420€ double; 330€–530€ junior suite. Métro: Madeleine. **Amenities:** Bar; bicycles; concierge; library; laundry; room service; iPads for guests; Wi-Fi (free).

INEXPENSIVE

Hôtel Alison ★★ While the lobby decor at this comfortable, family-run hotel hasn't changed since at least 1982 (think Almodóvar movies), it is impeccably clean and shiny, as are the relatively spacious rooms. There's nothing frumpy or musty about these crisp lodgings. The owners simply haven't felt the need to update the shiny white ceilings in certain rooms, or the square black headboards in others. However you feel about beige walls and chocolate carpets, you should be pleased with the generally high level of comfort here and the excellent location around the corner from the Madeleine and a short stroll to the Champs-Élysées and the Place de la Concorde. The owners are art fans, and the paintings hung throughout the hotel belong to their private collection; not surprisingly, the clientele includes a lot of people from the art world.

21 rue de Surène, 8th arrond. www.hotel-alison.com. ✆ **01-42-65-54-00.** 34 units. 142€–212€ double; 202€–212€ triple; 202€–364€ family suite. Métro: Charles-de-Gaulle–Etoile or George V. **Amenities:** Concierge; laundry service; Wi-Fi (free).

New Orient Hôtel ★★★ This lovely hotel offers comfortable rooms with high ceilings, 19th-century moldings, and antique headboards and armoires at a fraction of the price of a drab four-star nearby. While it may not be on top of the Champs-Élysées, it's not far, and it's close to stately Parc Monceau and a quick trot to the Saint Lazare train station. The friendly owners, who are inveterate flea-market browsers, have refinished and restored the antique furniture themselves. Rooms (many of which have small balconies) are small, but in tip-top shape, and bathrooms sparkle. Though there's an elevator, you'll have to negotiate stairs to get to it. Best rates are on the hotel website.

16 rue de Constantinople, 8th arrond. www.hotelneworient.com. ✆ **01-45-22-21-64.** 30 units. 110€–220€ double; 130€–248€ triple. Métro: Villiers, Europe, or St-Lazare. **Amenities:** Computer in lobby; concierge; Wi-Fi (free).

Opéra & Grands Boulevards (2nd & 9th Arrondissements)

The area just north of the Grands Boulevards (those wide throughways that Baron Haussman plowed through Paris in the 19th c.) and just below Montmartre is a lovely mix of hip bars and restaurants and old-time Paris, with a

The ultimate in upscale Parisian hospitality is the Palace Hotel, a rating given only to establishments able to symbolize "excellence and perfection, luxury and timelessness." It's here you'll find the Michelin-starred restaurants, spas, pools and the largest bedrooms. Palaces also usually occupy historically important buildings, like the **Peninsula** (http://paris.peninsula.com), where George Gershwin wrote "An American in Paris" in 1928. If you fancy splurging on a luxury night or two, here are our favorites: **The Plaza Athénée** (www.dorchester collection.com), for the trendy bar and Alain Ducasse's fantabulous fish restaurant; **Le Bristol** (www.lebristolparis. com), for its enduring elegance and three-Michelin-starred dining; and **Le Fouquet's Barrière** (www.hotelsbarriere. com), for the cruise-ship-style pool and the brasserie, where movie stars dine like royalty after the *Césars*, France's *equivalement* of the Oscars.

good sprinkling of small museums for a dose of culture. While you won't find too many big monuments around here, the area's upsides include lower room rates and a more neighborhood-y feel (at least, away from the boulevards).

MODERATE

Hôtel Arvor St Georges ★★   These spiffy lodgings are located in the charming "New Athens" neighborhood, where 19th-century Romantics like George Sand and Frédéric Chopin lived and worked. Maybe that's why Mme. Flamarion, of the famous French publishing house, decided to open this arty yet relaxed hotel, where fresh white walls show off modern photography and art prints. Rooms are a little small but simple and chic, with white walls, a splash of color, and a distinctive table or armchair. Those on the upper floors have nice rooftop views, and some of the suites offer a glimpse of the far-off Eiffel Tower. The airy lobby area, with large windows and shelves full of books, is an invitation to kick back and catch up on your reading. Along with the usual alcoholic drinks, the hotel bar officers Kusmi teas and fresh squeezed juices.

8 rue Laferrière, 9th arrond. www.hotelarvor.com. ℂ **01-48-78-60-92.** 30 units. 98€–195€ double; 143€–280€ suite. Métro: St-Georges. **Amenities:** Bar; room service, Wi-Fi (free).

Hôtel Langlois ★★   You won't be surprised to learn that this unusual hotel was once a bank: The lobby ceiling is so high you could easily walk around on stilts. The rooms are truly spacious, and some include bathrooms that are downright huge. The other atypical feature here is the furniture—many of the rooms have gorgeous Art Nouveau fittings that would make an antiques dealer foam at the mouth. All but one have pretty tiled fireplaces, and most have retained their old ceiling moldings. An antique wrought-iron elevator runs up the center of the building. It's no wonder that this hotel is a favorite for magazine photo shoots. *Note:* Beds are not standard sizes; those lovely old bedsteads were made before king-size mattresses came into style.

63 rue St-Lazare, 9th arrond. www.hotel-langlois.com. ℂ **01-48-74-78-24.** 27 units. 140€–180€ double; 290€ suite. Métro: Trinité. **Amenities:** Wi-Fi (free).

4

WHERE TO STAY | The Right Bank

INEXPENSIVE

Hôtel Chopin ★★ Nestled at the back of the delightful Passage Jouffroy, this budget hotel has remarkably quiet rooms considering its location in the middle of the rush and bustle of the Grands Boulevards. The staircase is a little creaky (you will have to climb a flight to get to the elevator), but recently refreshed rooms are clean and colorful and the bathrooms are spotless. Rooms on the upper floors get more light; many have nice views of Parisian rooftops. Across the street from the Passage Jouffroy entrance is Passage des Panoramas, a maze of hip bistros and shops.

10 bd. Montmartre or 46 passage Jouffroy, 9th arrond. www.hotel-chopin.com. *C* **01-47-70-58-10.** 36 units. 87€–147€ double; 147€ triple. Métro: Grands Boulevards or Richelieu-Drouot. **Amenities:** Wi-Fi (free).

Hôtel Tiquetonne ★ These cute, if basic lodgings are just around the corner from the chic Passage du Grand Cerf. This is definitely a budget hotel: The doors feel a little light and the carpets are a little worn, but the ceilings are high, and the atmosphere is homey. The old-fashioned bedspreads lay over firm mattresses, and rooms on the upper floors get lots of light. This is one of the few hotels left in Paris that still has cheap rooms with toilets on the landing; doubles with just a sink go for 65€ (there's a shower in the hall). For an in-suite toilet and shower, you'll pay just 80€. At these prices, don't expect TVs or toiletries. The hotel is just steps away from Les Halles and a block or so from the restaurants and food shops of rue de Montorgueil. Reserve well in advance.

6 rue Tiquetonne, 2nd arrond. www.hoteltiquetonne.fr. *C* **01-42-36-94-58.** 45 units. 65€–80€ double. Métro: Etienne Marcel; RER: Les Halles. **Amenities:** Wi-Fi (free).

Hôtel Vivienne ★★★ Right around the corner from restaurant-filled Passage des Panoramas, this family-run hotel offers comfortable, spotless lodgings at great prices. Most of the rooms have a modern decor and accents in purple, or, chocolate or grey; some have a more classic look with floral prints or stripes. A few rooms have balconies with space for a small table; some have connecting doors, and a handful of large suites are great for families. If you don't mind sharing a toilet, several doubles go for 90€. The service is friendly, as is the hotel's cat, Romero. Light sleepers should ask for a room facing the courtyard—the street can be a little noisy.

40 rue Vivienne, 2nd arrond. www.hotel-vivienne.com. *C* **01-42-33-13-26.** 44 units. 90€–165€ double; 190€–220€ suite for 2–4. Métro: Grands Boulevards or Richelieu–Drouot. **Amenities:** Concierge, Wi-Fi (free).

Montmartre (18th Arrondissement)

If you're looking for a romantic setting, you can't do much better than Montmartre. Once you get away from the tourist hordes that invade the Sacré Coeur and Place du Tertre, you'll find lovely little lanes and small houses, harkening back to the days when Picasso and the boys were at the Bateau Lavoir. Unfortunately, the pickings are a bit slim if you want to actually sleep here. If you

Ermitage Sacré-Coeur **5**
Hôtel des Arts
  Montmartre **3**
Hôtel Eldorado **1**
L'Hôtel Particulier **4**
Le Relais Montmartre **2**

||||| Steps
┿┿┿┿┿ Funicular
Ⓜ Métro station

0 ——— 200 y
0 ——— 200 m

are determined to stay up on the Butte, book early, as the few quality lodgings are generally in high demand. Another consideration: Although Montmartre is charming, it's on the northern edge of the city, so you'll need to budget extra time to get down the hill to the center of town.

EXPENSIVE

L'Hôtel Particulier ★★ If your vision of Montmartre involves secret little cobbled lanes and old townhouses with tree-filled gardens, this chic, arty hotel is for you. To get to it, you must buzz in from the street, then take a narrow, private path—Passage de la Sorcière (aka the "witch's alley")—to an elegant former mansion. Each of the five suites was designed by a different artist: One evokes a fancy bordello, with jewel-studded velvet walls; another has psychedelic floral wallpaper and stunning views over the garden; all are sumptuous. For extra pizazz, the loftlike, top-floor suite is awash in natural light and flaunts an open bathroom with a clawfoot bathtub. Into food? You may want to consider dining in: The hotel's on-site restaurant, **Mandragore,** offers exquisite French dishes with a modern twist, and serves afternoon tea

(Wed–Sun) in an *olde-worlde* courtyard—
a glorious treat on a sunny day.

23 ave. Junot (Pavillon D), 18th arrond. www.
hotel-particulier-montmartre.com. ⓒ **01-53-
41-81-40.** 5 units. 390€–590€ suite. Métro:
Lamarck Caulincourt. **Amenities:** Restaurant;
bar; garden; laundry service; room service;
Wi-Fi (free).

MODERATE

Le Relais Montmartre ★★   These
comfortable lodgings include small but
impeccable rooms decked out in light,
warm colors and a classic decor. Nothing
is particularly hip or stylish here, but
these are quality accommodations offering both tasteful floral prints and reliable
service. The one decorative quirk was the
decision to paint the exposed beams on
the ceilings shades of lavender or rust.
The hotel is located on a peaceful little

Art-themed room at L'Hôtel Particulier.

side street, right around the corner from a delicious stretch of food shops on
Rue Lepic. There are adjoining rooms for families, and a lovely little patio for
breakfasting in good weather.

6 rue Constance, 18th arrond. www.hotel-relais-montmartre.com. ⓒ **01-70-64-25-25.**
26 units. 139€–249€ double. Métro: Blanche. **Amenities:** Concierge service; laundry
service; iPad for guests; Wi-Fi (free).

INEXPENSIVE

Ermitage Sacré-Coeur ★★★   Built in 1890 by a rich gentleman for his
mistress, this elegant townhouse has been lovingly converted into intimate
guest lodgings. There may not much by way of amenities, but the ambience
is unique. Tucked behind the Sacré Coeur, this small mansion still feels like a
private home. In fact, it virtually is: The Canipel family has run these unconventional lodgings for over 40 years. Each of the five rooms is decorated with
different period prints and draperies, as well as handsome antique bedsteads
and armoires. The hallways and entry are done up in deep blues and gold leaf;
wall murals and paintings are the works of a local artist. The hotel has no
elevator and no TVs in the rooms. The Canipels also rent nearby studios and
apartments that sleep one to four. All reservations are made by e-mail.

24 rue Lamarck, 18th arrond. www.ermitagesacrecoeur.fr. ⓒ **06-12-49-05-15.** 5 units.
110€ double; 130€ triple; 140€ quad. Métro: Lamarck-Caulaincourt. Parking 25€. **Amenities:** Wi-Fi (free).

Hôtel Eldorado ★★   Though it's right outside the border, the soul of this
quirky hotel belongs in Montmartre. Funky and imaginative, the decor is the
work of the owner-artist who likes to use bright colors and offbeat details like

mosaic mirror frames and tiny sparkly chandeliers. The largest and most atmospheric rooms are in the "pavilion," a small, separate house behind the main building, with high ceilings and large windows. However, these rooms are separated by a pretty garden patio used by the in-house restaurant, **Bistrot des Dames,** which means that there can be noise until midnight in the warmer months. If you are a stickler for tidiness, you may not appreciate the occasional chipped paint or loose floor tiles; if you are young at heart, you will love the bohemian charm of the place. For those who don't mind sharing a bathroom, rates go as low as 60€ for a double and 70€ for a triple. The hotel has no elevator and no TV or telephone in the rooms.

18 rue des Dames, 17th arrond. www.eldoradohotel.fr. ℰ **01-45-22-35-21.** 33 units. 70€–120€ double; 90€–130€ triple. Métro: Place de Clichy. **Amenities:** Restaurant; bar; Wi-Fi (free).

Hôtel des Arts Montmartre ★★ On a narrow street just off lively rue des Abbesses, this unassuming hotel once hosted artists and sculptors and even a few dancers from the Moulin Rouge. Currently run by the third generation of the Lameyre family, today's guests are generally tourists, who enjoy the great rates, comfortable lodgings and welcoming atmosphere. Rooms are small, yet spotless, with firm mattresses and cheerful colors on the walls. A few have distant views of the Eiffel Tower over Parisian rooftops; the "Romantic" room comes with a bottle of champagne and has a small balcony. You'll pay more for these, but they are still a bargain. Montmartre's two remaining windmills, Moulin de la Galette and Moulin du Radet, are just up the street.

5 rue Tholozé, 18th arrond. www.arts-hotel-paris.com. ℰ **01-46-06-30-52.** 50 units. 80€–150€ double; 140€–200€ triple. Métro: Blanche or Abbesses. **Amenities:** Concierge; parking (19€); room service; Wi-Fi (free).

République, Bastille & Eastern Paris (11th & 12th Arrondissements)

Just north of the Marais, this shabby-chic, up-and-coming area offers low rates and proximity to the nightlife around Rue Oberkampf. Nearby, the Faubourg St-Antoine area is an Eldorado for exciting new restaurants, and has nice lodging options, even if it's less than central. This historic workers' neighborhood was where revolutionary fervor came to a head on July 14, 1789, when irate citizens stormed down the boulevard and took over the Bastille. Things have calmed down considerably since then, and outside of the festive bar and club scene around the Bastille and rue de Charonne, it's a pretty laid-back area.

MODERATE

Eden Lodge Paris ★★★ Hidden from the street in the back of a beautiful garden, this modern wooden structure combines environmental awareness with extremely comfortable lodgings. With only five rooms and a free breakfast, some might call this a bed and breakfast instead of a hotel. The warm

Guest room at Hôtel de la Porte Dorée.

smell of larch wood (the construction material) hits your nose when you enter the lobby, a glassed-in atrium with a staircase leading up to the rooms. Quality insulation, LED lighting, solar panels, and zero-carbon output give these lodgings its ecological creds, as well as self-cleaning tiles that absorb air-pollution. There's no skimping on comfort though: Rooms are chic, warm, and minimalist, with vintage-look furniture and high-tech Japanese toilets. A microwave and refrigerator are available for guests in the breakfast room, which is open all day. Bicycles on hand, as well as a 500m2 garden for communing with nature.

175 rue de Charonne, 11th arrond. www.edenlodgeparis.net. ✆ **01-43-56-73-24.** 5 units. 225€–250€ double; 350€–390€ suite. Métro: Alexandre Dumas. **Amenities:** Breakfast included; Wi-Fi (free).

Hôtel Paris Bastille Boutet ★ Around the corner from animated rue de Charonne, this hip hotel lures you in with a sumptuous Art Deco facade—a throwback to the building's time as a wood manufacturer—then pampers you with bright, classy rooms decked in oak and industrial era–style furniture. Ten have terraces, many with rooftop views over the city (request one when reserving), and there are connecting rooms for families. Other perks include a bar (perfect for a delicious pre-/post-dinner cocktail) and a great spa area, with a pool, a sauna, and a hammam.

22-24 rue Faidherbe, 11th arrond. www.accorhotels.com. ✆ **01-40-24-65-65.** 80 units. 199€–550€ double; 279€–630€ suite. Métro: Faidherbe-Chaligny. **Amenities:** Bar; laundry services; parking; Wi-Fi (free).

INEXPENSIVE

Cosmos Hotel ★★ Just around the corner from the animated Oberkampf neighborhood, this budget option is a terrific deal. The modern rooms are generally spotless, and everything from the bed linens to the floor covering looks spanking new. And such a deal: only 72€ to 82€ for a double. Furthermore, the staff is friendly and helpful. The only downside is possible weekend-night noise as people spill out of the busy bars and restaurants nearby.

35 rue Jean-Pierre Timbaud, 11th arrond. www.cosmos-hotel-paris.com. ⓒ **01-43-57-25-88.** 36 units. 72€–82€ double; 93€ triple; 98€ quad. Métro: Parmentier. **Amenities:** Wi-Fi (free).

Hôtel de la Porte Dorée ★★   True, it's a little out of the way, but these lovely lodgings are well worth the Métro fare. Soothing neutral tones, antique headboards, high ceilings, wood floors, and original curlicue moldings are all part of the package at this hotel, which is owned by a friendly Franco-American couple. The hotel goes the extra mile for both the environment (ecologically correct policies) and babies (toys, playpens, and even potty seats available). And you'll pay less for all this than you will for something utterly basic in the center of town. What's more, it is right next to the verdant Bois de Vincennes, where you can rent bikes or picnic. The nearby Métro will get you to the city center in about 15 minutes.

273 ave. Daumensil, 12th arrond. www.hoteldelaportedoree.com. ⓒ **01-43-07-56-97.** 43 units. 110€–185€ double; 125€–195€ triple. Métro: Porte Dorée. **Amenities:** Babysitting; bicycles; Wi-Fi (free).

Belleville, Canal St-Martin & La Villette (10th, 19th & 20th Arrondissements)

When historic arty neighborhoods like St-Germain and Montmartre became far too expensive for up-and-coming artists, many of them immigrated to these more proletarian neighborhoods, giving the area a funky, bohemian feel. Though it's gentrifying, Belleville is still known for artists' studios, while dozens of hip cafes and restaurants now line the Canal St-Martin and the Bassin de la Villette. The young and adventurous will appreciate this part of town, but you will need to use the Métro to get to the city's more central areas.

MODERATE

Le Citizen ★★   Maybe it's the smiling young staff in jeans or the ecological ethos, but there's something alternative in the air at this adorable boutique hotel on the Canal St-Martin. While the rooms are on the small side, they are light and airy, with lots of blond wood, clean lines, and views out onto the tree-lined canal. There are only two rooms per floor, ranging from the snug "City" to the spacious "Suite Zen," which can accommodate a couple with two children. On some floors, two rooms can be connected to form a large "apartment." When you check in, you'll be handed a loaner iPad loaded with information and apps on Paris, as well as restaurant recommendations. The buffet breakfast and movies on demand are included in your room rate.

96 quai de Jemmapes, 10th arrond. www.lecitizenhotel.com. ⓒ **01-83-62-55-50.** 12 units. 149€–296€ double; 250€–300€ suite; 400€–480€ apartment. Rates include breakfast. Métro: Jacques Bonsergent. **Amenities:** Loaner iPad; Wi-Fi (free).

Métro-themed breakfast area at the Generator hostel.

INEXPENSIVE

Generator Paris ★★ A 20-minute walk from Gare du Nord (the Eurostar terminal) and 5 minutes from the picturesque quays and bars of Canal St-Martin, this trendy establishment (opposite Oscar Niemeyer's iconic French Communist party's HQ) blurs the lines between hotel and hostel by offering both private rooms and dormitories (for up to 8 or 10 people). It also offers perks that many of the city's standard hotels can't provide: namely, a roof-top bar with views onto the Sacré Coeur and a Métro-themed basement "club" with a fab cocktail happy hour. Breakfast is served in a light-filled cafe overlooking a small urban garden. The bright dorms are filled with young, mostly English-speaking travelers, but the more expensive private rooms attract a more demanding set of mature clients with extras like terraces. Female-only dorms are available.

9-11 place du Colonel Fabien, 10th arrond. https://generatorhostels.com. ✆ **01-70-98-84-00.** 199 units. 23€–50€ per person in dormitories; 88€–150€ double. Métro: Colonel Fabien. **Amenities:** Cafe; bar; in-room lockers; laundromat; towel rental; Wi-Fi (free).

THE LEFT BANK

Latin Quarter (5th & 13th Arrondissements)

Central and reasonably priced, the Latin Quarter is a long-time favorite for travelers in search of affordable accommodations. As a consequence, a few corners of this famously academic neighborhood are overrun with tourists and trinket shops. The streets immediately surrounding the place St-Michel (especially around rue de la Huchette) are where you'll find the worst tourist traps, both hotel and restaurant-wise; better prices and quality are to be had in the quieter, and more authentic areas around the universities (College de France, La Sorbonne, Faculté de Sciences), a little farther from Notre-Dame but still within easy walking distance.

EXPENSIVE

Hotel Seven ★★★ Weird and wonderful, this luxury concept hotel is made for lovers in search of a night to remember. Mirrors and transparent

Left Bank Hotels (Eiffel Tower Area)

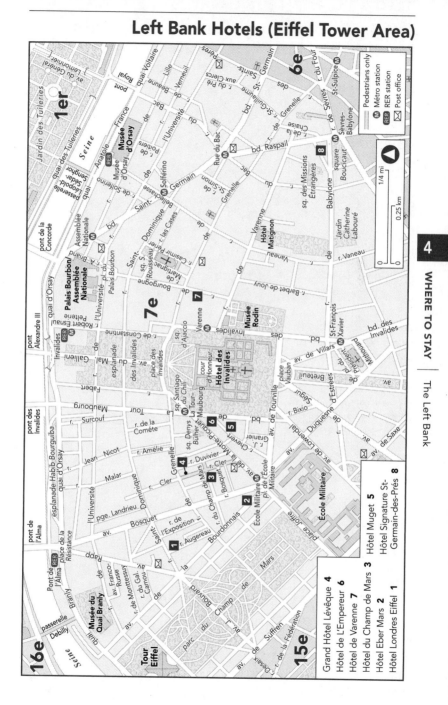

Pedestrians only
Ⓜ Métro station
RER RER station
☒ Post office

Grand Hôtel Lévêque **4**
Hôtel de L'Empereur **6**
Hôtel de Varenne **7**
Hôtel du Champ de Mars **3**
Hôtel Eber Mars **2**
Hôtel Londres Eiffel **1**
Hôtel Muget **5**
Hôtel Signature St-Germain-des-Prés **8**

Left Bank Hotels (Latin Quarter, St-Germain, Montparnasse)

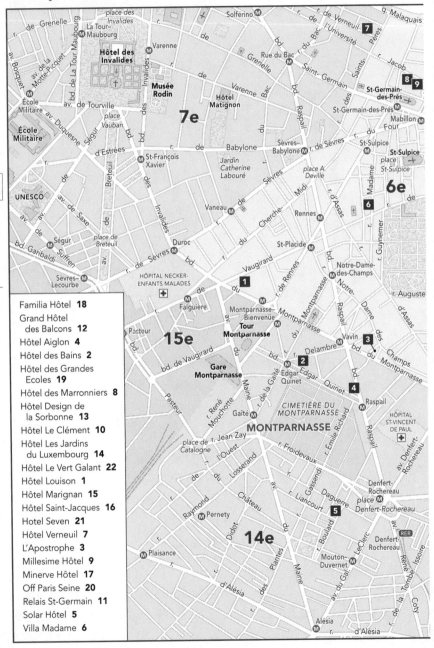

Familia Hôtel **18**

Grand Hôtel
des Balcons **12**

Hôtel Aiglon **4**

Hôtel des Bains **2**

Hôtel des Grandes
Ecoles **19**

Hôtel des Marronniers **8**

Hôtel Design de
la Sorbonne **13**

Hôtel Le Clément **10**

Hôtel Les Jardins
du Luxembourg **14**

Hôtel Le Vert Galant **22**

Hôtel Louison **1**

Hôtel Marignan **15**

Hôtel Saint-Jacques **16**

Hotel Seven **21**

Hôtel Verneuil **7**

L'Apostrophe **3**

Millesime Hôtel **9**

Minerve Hôtel **17**

Off Paris Seine **20**

Relais St-Germain **11**

Solar Hôtel **5**

Villa Madame **6**

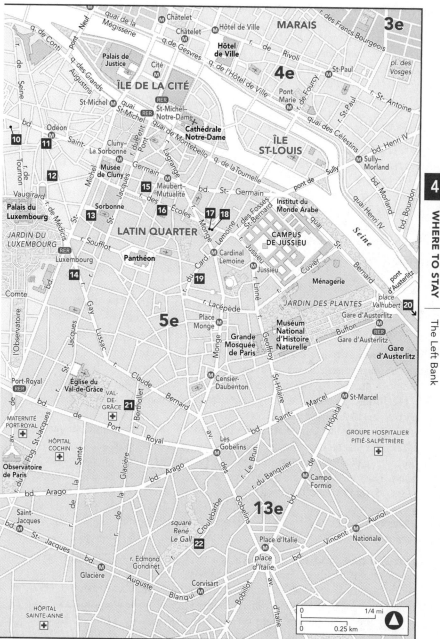

quai de la
Mégisserie
pont Neuf
q. de Conti
q. des Grands
Augustins
r. de Seine
bd.
Châtelet
Châtelet
q. de Gesvres
Palais de
Justice
Cité
ÎLE DE LA CITÉ
St-Michel
quai
St-Michel
quai du Petit Pont
RER
RER St-Michel–
Notre-Dame
Odéon
10
11
Saint-
Cluny–
La Sorbonne
Germain
Musée
de Cluny
r. de
Tournon
12
Vaugirard
Palais du
Luxembourg
Sorbonne
r. de Médicis
13
JARDIN DU
LUXEMBOURG
RER
Luxembourg
14
Comte
l'Observatoire
Port-Royal
RER
Église du
Val-de-Grâce
Gay Lussac
Jacques
de
bd.
MATERNITÉ
PORT-ROYAL
HÔPITAL
COCHIN
Observatoire
de Paris
bd. Arago
Saint-
Jacques
bd. St-Jacques
Faubg. St-Jacques
Santé
de la
Glacière
bd. Arago
la
de
Glacière
HÔPITAL
SAINTE-ANNE

Hôtel de Ville
Hôtel
de Ville
q. de l'Hôtel de Ville
r. de Rivoli
4e
Pont
Marie
St-Paul
r. St-Antoine
r. de la Tournelle
Cathédrale
Notre-Dame
q. de Montebello
q. de la Tournelle
Maubert-
Mutualité
15
r. des Écoles
16
17 18
Monge
Cardinal
Lemoine
19
r. Lacépède
Place
Monge
Grande
Mosquée
de Paris
Monge
Geoffroy
Censier-
Daubenton
Claude
Berthollet
VAL-
DE-
GRÂCE
21
Port
Royal
Bernard
St-
Germain
Lagrange
Jacques
Michel
bd.
St- Germain
r. des Fossés
St-Bernard
Institut du
Monde Arabe
quai
CAMPUS
DE JUSSIEU
Jussieu
Jussieu
Cuvier
Ménagerie
JARDIN DES PLANTES
Muséum
National
d'Histoire
Naturelle
Buffon
St-Hilaire
Les
Gobelins
Le Brun
des
Saint-
bd.
Marcel
St-Marcel
l'Hôpital
r. du Banquier
Campo
Formio
Gobelins
13e
square
René
Le Gall
22
r. Edmond
Gondinet
Corvisart
Blanqui
Auguste
place
d'Italie
Place d'Italie
Vincent
Nationale
Auriol
d'Italie
av.
Bobillot
GROUPE HOSPITALIER
PITIÉ-SALPÊTRIÈRE

MARAIS
r. des Francs Bourgeois
3e
r. de Fourcy
r. St-Paul
pl. des
Vosges
St-Paul
r. St-Antoine
quai des Célestins
bd. Henri IV
Sully-
Morland
bd. Morland
quai Henri IV
pont de Sully
Seine
bd. Bourdon
pont d'Austerlitz
place
Valhubert
20
Gare d'Austerlitz
RER
Gare d'Austerlitz
Gare
d'Austerlitz
Bernard

ÎLE DE LA CITÉ
LATIN QUARTER
Panthéon
Cardinal
Lemoine
5e
Souflot
JARDIN DU
LUXEMBOURG
ÎLE
ST-LOUIS

showers abound here, as do huge beds, theatrical lighting, and large sofas. Each of the creatively designed rooms and suites has a different theme: Some rooms are romantically space-age, with mobiles, pinpoint lights, and in-room transparent double showers, while the suites go all out: "Sublime" is all white with a round double bed under a feathery ceiling; "Nuit Chic" features a faux crocodile headboard and a black bathtub studded with Swarovski synthetic diamonds. Most have "levitation" beds, which are suspended horizontally. Your privacy will be enhanced by the fact that the hotel is far from the crowds, at the southern end of the Latin Quarter.

20 rue Berthollet, 5th arrond. www.sevenhotelparis.com. ℂ 01-43-31-47-52. 35 units. 297€–400€ double; 400€–879€ suite. Métro: Les Gobelins. **Amenities:** Bar; room service; laptop loans; massages by appointment; wine cellar; concierge; Wi-Fi (free).

MODERATE

Hôtel Design Sorbonne ★★   In the thick of the student quarter facing La Sorbonne, this cozy boutique hotel combines comfort with an unusual, but classy decor. Period furniture is covered in lively green, blue, and dark brown stripes; colorful wall fabrics put a modern spin on Victorian patterns, and excerpts from French literary classics are woven into the carpets. Each room has a desk with an iMac for guests' use. As pretty as they are, the rooms are small, and some have bathrooms that are downright tiny. If you need space, opt for a deluxe with a bathtub or the large room on the top floor with a view of the Sorbonne and the Pantheon.

6 rue Victor Cousin, 5th arrond. www.hotelsorbonne.com. ℂ 01-43-54-58-08. 38 units. 120€–380€ double; 180€–400€ top-floor double. Métro: Cluny–La Sorbonne. RER: Luxembourg. **Amenities:** Wi-Fi (free).

Hôtel des Jardins du Luxembourg ★★   Just around the corner from its glorious namesake and down the street from the university, these intimate lodgings are tucked away on a quiet impasse, making it a favorite with the professorial crowd. The building's claim to fame is that Sigmund Freud stayed here on his first visit to Paris. The 1940's look of the lobby and reading lounge invites deep reflection, or at least a nice rest in one of the plush armchairs. While the standard rooms are quite pretty, with curly wrought-iron headboards and puffy comforters, the superior rooms, which cost only a few euros more, have nicer views, small balconies, snazzy bathrooms, and designer fabric–covered walls. There's a sauna for guests' use on the ground floor.

5 impasse Royer-Collard, 5th arrond. www.les-jardins-du-luxembourg.com. ℂ 01-40-46-08-88. 26 units. 130€–198€ double. Métro: Cluny–La Sorbonne. RER: Luxembourg. **Amenities:** Sauna; Wi-Fi (free).

Hôtel Saint-Jacques ★★   The spacious rooms in this delightful hotel retain lots of architectural details from its Belle Epoque past. Most of the ceilings are adorned with masses of curlicues, and some have restored 18th-century murals to gaze upon while you laze in bed. Modern reproductions of famous French paintings hang on the walls, and Second Empire–themed murals decorate the lobby and breakfast room. The romantic decor has a light, feminine feel, in shades of light blue, cream, and grey—considerably more inviting than when the hotel served as a set for the Audrey Hepburn/Cary Grant classic, *Charade.* There is one pretty wheelchair-accessible room on the ground floor.

35 rue des Ecoles, 5th arrond. www.paris-hotel-stjacques.com. ⓒ **01-44-07-45-45.** 36 units. 100€–270€ double; 155€–286€ triple. Métro: Maubert-Mutualité. **Amenities:** Bar; babysitting; Wi-Fi (free).

OFF Paris Seine ★★★   Feel like taking a cruise but don't want to leave the city? Try Paris' first floating hotel, docked on the banks of the Seine at the foot of the Gare d'Austerlitz. Once inside, you'll feel like you're on a trendy ocean liner, especially when you are having a drink on one of the two decks that overlook the water. On warm days, you can even paddle in a narrow pool that separates the bar areas. The chic cabinlike rooms are small but well thought out; it's worth paying for a Seine-side room so you can gaze at the lights that reflect on the river at night. There's no room service per se, but if you pay at the bar in advance, you can have goodies delivered to your room.

20–22 Port d'Austerlitz, 13th arrond. www.offparisseine.com. ⓒ **01-44-06-62-65.** 58 units. 139€–239€ double; 250€–400€ suite. Métro: Gare d'Austerlitz or Gare de Lyon. **Amenities:** Bar; Wi-Fi (free).

INEXPENSIVE

Familia Hôtel ★★   Perfectly located, close to rue Mouffetard but far from the madding crowds, this is a budget hotel that doesn't feel like one. The rooms are snug, but every detail has been scrupulously considered, from the carved cherry wood headboards to the swags of period fabrics on the windows, to the top quality mattresses on the beds. Some have exposed beams, others have wall murals, and those on the second, fifth, and sixth floors have small balconies with lovely views of the Latin Quarter. The same meticulous management runs a slightly higher end version of itself next door, **Minerve Hôtel** (www.parishotelminerve.com; ⓒ **01-43-26-26-04**), with similar detailing and larger rooms (156€–275€ double; 212€ triple).

11 rue des Ecoles, 5th arrond. www.familiahotel.com. ⓒ **01-43-54-55-27.** 30 units. 90€–152 double; Métro: Jussieu or Cardinal Lemoine. **Amenities:** Wi-Fi (free).

Hôtel des Grandes Ecoles ★★★   Tucked into a private garden on the slope of the Montagne St-Geneviève, this lovely hotel gives you the impression you have just walked out of Paris and into the countryside. A path leads to a flower-bedecked interior courtyard, where birds chirp in the trees; the reception area adjoins an inviting breakfast room with potted plants and an upright piano. The spotless rooms are filled with country-style furniture and papered in old-fashioned prints; quilted bedspreads and framed etchings complete the look. Views from most windows are of either the garden or surrounding trees. The calm is such that the hotel has nixed TVs. What's more, this unique ambience comes at a reasonable price. Rooms in the "Garden

Building" are more modern, with newer bathrooms; families will appreciate the six suites that each sleep four.

75 rue de Cardinal-Lemoine, 5th arrond. www.hotel-grandes-ecoles.com. ℂ **01-43-26-79-23.** 51 units. 140€–165€ double; 185€ family room. Parking 30€. Métro: Cardinal Lemoine or Place Monge. **Amenities:** Wi-Fi (free).

Hôtel Le Vert Galant ★★ Located in a quiet green corner near the Manufacture Nationale des Gobelins (p. 173), this lovely haven is wrapped around a small garden. All the rooms in this family-run operation look out on greenery, and the hotel has an unfussy, country feel. Rooms have recently been renovated and now sport oak floors and Italian tiled showers. The Basque restaurant next door, **Auberge Etchegorry,** is run by the same

The garden at Hôtel des Grandes Ecoles.

management. You may feel like you have left the city center, but the hotel is only minutes away from rue Mouffetard and three Métro lines.

41 rue Croulebarbe, 13th arrond. www.vertgalant.com. ℂ **01-44-08-83-50.** 17 units. 120€–150€ double. Métro: Corvisart, Gobelins, or Place d'Italie. **Amenities:** Parking (15€); restaurant; Wi-Fi (free).

Hôtel Marignan ★★ A budget classic, these simple lodgings cater to travelers looking for reasonable, centrally located lodgings, who don't mind a little noise in the hallways. Not only is the price right, but there are extras like free washing machines and kitchen access (after your free breakfast is served) and a ton of sightseeing tips from the friendly management. Though still pretty basic, many of the rooms have been renovated as the owner gradually upgrades the establishment. The pretty ceiling moldings have been left intact, and the newly tiled bathrooms are spotless. Room sizes range from comfortable to enormous—this is one of the few hotels in Paris to offer rooms for up to five people. The cheapest rates involve sharing a toilet and/or shower. There is no elevator.

13 rue du Sommerard, 5th arrond. www.hotel-marignan.com. ℂ **01-43-54-63-81.** 30 rooms. 75€–105€ double; 105€–144€ triple; 122€–185€ quad; 133€–195€ quint. Rates include continental breakfast. Métro: Cluny–La Sorbonne. **Amenities:** Guest kitchen; washing machine and dryer (free); Wi-Fi (free).

St-Germain-des-Prés & Luxembourg (6th Arrondissement)

Sleek boutiques and restaurants abound in this legendary (and expensive) neighborhood; historic cafes and monuments lend plenty of atmosphere.

Unlike some other Parisian neighborhoods, this one is lively even late at night; it is also centrally located and within walking distance to many top sights. The highest concentration of noise and tourist traps is around boulevard St-Germain and Carrefour de l'Odéon; once you turn down a side street, things quiet down considerably.

EXPENSIVE

Relais St-Germain ★★★   Fashioned out of three adjoining 17th-century townhouses, this intimate hotel mixes old-world charm and jazzy modern ideas. Exposed beams abound in the spacious rooms, even the smallest of which is equipped with a comfortable sitting area. And yet there is nothing fussy or boring about the decor, which artfully blends period furniture with modern prints, like a Louis XV armchair covered in zigzagged leather. The effect is both stylish and deeply comforting. You'll want to fling yourself onto the king-size bed, cover yourself with a fake-fur throw, and just stare out the window at the lovely Carrefour de l'Odéon. There are some extra stairs between floors, so if you have mobility issues, make that clear when you reserve. Guests have priority at the hotel's restaurant, **Le Comptoir** (p. 114), where you might otherwise wait 6 months for a reservation. Rooms book up far in advance here.

9 carrefour de l'Odéon, 6th arrond. www.hotel-paris-relais-saint-germain.com. ✆ **01-44-27-07-97.** 22 units. 295€ double; 460€ suite. Rates include breakfast. Métro: Odéon. **Amenities:** Babysitting; concierge; laundry service; restaurant; room service; Wi-Fi (free).

Villa Madame ★★   These sleek lodgings offer spacious, modern rooms in subdued tones with a large dose of Parisian elegance. Tranquil shades of beige and white are punctuated with red cushions and detailing, giving the light-filled rooms a calm appeal—perfect for relaxing after pounding the

Blondin twin room at Relais St-Germain.

Parisian pavement. A few on the upper floors have balconies overlooking the neighborhood, which is just a short walk from the Jardin du Luxembourg; one large suite comes with a roomy terrace. Downstairs, there is a handicap-accessible room, as well as an interior courtyard where you can have breakfast or just lounge around with a drink in the evening surfing on the house iPad. When it's nippy out you can have tea by the fireplace in the salon.

44 rue Madame, 6th arrond. www.hotelvillamadameparis.com. © **01-45-48-02-81.** 28 units. 190€–420€ double; 300€–525€ suite. Métro: Rennes or St-Sulpice. **Amenities:** Bar; concierge service; laundry service; room service; Wi-Fi (free).

MODERATE

Hôtel des Marronniers ★★ If you are looking for old fashioned Parisian charm but have a limited budget, head for these cozy lodgings just a few minutes away from the church of St-Germain-des-Prés. Nestled in the back of a courtyard behind the galleries and antique stores of chic rue Jacob, rooms here feature rich fabrics, (mostly) high ceilings, warm colors, and reproduction antiques, as well as a dash of quirky *je ne sais quoi*. Rooms are so quiet it's hard to believe you are in the city center; those facing the garden get more light. While the bedrooms have all been renovated, bathrooms could use an overhaul. Guests are invited to have breakfast or just relax in the lush garden behind the hotel; if it's raining you can do the same on the covered veranda. The triples and quads are particularly well laid out for families.

21 rue Jacob, 6th arrond. www.paris-hotel-marronniers.com. © **01-43-25-30-60.** 36 units. 139€–220€ double; 185€–270€ triple; 232€–350€ quad. Métro: St-Germain-des-Prés. **Amenities:** Laundry service; library; Wi-Fi (free).

Hôtel Verneuil ★★★ Both historic and chic, this intimate hotel has conserved the exposed beams and architectural details of the 17th-century building it inhabits. In a nod to the neighborhood's literary roots, manuscripts and scrolls are tucked into niches in the walls, while neutral colors and cozy period touches give it the feel of a private home—perhaps that of an eminent editor. While the hallways painted in somber shades of brown and beige, the rooms are bright and friendly, if small. If you need to stretch out, go for the deluxe room, which has space for a desk and chairs to relax in; there are a few communicating rooms for families. Guests have use of loaner smart phones loaded with information and Internet access.

8 rue de Verneuil, 7th arrond. www.hotel-verneuil-saint-germain.com. © **01-42-60-82-14.** 26 units. 200€–350€ double; 230€–380€ triple. Métro: St-Germain-des-Prés or Rue du Bac. **Amenities:** Bar; babysitting; business corner with printer; massages by appt.; laundry service; room service; Wi-Fi (free).

Millesime Hôtel ★★ Completely overhauled in 2016, these cozy lodgings defy their historic surroundings with a set of modern, chic rooms in soothing shades of beige and grey. A 21st-century take on Parisian elegance that includes unusual wood headboards and soft flannel upholstery, the decor is contemporary without being overbearing. If you need to work or write, desks are unusually functional here, especially in the superior doubles and suites. Post-sightseeing drinks can be sipped in the small bar, or if the weather is nice, in the pretty courtyard patio.

15 rue Jacob, 6th arrond. www.millesimehotel.com. © **01-44-07-97-97.** 20 units. 160€–280€ double; 310€–450€ Suite. Métro: St-Germain-des-Prés. **Amenities:** Bar, concierge; iPhone docks; mobile phones for guests; room service; Wi-Fi (free).

INEXPENSIVE

Grand Hôtel des Balcons ★   For the neighborhood, the rooms in this simple hotel are remarkably spacious. Most also have small balconies, and if you look up the street you'll see the columns of the 18th-century Odéon theater. The roomy triples and quads are a good bet for families, and a handicap-accessible room is on the ground floor. The lobby has an Art Nouveau feel, and the well-kept rooms are impeccably clean, if not particularly stylish.

3 rue Casimir Delavigne, 6th arrond. www.balcons.com. © **01-46-34-78-50.** 49 units. 135€–180€ double; 240€ triple; 250€ quad. Métro: Odéon. **Amenities:** Wi-Fi (free).

Hôtel Le Clément ★★   Facing the chic boutiques of Marché St-Germain, these charming lodgings offer affordable comfort about 2 blocks away from St-Germain-des-Prés and a warren of restaurant-filled streets. This hotel offers exceptional value, considering the central location and the impeccably maintained rooms. Walls are covered in traditional prints, and beds are decked out in white quilted spreads. Doubles tend to be small, but the mini-suites are good for families. The Marché is closed at night, so all is calm in the evenings; rooms on the upper floors get the most light and enjoy views of Parisian rooftops. You'll need to be able to manage a few stairs to get to the elevator.

6 rue Clément, 6th arrond. www.hotelclementparis.com. © **01-43-26-53-60.** 28 units. 119€–180€ double; 148€–200€ triples and suites. Métro: Mabillon. **Amenities:** Babysitting; laundry service; room service; Wi-Fi (free).

Eiffel Tower & Nearby (7th Arrondissement)

For some reason, many visitors to Paris clamor for hotels that are right near the Eiffel Tower, perhaps under the impression that this is a central location. It isn't. Not only that, the 7th arrondissement is one of the grandest in Paris, filled with government ministries and posh residences—not exactly the ideal spot to experience a typical slice of Parisian life. That said, there's no denying it's a beautiful, quiet area, and that there is something magical about wandering out of your hotel and seeing the Eiffel Tower looming in the background.

EXPENSIVE

Hôtel de Varenne ★★   There is an atmosphere of refined serenity at this hotel, which caters to the ministerial crowd that frequents the area. Set back from the street, rooms noiseless, and there is a pretty garden patio for breakfast alfresco in the warmer months. The decor is stately without being stuffy; the custom-made furniture is inspired by Louis XVI and Empire styles. Infinite care has been taken to ensure that rooms stay in top condition; there is a handicap-accessible suite on the ground floor. Considering the quality of the lodgings and the self-importance of the neighborhood, rates here are very reasonable.

44 rue de Bourgogne, 7th arrond. www.hoteldevarenne.com. ℃ **01-45-51-45-55.** 26 units. 185€–290€ double; 250€–380€ triple; 340€–500€ suite. Breakfast is free when rooms are booked directly through the hotel's website. Métro: Varenne or La Tour Maubourg. **Amenities:** Concierge service; babysitting; laundry service; private parking (30€); Wi-Fi (free).

Hôtel Signature St-Germain-des-Prés ★★★ Run by the friendly Prigent family (who are also at the helm of the Hôtel Londres Eiffel; see below), this new boutique hotel has both stylish interiors and a homey charm. Bright colors on the walls blend harmoniously with subdued bedsteads and linens; vintage mid-century reproduction furniture and faux antique phones take the edge off sleek modern lines. The "Prestige" rooms cost more but are especially roomy (30 sq. m/323 sq. ft.), a rarity even in upscale Parisian hotels. In addition to particularly attentive service, this hotel is blessed with an excellent location for shopping addicts: It's just down the street from Bon Marché.

5 rue Chomel, 7th arrond. www.signature-saintgermain.com. ℃ **01-45-48-35-53.** 26 units. 169€–390€ double; 370€–420€ triple; 440€–540€ 2-room connecting family suite. Métro: Sèvres-Bablylone or St-Sulpice. **Amenities:** Concierge service; Wi-Fi (free).

MODERATE

Hôtel de L'Empereur ★★ All the rooms facing the street in this perfectly manicured hotel (run by the same meticulous management as the Hôtel Muguet; see below) have swell views of the nearby golden dome of Les Invalides, which hovers over the tomb of Napoleon (hence the name of the hotel). The best views are from the fifth and sixth floors. If views aren't your priority, consider the larger rooms facing the courtyard, which get lots of light and less street noise and are less expensive. The plush rooms are decorated with a modern take on Empire style. The hotel has connecting rooms for families.

2 rue Chevert, 7th arrond. www.hotelempereur.com. ℃ **01-45-55-88-02.** 31 units. 105€–290€ double; 350€ triple; 410€ quad. Métro: Ecole Militaire. **Amenities:** Concierge service; guest computer; Wi-Fi (free).

Hôtel Eber Mars ★★ When you walk in the door, chances are you will be greeted by none other than Monsieur Eber himself, who has spent the last decade lovingly renovating his hotel. Eber has opted for a 1930s-era decor that is low-key and specifically Parisian. Walls in the spacious rooms are papered in subtle period patterns in neutral colors, lit by authentic Art Deco hanging fixtures picked up at antiques fairs. Old-fashioned radiators have been scraped and lacquered; prints dating from the Universal Exposition of 1889 (which unveiled the Eiffel Tower—another decor theme) are hung on the walls. Rooms in this hotel are unusually large for Paris; the triples and communicating suites are ideal for families. Breakfast is served all day.

117 ave. de la Bourdonnais, 7th arrond. www.hotelebermars.com. ℃ **01-47-05-42-30.** 24 units. 100€–280€ doubles; 150€–300€ triples. Métro: Ecole Militaire. **Amenities:** Concierge service; Wi-Fi (free).

Hôtel Londres Eiffel ★★★ From the moment you enter, you feel like you are in a private home, and you'll probably be greeted by the friendly owners, the Prigents, as well as their dog, a polite golden retriever named Samba. Knickknacks line the wood bookshelves in the neo-retro lobby, an old-fashioned, yet cheerfully modern look that extends to the guest rooms. Walls are covered with tasteful printed fabrics featuring slightly kitsch 19th-century motifs, while the furniture harkens back to the 1940s, with lots of wood in soft shades of beige and brown. Two of the rooms have views of the Eiffel Tower (which is just steps away), but these book up early. For even more quiet and intimacy, request a spot in the Pavillion, a small elevator-less building in the back with just six rooms. Adjoining rooms are available for families.

1 rue Augereau, 7th arrond. www.londres-eiffel.com. ℂ **01-45-51-63-02.** 30 units. 160€–275€ double; 330€ triple. Métro: Ecole Militaire. **Amenities:** Wi-Fi (free).

Hôtel Muguet ★★★ Known for its impeccable service and comfort level, this personable hotel had a makeover in 2016, resulting in a more chic version of its classically cozy self. New modern wood headboards still have a lily-of-the-valley (*muguet*) motif, and spanking new bathrooms have vintage-style washstands and Italian showers. Rooms are relatively large for Paris, and the triples are downright spacious. Five doubles have a great view of the Eiffel Tower, two others of Les Invalides; needless to say, they book up months in advance. The others, which are less expensive, look out on either the quiet street or the courtyard. Two handicap-accessible rooms on the ground floor face directly into a small but lush garden.

11 rue Chevert, 7th arrond. www.hotelparismuguet.com. ℂ **01-47-05-05-93.** 40 units. 105€–280€ double; 250€–350€ triple; 410€ quad or quint. Métro: Varenne or La Tour Maubourg. **Amenities:** Computer and printer in lobby; concierge service; Wi-Fi (free).

INEXPENSIVE

Hôtel du Champ de Mars ★★ An adorable and affordable little inn right around the corner from the food shops of rue Cler—what more could you ask for? The impeccably maintained rooms are tastefully decorated with the kind of care people generally reserve for their own homes: thick cotton bedspreads, framed etchings, and printed fabrics in warm colors on the walls and windows. Two rooms have a tiny courtyard, while those on the upper floors get lots of light. *Note:* Food is not allowed in the rooms.

7 rue du Champ de Mars, 7th arrond. www.hotelduchampdemars.com. ℂ **01-45-51-52-30.** 25 units. 130€–170€ double. Métro: Ecole Militaire. **Amenities:** Concierge service; laptop loan for guests; Wi-Fi (free).

Montparnasse & Nearby (14th & 15th Arrondissements)

Montparnasse is more centrally located than it might seem—it's right on the border of St-Germain and close to the Luxembourg gardens. Also, the train station is a major transit hub for a bundle of Métro lines and bus routes. Though the utterly unaesthetic Tour Montparnasse now casts a shadow over this ancient artists' haunt (Henry Miller, Man Ray, Chagall, Picasso . . .), the neighboring streets are still full of personality.

MODERATE

Hôtel Aiglon ★★★   Once upon a time, the likes of Jean Paul Sartre, Luis Buñuel, and Albert Giacometti frequented this hotel, which is located at the heart of what was once the city's most vibrant artistic scene. While the hotel has since had a makeover, it is still a favorite of artists, film-makers and writers, as well as tourists looking for light-filled, airy rooms with a high comfort factor. Located close enough to the train station to be convenient but well out of the shadow of the Tour Montparnasse, south-facing rooms enjoy leafy views of the Montparnasse cemetery. While the rooms share a palette of discreet shades of grey, beige and blue, each boasts a different custom-made mosaic in the bathroom, the works a local artist. The hotel also offers 12 spacious family rooms that accommodate 3 to 4 people, as well as an apartment that sleeps 5.

232 blvd. Raspail, 14th arrond. www.paris-hotel-aiglon.com. © **01-43-20-82-42.** 46 units. 120€–350€ doubles; 210€–390€ triples; 260€–470€ quad; 300€–500€ apart for 5. Métro: Raspail. **Amenities:** Concierge; laundry service; parking (34€ per day); portable Wi-Fi routers; room service; Wi-Fi (free).

Hôtel Louison ★★   Hovering on the invisible border between the Montparnasse and Saint-Germain neighborhoods, this adorable hotel is a quick walk to the Luxembourg Gardens and the delights of the Bon Marché department store. While maintaining the original detailing and mood of this 19th-century building, the period decor is spiced up with contemporary colors and textures, like a gold and purple version of traditional *toile de jouy* wallpaper, or old-fashioned stripes cheered up with lush velvet pillows and contemporary headboards. Off the lobby, a cozy reading room is available for quiet pursuits and discussion; nearby the breakfast room is open all day with a microwave for guests who want to heat up a quick bite. There are connecting rooms for families, as well as a furnished apartment for rent by the week or the month.

105 rue de Vaugirard, 6th arrond. www.louison-hotel.com. © **01-53-63-25-50.** 42 units. 149€–199€ double; 199 triple. Métro: Duroc or Falguière. **Amenities:** Concierge; guest iPad; laundry service; parking (38€); Wi-Fi (free).

L'Apostrophe ★★   There's almost a bed and breakfast feel to this intimate "poem" hotel that honors the neighborhood's literary history (Henry Miller wrote across the way at La Coupole, and Hemingway set up shop at Closerie des Lilas down the street). Each of the 16 rooms has a theme: "Calligraphie" has Chinese characters splashed on royal blue walls, "Musique" features stenciled sheet music, instruments, and giant piano keys, and "Paris–Paradis" pays homage to the city's skyline. The larger rooms include a Jacuzzi bathtub right in the room—very romantic, but not for anyone who doesn't want to get naked in front of his or her roommate (the toilet is private). The other rooms come with jet-massage in the (private) shower.

3 rue de Chevreuse, 6th arrond. www.apostrophe-hotel.com. © **01-56-54-31-31.** 16 units. 110€–232€ double with jet-massage shower; 180€–260€ double with Jacuzzi. Métro: Vavin. **Amenities:** Bar; Wi-Fi (free).

INEXPENSIVE

Hôtel des Bains ★★★ With cute, comfortable rooms and excellent rates, this friendly hotel is one of the best deals on the Left Bank, especially for families. It offers several good-size, two-room suites for up to four people as well as comfortable doubles with high ceilings. The decor is simple, with fun original objects and artwork; several rooms have metal headboards and lamps resembling leafy vines. Some of these beauties come from the art market held on the nearby square every Sunday (where there is also an open-air market Wed and Sat mornings). Most rooms have wood floors, and a few have tiny balconies. The elevator stops at a landing between floors, so you will need to be able to manage a few stairs.

33 rue Delambre, 14th arrond. www.hotel-des-bains-montparnasse.com. ⓒ **01-43-20-85-27.** 42 units. 108€–126€ double; 150€–250€ suites for 2–4 people. Métro: Vavin, Edgar Quinet, or Montparnasse. **Amenities:** Wi-Fi (free).

Solar Hôtel ★ Declaring itself "the first ecological, economical, and activist hotel," these basic lodgings feature energy-efficient lighting, low water consumption, and composting and recycling. Breakfast, which is included in the low rate, is organic; bicycles are available for guests; and there is a nice garden for sipping your fair-trade tea. The bright rooms have a hostel-like feel (although they are private), but the mattresses are firm and everything is clean and tidy. Just around the corner from rue Daguerre, a cute pedestrian market street. There are two buildings: One has free Wi-Fi and small refrigerators in the rooms but no elevator; the other has an elevator but Wi-Fi only in the common areas.

22 rue Boulard, 14th arrond. www.solarhotel.fr. ⓒ **01-43-21-08-20.** 34 units. 89€ double. Rates include breakfast. Métro: Denfert-Rochereau. **Amenities:** Bicycles; Wi-Fi (free).

ALTERNATIVE LODGINGS

Hotels are all very well and good, but for some, nothing beats staying in a private home or apartment, particularly if you are a family on a budget. Fortunately, travelers with an independent streak have several options, including short-term rentals, B&Bs, and "*aparthotels.*"

Short-Term Rentals

In recent years there has been a boom in short-term rentals, and the Internet is now swimming in websites and agencies proffering hundreds of apartments smack in the center of the City of Light. Though the rates for two people can be close to what you'd pay at a hotel, the advantages include cooking some of your meals at home, saving yourself time and money. Other benefits are privacy, independence, and a chance to see what it's like to live like a Parisian, even if it's just for a week.

If you are more than two, and especially if you are traveling *en famille,* the benefits can be huge. Family suites and/or adjoining rooms are rare in Parisian hotels, so you'll often end up paying for two doubles—somewhere around 250€ to 500€ per night—whereas you could rent a one-bedroom apartment with a foldout couch and/or extra bed in the living room for anywhere from 600€ to 2,000€ per week, or 85€ to 285€ per night.

So how should you book? While established agencies like the ones listed below come with more services and guarantees, rates also tend to be more expensive than Internet rental platforms like **Airbnb.com, Flipkey.com, Homeaway.com,** and **VRBO.com,** as many of the rentals listed on these sites are done by the owners directly, so there's no middle man to pay. Agencies justify their costs by having cleaning staff, all-inclusive rates, and an office you can call when something goes wrong. They also can vet all of their apartments to make sure they are legal and that there is no funny business on the owners' side. That said, when this book went to print, Airbnb-style rentals, where individual apartment owners use the website to rent short-term, were legal in France, *as long as the apartment is the renter/owner's primary residence.* And there is no denying that thousands of people happily use Airbnb and similar sites and find great accommodations for very reasonable rates. The problem is that hugely popular sites like Airbnb cannot check up on every owner, so you cannot be entirely sure that your rental is legal.

Bottom line: If you want to minimize risk and are willing to pay more for it, go with a well-established agency like **Parisian Home** (www.parisian home.com; *✆* **01-45-08-03-37**), **France Lodge** (www.francelodge.fr; *✆* **01-56-33-85-85**), **Paris Attitude** (www.parisattitude.com; *✆* **01-42-96-31-46**), or **Paris Appartements Services** (www.paris-appartements-services. com; *✆* **01-40-28-01-28**). In most cases, you will deal directly with the agency (not the owners), and the minimum stay is 4 days to 1 week.

Bed & Breakfasts

Though bed-and-breakfasts (*chambres d'hôtes*) are extremely common in the French countryside, in the big city, where privacy and anonymity are treasured, they are still relatively rare. A terrific way to find a quality B&B is to visit the city's official B&B website: **Hôtes Qualité Paris** (www.hotesqualite paris.fr). A partnership with Paris's most well-established and trusted B&B agencies, the site offers a wide range of rooms for about 50€ to 140€ per person per night, based on double occupancy. A couple of other recommended agencies are **Good Morning Paris** (www.goodmorningparis.fr; *✆* **01-47-07-28-29**) and **Alcôve & Agapes** (www.bed-and-breakfast-in-paris.com; *✆* **07-64-08-42-77**).

Like apartment rentals (see above), these agencies and other B&B agencies are now in direct competition with massive Internet sites like **Airbnb.com** and **Wimdu.com,** which offer a stunning array of options at low prices. While the agencies listed above do not have as dazzling a variety of offers, their prices are competitive, and all have been in business a long time and know their clients. Knowing that your B&B hosts are on a first-name basis with a reliable agency can be a significant plus, and probably worth a few extra euros.

Aparthotels

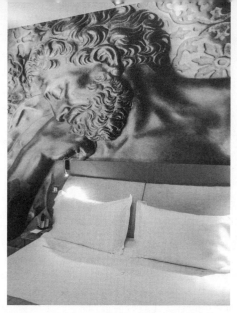

Every room at L'Apostraphe has a different design.

These utilitarian lodgings are a cross between a hotel and an apartment. Short on charm, *aparthotels* are decidedly practical: Units come with kitchenettes as well as hotel services like fresh towels, dry cleaning, and a concierge. Rates are generally higher than short-term rentals, but you do have the comfort of knowing you are dealing with a large company (if that makes you comfortable), with standardized apartments, organized websites, and customer service.

The best-known *aparthotel* company is **Citadines** (www.citadines.com; *©* **01-41-05-79-05**), which offers clean, comfortable units in excellent locations around the city. The cheapest rentals are the studios with pullout beds, which range from 125€ to 350€ a night depending on the season and location.

WHERE TO DINE

Everywhere you look in Paris, someone is doing his or her best to ruin your waistline. *Boulangeries* (bakeries) with buttery croissants and decadent pastries lurk on every street corner, open-air markets tempt the senses, and terrific restaurants with intriguing menus sprout up on every block. Following is just a sampling of Paris's gourmet delights. The best cafes, tearooms, and other places to find sinful sweets are listed at the end of this chapter.

In France, food is not a pastime; it's an art. Eating and drinking is a topic of serious discussion, the subject of radio shows, newspaper columns, and even feature films. So it's not surprising that Paris, navel of the French universe, should boast some of the best food on Earth. Fortunately, you don't have to have a king-size budget to dine like royalty. But you do have to choose wisely. Once upon a time, you could wander into just about any restaurant in Paris and sit down to a good meal; today, this is no longer the case. Try not to notice all the fast-food places that have popped up around the city, and don't even think about eating in one of the ubiquitous Chinese restaurants that serve a bland version of this marvelous Asian cuisine reheated in microwaves.

Fortunately, the guardians of good food are fighting back. Sick of the pressure and fuss of the temples of *haute cuisine,* about 15 years ago a bunch of famous chefs (like Christian Constant and Yves de Camdeborde) started what is now known as the "bistronomy" movement, opening dressed-down bistros that serve dressed-up versions of traditional workers' cuisine at relatively reasonable prices. Since then, a plethora of "neo-bistros" have opened up all over town, serving classic bistro dishes with a dash of contemporary *je ne sais quoi.* In general these restaurants are affordable, hip, and serve excellent food. One outgrowth of this movement is the obsession with "noble" ingredients, such as high-quality, regional produce or products, often from a specific small-scale farm or artisan, sometimes organic.

A French version of the Spanish tapas bar has recently appeared on the Parisian scene, where the tapas often come with a southwestern or Basque accent. And *pourquoi pas?* Since lunch is usually the big meal of the day, Parisians are happy to nibble something light at night, especially with a nice glass of wine.

There's also a puzzling interest in American food. Gourmet hamburgers are ubiquitous on bistro menus, and you'll find bagels and smoked salmon at "le brunch," a new-fangled meal (for the French) that is currently all the rage.

PRACTICAL MATTERS

Eating Hours & Annual Closings

In Paris, unless you see a sign that says SERVICE CONTINU, meals are usually restricted to set hours. This is one of the reasons it's a good idea to reserve, if you can (the other is that dining rooms tend to be small). Don't expect to wander in someplace for a bowl of soup at 4pm. Lunch is generally served between noon and 2pm (sometimes 2:30pm), and dinner is served from 7 to 10:30pm (sometimes 11pm). Many restaurants are closed on Sundays and/or Mondays, though some have started serving brunch on Sundays, which is generally served from 11am to 3pm. Cafes and restaurants with a bar tend to stay open between mealtimes serving drinks and coffee; if you are starving, you can usually order a light sandwich, or a *croque-monsieur* (a French take on a grilled ham and cheese sandwich). Some brasseries serve late into the night. For late-night dining options, see p. 93. Many restaurants close in August (normally for the first 2 weeks), and some shut down between Christmas and New Year's; see listings for details. *Tip:* If you didn't reserve and you want to avoid waiting in line, try to arrive at the very beginning of the service, noon or around 7:30pm. Most French people eat later than that, so you'll avoid the rush.

Reservations

Most restaurants in Paris are small, so if you have your heart set on eating at one in particular, reserving ahead, even if it is the same day, is essential. If you are looking to dine at one of Paris's hip neo-bistros or famous gourmet temples, you may have to reserve months in advance. Ask your hotel receptionist to help if you can't manage the telephone, or try reserving online through www.thefork.com (which also offers discounts). Otherwise, you can often reserve on the restaurant's site via e-mail.

Dejeuner sur L'Herbe (Picnics)

Although restaurants are all very well and good, there's a lot to be said for a quick and easy outdoor meal in one of Paris's many lovely parks and squares. Picking up picnic ingredients is a pretty easy affair, though there's a bit of terminology you should be familiar with. For good takeout food, look for the nearest *charcutier* (these specialize in smoked meat, pâtés, and other pork products) or *traiteur* (a store that sells prepared takeout dishes and salads). At almost any *boulangerie* (bakery), you can find what may well be **the best lunch bargain in the city:** their lunch *formule,* or set menu. For around 7€ or 8€, you can get a long sandwich (usually half a baguette), amply filled with chicken, ham, or tuna and *crudités* (tomato, lettuce, and other saladlike items), a drink, and a fresh pastry. Often you can substitute a slice of quiche for the sandwich. *Formules* and sandwiches are usually only available from 11am to 2pm. **Eric Kayser** (www.maison-kayser.com) and **Paul** (www.paul.fr) are reliable bakery chains serving salads, sandwiches, and even hot dishes. But your best bet is to use your *nez* and find a place on your own. Just be careful in tourist areas, like the Eiffel Tower, where you might pick a dud. The telltale signs of a good bakery are an attractive window display and a queue at mealtimes.

Choosing a Restaurant

Below is a selective list of restaurants, wine bars, and tearooms that serve the type of excellent food you came specifically to Paris to try. But seeing as how there are thousands of restaurants in the city, you just might wander into something wonderful and unexpected on your own. Finding a good restaurant is extremely subjective, taking into account any number of variables and a good dose of what the French call *le feeling.*

That said, I recommend you take some precautions if you go beyond the suggestions in this guide. Unfortunately, Paris has many restaurants geared solely to tourists that shovel out food that is at best, unmemorable, and at worst, indigestible. Look for places that are full of happy customers speaking French. And don't avoid places with lines out front (that's a *good* sign). Final strategy: Follow your nose. If there are delicious smells issuing from the kitchen, it's likely the food will be good (restaurants lacking in appetizing aromas may be relying on pre-packaged foods and microwaves).

THE RIGHT BANK

Louvre & Île de la Cité (1st Arrondissement)

Dining near the Louvre can be expensive and frustrating. Since almost every tourist visiting the city comes to this part of town, it's rife with overpriced, mediocre tourist restaurants (you can identify them by the fact that they offer menus in at least five languages). However, if you poke around some of the smaller streets away from the museum, you'll find more authentic eateries.

EXPENSIVE

Le Grand Véfour ★★★
CLASSIC FRENCH Back in the day, when the galleries of the Palais Royal were known for drinking, gambling, and revolutionary plotting (p. 141), what was then called the Café de Chartres was the place to see and be seen. Napoleon, Hugo, Colette, and Cocteau all dined in this magnificently preserved 18th-century dining room. Today, eating here is still a memorable event. Guy Martin, chef and owner for the past decade, offers up rightly celebrated signature dishes—like Prince Rainier III pigeon

The beautiful dining room at Le Grand Véfour.

and truffled oxtail parmentier—alongside sublime new creations that feature more contemporary flavors like sumac and star anise. All of the desserts are superb, but we have a special fondness for the *palet,* a thick biscuit with milk chocolate and hazelnuts, served with caramel and sea-salt ice cream. Reserve at least 2 weeks in advance. *Tip:* The lunch fixed-price menu is a third of the price of dinner (and just as good).

17 rue de Beaujolais, 1st arrond. www.grand-vefour.com. ✆ **01-42-96-56-27.** Main courses 98€–128€; fixed-price lunch 115€, fixed-price dinner 315€. Mon–Fri 12:30–1:45pm and 8–9:45pm. Closed Aug. Métro: Louvre–Palais-Royal or Pyramides.

Spring ★★★ MODERN FRENCH One of the city's most talked-about restaurants has a chef who is—gasp—American! Chef Daniel Rose, native of Chicago, pays utmost respect to all things French, while adding a dash of Yankee derring-do to his superb creations. The menu changes once a month, but it might start with zucchini with mint and curry oil, followed by quail with cherries and purée of almonds. Desserts might include a tea sorbet with grapefruit or chocolate with blackberries. You must order the four-course fixed-price menu but that doesn't seem to be a problem for diners, who fight for a

price CATEGORIES

Expensive	Main dishes 33€ and up
Moderate	Main dishes 18€–32€
Inexpensive	Main dishes under 18€

Right Bank West Restaurants

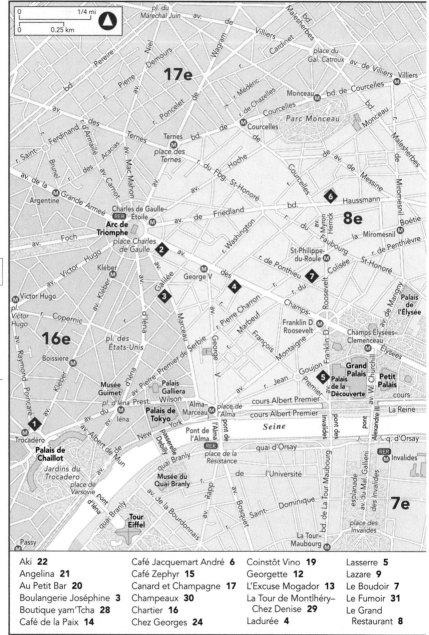

Aki **22**
Angelina **21**
Au Petit Bar **20**
Boulangerie Joséphine **3**
Boutique yam'Tcha **28**
Café de la Paix **14**

Café Jacquemart André **6**
Café Zephyr **15**
Canard et Champagne **17**
Champeaux **30**
Chartier **16**
Chez Georges **24**

Coinstôt Vino **19**
Georgette **12**
L'Excuse Mogador **13**
La Tour de Montlhéry–
  Chez Denise **29**
Ladurée **4**

Lasserre **5**
Lazare **9**
Le Boudoir **7**
Le Fumoir **31**
Le Grand
  Restaurant **8**

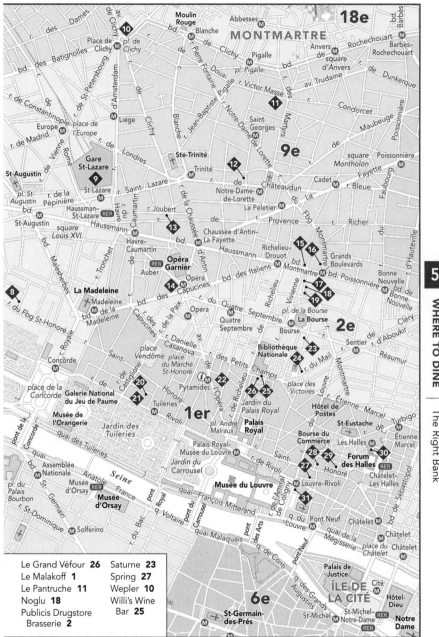

Le Grand Véfour **26**   Saturne **23**
Le Malakoff **1**   Spring **27**
Le Pantruche **11**   Wepler **10**
Noglu **18**   Willi's Wine
Publicis Drugstore   Bar **25**
  Brasserie **2**

seat here. Reserve at least 1 month in advance. *Note:* If you have dietary restrictions, alert your waiter so that the chef can tailor your meal.

6 rue Bailleul, 1st arrond. www.springparis.fr. ✆ **01-45-96-05-72.** Fixed-price dinner 84€. Tues–Sat 6:30–10:30pm. Métro: Louvre-Rivoli.

MODERATE

Champeaux ★ MODERN BRASSERIE   This is multi-Michelin-starred-chef Alain Ducasse's latest Parisian venture: a vintage-chic, train-station-inspired neo-brasserie set under the *canopée* (roof) of the new Halles shopping center. The place takes its name from a circa-1800s restaurant that once stood near Les Halles, and the menu also harks back to days gone by: onion soup, black pudding with apple salad, and the house specialty, soufflé, which comes in both sweet and savory varieties (think lobster, cheese, or caramel). Last order for food is at 11pm; after that, you'll have to make do with the excellent cocktails! Snacks such as *croque-monsieur* and cold meat platters are served all afternoon.

La Canopée, Forum des Halles, porte Rambuteau, 1st arrond. www.restaurant-champeaux. com. ✆ **01-53-45-84-50.** Main courses 16€–26€; afternoon snacks from 12€. Sun–Wed 11:30am–midnight; Thurs–Sat 11:30am–1am. Métro: Les Halles. RER: Châtelet–Les Halles.

La Brasserie de l'Ile Saint-Louis ★ TRADITIONAL BRASSERIE
Owned by the same family for three generations, this lovely, old-fashioned brasserie serves healthy portions of classic Alsatian dishes, like *choucroute garni*—a small mountain of sauerkraut topped with slices of ham, sausage, and other smoked meats—in a relaxed atmosphere. If sauerkraut isn't your game, try other classic brasserie fare like a tender entrecote (rib steak) or a breaded filet of haddock. The decor is blissfully kitsch with hunting trophies on the walls. Despite the location, many of the diners are regulars, including a handful of French celebrities. Eating's not a requirement; if you want, you can just enjoy a Mutzig (Alsatian beer) on the terrace and soak up a splendid view of the buttresses of Notre-Dame. Service is "nonstop."

55 quai de Bourbon, 4th arrond. www.labrasserie-isl.fr. ✆ **01-43-54-02-59.** Main courses 19€–34€. Thurs–Tues noon–10:30pm. Closed Aug. Métro: Pont Marie.

Right Bank East Restaurants

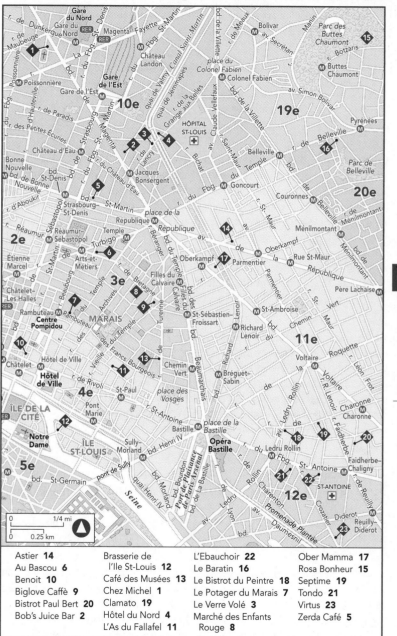

Astier **14**
Au Bascou **6**
Benoit **10**
Biglove Caffè **9**
Bistrot Paul Bert **20**
Bob's Juice Bar **2**

Brasserie de
  l'Ile St-Louis **12**
Café des Musées **13**
Chez Michel **1**
Clamato **19**
Hôtel du Nord **4**
L'As du Fallafel **11**

L'Ebauchoir **22**
Le Baratin **16**
Le Bistrot du Peintre **18**
Le Potager du Marais **7**
Le Verre Volé **3**
Marché des Enfants
  Rouge **8**

Ober Mamma **17**
Rosa Bonheur **15**
Septime **19**
Tondo **21**
Virtus **23**
Zerda Café **5**

La Tour de Montlhéry–Chez Denise ★★ TRADITIONAL FRENCH/BISTRO   One of the last remnants of the bustling atmosphere that used to surround the old Les Halles central market, Chez Denise stays open through the night until 5am and serves sturdy platters of *côte de boeuf* (a giant rib steak), grilled marrow bones, and brochettes of grilled meat so long they look like swords. The long-aproned waiters are used to encountering English speakers, but that hasn't changed the vibe, which is local and lively. If you are not a carnivore, the menu has a few fish dishes, and you can always enjoy the homemade fries, which are delicious.

5 rue des Prouvaires, 1st arrond. ✆ **01-42-36-21-82.** Main courses 23€–30€. Mon–Fri noon–3pm and 7:30pm–5am. Closed July 15–Aug 15. Métro: Les Halles.

Le Fumoir ★★ FRENCH-SCANDINAVIAN   With its high ceilings, subdued lighting, and large windows, this understatedly hip spot is a good place to regroup. During the day (except at lunchtime) dawdling is encouraged: Magazines and newspapers are available at the front entry, and a small lending library/book exchange is located in the back room. At night, well-dressed 30-somethings crowd around the magnificent wood bar—which in a former life stood in a Philadelphia speakeasy—as they wait for their table. You'll eat well here too: The offerings might include Nordic poached cod with smoked potato purée or a very French and very tender lamb navarin (stew) with fresh peas. On Sundays, there's a 26€ brunch complete with pancakes and eggs Benedict, and on Sunday nights, the Swedish chef (Henrik Andersson) returns to his roots with an all-Swedish menu.

6 rue de l'Amiral Coligny, 1st arrond. www.lefumoir.com. ✆ **01-42-92-00-24.** Main courses 13€–28€; fixed-price menu lunch 24€–28€, fixed-price menu dinner 35€–39€. Daily 11am–2am; lunch noon–3pm, dinner 7:30–11pm. Métro: Louvre-Rivoli.

Willi's Wine Bar ★ MODERN BISTRO/WINE BAR   Contrary to what you may expect, Willi was a dog. The owner's basset hound, to be exact. But he graciously lent his illustrious name to this wine bar, which has been thrilling taste buds for over 30 years. You'll hear a lot of English spoken here, but that doesn't mean it's a tourist joint (it's a favorite of the British and American expat community living in Paris)—in addition to a terrific selection of wines, you can indulge a variety of delicious dishes like roasted cod with fresh peas and sherry or veal with preserved lemons and ginger. If you'd just like to nibble something with your glass of wine, Willi's serves a selection of Spanish ham and finger food, too (4€–8€).

13 rue des Petits Champs, 1st arrond. www.williswinebar.com. © **01-42-61-05-09.** Main courses 16€–24€; fixed-price lunch 26€, fixed-price dinner 36€. Mon–Sat noon–2:30pm and 7–10:30pm; wine bar noon–midnight. Métro: Pyramides or Bourse.

INEXPENSIVE

Aki ★★ JAPANESE Aki specializes in *okonomiyaki*, a sort of grilled omelet topped with meat or seafood and a yummy sauce. Watch the cooks create yours on a griddle in the open kitchen before diving into your meal. You can also order excellent udon or soba noodles. Get here early or be prepared to stand in line. For other recommended Japanese restaurants, see box below.

11bis rue Sainte Anne, 1st arrond. www.akirestaurant.fr. © **01-42-97-54-27.** Main courses 12€–15€; fixed-price lunch or dinner 13€–16€. Mon–Sat 11:30am–10:45pm. Métro: Pyramides.

Au Petit Bar ★★ TRADITIONAL FRENCH Tucked on a small street right behind the illustrious Rue de Rivoli, this old-fashioned mom-and-pop restaurant has somehow survived the onslaught of chic that has inundated the neighborhood. Mom and Pop really are in the kitchen, while their son is behind the bar bantering with the customers, most of whom he knows by name. The food is simple and solid—you might start with mackerel in white wine, followed by steak-frites, and finish up with a chocolate mousse, for example. Prices are extremely reasonable, considering the close proximity to the ritzy place Vendôme; in fact, this is probably one of the cheapest cups of coffee on the Right Bank. No credit cards accepted.

7 rue Mont Thabor, 1st arrond. © **01-42-60-62-09.** Main courses 8€–13€. Mon–Sat 7am–8pm. Closed Aug. Métro: Tuileries.

Boutique yam'Tcha ★★★ FRENCH-ASIAN STREET FOOD Book a table at renowned chef Adeleine Grattard's Michelin-starred restaurant

---

Japantown, Paris-Style

You are wandering around the streets near the Opéra, when you take a sharp turn onto the rue Ste-Anne. Suddenly, everything is in Japanese, and there are noodle shops everywhere! Plunge into a bowl at one of these restaurants:

○ **Udon Jubey,** 39 rue Ste-Anne, 1st (© **01-40-15-92-54;** Métro: Pyramides), makes some of the best Udon noodles in town; slurp at the counter grab one of the limited number of tables.
○ **Higuma,** 32 bis rue Ste-Anne, 1st (www.higuma.fr; © **01-47-03-38-59;**

Métro: Pyramides), features an open kitchen, ramen soups, and a long line out the front door.
○ **Aki Boulangerie,** 16 rue Ste-Anne, 1st (http://akiboulanger.com; © **01-40-15-63-38**), is a bakery-tearoom run by the same management as the restaurant (described above). Excellent Japanese teas and savory goodies, as well as terrific Franco-Japanese pastries, such as asuki bean tarts and matcha tea éclairs, are all on offer.

yam'Tcha and you'll certainly have a fabulous meal (121 rue St. Honore, 1st arrond.; ℭ 01-40-26-08-07; tasting menus from 65€, reservations 2 months in advance): Grattard works miracles with simple ingredients such as lobster, seabass, truffles and pork. But her second place near the Louvre—a duel take-out *bao* bar (steamed Taiwanese brioches) and a tearoom—lets you taste her cooking for a fraction of the price. The bar section is a window open to the street, where foodies queue for bao buns filled with delectables such as smoked tofu or crab with vegetables, plus unexpected mixes like stilton and cherries. The tearoom, run by Grattard's Hong Kong-born husband Chi Wah Chan (a veritable tea guru who pairs teas with dishes in the same way sommeliers pair wines) serves excellent main courses such as Peking soup and fish tartare, both for around 14€.

4 rue Sauval, 1st arrond. www.yamtcha.com. ℭ **01-40-26-06-06.** Bao buns 5€–7€, Main courses 8€–14€. Wed–Fri noon–6pm; Sat noon–8pm. Métro: Louvre-Rivoli.

Le Marais (3rd & 4th Arrondissements)

You should have no trouble finding good things to eat in the Marais. Between its working-class roots and its more recent gentrification, the Marais has a wide range of choices, from humble falafel joints to trendy brasseries. Unlike the shops here, which have become so hip it hurts, there is still a good selection of midrange restaurants that attract both the sleek set and just regular folks.

EXPENSIVE

Benoit ★ TRADITIONAL FRENCH   This historic restaurant had hosted a century's worth of Parisian notables when renowned chef Alain Ducasse took the helm in 2005. The venerable dining room is still lined with mirrors, zinc, and tiles, while the menu features beautifully executed bistro classics. Escargots (snails) in garlic butter, and brill braised with Jura wine share the stage with homemade cassoulet and beef filet bordelaise. Save room for the profiteroles, puff pastry filled with ice cream and drizzled with chocolate sauce.

20 rue St-Martin, 4th arrond. www.benoit-paris.com. ℭ **01-42-72-25-76.** Main courses 26€–54€; fixed-price lunch 39€. Mon–Thurs noon–2pm and 7:30–10pm; Fri–Sun noon–2pm and 7–10pm. Closed first 3 weeks of Aug. Métro: Hôtel-de-Ville.

Eating Vegetarian in Paris

Though the French still love their meat, time are a-changing and an increasingly large number of Parisian restaurants now cater to vegetarians, offering at least a couple of appropriate dishes on the menu. Even basic cafes will usually serve *salades composées*, meal-size salads that often come in meat-free versions. If you eat fish, most restaurants offer at least one or two pescatarian selections too. And, of course, Paris does have vegetarian restaurants. We've listed a few (**Bob's Juice Bar,** p. 106; **Le Potager du Marais,** p. 91; **Noglu,** p. 99; and **Jardin des Pâtes,** p. 114), but space limitations make it hard to go into depth. For more options, visit the Happy Cow (www.happycow.net), a veggie online network with extensive listings for Paris.

Many restaurants in Paris serve a set-price menu at lunch that is considerably cheaper than the same food served at dinnertime. It is not unusual to find a two- or three-course lunch prix-fixe, called alternately a *formule*, or a menu for 17€ to 28€. The only downside is that your choice of dishes will usually be limited on the *formule*. **Note:** Set-price lunches are usually only served Monday through Friday.

MODERATE

Au Bascou ★★ BASQUE Basque cuisine, like the province, is not entirely French. Using lots of tomatoes, onions, and sweet Espelette pepper, Basque dishes have a decidedly different tang to them. But while the name of this restaurant refers to Basque country, the menu covers the entire southwest. Traditional Basque dishes like *pipérade* (a tasty omelet loaded with peppers and onions) and *axoa* (a stew of veal shoulder, peppers, and onions) mingle with southwestern classics like duck foie gras and roast *palombe* (wood pigeon). Everything is handled with great care by the chef, who used to be the right-hand man of Alain Sederens.

38 rue Réaumur, 3rd arrond. www.au-bascou.fr. ℂ **01-42-72-69-25.** Main courses 18€–26€; fixed-price lunch menu 18€ and 25€. Mon–Fri noon–2pm and 8–10:30pm. Closed between Christmas and New Year's and in Aug. Métro: Arts-et-Métiers.

Café des Musées ★ TRADITIONAL FRENCH/BISTRO Weary culture vultures who've tried to do both the Picasso museum and the Musée Carnavalet on the same day will appreciate this bustling corner cafe with its appealing sidewalk tables. We recommend it not just for the atmosphere, however, but because the young chef does terrific things with bistro classics like steak-frites with béarnaise sauce, or *andouillette* (tripe sausage) as well as lighter fare like seasonal vegetable casserole with basil oil, or a *grand aioli*, poached cod with aioli mayonnaise and vegetables. The lunch fixed-price menu is particularly good value.

49 rue de Turenne, 3rd arrond. www.lecafedesmusees.fr. ℂ **01-42-72-96-17.** Main courses 15€–27€; fixed-price lunch 17€. Daily noon–3pm and 7–11pm. Closed last 2 weeks of Aug. Métro: St. Paul or Chemin Vert.

Le Potager du Marais ★ VEGAN The shoe-box-size dining room fills up quickly, as there aren't all that many vegan eateries in Paris. But even omnivores enjoy the delicious veggie offerings here, which include *seitan bourguignon,* mushroom pâté, and pumpkin parmentier. Many items are gluten-free. Finish off with a simple but scrumptious apple compote. A handy takeout version is located at 48 bd. du Temple, 11th arrond. between République and Oberkampf métros.

24 rue Rambuteau, 3rd arrond. www.lepotagerdumarais.fr. ℂ **01-57-40-98-57.** Main courses 16€–20€. Wed–Sun noon–3pm and 7–11pm. Métro: Rambuteau.

5

WHERE TO DINE | The Right Bank

Over the past few years, many sandwich bars have popped up all over town:

o **Cojean** (20 locations; www.cojean.fr). These airy, modern boutiques serve fresh, healthy food, including innovative salads, quiches, sandwiches, and fresh-squeezed juices. Many veggie options. You can eat on-site at comfortable tables. Open until 4 or 5pm in most locations.

o **Exki** (11 locations; www.exki.com). This Belgian chain (pronounced ex-*key*, like the French word for "exquisite") offers a terrific array of healthy sandwiches, soups, and desserts (including vegetarian choices), usually until 9 or 10pm. They use lots of organic, free-trade ingredients and have a low ecological footprint.

o **Boco** (3 locations; www.boco.fr). This one is almost too good to be true: organic takeout by Michelin-starred chefs for under 15€. Hot food, cold food, light meals, and desserts until 8 or 10pm (St-Lazare location, lunch only). Main dishes cost 7€ to 10€.

INEXPENSIVE

Biglove Caffé ★ ITALIAN   Jars of preserved fruit line the walls, and hams hang from the ceiling—yes, you're still in Paris, but this place sure feels like Napoli. It tastes like it, too. For breakfast patrons tuck into pancakes with bufflonne ricotta and passion fruit, for brunch a highlight are eggs benedict with 24-month-matured parma ham, and most any other time of day, pizza reigns supreme (the gluten-free versions are just as good), as does pasta. Whatever you choose, everything is made with only the choicest and freshest of ingredients, many of them direct from "petits producteurs" (small producers) in Italy. Set in a frighteningly hip part of the northern Marais, it is a popular place. Biglove doesn't take reservations, so if you come for brunch, arrive as early as possible—especially on weekends when this neighborhood is a brunch hotspot.

30 rue Debelleyme, 3rd arrond. ℂ **01-42-71-43-62.** Main courses 10€–16€. Daily 9am–4:30pm and 7–10:30pm. Métro: Filles de Calvaire.

L'As du Fallafel ★★ FALAFEL/ISRAELI   This Marais institution offers, without a doubt, the best falafel in Paris. And they're kosher yet. True, falafel joints are scarce in this city, but that doesn't take away from the excellence of these overstuffed beauties, brimming with cucumbers, pickled turnips, shredded cabbage, tahini, fried eggplant, and those crispy balls of fried chickpeas and spices. Other arrangements of similar ingredients *sans* pita can be found in the *assiettes* (platters). Wash it down with an Israeli beer. Service is fast and furious, but basically friendly—just be prepared to deal with hordes of tourists and locals at lunch. It's closed Friday afternoon and all day Saturday.

34 rue des Rosiers, 4th arrond. ℂ **01-48-87-63-60.** Main courses 8€–20€. Sun–Thurs 11am–midnight; Fri 11am–3pm. Métro: St. Paul.

Marché des Enfants Rouge ★★ STREET FOOD   On rue de Bretagne, this quaint, 400-year-old food market (the oldest in Paris) is a bustling, fragrant labyrinth of ready-to-eat food stalls hawking everything from Caribbean curries to couscous, sushi, and pasta. A hugely popular spot (if the queues are anything to go by) is Alain Miam Miam's organic crêpe stand, which serves made–to-order paninis and pancakes dripping in tasty cheese and ham. This is also where you'll find some of the best burgers in town: Burger Fermier makes the bread on-site, slathers the burgers in French cheese such as cider-infused Tomme, and only uses hand-picked beef from a farm in northern France. Come late afternoon and you can join the post-shopping crowd over a glass of wine.

39 rue de Bretagne, 3rd arrond. http://marchedesenfantsrougesfr.com. No phone. Main courses 7.50€–16€. Tues–Sat 8am–8:30pm; Sun 8:30am–5pm. Métro: Saint Sébastien-Froissart.

Champs-Élysées & Western Paris (8th, 16th & 17th Arrondissements)

Mobbed with tourists, oozing with opulence, the Champs-Élysées is a difficult place to find a good meal, unless you are willing to spend a lot of money. Mediocre chain restaurants abound on the grand avenue itself; kebab joints mingle with frighteningly expensive gourmet palaces on the surrounding side streets. If you have no strings attached to your wallet, you can explore dinners in the many two- and three-Michelin star restaurants in the area; if you are like the rest of us, consider splurging on lunch in one of these same eateries for half the price.

EXPENSIVE

Lasserre ★★★ GOURMET FRENCH   André Malraux, Salvador Dali, Audrey Hepburn, Marlene Dietrich . . . the list of celebrities who have dined at this legendary restaurant is understandably long—what famous person wouldn't want to eat in this superb dining room, where the ceiling opens when the weather is willing, and the food will send you swooning? A silk-draped, arch-windowed affair, the room glistens with fine porcelain, silver knick-knacks, and crystal candelabras. When it's closed, you can still admire the

---

Dining After Hours

There aren't many restaurants that stay open until the wee hours of the Parisian night, but there are a few stalwarts around Les Halles. **Le Tambour,** 41 rue de Montmartre, 2nd arrond. (✆ **01-42-33-06-90;** Métro: Les Halles), serves reliable dishes like steak-frites (main courses 16€–20€) from noon to 5:30am every day in a dining room filled with kitschy Paris memorabilia. Nearby, **Au Pied de Cochon,** 6 rue Coquillière, 1st

arrond. (www.pieddecochon.com; ✆ **01-40-13-77-00;** Métro: Les Halles), is a brasserie open 24/7 that specializes in pork and more pork (main courses 22€– 50€). Au Pied du Cochon also has some good seafood dishes and a restorative onion soup that's ideal at 4am after a night on the town. For a late-night beef fix, head to **La Tour de Montlhéry– Chez Denise** (p. 88; open until 5am), where the steak is as juicy as it is huge.

Le Grand Restaurant.

ceiling, which is painted with white clouds and a cerulean sky. Along with the restaurant's classics, like Challans duck and filet of beef Rossini, you can find more modern creations, like sea bass with vegetables in chardonnay, and roasted lamb confit with artichokes and apples. Reserve at least 2 weeks ahead. Dinner jackets required for men.

17 ave. Franklin D. Roosevelt, 8th arrond. www.restaurant-lasserre.com. © **01-43-59-02-13.** Main courses 50€–103€; fixed-price lunch 90€, fixed-price dinner 190€, tasting menu with wine 340€. Tues–Wed and Sat 7–10pm; Thurs–Fri noon–2pm and 7–10pm. Closed Aug. Métro: Franklin Roosevelt.

Le Grand Restaurant ★★★ MODERN FRENCH Chef Jean-François Piège is—in our humble opinion—the most exciting chef in France right now. His ultra-modern take on traditional "bourgeois" cuisine is playful, delicious, and wholly unlike anything you'll taste anywhere else. Book ahead for a table in his swish, grey dining room (decked in concrete walls and geometric ceiling panels that wouldn't look amiss in Kubrick's *2001: A Space Odyssey*), then sit back for a rollercoaster ride of haute cuisine: shellfish-stuffed potato with caviar, Parmesan-infused spaghetti with truffles and fall-off-your-fork pork, and a delightful bergamot-flavored custard cream to finish. Don't be fooled by the simplicity of the descriptions; Piège's cooking is as complex as it is satisfying. His place is near the Élysée palace, so don't be surprised if you spot politicians out for a business meal—though Piège's devoted fans are never far away.

7 rue d'Aguesseau, 8th arrond. www.jeanfrancoispiege.com. © **01-53-05-00-00.** Main courses 72€–155€; fixed-price lunch 85€, fixed-price dinner 195€ and 255€. Mon–Fri 12:30–2pm and 7:30–9pm. Closed 3 weeks in Aug and last week in Dec. Métro: Concorde or Madeleine.

MODERATE

Lazare ★★★ MODERN BISTRO Before the Gare St-Lazare train station had its recent makeover, about the only thing you could get to eat was a limp sandwich. Today, you can eat like a king as you wait for your train to come in, and we're not talking about the Burger King that opened up on the main level. Eric Frechon, one of those Michelin-starred chefs, is the great mind behind this gourmet enterprise, which serves as cafe, bar, and restaurant. The lofty ceilings, wood furnishings, and white walls give the place a relaxed air, as does the menu, which features French comfort food like boeuf bourguignon, cod *brandade* (a sort of fish shepherd's pie), and Toulouse sausage with mashed potatoes. Don't be fooled, though; granny is definitely not in the kitchen. A gaggle of young, intense cooks bustle about, preparing each dish with the best ingredients and designing each plate with care. Breakfast is served from 7:30 to 11am, and tea time is 3 to 6pm.

Inside the Gare St-Lazare shopping gallery, 8th arrond. www.lazare-paris.fr. ℂ **01-44-90-80-80.** Main courses 19€–22€; fixed-price lunch (Sun only) 39€. Daily 7:30–midnight, lunch served noon–3pm, dinner 7–11pm. Métro: Gare St-Lazare.

Le Boudoir ★★ TRADITIONAL FRENCH This intimate restaurant features three different settings for your gustatory pleasure: a chic restaurant in shades of red; a cozy dining room upstairs; and a *fumoir,* or cigar salon, where you can smoke without driving your neighbors mad. But the main event here is the food, which reaches gourmet heights at a relatively earthbound price. A minimalist menu features French classics like chateaubriand Rossini and sautéed scallops cooked to perfection and served with intriguing vegetable accompaniments like squash risotto. If you can't decide, order the tasting menu (evenings only; 55€) and sample two appetizers, two main courses, and a dessert. On Saturday nights, Le Boudoir becomes a wine bar, serving tapas and charcuterie to go along with your glass of red (or white, or rosé . . .).

25 rue du Colisée, 8th arrond. www.boudoirparis.fr. ℂ **01-43-59-25-29.** Main courses 27€–35€; fixed-price dinner 55€. Mon–Fri noon–2pm and 8–10pm; Sat (wine bar only) 8–10pm. Closed 2 weeks in Aug. Métro: St-Philippe-du-Roule.

Le Malakoff ★ BRASSERIE While the brasseries on the Place du Trocadéro are generally overpriced and sniffy, this one is accessible, both in terms of price and service. The menu is standard Parisian brasserie fare—steak tartare, grilled chicken, *choucroute garni,* steak-frites—executed with skill, and supplemented with a wide variety of tasty *salades composées* (meal-size salads). Best of all, you get a front row view of the grandiose Place and the Palais de Chaillot (and, if you lean over, the Eiffel Tower). The same management runs **Le Wilson** (www.le-wilson.fr), a smaller operation at 2 place du Trocadéro at the corner of ave. du Président Wilson, which offers a similar menu.

6 place du Trocadéro, 16th arrond. www.le-malakoff.com. ℂ **01-45-53-75-27.** Main courses 13€–24€. Mon–Fri 7:30am–1am; Sat–Sun 8:30am–1am. Métro: Trocadéro.

Publicis Drugstore Brasserie ★★ MODERN BRASSERIE You won't find toothpaste at this "drugstore," whose name comes from a former 1950s incarnation that consisted of a warren of shops, restaurants, and services "à l'americaine." This ultra-modern, oh-so-chic complex has replaced the funky original, keeping the multifunctional concept intact with shops, restaurants, and a cinema. The Brasserie is the most accessible eating option: a light-filled expanse with an incredible street-side view of the Champs-Élysées and the Arc de Triomphe. The food is high-end casual, featuring items like gourmet hamburgers, grilled fish, steak tartare, and filet of sole delivered by a young and beautiful wait staff. Meals are served nonstop until 2am, and an "early lunch" deal is offered during the week from 11:30am to 12:30pm for 15€ to 20€. There's also a terrific buffet brunch on Sundays from 11am to 4pm.

133 ave. des Champs-Élysées, 8th arrond. www.publicisdrugstore.com. (C) **01-44-43-77-64.** Main courses 22€–42€; fixed-price "early lunch" 15€–20€; Sunday brunch 38€. Mon–Fri 8am–2am; Sat–Sun 10am–2am. Métro: Charles de Gaulle–Etoile.

INEXPENSIVE

Boulangerie Joséphine ★ BAKERY/SANDWICHES/FRENCH This terrific bakery near the Arc de Triomphe does double duty as a lunch spot, with a nice outdoor terrace and a pretty upstairs dining room that fills quickly with local office workers and business people. You can buy sandwiches and salads (and desserts, of course) to go or sit down for table service (noon–3pm), which gives you the option of trying one of the excellent daily specials, like stuffed vegetables, roast chicken, or osso buco. It's also open for breakfast, including a mini brunchlike offering of omelet, pastries, and coffee for 15€ (8–11am).

69 ave. Marceau, 8th arrond. www.josephine-boulangerie.com. (C) **01-47-20-49-62.** Main courses 5€–15€. Mon–Fri 8am–8pm. Closed 2 weeks in mid-Aug. Métro: Charles de Gaulle–Etoile.

Opéra & Grands Boulevards (2nd & 9th Arrondissements)

Buzzing with cafes and theaters in the 19th century, the long-overlooked Grands Boulevards are finally coming back to life, especially where these wide avenues intersect with the Opéra and the hip and happening part of the 9th arrondissement that borders Montmartre. Less trendy, but also less expensive, the little streets around the Bourse (the French stock exchange) have a wide range of restaurant options, especially at lunchtime. The covered passages that crisscross parts of the 2nd arrondissement (p. 218) also harbor some excellent dining options.

EXPENSIVE

Chez Georges ★★ TRADITIONAL FRENCH A step back in time, this is how Parisian restaurants were before cuisine became nouvelle, or vanilla infusions were allowed to touch a fish dish. The room is crowded and lively, the cooking old-fashioned and delicious. Many of the customers are regulars who work in nearby offices. The handwritten menu features beautifully executed classics like filet of sole, *pot-au-feu* (beef simmered with vegetables), and sweetbreads with morels. Save room for the profiteroles at dessert.

1 rue du Mail, 2nd arrond. (C) **01-42-60-07-11.** Main courses 20€–43€. Mon–Fri noon–2:30pm and 7–11pm. Closed Aug and the last week of Dec. Métro: Bourse.

Saturne ★★★ MODERN FRENCH   There are not very many glass-roofed restaurants in Paris, and even fewer with a kitchen like this one. The chef's Scandinavian roots are evident in the decor, with its sleek blond wood and white walls. But it's what's on the plate that makes it difficult to get a reservation here: exquisitely refined combinations of flavors and textures, described on the menu as a list of ingredients. Resembling works of contemporary art, dishes might combine gnocchi, chestnuts, and truffles; or guinea hen with purple artichokes and spring garlic; and could be followed with a concoction of carrots, citrus, and olives. At lunch you can choose between a menu of three or six dishes, or à la carte; at dinner, there's a choice-free fixed-price menu for one and all.

17 rue Notre-Dame-des-Victoires, 2nd arrond. www.saturne-paris.fr. © **01-42-60-31-90.** Fixed-price lunch 45€–85€, fixed-price dinner 85€, with wines 150€. Mon–Fri noon–1:30pm and 7:30–10pm. Closed 3 weeks in Aug. Métro: Bourse.

MODERATE

Canard et Champagne ★★ MODERN BISTRO   Tucked away in the old-world Passage des Panoramas, this delightful spot attracts the eye with a giant wall mural of French actor Louis de Funès (in his iconic role as Mr. Septime in the 1966 movie *Le Grand Restaurant*), then reels patrons in with fabulous duck dishes—foie gras, *confit de canard,* and *magret*—all washed down with hand-picked champagne from the region's best small producers. The concept is fabulous, especially since it won't break the bank: The set menus, which include two or three courses and up to three glasses of champagne, start at 32€. Reserve in advance or arrive early (noon for lunch, 7pm for dinner).

57 passage des Panoramas, 2nd arrond. http://frenchparadox.paris. © **09-81-83-95-69.** Fixed-price lunch 18€–21€, fixed-price dinner 26€, fixed-price dinner with champagne 32€–62€. Tues–Sun noon–midnight. Closed 2 weeks in Aug. Métro: Bonne Nouvelle.

Le Pantruche ★★ TRADITIONAL FRENCH/BISTRO   The name is old-fashioned slang for Paris, but this little bistro has a decidedly modern feel to it. Maybe it's the mirrored column near the bar. In yet another case of runaway chefs from Michelin-starred restaurants, here you'll find flavorful updated bistro fare like braised sweetbreads with carrots in a licorice glaze, or suckling pig with pears, celery root, and chestnuts. It's hard to resist indulging in dessert when the Grand Marnier soufflé is on the menu. The fixed-price menus at lunch and dinner are a terrific value and the tiny dining room fills quickly, so definitely reserve ahead.

3 rue Victor Massé, 9th arrond. © **01-48-78-55-60.** Main courses: 19€–26€; fixed-price lunch 19€, fixed-price dinner 35€. Mon–Fri 12:30–2:30pm and 7:30–9:30pm. Closed first 3 weeks of Aug. Métro: Pigalle.

INEXPENSIVE

Café Zephyr ★ TRADITIONAL BISTRO   This large, old-fashioned bistro sprawls out on the sidewalk of one of the Grands Boulevards. It's nowhere near as hip as the new restaurants in the Passage des Panoramas

A WORD ABOUT kids IN RESTAURANTS

Many foreigners wonder how French people manage to make their kids behave so well in restaurants. While the ritual of long Sunday family lunches probably trains them to sit still at an early age, there's also the fact that childhood rowdiness is not well tolerated in eating establishments. If the kids can't sit still, the parents simply don't eat out with them. It's rare to find crayons, puzzles, and other kid-friendly items in Parisian restaurants, though they usually have high-chairs (*chaise-haute*, shehz-oht), if not booster seats (*réhausseur*, ray-hoh-sur). That said, by and large French people are kid-friendly, so small, family-owned restaurants will usually be pretty understanding, as long as you don't let your kids run wild. Ask if there's a kids' menu (*menu enfant*). While not particularly nutritious, they'll usually keep small ones busy with plenty of French fries. Below is a short list of some restaurants that are particularly amenable to the kid contingent:

o **Restaurant Polidor** (p. 118) With its red-checked tablecloths and family-style cooking, this is a good place for an introduction to bistro food.

o **Crêperie Saint Malo** (p. 124) This (a sit-down restaurant, not a stand on the street) is a great option for kids because they offer early-dinner seating and easy prices. And what kid doesn't love a crepe?

o **Le Relais de l'Entrecôte** (p. 116) Serving unlimited helpings of steak and fries, this lively place is a no-brainer for the kid set.

o **Rosa Bonheur** (p. 107) Located inside the Parc des Buttes-Chaumont, this cool cafe has a beautiful outdoor terrace where parents can nibble on tapas while watching their kids roll down the hill.

across the street, but the joy of the Zephyr is all in the atmosphere. It's a friendly, noisy place to stop for a *salade composé* (meal-size salad) or a steak-frites, or just to sip a drink and watch the world go by. At night, the pool table becomes a focus of attention for some; others come here to dine before seeing a show at the nearby Opéra Comique. There's a nice brunch on Sundays.

12 bd. Montmartre, 9th arrond. ✆ **01-47-70-80-14.** Main courses 12€–16€; brunch 19€. Daily 8am–2am. Métro: Grands-Boulevards or Richelieu–Drouot.

Chartier ★ TRADITIONAL FRENCH This gargantuan restaurant claims to have served some 50 million meals since it opened in 1896, and considering the fact that the dining room can seat over 300 people, it seems entirely possible. It's one of the last of the *bouillons,* or workers' restaurants, that used to be found all over Paris back in the 19th century. The idea was to serve good food at modest prices, an idea that still speaks to working Parisians more than 100 years later, if the line out the door is any indication. You come here for the experience, more than for the food, which is tasty but certainly won't win any prizes. The menu covers a wide variety of traditional dishes like roast free-range chicken with fries or rump steak with pepper sauce. Service is fast and furious (how could it not be with this many tables?), but it's all part of the atmosphere, which is something that belongs to another time and place. Chartier takes no reservations, so be prepared to wait.

7 rue du Faubourg Montmartre, 9th arrond. www.bouillon-chartier.com. © **01-47-70-86-29.** Main courses 8.50€–14€. Daily 11:30am–10pm. Métro: Grands-Boulevards.

Coinstôt Vino ★★ WINE BAR   What's in a name? In this case, an amalgam of French and Italian words for "corner bistro" and "wine," which pretty much sums things up. This tiny place, which sits on the corner of two covered alleyways in the lovely Passage des Panoramas, has a generous and excellent selection of wines. While much of the menu is top-quality nibbles to enjoy while you savor your wine, like oysters, plates of smoked ham, pâté, and cheese, there are also a few *plats du jour* (daily specials) like grilled sea bass and steak with mushrooms. In season, the oysters come from Utah Beach, of Normandy landings fame. A pizza chef was recently imported from Italy, and you can sample his excellent wares with your glass of *vino*.

26 bis passage des Panoramas, 2nd arrond. © **01-44-82-08-54.** Main courses 15€–25€; fixed-price lunch 16€–19€. Mon–Fri noon–2pm and 6–11pm; Sat 6–11pm. Closed first 3 weeks of Aug and last week of Dec. Métro: Grands-Boulevards or Bourse.

Georgette ★★ MODERN BISTRO   Cozy and low-key with neo-retro Formica tables and soft banquettes, this is a delightful spot for a meal that is both affordable and delicious. We could tell you what is on the menu, which sticks close to traditional bistro fare (steak with sautéed potatoes, marinated salmon, etc.), but that wouldn't take into account the terrific specials, which vary according to what produce and meats are at the market that day. You can be sure of fresh, top-quality ingredients and a light touch, for Georgette is indeed in the kitchen, and at times she is also the waiter who serves your food. Reserve online if you want to be sure to have a table.

29 rue St-Georges, 9th arrond. http://restaurantgeorgette.fr/en. © **01-42-80-39-13.** Main courses 13€–18€; fixed-price lunch 20€. Tues–Fri noon–2:45pm and 7:30–11pm. Closed Aug. Métro: Notre-Dame-de-Lorette.

L'Excuse Mogador ★ CREPES   In the hustle-bustle of clothing stores and lunch spots that line the streets in this crowded quarter, this tiny crêperie is a standout. The crepes are generously filled with fresh ingredients like goat cheese, spinach, eggplant, and of course, ham and cheese; the zinc bar and vinyl banquettes make the ambience that much more Parisian. It's open only at lunchtime, when it fills up quickly with shoppers and office workers.

21 rue Joubert, 9th arrond. © **01-42-81-98-19.** Main courses 6€–11€. Mon–Sat 11:30am–4pm. Métro: Havre-Caumartin, RER Auber.

Noglu ★★ GLUTEN-FREE   Hidden down one of the foodiest covered passageways in Paris—the Passage des Panoramas—this tiny restaurant is where gluten-intolerant people bring their friends, quite simply because the home-cooked gluten-free food is so tasty you don't have to have a food allergy to appreciate it. Dishes might include cod with lentils, vegetable lasagna, and warm chocolate cake. Though not vegetarian per se, Noglu always has meat-and fish-free dishes on the menu. If you're in a hurry, the takeout section (just opposite) is a handy address to have up your sleeve, and doubles as a tiny cafe—the perfect spot for afternoon coffee and cake. There are now two new addresses elsewhere in Paris too: In the Marais (38 rue Saintonge, 3rd arrond.) and on the Left Bank (69 rue de Grenelle, 7th arrond.).

16 passage des Panoramas, 2nd arrond. www.noglu.fr. ℰ **01-40-26-41-24.** Main courses 11€–13€; fixed-price lunch 22€; Sat brunch 24€. Mon noon–2:30pm; Tues–Sat noon–2:30pm and 7:30–10:30pm. Closed 2 weeks in Aug. Métro: Bonnes Nouvelles.

Montmartre (18th Arrondissement)

When you get away from the tourist traps of Place du Tertre, you start to understand why people love this neighborhood, and why it's become a favorite with the arty-hipster set. To the north and west of the basilica is where you will find the villagey atmosphere you've heard so much about; to the east and south, Montmartre gives way to Barbès, a lively immigrant neighborhood where you are just as likely to see women in Indian saris and African prints as in smart Parisian apparel. Either way, you're bound to come across good food.

MODERATE

Le Coq Rico ★★★ ROTISSERIE   At the top of the Butte de Montmartre, this popular rotisserie is where renowned chef Antoine Westerman proves that poultry can go way beyond the nugget. When raised in the right conditions (in the open-air, with space and with nutritious food), poultry can be just as delicious as the finest cut of beef. On the menu are such delicacies as guinea fowl in a hazelnut crumb, succulent whole duck from the Dombes region (to share) and tantalizingly juicy Challans chicken—the lot accompanied by crispy, hand-cut fries or macaroni and cheese. The desserts are worth leaving space for, too: lemon crumble, caramelized brioche with poached pears and beer ice-cream, and one of the best chocolate mille-feuille (layers of pastry and chocolate) in town.

98 rue Lepic, 18th arrond. http://en.lecoqrico.com. ℰ **01-42-59-82-89.** Main courses 22€–41€; whole birds to share 85€–98€. Daily noon–2:30pm and 7pm–midnight. Métro: Abbesses or Lamarck-Caulincourt.

Wepler ★★ FRENCH BRASSERIE   Picasso and Modigliani used to hang out at this venerable brasserie on Place de Clichy, as did writer Henry Miller, who made it his headquarters. "I knew it like a book," he wrote. "The faces of the waiters, the managers, the cashiers, the whores, the clientele, even the attendants in the lavatory, are engraved in my memory as if they were illustrations in a book which I read every day." Today the atmosphere is quite sedate, but it's still a wonderful place to sit and watch the world go by, and the prices are accessible enough that it is still frequented by artists and writers. The

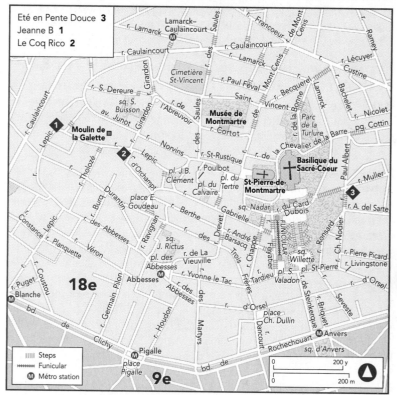

Eté en Pente Douce **3**
Jeanne B **1**
Le Coq Rico **2**

Lamarck–Caulaincourt

Moulin de la Galette

Musée de Montmartre

Basilique du Sacré-Coeur

St-Pierre-de-Montmartre

18e

9e

IIIII Steps
⊷⊷⊷⊷ Funicular
Ⓜ Métro station

0   200 y
0   200 m

menu is classic brasserie (steak tartare, shellfish platters, poached haddock in *beurre blanc*) but with a light, gourmet touch. If you don't want a big meal, ask for the less expensive cafe menu, which features delicate omelets, a *plat du jour,* and meal-size salads served on the covered terrace.

14 place de Clichy, 18th arrond. www.wepler.com. ℂ **01-45-22-53-24.** Main courses 18€–30€; fixed-price lunch or dinner 26€–32€. Daily 8am–12:30am. Métro: Place de Clichy.

INEXPENSIVE

Jeanne B ★★ BISTRO/ROTISSERIE   If you are flagging and have kids in tow, here's a relaxed place to eat that also happens to have excellent-quality goods. Run under the same umbrella as **Astier** (p. 102), at lunchtime this comfy cafe and rotisserie offers roast chicken with gratin of potatoes dauphinois and dessert for 15€ at lunch, ideal for hungry youngsters (or yourself). The menu also has other delectable roasted meat dishes (lamb, duck, beef), as well as salads and quiches. Service is *continue,* meaning there are no fixed hours for meals. You can also come by at the *apèro* hour (late afternoon to early evening) and order a platter of yummy nibbles to accompany your drink.

61 rue Lepic, 18th arrond. www.jeanne-b-comestibles.com. © **01-42-51-17-53.** Main courses 16€–19€; fixed-price lunch 19€–24€, apèro platters 7€–19€, fixed-price dinner 25€–29€. Daily 10am–10:30pm. Métro: Lamarck-Caulaincourt or Blanche.

République, Bastille & Eastern Paris (11th & 12th Arrondissements)

With a mix of working-class families, hipsters, and *bobos* (bourgeois bohemians), the area between République and Nation is diverse, young, and fun. It's also one of the most exciting places for food right now, with a plethora of young chefs opening restaurants that Parisians cross the city for.

EXPENSIVE

Septime ★★★ MODERN FRENCH   With its seafood tapas bar next door (**Clamato**) and its tiny wine bar across the street (**Septime la Cave**), Septime has done more to gentrify this stretch of the 11th arrond. than years of town planning ever could. People cross the entire city for a table in Bertrand Grébaut's retro-chic neo-bistro (including Beyoncé, Jay Z, and Gwyneth Paltrow), reserving months in advance. But that's not why you should come. The progressive, seasonal dishes—anything from line-caught squid with mustard and leek sauce to pigeon with beetroot and Morello cherries—are consistently delicious, and the menus change daily according to what's freshest in the produce market. If you can't score a dinner reservation, try lunchtime. And if all else fails, nip next door to Clamato, where fabulous small plates of crab fritters, clams, or trout roe are washed down with lip-smacking wine that starts for as little as 5.50€ a glass. You won't be disappointed.

80 rue de Charonne, 11th arrond. www.septime-charonne.fr. © **01-43-67-38-29.** Fixed-price lunch 35€, fixed-price dinner 65€. Tues–Fri 12:15–2pm and 7:30–10pm; Mon 7:30–10pm. Closed Aug. Métro: Charonne or Ledru-Rollin.

MODERATE

Astier ★★ TRADITIONAL FRENCH/BISTRO   This handsome old restaurant has kept up its polished wood and checked tablecloths as well as its classic menu. Wild boar terrine, rabbit in mustard sauce, rib steak with anchovy toasts, pike *quenelles* (a sort of elegant dumpling), and *tarte tatin* (caramelized apple tart) are menu regulars, plus the legendary cheese tray. It's a picture-postcard version of a Paris bistro, without the surly waiters. The wine list is delectable, too. There is a *plat canaille,* or daily special, at lunch for 15€.

44 rue Jean-Pierre Timbaud, 11th arrond. www.restaurant-astier.com. © **01-43-57-16-35.** Main courses 22€–26€; fixed-price lunch/dinner 35€ and 45€. Mon–Fri 12:15–2:15pm and 7–10:30pm; Sat 12:15–2:15pm and 7–11pm; Sun 12:30–2:15pm and 7–10:30pm. Métro: Parmentier or Oberkampf.

Bistrot Paul Bert ★★★ BISTRO/TRADITIONAL FRENCH   There are so many beautiful old bistros in this part of town that it's hard to choose just

Clamato Restaurant.

one, but when in doubt, you can't go wrong here. Even the most hard-nosed food critics get misty-eyed about this place, which specializes in the kind of cooking that reminds people of the good old days, even if they aren't that old. You might find comfortable classics like *onglet* (a type of beef steak) with shallots, or something a little more challenging, like roast venison with cranberries. This is definitely a meat-eater's hangout, though you can find lighter fare on the ever-changing menu, like roast pigeon or monkfish with creamy rice. The wine list features many unusual and affordable bottles from small wine producers.

18 rue Paul Bert, 11th arrond. © **01-43-72-24-01.** Main courses 27€; fixed-price lunch 18€ and 38€, fixed-price dinner 38€. Tues–Sat noon–2pm and 7:30–11pm. Closed 3 weeks in Aug. Métro: Faidherbe-Chaligny.

Tondo ★★ BISTRO/MODERN FRENCH   On a narrow street filled with eateries behind the Aligre Market (p. 221), this place stands out for its 1930s Art Deco decor and the beautifully presented food, which might include tempura-battered mushrooms with garlic butter, beetroot gnocchi, and chicken with creamy courgette purée. If it's on the menu (and you're not put off by raw beef), try the delicious carpaccio, dry-aged for 4 weeks and served with Corsican goat cheese—simple and yet wonderfully tasty. Cap off your meal with the moist orange cake. And don't forget the wine: The sommelier has some surprising *cépages* (grape varieties) that will pair perfectly with whatever you order—especially if you come along for the 95€ evening tasting menu, which includes a glass with every course.

29 rue de Cotte, 12th arrond. http://tondo-paris.com. © **01-40-21-19-21.** Main courses 17€–28€; fixed price lunch 25€; fixed-priced dinner 45€–115€. Thurs–Sat 12:15–2pm and 7:30–10pm; Tues–Wed 7:30–10pm. Métro: Ledru Rollin.

Virtus ★★★ BISTRO   This discreet little place, tucked away on a gentrifying street in a residential part of the 12th arrond., draws food-savvy locals with impressively executed dishes like scallops in hazelnut butter, succulent roast lamb with peas, and lip-smacking passion fruit mousse with yogurt ice-cream. The descriptions sound simple, but the result is wonderfully complex, with layers of flavors that explode in your mouth. A good time to visit is lunchtime, when the 17€ menu (dish of the day and a plate of cheese) is an absolute steal. If you come along for dinner, you're in for a wonderful 6-course ride with the obligatory tasting menu, which may include delights like asparagus with strawberries and burrata, and pollack in anchovy emulsion—the lot washed down with wine served by the resident sommelier who doubles as your waiter.

8 rue Crozatier, 12th arrond. www.virtus-paris.com. ℂ **09-80-68-08-08.** Main courses 17€–20€; fixed-price dinner 60€. Tues–Sat noon–2pm and 8–10:30pm. Closed part of Aug. Métro: Reuilly-Diderot, Montgallet, or Gare de Lyon.

INEXPENSIVE

L'Ebauchoir ★★★ MODERN FRENCH   Located in an unlikely corner of the 12th arrondissement, this crowded neighborhood hangout offers a fab selection of modern bistro cooking at decidedly reasonable prices. The high ceilings, sunny yellow walls, and wooden fixtures create a warm and friendly environment for vaguely Mediterranean-inspired dishes like roast lamb with sweet spices and Thai basil, or *magret* (breast) of duck with vanilla and pineapple. There's usually a nice vegetarian option here, like a vegetable "cake" with sautéed shitake mushrooms, asparagus, and hummus. With a three-course lunch deal at 16€, this place gets jammed at noon, so try to reserve.

43 rue des Citeaux, 12th arrond. www.lebauchoir.com. ℂ **01-43-42-49-31.** Main courses dinner 18€–24€; fixed-price lunch 14€–25€. Mon 8–11pm; Tues–Fri noon–2:30pm and 8–11pm; Fri–Sat noon–2:30pm and 7:30–11pm. Closed 1 week mid-Aug. Métro: Faidherbe Chaligny or Reuilly Diderot.

Ober Mamma ★★★ ITALIAN/PIZZA   Arrive at 5:45pm for the early sitting or after 9:30pm for the late one. Any other time, you'll have to queue. But the wait'll be worth it, because Ober Mamma (along with its sister restaurant, **East Mamma,** 133 rue du Faubourg Saint Antoine, and **Biglove Caffè;** p. 92) serves superlative Italian cuisine using only the choicest of ingredients from small Italian producers. Share a *stracciatella fondante fumée* (the smoked, creamy innards of a burata) served in a little metal dish, or the melt-in-mouth *bresola* (dried, salted beef). The wood-oven pizzas and pastas are staples, as is the Tigramisu (traditional tiramisu named after Tigrane, the owner). Don't forget to try a cocktail from the bar at the entrance: The Big Mamma (vodka, lime, ginger beer, and fresh fruit) is dangerously moreish.

107 bd. Richard Lenoir, 11th arrond. www.bigmammagroup.com. ℂ **01-43-41-32-15.** Main courses 12€–16€. Mon–Sat noon–2:15pm and 6–11pm. No reservations. Métro: Oberkampf.

Belleville, Canal St-Martin & Northeast Paris (10th, 19th & 20th Arrondissements)

Between the two parks of Belleville and Buttes Chaumont and along the Canal St-Martin lie some of the city's most quirky and delightful restaurants. One of the last strongholds of Paris's bohemian set, here you can find both gourmet bistros and funky cheap eats, as well as a good number of wine bars that serve nibbles along with the fruit of the vine.

MODERATE

Chez Michel ★★★ BRETON/SEAFOOD   Diners come from all over Paris, as well as across the channel (via the nearby Eurostar train hub at Gare du Nord), to sample Thierry Breton's superb cooking at affordable prices that have barely budged in a decade. A native of Brittany, Breton improvises on recipes from back home, including lots of seafood dishes like *kaotriade,* a Breton ("Breton" means from Brittany, by the way) fish stew, and fresh crab salad. For dessert, try the copious rice pudding or the awe-inspiring Paris-Brest (a choux pastry filled with praline cream).

10 rue de Belzunce, 10th arrond. ✆ **01-44-53-06-20.** Fixed-price lunch 29€, fixed-price dinner 35€. Tues–Fri noon–2pm; Mon–Fri 7pm–midnight. Closed Aug. Métro: Gare du Nord.

Hôtel du Nord ★★ FRENCH   Overlooking Canal St-Martin, just across from where Amélie threw pebbles in Jean-Pierre Jeunet's acclaimed 2001 movie, this vintage bistro is an atmospheric place for a meal. For casual dining, book the front section, reminiscent of a 1930s cafe with tiled floors and an Art Deco zinc bar; for something more sophisticated, the back section's red banquettes, white tablecloths, and mirrors create a boudoir-chic ambience.

Ober Mamma.

Hôtel du Nord.

Wherever you sit, the food is good: classic dishes like beef carpaccio with fries, and sausage-rich cassoulet, or vegetarian options such as ricotta and spinach ravioli. The 25€ brunch is popular on Sundays, when the streets outside become pedestrian-only.

102 quai de Jemmapes, 10th arrond. www.hoteldunord.org. ℂ **01-40-40-78-78.** Main courses 13€–29€; fixed-price lunch 16€–20€. Daily 10:30am–1am. Métro: Jacques Bonsergent.

Le Baratin ★★ TRADITIONAL FRENCH/BISTRO For some time, people have been crowding into this bistro to sample the cooking of Argentina-born Chef Raquel Carena's down-home bistro fare. You can find modern treats like smoked mackerel tartare and duck with ginger and gooseberry jelly, as well as more traditional fare. Lunch is a fantastic deal, only 19€ for the fixed-price menu. The impressive wine cellar is managed by Raquel's famously grumpy husband, Philippe Pinoteau.

3 rue Jouye-Rouve, 20th arrond. ℂ **01-43-49-39-70.** Main courses 19€–32€; fixed-price lunch 19€. Tues–Sat noon–2:30pm and 8–11:30pm. Closed last 3 weeks in Aug and first week of May. Métro: Pyrenées.

Le Verre Volé ★ WINE BAR/MODERN FRENCH The sun is shining, the leafy trees are posing prettily along the Canal St-Martin, and you are walking over one of the Japanese-eque bridges that curve over the water. All that's missing is a table and a glass of wine. Luckily, this wine bar/restaurant is on hand to delight you with a vast selection of bacchic and gustatory delights. You could just share a plate of sliced smoked meats and sausage, the usual accompaniment to a glass of red, or you can explore the menu, which might include a slice of milk-fed veal or mullet ceviche. Then select a bottle of wine from the shelves that line the walls, and enjoy it (for a nominal corkage fee) in this informal, if crowded, setting.

67 rue de Lancry, 10th arrond. www.leverrevole.fr. ℂ **01-48-03-17-34.** Main courses lunch 17€, dinner 25€–27€. Daily 12:30–2pm and 7:30–10:30pm; wine bar 9:30am–1am. Métro: Jacques Bonsergent.

INEXPENSIVE

Bob's Juice Bar ★ VEGETARIAN Hipsters are tripping all over themselves to try "smoossies" (that is, smoothies) and juices these days, and some of the best can be found at this terrific vegetarian restaurant, which has become *the* place to sample muffins, bagels, soups, and other delicious vegetarian goodies. The brainchild of Marc Grossman (alias "Bob"), an erstwhile New Yorker, this may not be the most authentically French experience, but it certainly is a tasty one. You can sit down or take out here, or try the larger **Bob's Kitchen** in the Marais (74 rue des Gravilliers) or **Bob's Bake Shop** in the 18th (Halle Pajol, 12 Esplanade Nathalie Sarraute), both of which are open on Sundays.

15 rue Lucien Sampaix, 10th arrond. www.bobsjuicebar.com. (C) **09-50-06-36-18.** Smoothies and juices 5€–7.50€; main courses 6€–8€. Mon–Fri 7:30am–3pm; Sat 8:30am–4pm. Métro: Jacques Bonsergent.

Rosa Bonheur ★ TAPAS   This unconventional space is named after an unconventional 19th-century painter/sculptress. Yes, it's a tapas bar, but it's also a sort of off-the-wall community center, hosting various expositions and events, not to mention its own chorus and soccer team. Located in an old *buvette* (refreshment pavilion) inside the Parc des Buttes Chaumont that dates from the Universal Exposition of 1900, the restaurant boasts a sprawling terrace and one of the best panoramic views in town. A huge crowd gathers to drink and nibble tapas both indoors and out. The ambience is relaxed and friendly, and coming here is a good excuse to stroll through the lush Buttes Chaumont park. That park, plus an indoor play area and kids' menu, makes Rosa Bonheur a great family option. There is a second location on a docked barge on the Seine, **Rosa Bonheur Sur Seine** (right near the Pont des Invalides on the Left Bank). The barge is open year-round; from April to October it has outdoor seating and a pizza stand on the quay.

2 allée de la Cascade, 19th arrond. www.rosabonheur.fr. (C) **01-42-00-00-45.** Tapas 4€–9€. Wed–Fri noon–midnight; Sat–Sun 10am–midnight. Closed first 2 weeks in Jan. Métro: Botzaris.

Rosa Bonheur, inside the Parc des Buttes Chaumont.

Zerda Café ★★ NORTH AFRICAN/COUSCOUS Intricately carved Moorish designs cover the walls of this friendly restaurant, which serves some of the best couscous (grains of semolina) in Paris. A steaming heap of fine couscous, a savory bouillon with vegetables, and delicately grilled or roasted meat are the three main components of this dish, originally imported from North Africa and now wildly popular in France. Zerda offers a choice of lamb, chicken, and *merguez* (spicy lamb sausage) versions; our favorite is the meltingly tender "lamb cooked in sauce," but all are good. If you prefer one of the scrumptious *tagines* (stews seasoned with such ingredients as dried fruits, olives, or preserved lemons), be patient: They take 20 minutes to prepare. A second location recently opened up at 125 rue de Tocqueville in the 17th arrondissement, and offers a 19€ fixed-price lunch.

15 rue René Boulanger, 10th arrond. www.zerdacafe.fr. ⓒ **01-42-00-25-15.** Main courses 15€–22€. Mon and Sat 7pm–midnight; Tues–Fri and Sun noon–4pm and 7pm–midnight. Closed 2 weeks in Aug. Métro: Strasbourg–St-Denis.

THE LEFT BANK
Latin Quarter (5th & 13th Arrondissements)

For more than 700 years, this lively neighborhood has been overrun with students, a population that is forever on the lookout for a good, cheap meal. As a result, the area is full of inexpensive snack shacks of varying quality, from souvlaki huts to Vietnamese noodle shops to Breton crêperies. Steer clear of the unbearably touristy area around rue de la Huchette, where you are bound to pay too much for a mediocre product, and be wary of rue Moufftard, which was once a good bet for good food but has since become a victim of its own success. If you want to eat well, you'll need to venture a little farther afield, where innovative restaurateurs have been cultivating a knowledgeable clientele of professors, professionals, and savvy tourists.

EXPENSIVE

La Truffière ★★ CLASSIC FRENCH An atmospheric 17th-century dining room near the Seine, with exposed stone walls and wooden beams is the setting for the sort of French cuisine you crave for when you think of Paris—langoustines, suckling lamb, ultra-ripe cheeses, and the *black diamonds* (truffles) that the restaurant takes its name from, prepared with panache by talented chef Charistophe Poard. If you're into wine, you'll be hard-pushed to find a better restaurant: There are some 3,200 bottles on the menu. Thank goodness for the sommelier who takes into account both your budget and the dishes you've ordered. Tasting menus costs up to 125€ in the evening, so the 32€ lunch menu is one of the best deals in town.

4 rue Blainville, 5th arrond. www.la-truffiere.fr. ⓒ **01-46-33-29-82.** Main dishes 65€–143€; fixed-price lunch 32€, fixed-price dinner 65€–125€. Daily noon–2pm and Tues–Sat 7–10:30pm. Closed Aug. Métro: Place Monge or Cardinal Lemoine.

Left Bank Restaurants (Eiffel Tower Area)

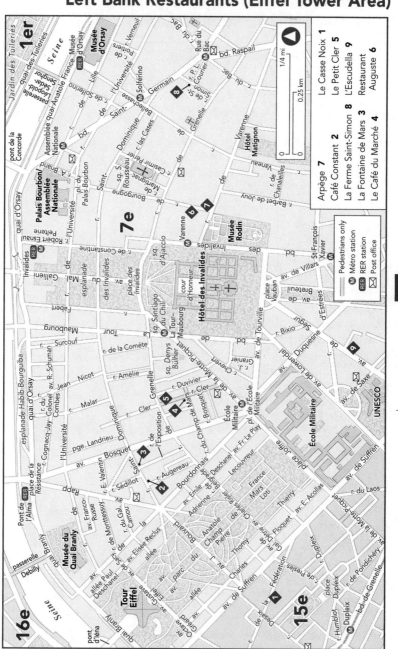

Arpège **7**
Café Constant **2**
La Ferme Saint-Simon **8**
La Fontaine de Mars **3**
Le Café du Marché **4**

Le Casse Noix **1**
Le Petit Cler **5**
L'Escudella **9**
Restaurant
Auguste **6**

Left Bank Restaurants (Latin Quarter, Saint Germain, Montparnasse)

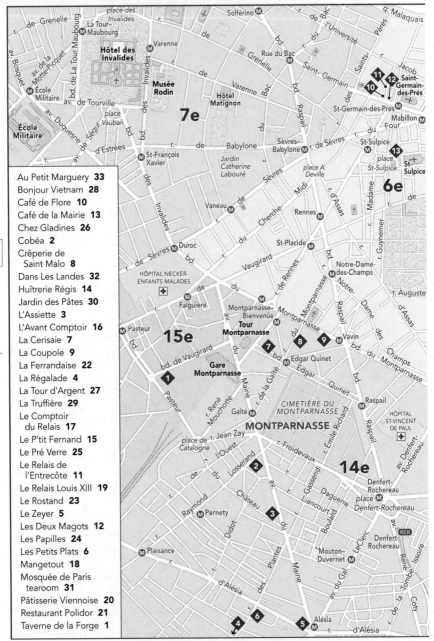

Au Petit Marguery **33**
Bonjour Vietnam **28**
Café de Flore **10**
Café de la Mairie **13**
Chez Gladines **26**
Cobéa **2**
Crêperie de
Saint Malo **8**
Dans Les Landes **32**
Huîtrerie Régis **14**
Jardin des Pâtes **30**
L'Assiette **3**
L'Avant Comptoir **16**
La Cerisaie **7**
La Coupole **9**
La Ferrandaise **22**
La Régalade **4**
La Tour d'Argent **27**
La Truffière **29**
Le Comptoir
du Relais **17**
Le P'tit Fernand **15**
Le Pré Verre **25**
Le Relais de
l'Entrecôte **11**
Le Relais Louis XIII **19**
Le Rostand **23**
Le Zeyer **5**
Les Deux Magots **12**
Les Papilles **24**
Les Petits Plats **6**
Mangetout **18**
Mosquée de Paris
tearoom **31**
Pâtisserie Viennoise **20**
Restaurant Polidor **21**
Taverne de la Forge **1**

5

WHERE TO DINE | The Left Bank

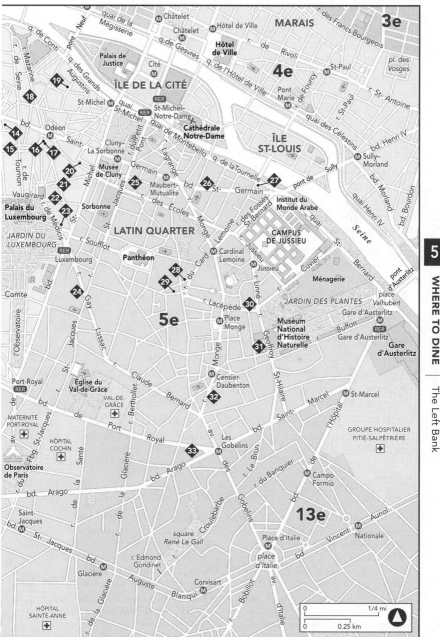

La Tour d'Argent ★★★ CLASSIC FRENCH Everyone from Queen Elizabeth II to Orson Welles has dined in this venerable restaurant, famed for its history (there has been a restaurant here since 1582), its impeccable service and its sweeping view of Notre-Dame's flying buttresses. And since the appointment of chef Philippe Labbé in 2016, the food's back on track again (after a dip in quality), wooing well-dressed crowds with the promise of inventive French cuisine and the establishment's coveted signature dish of pressed duck (each duck has been numbered since 1890). Five or six different waiters will visit your table at one time or another, accomplishing various tasks (opening wine bottles, pulling out your chair, and even leading you to the bathroom) with utmost professionalism and not a hint of snobbery. They then discreetly disappear into the rich decor as you gaze through the huge windows. The fixed-price lunch is a good way to enjoy this singular experience without busting your budget. Be sure to reserve at least a week in advance; jackets are required for men at dinner.

15–17 quai de la Tournelle, 5th arrond. www.latourdargent.com. ⓒ **01-43-54-23-31.** Main courses 70€–140€; fixed-price lunch 105€, fixed-price dinner 350€ and 370€. Tues–Sat noon–1pm; Tues–Sat 7–9pm. Closed Aug. Métro: St-Michel or Maubert-Mutualité.

MODERATE

Au Petit Marguery ★★ TRADITIONAL FRENCH/BISTRO This place has everything you always wanted in a French bistro: antique tile floors, banquettes, vested waiters, and a dark rose color scheme. The menu also reflects the traditions of yesteryear, with an emphasis on game dishes in autumn and fresh produce in summer. Appetizers include several different terrines, including homemade foie gras; main dishes feature meaty items like 7-hour lamb and lighter fare like sea bream with fennel and star anise. Top it all off with a Grand Marnier soufflé (a specialty of the house). The restaurant has a smaller and more relaxed version of itself next door, the **Comptoir Marguery,** where prices are lower and the menu is a little more basic, and another outpost of the main restaurant, **Au Petit Marguery Rive Droite,** is at 64 avenue des Ternes on the Right Bank.

9 bd. du Port-Royal, 13th arrond. www.petitmarguery.com. ⓒ **01-43-31-58-59.** Fixed-price lunch 24€–29€, fixed-price dinner 42€. Daily noon–2:15pm and 7–10:15pm. Métro: Gobelins.

Chinatown, Paris-Style

Paris actually has two Chinatowns: the more established one, among the ugly apartment towers between avenues d'Ivry and Choisy in the 13th arrondissement (about a 5-min. walk from Place d'Italie), and another newer one in Belleville in the 20th. Neither Chinatown is strictly Chinese—the population also includes communities from Vietnam, Cambodia, and other Asian countries. There are dozens of good restaurants in the 13th's Chinatown. A couple of our favorites for Chinese food are **Imperial Choisy,** 32 ave. de Choisy, 13th arrond. (ⓒ **01-45-86-42-40**), and across the street, **Likafo,** 39 ave. de Choisy, 13th arrond. (ⓒ **01-45-84-20-45**), for great shrimp ravioli soup.

Dans Les Landes ★ SOUTHWESTERN FRENCH/TAPAS   Les Landes is a region in the southwest of France blessed with green forests, sandy beaches, and lots of great food. Chef Julien Duboué takes inspiration from his native homeland and neighboring Basque country to create luscious tapas to be sampled with (many) glasses of great regional wines. Fried *chipirions* (small squid that are crisp, golden, and dusted with smoky pepper), polenta with smoked duck breast, Basque-style mussels—the list is long and tempting. The place is packed at night, so get there early or reserve a table.

119 bis rue Monge, 5th arrond. http://dansleslandes.fr. ℂ **01-45-87-06-00.** Tapas 8€–29€, salads 13€–15€. Daily noon–11pm. Closed last week of Dec and first week of Jan. Métro: Censier-Daubenton.

Le Pré Verre ★★ MODERN FRENCH/ASIAN FUSION   This laid-back gourmet wine bar is the work of the Delacourcelle brothers (Philippe is the chef, Marc is the wine maven), trailblazers in the bistronomy movement. One of the first restaurants to offer a reasonably priced, easy-to-understand menu of gourmet goodies, this crowded and convivial place offers dishes that are a scrumptious blend of traditional French and exotic ingredients. Your main course could be a meltingly tender *cochon de lait* (milk-fed pork) served with a smooth cinnamon-infused sauce and a delectably crunchy mass that turns out to be cabbage. Or it might be tournedos of salmon with an herbed vegetable casserole. Dessert could follow with strawberries with parsley ice cream. The weekday lunch menu is a particularly great deal: appetizer and main dish (chef's choice) plus a glass of wine and coffee for 15€.

8 rue Thenard, 5th arrond. www.lepreverre.com. ℂ **01-43-54-59-47.** Main courses 19€–29€; fixed-price lunch 15€, fixed-price dinner 32€. Tues–Sat noon–2pm and 7:30–10:30pm. Closed last week of Dec. Métro: Maubert-Mutualité or Cluny-La Sorbonne.

Les Papilles ★★ BISTRO/WINE BAR   Lined with shelves upon shelves of delectable bottles, this bustling wine shop/bistro/gourmet grocery matches simple but excellent fare with terrific samples of the fruit of the vine. At dinnertime, the fixed-price menu offers great value—four courses for 35€—but no choices. If you don't want the menu, try the *marmite du marché*, the stew of the day served in a cast-iron pot (20€). At lunch you can choose between a fixed-price menu or lighter fare: a variety of salads, open-faced sandwiches, and charcuterie plates. Wine is available by the glass, but patrons are encouraged to choose a bottle from the nearby shelves and pay just a small corkage fee—a great way to try a good bottle without the usual restaurant markup on the wine.

30 rue Gay-Lussac, 5th arrond. www.lespapillesparis.fr. ℂ **01-43-25-20-79.** Main courses 20€; fixed-price lunch 28€, fixed-price dinner 35€. Tues–Sat 9:30am–midnight. Closed in Aug and between Christmas and New Year's. RER: Luxembourg.

INEXPENSIVE

Bonjour Vietnam ★★ VIETNAMESE   This postage stamp of a restaurant serves deliciously authentic Vietnamese dishes like *bò bún*, a heap of rice vermicelli, sliced beef, and crispy spring rolls in a tangy sauce, or a steaming bowl of *pho*, beef broth with vegetables and noodles, topped with fresh basil, mint, and bean sprouts. The less adventurous might prefer caramel pork or ginger chicken, both featured on the 12€ lunch set menu. Most everyone enjoys the steamed raviolis as a starter. These fresh dishes are made to order, so don't expect instant service.

6 rue Thouin, 5th arrond. ℭ **01-43-54-78-04.** Main courses 12€–14€; fixed-price lunch 12€. Wed–Mon noon–3pm and 7–11pm. Métro: Cardinal Lemoine.

Chez Gladines ★ SOUTHWESTERN   Hungry? Come here for enormous and tasty portions of rib-sticking French southwestern specialties. That means crispy duck confit with sautéed potatoes; Basque-style chicken (with tomatoes and bell peppers); *pipérade* (a casserole of eggs with smoked ham, sliced and sautéed potatoes, bell peppers, and a bright tomato sauce); and the like. Even the salads are gargantuan, filled with goodies like bacon, goat cheese, smoked ham, and foie gras. The success of the original Gladines in the 13th arrondissement (30 rue des Cinq Diamants) has spawned four other locations: 11 bis rue des Halles, 1st arrond.; 74 bd. des Batignolles, 17th arrond.; 140 rue du Faubourg St. Martin, 10th arrond.; and 64–66 rue de Charonne, 11th arrond.

44 bd. St-Germain, 5th arrond. www.gladines.com. ℭ **01-46-33-93-88.** Main courses 10€–15€. Mon–Thurs noon–11pm; Fri–Sat noon–midnight; Sun noon–11:30pm. Métro: Maubert-Mutualité.

Jardin des Pâtes ★ PASTA/VEGETARIAN   This light-filled restaurant specializes in pasta. But this is no ordinary pasta—not only are the rice, wheat, rye, and barley noodles made fresh every day, but the organic flour that goes into them is ground daily on the premises. The focus on wholesome ingredients is menu-wide; even the ice cream is 100% natural. While you won't find the usual Italian sauces, you will find original creations like rye pasta with ham, cream, sweet onions, white wine, and Comté cheese or barley pasta with fresh salmon, leeks, seaweed, and crème fraîche. There are lots of vegetarian choices here, and the relaxed atmosphere makes it a good place to bring (well-behaved) kids. Pastas are made to order, so don't be in a hurry.

4 rue Lacépède, 5th arrond. ℭ **01-43-31-50-71.** Main courses 13€–15€. Daily noon–2:30pm and 7–11pm. Métro: Place Monge.

St-Germain-des-Prés (6th Arrondissement)

St-Germain is a mix of expensive eateries that only the lucky few can afford and smaller bistros that bring back the days when intellectuals and artists frequented the Café de Flore. Overpriced tourist restaurants cluster around Boulevard St-Germain near the Carrefour de l'Odéon; as you head south and north of this major boulevard, your choices will expand. Though the Marché St-Germain has been transformed into a type of mall, the restaurants hugging its perimeter offer a wide range of possibilities.

EXPENSIVE
Le Comptoir du Relais ★★★ TRADITIONAL FRENCH/BISTRO   The brainchild of super-chef Yves de Camdeborde, this small and scrumptious bistro is still bringing in the crowds more than a decade after it opened.

Camdeborde is often credited with starting the bistronomy movement in the 1990s when he walked out on the Crillon and opened up his own bistro where he could offer the French equivalent of "down home" cooking, using the best ingredients and charging affordable prices. During the day, the Comptoir is a bistro, serving relatively traditional fare, like a slice of lamb with thyme sauce or *panier de cochonaille,* a basket of the Camdeborde family's own brand of sliced smoked ham, dried sausage, and other pork-based delectables. On weeknights, it's a temple to haute cuisine, with a tasting menu that includes as many as five different dishes. Reserve far (i.e., months) in advance for this fixed-price meal, which changes every night. There are no reservations at lunch or on the weekends when the bistro menu is served from noon to 11pm, so arrive early or be prepared to wait.

9 carrefour de l'Odéon, 6th arrond. www.hotel-paris-relais-saint-germain.com. ℚ **01-44-27-07-50.** Main courses weekends and weekdays 15€–29€; fixed-price dinner weeknights 60€. Daily noon–11pm. Métro: Odéon.

Le Relais Louis XIII ★★★ TRADITIONAL FRENCH   In an ancient building on the site where Louis XIII was crowned back in 1610, this acclaimed restaurant pays homage not only to the monarch, but to traditional French cuisine at its most illustrious. No tonka beans or reduced licorice sauce here—Chef Manuel Martinez trains his formidable talents on classic sauces and time-honored dishes like sea-bass *quenelles* and roast duck, though he's not opposed to topping off the meal with a little lemon-basil sherbet at dessert. Signature dishes include lobster and foie gras ravioli and braised sweetbreads with wild mushrooms. The atmospheric dining room, crisscrossed with exposed beams and ancient stonework, makes you wonder if the Three Musketeers might not tumble through the doorway bearing your mille-feuille with bourbon vanilla cream.

8 rue des Grands-Augustins, 6th arrond. www.relaislouis13.fr. ℚ **01-43-26-75-96.** Main courses 60€; fixed-price lunch 60€, fixed-price dinner 90€–140€. Tues–Sat 12:15– 2:30pm and 7:30–10:30pm. Closed Aug. Métro: Odéon or St-Michel.

MODERATE

Huîtrerie Régis ★ OYSTERS/SEAFOOD   Like oysters on the half shell? Good, because that's pretty much all they have here: delicious bivalves that come straight from the Marennes-Oléron region on France's Atlantic coast. The brief and to-the-point menu gives you a choice of various sizes and grades of oysters, as well as sea urchins, clams, and shrimp. You'll have to order at least a dozen oysters to sit down in the tiny restaurant; considering the price, you may as well order a *formule,* or fixed-price menu, which include various combinations of oysters, wine, and coffee. These oysters are fresh, oceany mouthfuls of flavor that deserve a good glass of Sancerre.

3 rue de Montfaucon, 6th arrond. www.huitrerieregis.com. ℚ **01-44-41-10-07.** Oysters per dozen 26€–64€; fixed-price lunch or dinner 30€–40€. Mon–Fri noon–2:30pm and 6:30–10:30pm; Sat and Sun noon–10:45pm. Closed mid-July to mid-Sept. Métro: Mabillon or St-Germain.

Poilâne: The Mecca of Bread

Even the most stylish locals humbly bow their heads when they step inside this temple of baked goods. The store is tiny and unassuming, but the orders are meted out like communion wafers. You ask for your bread and wait silently while the baker solemnly counts out the slices (yes, you order by the slice). Then you meekly pay and leave room for the next suppliant.

This isn't just bread; it's history. Pierre Poilâne opened his store in 1932, serving country-style bread made with stone-ground flour in a wood-burning oven. Success was such that the recipe hasn't changed an iota, and today the round loaves are shipped all over the world. Not many breadmakers rub shoulders with the jet set: In 1969, son Lionel even made Salvador Dalí a bedroom made out of bread. Today granddaughter Apollonia guides the mothership with a firm hand, making sure the tradition continues. Poilâne is at 8 rue du Cherche-Midi, 6th arrond. (www.poilane.com; ℭ **01-45-48-42-59;** two other locations in the Marais and near the Eiffel Tower).

La Ferrandaise ★★ TRADITIONAL FRENCH/BISTRO   Named after a particularly tasty breed of cow, the beef at this carnivore's paradise comes direct from Puy du Dôme, the center of France's green heartland. The young chef is also a great believer in local products (all vegetables are local and/or organic) and authentic bistro cuisine. Menu highlights could include shoulder of lamb with spinach, or a juicy steak with sautéed carrots, but if meat is not your game, there are also scrumptious fish and poultry dishes. To finish off, try a fresh Auvergne cheese like Saint Nectaire or Fourme d'Ambert. Bring your appetite, as you must order one of the three-course fixed-price menus; there's no à la carte.

8 rue de Vaugirard, 6th arrond. www.laferrandaise.com. ℭ **01-43-26-36-36.** Fixed-price lunch 16€–37€, fixed-price dinner 37€ and 55€. Mon–Fri noon–2:30 and 7–10:30pm; Sat 7–11pm. Closed evenings in August. Métro: Odéon.

Le P'tit Fernand ★★ TRADITIONAL FRENCH/BISTRO   This tiny slice of restaurant packs a flavorful punch. Red-checked tablecloths provide a homey background for excellent bistro dishes like thick steak with a confit of shallots and creamy mashed potatoes, or duck *magret* (breast) served with morello cherry sauce. You could start with a nice light beet and rhubarb gazpacho, or go nuts and order the homemade terrine of foie gras. Whatever it is, it will be executed with loving care and quality ingredients, which is why this restaurant has a devoted clientele.

7 rue Lobineau, 6th arrond. ℭ **01-40-46-06-88.** Main courses 18€–26€. Daily noon–2pm and 7–10:30pm. Métro: Mabillon.

Le Relais de l'Entrecôte ★ TRADITIONAL FRENCH/STEAK   You won't have to trouble yourself with deciding what to eat here: The only thing on the menu is steak. Just tell the waiter how you want it cooked (*bien cuit* for medium-well, à point for medium-rare, or *saignant* for rare) and sit back and wait. First comes a fresh green salad, and then the main event: a giant silver platter of steak, doused in an addictive "secret sauce," and served with crispy golden fries. Expect to see your server return with a second helping once you've finished. Desserts, if you can find the strength, are classic and delicious, including profiteroles and crème brûlée. Get here early; you can't reserve and there is often a line out the door. If the line looks too long, you can try one of the two other locations: 101 bd. Montparnasse in the 6th, or 15 rue Marbeuf in the 8th.

20 rue St. Benoît, 6th arrond. www.relaisentrecote.fr. © **01-45-49-16-00.** Daily noon–2:30pm and 7–11:30pm. Fixed-price lunch and dinner 27€. Métro: St-Germain-des-Prés.

Mangetout ★★★ MODERN FRENCH This affordable taste treat comes courtesy of award-winning chef Alain Dutournier. Considering the quality of the fare, the price is most definitely right. Your feast could start with mushroom-infused scallops in herbs, proceed to milk-fed lamb with spring vegetables, and finish with a decadent chestnut cream *Mont Blanc* and still get out for under 50€. The dining room is tiny, so dinner reservations are essential.

82 rue Mazarine, 6th arrond. www.alaindutournier.com/wp/mangetout. © **01-43-54-02-11.** Main courses 13€–29€. Tues–Sat noon–2pm and 7–10:30pm. Closed in Aug. Métro: Mabillon or Odéon.

INEXPENSIVE

L'Avant Comptoir ★ WINE BAR/TAPAS/CREPES This shoebox-size wine-bar-*cum*-crêpe stand is an outcropping of the venerable Comptoir du Relais next door. Hungry diners descend on the bar-and-tapas component while waiting for a table at the restaurant; those in search of quick and portable bites can order takeout crêpes and salads (note that if you order from the takeout menu, you give up your right to stand and eat at the counter). There is a decidedly hip atmosphere here, despite the low-key "this is just a typical southwestern bar" decor. Goodies include fried croquettes stuffed with Iberian ham, *brandade* (mashed potatoes with cod), oxtail canapés with horseradish cream, and chicken hearts grilled with garlic and parsley.

3 carrefour de l'Odéon, 6th arrond. www.hotel-paris-relais-saint-germain.com. No phone. Tapas 7€–10€. Daily noon–midnight. Métro: Odéon.

Pâtisserie Viennoise ★★ BAKERY Squeezed between two medical schools, this old-fashioned pastry shop gets its share of students and professors in need of a nosh. And this is a nosher's heaven: It has a huge selection of pastries, including Viennese classics like Linzer torte and strudel, and the hot chocolate is one of the best in the city (3€–4€). It's thick and dark and bitter—sugar cubes are provided so you can adjust the sweetness—and if you ask for it à la viennoise, it will come with a dollop of real whipped cream. The tiny dining area looks like it hasn't changed in at least 50 years: a collection of wooden booths and small tables that might have been shipped in from

Vienna. You can also lunch here on a variety of inexpensive quiches, salads, and pasta dishes, including some nice vegetarian choices.

8 rue de l'Ecole de Médecine, 6th arrond. © **01-43-26-60-48.** Main courses 7€–9€; pastries 3.50€–6€. Mon–Fri 8:30am–7:30pm. Closed mid-July through 3rd week of Aug. Métro: Odéon or Cluny La Sorbonne.

Restaurant Polidor ★ TRADITIONAL FRENCH/BISTRO An unofficial historic monument, Polidor is not so much a restaurant as a snapshot of a bygone era. The decor has not changed substantially for at least 100 years, when Verlaine and Rimbaud, the bad boys of poetry, would come here for a cheap meal. The bistro would continue to be a literary lunchroom for decades: In the 1950s, it was dubbed "the College of

Restaurant Polidor.

Pataphysics" by a rowdy group of young upstarts that included Max Ernst, Boris Vian, and Eugene Ionesco; André Gide and Ernest Hemingway were reputed regulars. The menu features hefty bistro standbys like *boeuf bourguignon* and *blanquette de veau* (veal stew with white sauce), but if you look carefully you'll also find lighter fare like salmon with basil and chicken breast with morel sauce. These days, the arty set has moved elsewhere; you'll probably be sharing the long wood tables with other tourists, along with a dose of locals. Though the food is not particularly memorable, the ambience is unique.

41 rue Monsieur-le-Prince, 6th arrond. www.polidor.com. © **01-43-26-95-34.** Main courses 12€–20€; fixed-price menu 22€–35€. Mon–Sat noon–2:30pm and 7pm–12:30am; Sun noon–2:30pm and 7–11pm. Métro: Odéon.

Eiffel Tower & Nearby (7th Arrondissement)

Crowded with ministries and important people, this neighborhood is so grand, you half expect to hear trumpets blowing each time you turn a corner. While you will have no problem finding chic gourmet restaurants, eating here on a budget takes some skill, or at least a bit of insider knowledge. Though this is a rather staid neighborhood, a few streets are fairly lively, namely rue Cler, a pretty market street, and rue St-Dominique, home to some of the best restaurants on this side of the Seine. You're likely to get fleeced if you insist on eating right next to the Eiffel Tower—that is, if you can find a restaurant, as the pickings are pretty slim in the Iron Lady's immediate vicinity. If it's a nice day, buy a sandwich at a bakery and have a picnic on the Champs de Mars, where you can't beat the price or the view.

EXPENSIVE

Arpège ★★★ MODERN FRENCH   Chef Alain Passard made waves when he decided to put vegetables, not meat, in the spotlight at his acclaimed restaurant. You can still find meat on the menu, but it takes a back seat to carrots, turnips, sweet peas, or whatever other lovely plant life is in season. This pristine produce, which comes from Passard's organic farm near Le Mans, is often picked in the morning and ends up on diners' plates the same evening. Uneaten food makes the return journey and becomes compost. Food politics aside, the flavors that Passard coaxes from these vegetables are truly remarkable. The menu comes in two sections: the "grand crus" of the vegetable garden, and the "memory" dishes, medallions of lobster in honey with a "transparence" of Atlantic turnip, or a creamy risotto with "garden treasures." Service is discreet, as one expects at a restaurant frequented by diplomats and executives, and the dining room, with etched glass, burnished steel, and pearwood paneling, is beautiful. Don't miss the *tarte aux pommes bouquet de roses* (a tart composed of apple ribbons rolled into tiny rosettes). Reservations required at least 2 weeks in advance.

84 rue de Varenne, 7th arrond. www.alain-passard.com. ℂ **01-47-05-09-06.** Main courses 74€–165€; fixed-price lunch 145€, fixed-price tasting menu (lunch and dinner) 320€ and 390€. Mon–Fri noon–2pm and 7–10:30pm. Métro: Varenne.

La Ferme Saint Simon ★★★ TRADITIONAL FRENCH   Off the beaten track, down a quiet side street, this gourmet restaurant feels like a secret, attracting only those in the know—generally ambassadors from the nearby embassies and other locals. The menu treats classic dishes with kindness and care, giving each a dash of delicious originality. We've been impressed with the roast monkfish with bacon, horseradish and turnip, the rib of beef in red wine sauce, and the frogs' legs in parsley sauce—and for dessert, the out-of-this-world chocolate soufflé.

6 rue de Saint Simon, 7th arrond. www.fermestsimon.com. ℂ **01-45-48-35-74.** Main courses 29€–84€; fixed-price lunch menu 39€. Mon–Fri noon–2:30pm; Mon–Sat 7–10pm. Métro: Ru du Bac or Solférino.

Arpège's tarte bouquet de roses.

Restaurant Auguste ★★ MODERN FRENCH/SEAFOOD   It's not every famous chef that can call himself "Mr. Goodfish." Gael Orieux's love of the sea and everything in it has led him to become spokesperson for an association dedicated to protecting the oceans. Naturally, that means that

Pate in pastry at La Ferme Saint Simon.

what you see on your plate is not only delicious, but also ecologically correct. Let's hope he makes an impact on his clientele, many of whom are politicians taking a break from the nearby Assemblée Nationale. Aside from protecting fish, Orieux cooks it, serving some of the best seafood in town, and plates it with real flair. A dish of scallops with foie gras and enoki mushrooms might look like a Jackson Pollock abstract; a lacquered monkfish with lobster oil and nutmeg will be equally as artistic. Meat eaters are taken care of with dishes like blackened lamb with Cajun spices, white cherry juice, and yellow zucchini.

54 rue de Bourgogne, 7th arrond. www.restaurantauguste.fr. ℰ **01-45-51-61-09.** Main courses 40€–54€; fixed-price lunch 37€, fixed-price dinner 88€, fixed-price dinner with wine 154€. Mon–Fri noon–2:30pm and 7–10:30pm. Closed 3 weeks in Aug. Métro: Varenne.

MODERATE

La Fontaine de Mars ★★ BISTRO/SOUTHWESTERN FRENCH   Red and white checks are everywhere at this old-school bistro: on the tablecloths, the wicker chairs, and even the curtains. A venerable institution since it first opened in 1908, it continues to draw in the crowds with its classy, low-key decor and traditional menu. The kitchen turns out reliable and succulent southwestern dishes like cassoulet, foie gras, and duck breast with black cherry sauce. Starters include escargots (snails) and *oeufs au Madiran* (eggs baked with red wine and bacon). The dessert list is full of such classics as île flottante ("floating island," a puffy meringue floating on vanilla cream), crème brûlée, and dark chocolate mousse.

129 rue St-Dominique, 7th arrond. www.fontainedemars.com. ℰ **01-47-05-46-44.** Main courses 17€–49€. Daily noon–3pm and 7:30–11pm. Métro: École Militaire.

Le Casse Noix ★★ TRADITIONAL FRENCH/BISTRO   Chef Pierre-Olivier Lenormand brings his high-caliber food to a casual, affordable setting. The decor is nostalgic (note the nutcracker collection and vintage advertisements) and the traditional French cooking is sincere and generous. Perhaps a roast pork shoulder Ibaïona with olive purée will fill the bill? Or try a classic *petit salé* (lentils with smoky ham) followed by a crowd-pleasing dessert like île flottante. About a 10-minute walk from the Eiffel Tower, this is a good bet for those looking for a bit of authenticity in an otherwise very touristy neighborhood. At dinnertime, the fixed-price menu is *obligatoire;* there is no à la carte ordering. Lunch is more flexible.

56 rue de la Fédération, 15th arrond. www.le-cassenoix.fr. ℂ **01-45-66-09-01.** Main courses at lunch 19€–23€; fixed-price lunch 22€ and 26€, fixed-price dinner 36€. Mon–Fri noon–2:30pm and 7–10:30pm. Closed Aug and between Christmas and New Year's. Métro: Dupleix.

L'Escudella ★★ MODERN FRENCH This smart neo-bistro is located on a quiet residential street between UNESCO and Les Invalides. Its name means "plate" in Occitan—a nod to both chef Paul-Arthur Berlan's origins and the southwest-inspired dishes you're about to tuck into: delights like tomato and mustard gazpacho, sea bass with chorizo and artichoke risotto, and lip-smacking Paris-Carcassonne (choux pastry filled with hazelnut cream, a southwest version of the Paris-Brest). If you fancy sharing starters, L'Escudella serves excellent tapas: homemade paté, jambon de bayonne (cured ham), or spicy wagyu beef chorizo. The lunchtime dish of the day is an absolute steal at 16€: Details are posted daily on the restaurant's Facebook page. In fact, this place is so lovely, it's a mystery it hasn't attracted more attention—especially since the chef was a semifinalist on France's version of *Top Chef,* the American TV cooking show.

41 ave. de Ségur, 7th arrond. www.facebook.com/LEscudella-618124075008370. ℂ **09-82-28-70-70.** Main courses 18€–29€; fixed-price lunch 16€. Mon–Fri 11:30am–3pm and 7pm–midnight. Métro: École Militaire or Saint François Xavier.

INEXPENSIVE

Café Constant ★★ TRADITIONAL FRENCH/BISTRO At this relaxed bistro you are quite likely to find the chef and owner Christian Constant himself at the bar during his off hours. The restaurant serves a modern version of French comfort food like tangy poached cod with aioli, melt-in-your-mouth beef *daube* (stew) with carrots, or steak with shallots and creamy potato purée. While the low prices and great food are no longer a traveler's secret (you might be sharing the dining room with Asian and American tourists), that's no reason not to make the most of it: This is still one of the best deals in town. At lunch on weekdays you can even get a two-course meal (chef's choice) for 17€—a terrific deal for this level of quality. Reservations are not accepted.

139 rue Saint-Dominique, 7th arrond. www.maisonconstant.com. ℂ **01-47-53-73-34.** Main courses 16€–29€; lunch fixed-price menu 17€–24€. Daily 7–11am and noon–11pm. Métro: École Militaire.

Le Café du Marché ★ TRADITIONAL FRENCH/BISTRO Located on the rue Cler, a pedestrian market street, this bustling cafe has one of the nicest sidewalk terraces in the area. You can do some serious people-watching here without inhaling excess car exhaust. The menu features simple bistro dishes like crispy duck confit and thick slabs of grilled lamb, as well as more modern turns like salmon brochettes with balsamic vinegar and ginger. Meals are served "nonstop" all day. *Note:* Prices vary by 2€ to 3€, depending on what time of day you eat; the fluctuations are detailed on the menu.

38 rue Cler, 7th arrond. ℭ **01-47-05-51-27.** Main courses 10€–17€. Mon–Sat noon–11pm; Sun noon–3:30pm. Métro: École Militaire.

Le Petit Cler ★ TRADITIONAL FRENCH/BISTRO   This cute little cafe tumbles out on to the rue Cler pedestrian market street and serves high quality but simple food at very reasonable prices. While you won't find as many red and white checks, you will find classic cafe fare (steaks with sautéed potatoes, omelets, open-faced grilled sandwiches, and the like) as well as a daily special, which might be roast chicken (Sun) or fresh fish (Fri, natch). You can also get a complete breakfast (including eggs) for 13€, and (later in the day) cheese and cold meat platters (from 7.50€) to soak up all the wine on the menu.

29 rue Cler, 7th arrond. www.lepetitcler.com. ℭ **01-45-50-17-50.** Main courses 11€–18€. Daily 8am–11pm. Closed 2 weeks in Aug. Métro: École Militaire.

Montparnasse & Nearby (14th & 15th Arrondissements)

The famous cafes (Le Dôme, Le Select, La Coupole, and so on) where struggling writers and artists like Picasso, Hemingway, and Chagall once hung out are now much too expensive for most ordinary mortals, much less struggling artists, so having a drink and soaking up the atmosphere is probably the most affordable way to enjoy them. This is also the most Breton (that is, from Brittany) section of Paris. The trains from Brittany arrive and depart from Montparnasse, and the story goes that between the Wars, fresh-off-the-train Bretons, not knowing where else to go, settled in the immediate vicinity. Hence the high density of crêperies (the crepe having its origins in Brittany). In recent years, the neighborhood has woken up, gastronomically speaking, and a bundle of new gourmet bistros are tantalizing local taste buds.

EXPENSIVE

Cobéa ★★★ MODERN FRENCH   Grey and white elegance greets diners when they enter this pretty little house (a throwback to when southern Montparnasse was part of the countryside). Chef Philippe Bélissent invents concoctions that are as delicate and refined as the dining room. Perfectly cooked veal with fava beans and polenta, freshly caught John Dory, or pigeon with artichokes and olives might show up on the mix-and-match menu. The concept at dinner is as follows: There is one menu, from which you decide whether you'd like to try four (85€), six (105€), or eight (120€) courses. Service is impeccable.

11 rue Raymond Losserand, 14th arrond. www.cobea.fr. ℭ **01-43-20-21-39.** Fixed-price lunch 50€–82€, fixed-price dinner 85€–120€. Tues–Sat 12:15–1:15pm and 7:15–9:15pm. Closed Aug. Métro: Gaîté or Pernety.

MODERATE

L'Assiette ★★ TRADITIONAL FRENCH   There's a whiff of the Belle Epoque in this old-fashioned dining room, which has its share of mirrors and ceiling ornaments. The menu appeals to culinary nostalgia as well, with dishes like homemade cassoulet, pike quenelles (long and delicate fish dumplings) with Nantua sauce, as well as escargots and homemade foie gras for starters. For dessert, indulge in crème caramel made with salted butter or profiteroles with chocolate sauce. The restaurant also hosts workshops for tea-lovers, where you can explore the secrets of gourmet teas (more information at www.thesdelassiette.com).

181 rue du Château, 14th arrond. www.restaurant-lassiette.com. ⓒ **01-43-22-64-86.** Main courses 25€–38€; fixed-price lunch 23€. Wed–Sun noon–2:30pm and 7:30–10:30pm. Closed Aug. Métro: Gaîté.

La Cerisaie ★★ SOUTHWESTERN FRENCH/BISTRO   This shoebox-size dining room near the Tour Montparnasse serves a classy version of the soul-warming cuisine of southwestern France. In autumn and winter, Chef Cyril Lalanne does amazing things with wild game, and his menu features every animal in the forest from hare to partridge to boar. Other regional dishes include breast of goose with roasted pears and sautéed foie gras. Finish with the incredible Armagnac (as opposed to rum) baba, which comes with a scoop of luscious vanilla *crème fouettée*. It's best to reserve ahead, but if you can't, you can line up for one of the two seatings, at 7pm and 9pm.

70 bd. Edgar-Quinet, 14th arrond. www.restaurantlacerisaie.com. ⓒ **01-43-20-98-98.** Main courses 16€–21€. Mon–Fri noon–2pm and 7–10pm. Closed mid-July to mid-Aug. Métro: Montparnasse-Bienvenüe or Edgar Quinet.

La Régalade ★★★ TRADITIONAL FRENCH/BISTRO   This sweet little bistro, with its cracked tile floors, polished wood, and burgundy banquettes, was one of the first outposts in the bistronomy movement. It is currently owned by chef Bruno Doucet, who has maintained the tradition of simplicity and quality. The menu changes regularly, but starters could include foie gras in asparagus bouillon or marinated sea scallops with basil and Parmesan. Main dishes are generally variations on French comfort food, such as a succulent pork breast with sweet peas, or lively innovations like a creamy squid risotto with sautéed prawns. Dessert could be a stinky Reblochon cheese, a molten Guanaja chocolate cake, or the house specialty, rice pudding. Reserve a week in advance.

14 ave. Jean-Moulin, 14th arrond. ⓒ **01-45-45-68-58.** Fixed-price menu 37€. Tues–Fri noon–2:30pm; Mon–Fri 7–11pm. Closed first 3 weeks of Aug. Métro: Alésia.

Les Petits Plats ★★ MODERN FRENCH/BISTRO   Not especially hungry but you still want to eat well? This friendly bistro offers all of its main courses in full or half-sizes (at full and half-prices). The blackboard lists the day's offerings, which might include a juicy slab of Aubrac beef, lightly sizzled cod with compote of roasted fresh vegetables, or sautéed squid and scallops with black rice. Finish it off with a meltingly rich chocolate *mi-cuit* (a not-quite-cooked cake). The ambience is relaxed and the young staff is downright charming. At dinner a tasting menu of five different dishes costs 45€.

39 rue des Plantes, 14th arrond. ⓒ **01-45-42-50-52.** Main courses 22€–26€; half-dishes 11€–15€; fixed-price lunch 18€, fixed-price dinner 37€–46€. Mon–Sat noon–2pm and 7:30–10pm. Closed 3 weeks in Aug. Métro: Alésia.

This is a particularly tough call, since new pastry shops are opening up all the time, but here are a few classic outlets where not even the snootiest gourmands will turn their noses up.

o **Dalloyau,** 101 rue du Faubourg St-Honoré, 8th arrond. (www.dalloyau.fr; *Ⓒ* **01-42-99-90-00;** Métro: St-Philippe du Roule), has been in business since Napoleon was in power and supplies pastries to the Élysée Palace (the French White House). Known for *Le Dalloyau,* a light praline cake filled with almond meringue.

o **Pierre Hermé,** 72 rue Bonaparte, 6th arrond. (www.pierreherme.com; *Ⓒ* **01-43-54-47-77;** Métro: St-Sulpice),

may look like a chic jewelry store, but the goods are edible here. Exquisite and fashionable pastries include the Ispahan series, based on litchi, rose, and raspberry flavors.

o **Stohrer,** 51 rue Montorgueil, 2nd arrond. (www.stohrer.fr; *Ⓒ* **01-42-33-38-20;** Métro: Sentier or Les Halles), was opened by Louis XV's pastry chef in 1730. This is the place to sample the ultimate *baba au rhum* (a rum-soaked sponge cake); Stohrer invented it in the 18th century.

For a complete rundown on where to find delicious goodies, take a look at **The Paris Pastry E-Guide** app by local blogger and pastry chef David Lebovitz (www.paris-pastry.com).

5

WHERE TO DINE | The Left Bank

INEXPENSIVE

Crêperie Saint Malo ★★ CRÊPERIE   Of the dozens of crêperies concentrated near the Montparnasse train station, this is one of the best. The *galettes* and crepes are perfectly cooked with lacy, crispy edges, and what's more, they use organic flour. Try to save room for a sweet crepe after. Tradition demands that this meal be accompanied by a bowl of "brut" cider (low alcohol content, for adults only). The friendly service and easy-going atmosphere make this a good choice for families with kids.

53 rue du Montparnasse, 14th arrond. www.creperie-saintmalo.com. *Ⓒ* **01-43-20-87-19.** Main courses 3.10€–14€; fixed-price menu 14€. Daily 11:30am–2:30pm and 6:30–11:30pm. Métro: Edgar Quinet.

Taverne de la Forge ★ ALSATIAN   The menu and the decor at this woodsy tavern honor Alsace, an eastern region that shares a border with Germany. Decked out with a chalet interior and a wood-burning oven, this cozy restaurant serves up delicious specialties like *flammekueches,* the Alsatian version of pizza. The delicate, thin crust is dotted with sautéed onions, smoked ham, mushrooms, or a variety of other goodies like potatoes or smoked salmon. Other regional specialties include variations on the cheese-on-potatoes-and-ham theme, as well as choucroute, smoked meats on a heap of cooked and shredded cabbage, and a selection of standard bistro fare. Right next to the Montparnasse station, and with "nonstop" service all day, this is a good place to grab a bite while you are waiting for your train.

63 bd. de Vaugirard, 15th arrond. www.laforgemontparnasse.fr. *Ⓒ* **01-43-20-87-10.** Flamekueches 8.50€–12€, other main dishes 11€–23€. Mon–Sat noon–10:30pm; Sun noon–10pm. Métro: Montparnasse–Bienvenüe.

THE TOP TEAROOMS

It may surprise you to know that despite their famous cafe culture, many French people are closet tea fanatics. So it is only fitting that some of the world's loveliest tearooms are in Paris. Here is a sampling of some of the city's finest tea temples.

Angelina ★★ TEAROOM   This Belle Epoque beauty under the arcades on the rue de Rivoli was once frequented by Proust and Coco Chanel, among other notables. Famous for its hot chocolate and its chestnut-y Mont Blanc pastry, this is also a great spot for a chic breakfast or lunch.

226 rue de Rivoli, 1st arrond. www.angelina-paris.fr. ℰ **01-42-60-82-00.** Main courses 16€–29€; fixed-price breakfast 20€–30€; brunch 40€. Mon–Thurs 7:30am–7pm; Fri 7:30am–7:30pm; Sat–Sun 8:30am–7:30pm. Métro: Tuileries.

Café Jacquemart-André ★★ TEAROOM   Peek up at the Tiepolo ceiling as you sip your tea in what was once the dining room of Edouard André and Nélie Jacquemart. This beautiful tearoom serves excellent teas and delicious pastries from Stroher and La Petite Marquise. Lunch (or brunch Sat–Sun) from 11:45 to 3pm, tea and pastries 3 to 5:30pm. No reservations.

Musée Jacquemart-André, 158 bd. Haussmann, 8th arrond. www.musee-jacquemart-andre.com. ℰ **01-45-62-11-59.** Main courses 15€–20€; fixed-price lunch 19€–24€; brunch 30€. Daily 11:45am–5:30pm. Métro: Miromesnil or Saint-Augustin.

Ladurée ★ TEAROOM   This luxury pastry shop has boutiques everywhere these days, but there's nothing quite like a cup of tea and macarons (Ladurée's famous light-as-air filled cookies) in one of its elegant Parisian tearooms. The rue Royale location, with its original 1862 *boiseries* (decorative wood paneling), and the grandiose Champs-Élysées site with its upstairs salon, are the most impressive.

Angelina tearoom.

75 ave. des Champs-Élysées, 8th arrond. www.laduree.fr. ℰ **01-40-75-08-75.** Main courses 18€–40€; fixed-price lunch and dinner 29€–42€; brunch 49€. Mon–Thurs 7:30am–11:30pm; Fri 7:30am–12:30am; Sat 8:30am–12:30am; Sun 8:30am–11:30pm. Métro: George V.

Mosquée de Paris ★ TEAROOM   For an altogether different cup of tea, have a seat at this lovely tearoom attached to the grand Paris Mosque. Sip a glass of sweet mint tea and nibble on a *corne de gazelle* (a crescent-shaped, powdered-sugar-covered delight) or another pastry on the patio or in the beautifully tiled tearoom and dream that you're in the Casbah. Couscous is served, too (17€). Note that the entry is not the same as the one for the mosque.

39 rue Geoffroy St-Hilaire, 5th arrond. www.la-mosquee.com. ℭ **01-43-31-38-20.** Mint tea 2€; 3 pastries 7€; main courses 17€. Daily 9am–midnight. Métro: Censier-Daubenton.

THE TOP CAFES

It would be a crime to come to Paris and not stop for a coffee (or other drink) in a cafe. Cafe life is an integral part of the Parisian scene, and it simply won't do to visit the capital without at least participating once. *Important note:* Cafes are not bars in the North American sense—though they generally serve alcohol, they are not places where people come to get smashed. They are places where people come to just "be," to sip a drink, to take a break, to read a book, or to simply watch the world go by. Perhaps that's why the great Existentialist himself, Jean-Paul Sartre, spent so many of his waking hours in cafes. Most cafes open very early in the morning and close between midnight and 2am.

There must be thousands of cafes in Paris, and a thorough rundown would easily fill a book. Though you could probably have a primal cafe experience in just about any corner operation, here are a few surefire options to choose from.

Historic Cafes

Café de Flore ★★★ CAFE   A monument to the St-Germain quarter's intellectual past, Café de Flore is a must-sip on the cafe tour circuit. Seemingly every great French intellectual and artist seems to had his or her moment here: Poets Apollinaire and André Breton wrote here; artists Zadkine, Picasso, and Giacometti came to take refuge from Montparnasse; literary and theatrical stars came to preen; and of course, philosophers gathered to figure out the meaning (or nonmeaning) of life. During the war, Simone de Beauvoir and Jean-Paul Sartre more or less moved in, and Sartre is said to have written his trilogy *Les Chemins de la Liberté* (*The Roads to Freedom*) here. The atmosphere now is less thoughtful and more showbiz, but it still may be worth an overpriced cup of coffee just to come in and soak it up.

172 bd. St-Germain, 6th arrond. www.cafedeflore.fr. ℭ **01-45-48-55-26.** Daily 7am–2am. Métro: St-Germain-des-Prés.

Café de la Paix ★ CAFE   A Parisian institution ever since it was inaugurated by Empress Eugenie in 1862, this is the home of what is quite possibly the most expensive cup of coffee in the city (6€). Everyone from Emile Zola to Yves Montand has done time at this Second Empire marvel, whose gold leaf and curlicues have recently been meticulously renovated. Its outdoor terrace offers a magnificent view of the Palais Garnier—the perfect place for a drink before a night at the Opéra. It won't be cheap, but it will be memorable.

Corner of Place de l'Opéra and Boulevard des Capucines. www.cafedelapaix.fr. ℭ **01-40-07-36-36.** Daily 9am–midnight. Métro: Opéra.

coffee TALK

Ordering a cup of coffee in Paris is not quite as simple as it sounds. There is a multitude of delightful caffeinated (and decaffeinated) java possibilities at most any cafe. Cappuccinos, by the way, are rare in Parisian cafes, and when you do get one, chances are it won't resemble anything you'd get in Italy. **Important tip:** Drinks at the bar (coffee or otherwise) can cost half what you will pay sitting down at a table—as little as 1€ for an expresso.

The following miniglossary will help you navigate once your waiter makes it over to your table.

Café (ka-*fay*): Coffee. This is pure, black espresso, albeit lighter than the Italian version, served in a small demitasse cup. The equivalent of a "long shot," in Starbucks-speak.

Décaf (*day*-ka): Decaf, or decaffeinated coffee. An unleaded version of the above.

Café serré (ka-*fay* sehr-*ay*): Smaller in volume, but packs a bigger punch. Resembles an Italian espresso.

Noisette (*nwa*-zet): A café with a dash of steamed milk (my favorite).

Café crème (crem): A café with an equal amount of steamed milk, served in a larger cup.

Café au lait (ka-*fay* oh lay): Virtually identical to the above, sometimes with a bit more milk. The biggest difference is the time of day; in the morning, they call it a café au lait, in the afternoon a crème.

La Coupole ★★ CAFE   The artistic legacy of this brasserie is almost as vast as its square footage: Marc Chagall, Josephine Baker, Henry Miller, Salvador Dalí, and Ernest Hemingway are just some of the stars that lit up this converted charcoal depot. One of the largest restaurants in France, this Art Deco mastodon first opened in 1927 and has been hopping ever since. Thirty-three immense painted pillars hold up the ceiling; huge murals and paintings cover the walls. Though the food is decent (the lamb curry is the signature dish), it's best to just come here for a drink or a snack, grab a table by the windows, and watch the world go by. It's also a fun place to have breakfast.

102 bd. du Montparnasse, 14th arrond. www.lacoupole-paris.com. ℭ **01-43-20-14-20.** Tues–Sat 8:30am–midnight; Sun–Mon 8:30am–11pm. Métro: Vavin.

Les Deux Magots ★★ CAFE   After the war, de Beauvoir and Sartre moved from Café de Flore to this nearby artists' haunt, where they continued to write and think and entertain their friends for a good chunk of the rest of their lives. The literary pedigree here is at least as impressive as that of its neighbor: Poets Verlaine and Rimbaud camped out here, as did François Mauriac, André Gide, Paul Eluard, Albert Camus, and Ernest Hemingway. Since 1933, Les Deux Magots has been handing out a literary prize (in 1994, the Flore came up with its own). The outdoor terrace is particularly pleasant early in the morning before the crowds wake up.

6 place St-Germain-des-Prés, 6th arrond. www.lesdeuxmagots.fr. ℭ **01-45-48-55-25.** Daily 7:30am–1am. Métro: St-Germain-des-Prés.

Cafes with Decor

Le Bistrot du Peintre ★★ CAFE   Artists, hipsters, and other fauna from the bustling rue de Charonne area crowd in to this popular spot, which sports an authentic Art Nouveau interior with the original peeling paint. Lean up against the zinc bar and admire yourself and others in the vast mirror behind the barman, or simply slouch at one of the tiny tables that tumble onto the sidewalk.

116 ave. Ledru-Rollin, 11th arrond. www.bistrotdupeintre.com. ✆ **01-47-00-34-39.** Daily 7am–2am. Métro: Ledru-Rollin.

Le Zeyer ★ CAFE   After a hard day of shopping in the discount stores on rue d'Alesia, nothing could be nicer than a steaming café crème at this gorgeous Art Deco brasserie. One of the last of its kind that hasn't been turned into a tourist trap, this local hangout has a spacious covered terrace—the perfect spot for a rainy afternoon.

62 rue d'Alesia, 14th arrond. www.lezeyer.com. ✆ **01-45-40-43-88.** Daily 8am–midnight. Métro: Alésia.

Cafes for People-Watching

Café de la Mairie ★★ CAFE   What could be nicer than sitting in a wicker chair at a sidewalk cafe on the Place St-Sulpice? Relatively free of car exhaust (there's one lane of traffic between you and the place), in good weather cafe tables on the wide sidewalk are much in demand; you may have to hover a while to get one. Indoors, it's a 1970s archetype: Formica bar, boxy chairs, and an odd assortment of pensioners, fashion victims, students, and would-be novelists.

8 place St-Sulpice, 6th arrond. ✆ **01-43-26-67-82.** Mon–Fri 7am–2am; Sat 8am–2am; Sun 9am–2am. Métro: Mabillon or St-Sulpice.

Eté en Pente Douce ★ CAFE   On a delightful corner facing the tranquil eastern side of Sacré Coeur, this colorful cafe features a lovely sidewalk terrace where you can relax away from the tourist hordes. Don't bother with the food here, which is fair to middling; just order a café or a nice cool beer, look out on the greenery, and watch people huffing and puffing up the stairs to the basilica. You'll have to huff and puff a little yourself to get here.

23 rue Muller, 18th arrond. www.parisresto.com. ✆ **01-42-64-02-67.** Daily noon–midnight. Métro: Anvers.

Le Rostand ★★ CAFE   This quintessentially Parisian cafe has a swell terrace directly opposite the entrance to the Jardin du Luxembourg, and despite its touristy location, it draws oodles of chic locals. It's the ideal spot for a before- or after-promenade drink, a book-reading session, or just taking a load off after a visit to the park or the Panthéon.

6 place Edmond Rostand, 6th arrond. ✆ **01-43-54-61-58.** Daily 8am–midnight. RER: Luxembourg.

EXPLORING PARIS

With more than 130 world-class museums to visit, scores of attractions to discover, extraordinary architecture to gape at, and wonderful neighborhoods to wander, Paris is an endless series of delights. The hardest part is figuring out where to begin. Fortunately, you can have a terrific time even if you don't see everything. Some of your best moments may be simply roaming around the city without a plan. Lolling on a park bench, dreaming over a drink at a sidewalk cafe, or noodling around an unknown neighborhood can be the stuff of your best travel memories.

Area by area, the following pages will highlight the best that Paris can offer, from iconic sights known the world over to quirky museums and hidden gardens, from 1,000-year-old castles to galleries celebrating the most challenging contemporary art, and from the must-sees to the only-if-you've-seen-everything-else-sees. Here, then, is the best of Paris's attractions.

THE RIGHT BANK

Louvre & Île de la Cité (1st Arrondissement)

This is where it all started: Back in its misty and uncertain beginnings, the Parisii tribe set up camp on the right bank of the Seine, and then started hunting on the **Île de la Cité.** Many centuries later, the **Louvre** popped up, first as a fortress, and now one of the world's mightiest museums. The city's epicenter, this area packs in a high density of must-see monuments and museums, but don't miss the opportunity for aimless strolling in the magnificent **Tuileries Gardens** or over the **Pont Neuf.** This section includes the entire Île de la Cité, though technically half of it lies in the 4th arrondissement.

Cathédrale de Notre-Dame ★★★ CATHEDRAL   One of France's most brilliant expressions of medieval architecture, this remarkably harmonious ensemble of carved portals, huge towers, and flying buttresses has survived close to a millennium's worth of French history and served as a setting for some of the country's

Right Bank Attractions

Arc de Triomphe **2**
Basilique du
  Sacré Coeur **22**
Cathédrale de
  Notre-Dame **36**
Centre Pompidou **38**
Cimetière du
  Père-Lachaise **48**
Cité de l'Architecture
  et du Patrimoine **5**
Cité des Sciences et
  de l'Industrie **50**
Conciergerie **33**
Crypte Archéologique
  du Parvis Notre-
  Dame **35**
Espace Dalí **20**
Fondation Louis
  Vuitton **1**

Gaîté Lyrique **31**
Galerie-Musée Baccarat **3**
Grand Palais **13**
Hôtel de Ville **37**
Jardin des Tuileries **19**
La Madeleine **16**
La Promenade Plantée **47**
Maison de Balzac **6**
Maison de Victor Hugo **45**
Musée Carnavalet **43**

Musée Cognacq-Jay **42**
Musée d'Art et Histoire
  du Judaïsme **39**
Musée d'Art Moderne
  de la Ville de Paris **9**
Musée de l'Homme **6**
Musée de l'Orangerie **17**
Musée de la Chasse
  et de la Nature **40**

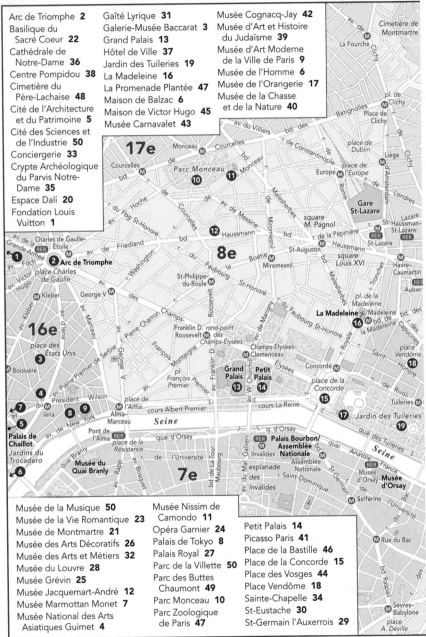

Musée de la Musique **50**
Musée de la Vie Romantique **23**
Musée de Montmartre **21**
Musée des Arts Décoratifs **26**
Musée des Arts et Métiers **32**
Musée du Louvre **28**
Musée Grévin **25**
Musée Jacquemart-André **12**
Musée Marmottan Monet **7**
Musée National des Arts
  Asiatiques Guimet **4**

Musée Nissim de
  Camondo **11**
Opéra Garnier **24**
Palais de Tokyo **8**
Palais Royal **27**
Parc de la Villette **50**
Parc des Buttes
  Chaumont **49**
Parc Monceau **10**
Parc Zoologique
  de Paris **47**

Petit Palais **14**
Picasso Paris **41**
Place de la Bastille **46**
Place de la Concorde **15**
Place des Vosges **44**
Place Vendôme **18**
Sainte-Chapelle **34**
St-Eustache **30**
St-Germain l'Auxerrois **29**

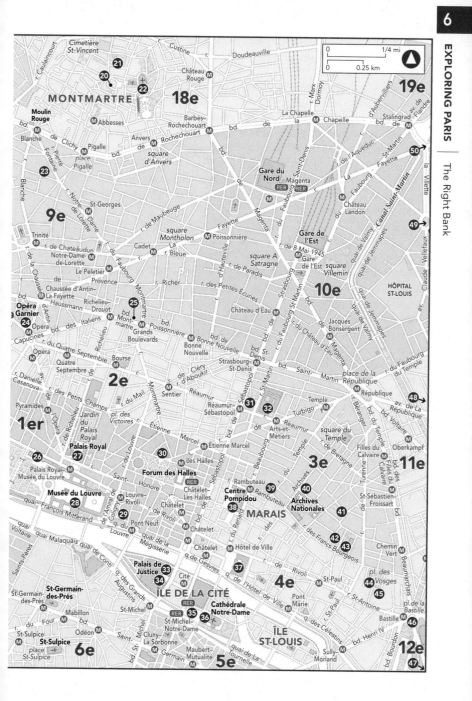

0   1/4 mi

0   0.25 km

Cimetière
St-Vincent

21

20

22

Custine

Doudeauville

Château
Rouge

MONTMARTRE   **18e**

**Moulin
Rouge**

Abbesses

Barbès-
Rochechouart

La Chapelle   Chapelle

19e

Stalingrad

50

Blanche

Pigalle

Anvers
square
d'Anvers

Rochechouart

**Gare du
Nord**
RER

Magenta
RER

Château
Landon

49

23

St-Georges

9e

Trinité

Notre-Dame-
de-Lorette

Le Peletier

Chaussée d'Antin-
La Fayette

**Opéra
Garnier**

24 Opéra

Opéra

Capucines

Opéra

Quatre
Septembre

Pyramides

1er

26

27

Palais Royal-
Musée du Louvre

Musée du Louvre

28

square
Montholon

Poissonnière

Cadet

r. Bleue

Richelieu-
Drouot

25

Grands
Boulevards

2e

Bourse

Sentier

Réaumur

**Gare de
l'Est**

Gare
de l'Est

Poissonnière

Bonne Nouvelle

Bonne
Nouvelle

Strasbourg-
St-Denis

St-
Denis

Réaumur-
Sébastopol

31   32

Étienne

Marcel

Étienne Marcel

square A.
Satragne

square
Villemin

10e

Château d'Eau

**HÔPITAL
ST-LOUIS**

Jacques
Bonsergent

Temple

Turbigo

Réaumur

Arts-et-
Métiers

3e

place de la
République

République

48

11e

Oberkampf

29

Louvre-
Rivoli

Pont Neuf

Palais Royal

Jardin
du
Palais
Royal

Palais Royal

30

Les Halles

Forum des Halles
RER

Châtelet-
Les Halles

Sébastopol

Rambuteau

**Centre
Pompidou**

38

39

MARAIS

**Archives
Nationales**

40

41

square du
Temple

Filles du
Calvaire

St-Sébastien-
Froissart

St-Paul

42 43

Châtelet

Châtelet

**Palais de
Justice** 33

34

ÎLE DE LA CITÉ

**St-Germain-
des-Prés**

Mabillon

St-Sulpice

St-Sulpice

Odéon

6e

St-Michel

RER 35

36

St-Michel-
Notre-Dame

Cluny-
La Sorbonne

Cité

37

**Cathédrale
Notre-Dame**

Hôtel de Ville

4e

St-Paul

Pont
Marie

Maubert-
Mutualité

5e

**ÎLE
ST-LOUIS**

Sully-
Morland

44

45

Bastille

46

12e

47

pl. des
Vosges

pl. de la
Bastille

most solemn moments. Napoleon crowned himself and Empress Josephine here, Napoleon III was married here, and some of France's greatest generals (Foch, Joffre, Leclerc) had their funerals here. In August 1944, the liberation of Paris from the Nazis was commemorated in the cathedral, as was the death of General de Gaulle in 1970.

The story of Notre-Dame begins in 1163, when Bishop Maurice de Sully initiated construction, which lasted over 200 years. (The identity of the architect who envisioned this masterpiece remains a mystery.) The building was relatively untouched up until the end of the 17th century, when monarchs started meddling with its windows and architecture. By the time the Revolutionaries decided to convert it into a "Temple of Reason," the cathedral was already in sorry condition—and the pillaging that ensued didn't help. The interior was ravaged, statues were smashed, and the cathedral became a shadow of its former glorious self.

We can thank the famous "Hunchback" himself for saving Notre-Dame. Victor Hugo's novel, *The Hunchback of Notre-Dame,* drew attention to the state of disrepair, and other artists and writers began to call for the restoration of the edifice. In 1844, Louis-Phillipe hired Jean-Baptiste Lassus and especially architect/archeologist/writer/painter Viollet-le-Duc to restore the cathedral, which they finished in 1864. Though many criticized Viollet-le-Duc for what they considered to be overly romantic and unauthentic excesses, he actually took extreme care to remain faithful to the historic gothic architecture. His addition of a 45m (148-ft.) spire, for example, was in fact a re-creation of one that existed in the 13th century. Made out of lead-covered oak (*chene*), it weighs 750 metric tons (827 U.S. tons).

Begin your visit at **Point Zéro,** just in front of the building on the *parvis* (the esplanade). It is the official center of Paris and the point from which all distances relative to other French cities are calculated. Before you are three enormous **carved portals** depicting (from left to right) the Coronation of the Virgin, the Last Judgment, and scenes from the lives of the Virgin and St-Anne. Above is the **Gallery of the Kings of Judah and Israel**—thought to be portraits of the kings of France, the original statues were chopped out of the facade during the Revolution; some of the heads were eventually found in the 1970s and now are in the Musée National du Moyen Age/Thermes de Cluny (p. 177). Above this is a superb **rose window,** over which soar the two bell **towers** of Quasimodo fame.

Upon entering the cathedral, you'll be immediately struck by two things: the throngs of tourists clogging the aisles, and then, when you look up, the heavenly dimensions of the pillars holding up the ceiling. Soaring upward, these delicate archways give the impression that the entire edifice is about to take off into the sky. Up there in the upper atmosphere are the three remarkable stained-glass **rose windows,** one for each of the west, north, and south ends of the church. The north window retains almost all of its 13th-century

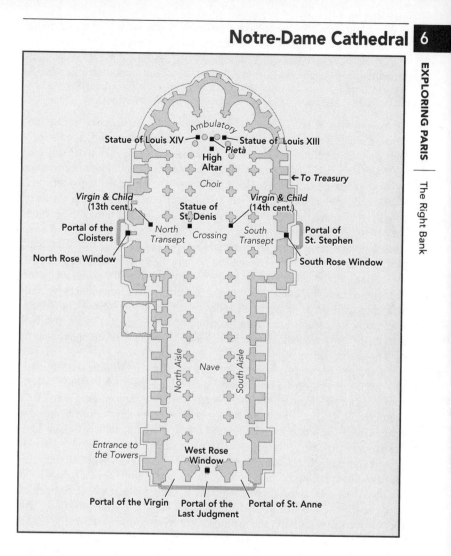

Statue of Louis XIV

Ambulatory

Statue of Louis XIII

Pietà

High Altar

← To Treasury

Choir

Virgin & Child (13th cent.)

Virgin & Child (14th cent.)

Statue of St. Denis

Portal of the Cloisters

North Transept

Crossing

South Transept

Portal of St. Stephen

North Rose Window

South Rose Window

North Aisle

Nave

South Aisle

Entrance to the Towers

West Rose Window

Portal of the Virgin

Portal of the Last Judgment

Portal of St. Anne

stained glass; the other two have been heavily restored. The impressive **treasury** is filled with relics of various saints including the elaborate cases for the **Crown of Thorns,** brought back from Constantinople by Saint Louis in the 13th century. The crown itself is not on display; however, it can be viewed, along with a nail and some pieces of the Holy Cross, on the first Friday of the month (3pm), every Friday during Lent (3pm), and Good Friday (10am–5pm). For a detailed look at the cathedral, take advantage of the **free guided tours in English** (Mon, Tues, Sat 2:30pm; Wed–Fri 2pm) or rent an **audioguide** for 5€.

When you leave, be sure to take a stroll around the outside of the cathedral to admire the other portals and the famous flying buttresses.

Place du Parvis Notre-Dame, 4th arrond. www.notredamedeparis.fr. ✆ 01-42-34-56-10. Admission free to cathedral. Treasury 4€ adults, 2€ 25 and under. Cathedral Mon–Fri 8am–6:45pm, Sat–Sun 8am–7:15pm. Treasury Mon–Fri 9:30am–6pm, Sat 9:30am–6:30pm, Sun 1:30–6:30pm. Métro: Cité or St-Michel. RER: St-Michel.

Conciergerie ★ HISTORIC SITE   A relic of the darker side of the Revolution, the Conciergerie was where some of its most famous participants spent their final days before making their way to the guillotine. Danton, Desmoulins, Saint-Just, and Charlotte Corday passed through these doors, but perhaps its most famous guest was Marie Antoinette, who spent her time here in a dismal cell, reading and praying while she awaited her fate. After doing away with the monarchy, the Revolution began to eat itself alive; during the particularly bloody period known as the Terror, murderous infighting between the various revolutionary factions engendered panic and paranoia that led to tens of thousands of people throughout the country being arrested and executed. Twenty-two of the leaders of one of the leading factions, the Girondins, were condemned to death; legend has it that on the eve of their execution they drank and sang until dawn in their cell (now called the Chapelle des Girondins). Eventually Robespierre, the main force behind the Terror and an ardent advocate for Marie-Antoinette's execution, found himself in the cell next door to the one she stayed in.

Though it's been a prison since the 15th century, the building itself is actually what remains of a 14th-century royal palace built by Philippe le Bel. Even before the Revolution, the Conciergerie was notorious: Henry IV's murderer, Ravaillac, was imprisoned here before an angry crowd tore him apart alive. The enormous **Salle des Gens d'Arms,** with its 8.4m-high (28-ft.) vaulted ceiling, is an impressive reminder of the building's palatial past. As for the prison itself, though the cells have been outfitted with displays and re-creations of daily life (including wax figures), it's a far cry from the dank hell it once was. Fresh paint and lighting make it a little difficult to imagine what it was like in the bad old days, but a few areas stand out, like the **Cours des Femmes** (the women's courtyard), which virtually hasn't changed since the days when female prisoners did their washing in the fountain. **Marie Antoinette's cell** was converted into a memorial chapel during the Restoration; a re-creation of her cell, containing some original objects, is on display. There are some worthwhile historical exhibits, including a list of the names of all those guillotined during the Revolution, 2,780 in Paris alone. The Conciergerie can be visited in conjunction with the **Sainte-Chapelle,** which lies along the same road, or Notre-Dame's towers (p. 143 and p. 129; joint tickets 15€ adults, 12€ ages 18–25).

2 bd. du Palais, 1st arrond. www.monuments-nationaux.fr. ✆ **01-53-40-60-80.** Admission 9€ adults, 7€ ages 18–25, free 17 and under. Daily 9:30am–6pm. Métro: Cité, Châtelet, or St-Michel. RER: St-Michel.

Passing on the Passes

Paris is a walkable city with numerous free museums and serendipitous experiences, so paying for a travel and museum pass doesn't always make sense. It comes down to math. The Paris Passlib' sightseeing package comes in 2-, 3-, and 5-day options, costing 109€, 129€ and 155€ respectively. Each includes unlimited public transport (zones 1–3), an hour's boat cruise and a 1-day bus tour, as well as free, skip-the-line entry to many of the city's major museums, including the **Louvre,** the **Pompidou Center,** and the **Musée d'Orsay.** This may sound like a good deal, but remember that the average adult museum entry fee ranges around 10€ to 14€, a *carnet* (pack) of 10 metro tickets is 15€, a boat trip is around 14€ and a 1-day bus tour costs about 32€. So if you buy the 2-day pass, you'll need to visit four museums to make it worth your while, *and* take the bus tour *and* take a boat tour. That's not only an overload of cerebral stimulation it's near impossible to do since it's a 1-day long bus tour. The 3-day and 5-day passes make a little more sense: You'll only need to see a maximum of two museums per day (and do the bus and boat tours) to make back your investment—still a lot, but doable. In short, if you are serious museum fan, and want to take a boat and bus tour, consider a pass. If not, do without. For more info, visit www.parisinfo.com.

Crypte Archéologique du Parvis Notre-Dame ★ ARCHEOLOGICAL SITE   Back in the 1960s, construction of an underground parking lot revealed a vast array of archeological ruins under the esplanade in front of Notre-Dame. Specialists were called in and the site was preserved and made accessible to visitors. The ruins are a jumble of centuries of Parisian history, including Roman baths, medieval ramparts, and an ancient port. Explanatory displays have been translated into English, and spiffy 3D displays have been installed to show what Paris looked like during various epochs, which brings many parts of the ruins to life. For some, it'll still be just a pile of rocks; for others, it's a fascinating look into the city's history.

7 parvis Notre-Dame, 4th arrond., entrance at the western end of the esplanade in front of Notre-Dame. www.crypte.paris.fr. © **01-55-42-50-10.** Admission 8€ adults, 6€ ages 18–26, free 17 and under (and students under 26s with ID). Tues–Sun 10am–6pm. Métro: Cité or St-Michel. RER: St-Michel-Notre-Dame.

Jardin des Tuileries ★★★ PARK   This exquisite park spreads from the Louvre to the Place de la Concorde. One of the oldest gardens in the city—and the first to be opened to the public—it's also one of the largest. In the Middle Ages, a factory here made clay tiles (*tuiles*), a word that was incorporated into the name of the palace that Catherine de Medicis built at the far end of the Louvre in 1564. Such a grand palace needed equally splendid Italian gardens; later in the mid-1600s, Louis XIV had master landscape artist André Le Nôtre—the man behind the gardens of Versailles—give them a more French look. Le Nôtre's elegant geometry of flowerbeds, parterres, and groves of trees made the Tuileries Gardens the ultimate stroll for well-to-do Parisians.

Jardin des Tuileries, outside the Louvre.

Though the Tuileries Palace burned down during the Paris Commune in 1871, the landscaping lived on. During World War II, furious fighting went on here, and many statues were damaged. Little by little in the post-war years the garden put itself back together. Seventeenth- and 18th-century representations of various gods and goddesses were repaired, and the city added new works by modern masters such as Max Ernst, Alberto Giacometti, Jean Dubuffet, and Henry Moore. Rodin's "The Kiss" and "Eve" are here, as well as a series of 18 of Maillol's curvaceous women, peeking out of the green **labyrinth** of hedges in the Carousel Gardens near the museum.

Pulling up a metal chair and sunning yourself on the edge of the large **fountain** in the center of the gardens (the **Grande Carrée**) is a delightful respite for tired tourists after a day in the Louvre; cranky tots will enjoy playing with one of the wooden **toy sailboats** that you can rent from a stand (2.50€ for a half-hour).

Near Place de la Concorde, 1st arrond. Free admission. Daily 7:30am–dusk. Métro: Tuileries or Concorde.

Musée de l'Orangerie ★★ MUSEUM Since 1927, this former royal greenhouse has been the home of Monet's stunning "Nymphéas," or water lilies, which he conceived as a "haven of peaceful meditation." Two large oval rooms are dedicated to these masterpieces, in which Monet tried to replicate the feeling and atmosphere of his garden at Giverny. He worked on these enormous canvases for 12 years, with the idea of creating an environment that would soothe the "overworked nerves" of modern men and women—in what might be called one of the world's first art installations.

The other highlight here is the Guillaume collection, an impressive assortment of late-19th- and early-20th-century paintings. It's on the lower level, where the first, light-filled gallery displays mostly portraits and still-lifes, like Renoir's glowing, idyllic "Femme Nu dans un Paysage," and Cézanne's rather dour-looking "Madame Cézanne." The rest of the collection is under artificial lights: slightly sinister landscapes by Rousseau, enigmatic portraits by Modigliani, distorted figures by Soutine, as well as some kinder, gentler Picassos ("Les Adolescents" bathed in pink and rust tones). This collection has a stormy history—after Guillaume's death, his rather flamboyant wife rearranged the collection to her own taste, selling off some of the more "difficult" paintings. The result is a lovely collection that lacks a certain bite; truly impressive works by these masters can be seen elsewhere.

Jardin des Tuileries, 1st arrond. www.musee-orangerie.fr. ⓒ **01-44-77-80-07.** Admission 9€ adults, 6.50€ ages 18–25, free 17 and under. Wed–Mon 9am–6pm. Métro: Concorde.

Musée des Arts Décoratifs ★★ MUSEUM   Possessing some 150,000 items in its rich collection, this fascinating museum offers a glimpse of history through the prism of decorative objects, with a spectrum that ranges from medieval traveling trunks to Philippe Starck stools. The collection is organized in more or less chronological order, so on your journey you will pass by paintings from the First Italian Renaissance, through a room filled with exquisite 15th-century *intarsia* ("paintings" made out of intricately inlaid wood), before gaping at huge, intricately carved 17th-century German armoires. Other highlights include a tiny room covered in gilded woodwork from an 18th-century mansion in Avignon, a stunning Art Nouveau dining room and fashion designer Jeanne Lanvin's decadent, purple Art Deco boudoir. While the objects themselves are beautiful, the link between style and historic context is illuminating; the endless curlicues of the rococo style, which perfectly reflected the excesses of Louis XV's court, for example, gives way to more

The Two Towers

The lines are long and the climb is longer, but the view from the **rooftop balcony** (www.tours-notre-dame-de-paris.fr; ⓒ **01-53-40-60-80;** 10€ adults, 8€ under 26, free under 18 [and under 26 from EU countries]; Apr–June and Sept 10am–6:30pm, July–Aug Sun–Thurs 10am–6:30pm, Fri–Sat 10am–11pm, Oct–Mar 10am–5:30pm) at the base of the cathedral's towers is possibly the most Parisian of all views. After trudging up some 255 steps (a narrow, winding staircase with a handrail—not for small children or anyone with mobility concerns), you'll be rewarded with a panorama that not only encompasses the Île de la Cité, the Eiffel Tower, and Sacré Coeur, but is also framed by a collection of photogenic **gargoyles.** These

fantastic monsters, composed of various portions of apes, birds, and even elephants, came directly from the imagination of Viollet-le-Duc, who placed them during the restoration of the cathedral. One of the most famous is the **Stryga,** a horned and winged beasty holding his head in his hands, pensively sticking his tongue out at the city below. Squeeze around the narrow first balcony to the entrance to the belfry, Quasimodo's old haunt; its massive wood beams hold up a 14-ton bell. Another 147 steps up another stairway lead to the summit of the **south tower,** from which there is an endless view of Paris. To minimize the wait, come 20 minutes before opening in the morning before the crowds get thick.

puritanical neoclassicism, which developed during the Enlightenment, when unrestrained frivolity began to look degenerate.

Two other collections worthy of your time are the Publicité/Graphisme collection, which takes on the history of advertising, and the Mode/Textile fashion displays. While the former will mostly be of interest to those who are in the biz, the latter hosts a terrific range of works from famous couture houses like Jean-Paul Gaultier and Dior. Another intriguing addition is a collection of wallpaper through the ages—the earliest of which dates from 1864 and depicts a bucolic hunting scene. *Note:* The visit starts on the third, not the first, floor.

Palais du Louvre, 107 rue de Rivoli, 1st arrond. www.lesartsdecoratifs.fr. © **01-44-55-57-50.** Admission 11€ adults (audioguide included), 8.50€ ages 18–25, free 17 and under. Tues–Sun 11am–6pm (until 9pm Thurs for temporary exhibitions only). Métro: Louvre-Palais-Royal or Tuileries.

Musée du Louvre ★★★ MUSEUM The best way to thoroughly visit the Louvre would be to move in for a month. Not only is it one of the largest museums in the world, with more than 35,000 works of art displayed over 60,000 sq. m (645,835 sq. ft.), but it's packed with enough artistic masterpieces to make the Mona Lisa weep. Rembrandt, Reubens, Botticelli, Ingres, and Michelangelo are all represented here; subjects range from the grandiose (Antoine-Jean Gros's gigantic "Napoleon Bonaparte Visiting the Plague-Stricken in Jaffa") to the mundane (Vermeer's tiny, exquisite "Lacemaker"). You can gape at a diamond the size of a golf ball in the gilded Galerie d'Apollon or marvel over exquisite bronze figurines in the vast Egyptian section. There's something for everyone here.

Today, the building is divided into three wings: Sully, Denon, and Richelieu, each one with its own clearly marked entrance, found under I. M. Pei's glass pyramid. Get your hands on a museum map, choose your personal

---

Leaping over the Louvre Line

Don't want to wait in line for tickets to the Louvre? The easiest option is to buy tickets in advance online (in English) at **www.ticketlouvre.fr** and print them out. Or try **www.fnactickets.com**; you can print out your tickets, get them mailed to you, or pick them up at any French branch of the Fnac bookstore chain. (Also note that the Louvre is open until 9:30pm on Wed and Fri—usually a quiet time to visit.) If you are of an improvisational bent and prefer to pick up tickets at the entrance, there are four ways to avoid the lines that often

snake around the glass pyramid entryway. Either:

- Enter directly from the Palais Royal–Musée du Louvre metro stop.
- Take one of the two staircases on either side of the Arc du Carrousel in the Tuileries Gardens that lead directly down to the ticketing area.
- Buy your ticket from the Civette du Carousel tobacconist in the Carousel du Louvre shopping center (99 rue de Rivoli) where there's never a wait.
- Enter at the Porte des Lions (in the Denon wing), open until 5:30pm.

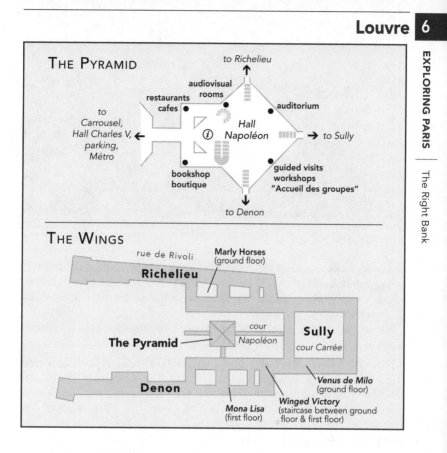

THE PYRAMID

to Richelieu

audiovisual rooms

restaurants cafes

auditorium

to Carrousel, Hall Charles V, parking, Métro

Hall Napoléon

ⓘ

to Sully

bookshop boutique

guided visits workshops "Accueil des groupes"

to Denon

THE WINGS

rue de Rivoli

Marly Horses (ground floor)

Richelieu

cour Napoléon

The Pyramid ←

Sully

cour Carrée

Denon

Venus de Milo (ground floor)

Mona Lisa (first floor)

Winged Victory (staircase between ground floor & first floor)

"must-sees," and plan ahead. There's no way to see it all; you'll be an instant candidate for early retirement if you try. Mercifully, the museum is well organized and has been very reasonably arranged into color-coded sections. If you're really in a rush, or you just want to get an overall sense of the place, you can take the introductory guided tour in English (1½ hr.; 11am and 2pm Wed–Mon; 12€; ℭ **01-40-20-52-63**). You won't see as much as you would on your own, but at least you'll know what you are seeing. Reserve at least 14 days in advance to secure a place.

The museum's three biggest stars are all located in the Denon wing. "La Joconde," otherwise known as the **"Mona Lisa"** (see the "Men Have Named You . . ." box, below), now has an entire wall to herself, making it easier to contemplate her enigmatic smile. Another inscrutable female in this wing is the **"Venus de Milo,"** who was found on a Greek isle in 1820. Possibly the most photographed woman in the world, this armless marble goddess gives no hint of the original position of her limbs or her exact identity. Recently restored and lovelier than ever, the **"Winged Victory of Samothrace,"** is the

Courtyard of the Louvre Museum.

easiest to locate. Standing at the top of a majestic flight of stairs, her powerful body pushing forward as if about to take flight, this headless yet magnificent Greek sculpture once guarded the Sanctuary of the Great Gods on the island of Samothrace.

Because a complete listing of the Louvre's highlights would fill a book, below is a decidedly biased selection of our favorite areas:

13TH- TO 18TH-CENTURY ITALIAN PAINTINGS A few standouts in the immense Italian collection include Botticelli's delicate fresco **"Venus and the Three Graces Presenting Gifts to a Young Woman,"** Veronese's enormous **"Wedding Feast at Cana,"** and of course, the **"Mona Lisa."** The Divine Miss M is in a room packed with wonders, including several Titians and Tintorettos. Once you've digested this rich meal, stroll down the endless Grande Galerie, past more da Vincis ("Saint John the Baptist," "The Virgin of the Rock"), as well as works by Raphael, Caravaggio, and Gentileschi.

GREEK & ROMAN SCULPTURE While the **"Winged Victory of Samothrace"** and the **"Venus de Milo"** are not to be missed, the Salle des Caryatides (the room itself is a work of art) boasts marble masterworks like Artemis hunting with her stag and the Sleeping Hermaphrodite, an alluring female figure from behind—and something entirely different from the front.

THE GALERIE D'APOLLON The gold-encrusted room is an excellent example of the excesses of 17th-century French royalty. Commissioned by Louis XIV, aka "The Sun King," every inch of this gallery is covered with gilt stucco sculptures and flamboyant murals invoking the journey of the Roman sun god Apollo (ceiling paintings are by Charles Le Brun). The main draw here is the collection of crown jewels. Among necklaces bedecked with quarter-sized sapphires and tiaras dripping with diamonds and rubies are the **jewel-studded crown** of Louis XV and the **Regent,** a 140-carat diamond that he used to decorate his hat.

THE EGYPTIANS   This is the largest collection outside of Cairo, thanks in large part to Jean-François Champollion, the 19th-century French scientist and scholar, who first decoded Egyptian hieroglyphs. Sculptures, figurines, papyrus documents, steles, musical instruments, and of course, mummies, fill numerous rooms in the Sully wing, including the colossal **statue of Ramses II** and the strangely moving **Seated Scribe.** He gazes intently out of intricately crafted inlaid eyes: A combination of copper, magnesite, and polished rock crystal creates a startlingly lifelike stare.

LARGE-FORMAT FRENCH PAINTINGS   Enormous floor-to-ceiling paintings of monumental moments in history cover the walls in these three rooms. The overcrowded and legendary **"Coronation of Napoléon"** by Jacques-Louis David depicts the newly minted Emperor crowning Josephine, while the disconcerted pope and a host of notables look on. On the facing wall, **"Madame Récamier"** (also by David), one of Napoleon's loudest critics, reclines fetchingly on a divan. Farther on are several tumultuous canvases by Eugène Delacroix, including **"Liberty Guiding the People,"** which might just be the ultimate expression of French patriotism. In the painting, which evokes the events of the revolution of 1830, Liberty—breast exposed, a rifle in one hand, the French flag in the other—leads the crowd over a sea of dead bodies. High ideals and gore—sort of sums up the French revolutionary spirit.

Note: When visiting the museum, **watch your wallets and purses**—there has been an unfortunate increase in pickpockets; thieves even use children to prey on unsuspecting art lovers. On a more positive note, the Louvre has made great strides in improving **accessibility for handicapped visitors** in recent years, including special programs, ramps, free wheelchairs, and folding chairs. For more info, click "accessibility" at the top of the museum's website.

Quai du Louvre, 1st arrond. Main entrance in the glass pyramid, cour Napoléon. www.louvre.fr. Ⓒ **01-40-20-50-50.** Admission 17€, free 17 and under (and 25s and under from the EU). Sat–Mon and Thurs 9am–6pm; Wed and Fri 9am–9:30pm. Métro: Palais-Royal–Musée du Louvre.

Palais Royal ★★ HISTORIC SITE/GARDEN   The gardens and long arcades of the Palais Royal are not only a delight to stroll through, but were also witnesses to one of the most important moments in French history.

But first the backstory: Built by Cardinal Richelieu, the lavish palace was left to the king upon his prime minister's death. It was subsequently occupied by a number of royal family members (including Louis XIV as a child) until it came into the hands of a certain Duke Louis Phillippe d'Orleans at the end of the 18th century. An inveterate spendthrift, the young lord soon found himself up to his ears in debt. To earn enough money to pay off his creditors, he came up with the shockingly modern idea of opening the palace gardens to development, building apartments on the grounds. The bottom floor of these lodgings, which make up three sides of the enclosure you see today, were let out as shops, cafes, and boutiques. Though the neighbors screamed, their cries

MEN HAVE named YOU . . .

Everything about the "Mona Lisa" is mysterious—the identity of the sitter, how long it took to paint, and how it got into the French royal collection, among other things. Most scholars agree that it is a portrait of Lisa Gheradini, the wife of one Francesco del Giocondo, but Ms. Lisa could also be Isabella of Aragon (as suggested by the patterning of her dress) or simply an embodiment of beauty and happiness (hence the smile), as suggested by the Italian word *gioconda*.

A few years ago, researchers found evidence of a fine, translucent veil around the subject's shoulders, a garment women in Renaissance Italy wore when they were expecting, provoking an onslaught of speculation that her secret smile had to do with her being pregnant.

What's certain is that the painting created a sensation. The overall harmony of the composition, the use of a distant landscape in the background, the lifelike quality of the subject, had a huge impact on early-16th-century Florentine art. As Giorgio Vasari, a Renaissance painter and biographer lamented, "It may be said that it was painted in such a manner as to make every valiant craftsman, be he who he may, tremble and lose heart."

The painting's history is action packed. One morning in 1911, an artist named Louis Béroud came in to the museum to sketch a copy of the famous portrait, and found a bare spot with four hooks in the wall. After a concerted effort, he convinced the lackadaisical guard to find out what happened. In fact, the "Mona Lisa" had been stolen. The thief had entered the museum posing as a visitor, hid in the building overnight, and in the morning disguised himself as a workman and made off with the painting while the guard went out to smoke a cigarette. Needless to say, panic ensued. There was a nationwide

investigation, and the borders were sealed. What the police didn't realize is that the painting was at first hidden only a mile from the Louvre. Conspiracy theories spread through the newspapers—some thought it was merely a publicity stunt. There was a lot of criticism about the Louvre's lax security, in particular from the poet Apollinaire. He soon found himself arrested as a suspect, and his friend Pablo Picasso was also brought in for questioning after they were caught in possession of some other art objects of dubious origins. After they both broke down in tears before the bench, the judge let them go with a slap on the wrist.

After 2 years of false leads and bungled investigations, the "Mona Lisa" was finally found when the thief, Vincenzo Perugia, tried to sell it to an art dealer in Florence. What was the motive for the crime? It seems that Perugia, an Italian patriot who had once worked at the museum, simply felt that the "Mona Lisa" belonged in her country of birth, Italy. During his trial, Perugia claimed to have been bewitched by the painting—and indeed, who hasn't been?

The life of a superstar certainly isn't easy. With millions of admirers around the world, at least a couple are bound to have a few screws loose. Once she was back at the museum (under increased security), things calmed down until 1956, when a deranged visitor threw acid on the painting, severely damaging its lower half (restoration took several years). A few months later, someone threw a rock at her. The painting is now covered with bulletproof glass, and a full-time guard stands at the ready. So be patient with the lines and velvet ropes—if "Mona Lisa" gets the kind of security usually reserved for rock stars or heads of state, she has certainly earned it.

were drowned out by the success of the new project, which made the area into a commercial hub. What's more, since the police had no power over these royal grounds, all sorts of usually illegal activities were given free reign here. Gambling houses and bordellos sprang up between the shops and cafes, and the gardens became the central meeting place for revolutionaries. Things came to a head on July 12, 1789, when Camille Desmoulins stood up on a table in front of the Café de Foy and called the people to arms—2 days later, the mob would storm the Bastille, igniting the French Revolution.

The glory days of the Palais Royal would come to an abrupt end in 1815, when a new Louis-Philippe showed up, decided this was not the way to treat the home of his ancestors, and kicked everyone out. Once the royals finally left in the 19th century, the palace was taken over by various government ministries, and the apartments in the galleries were let out to artists and writers, among them Collette and Jean Cocteau.

Today the shops in the arcades are very subdued, and very expensive—mostly a smattering of high-end designer clothes, and a couple of pricey restaurants, including the legendary **Grand Véfour** (p. 83). The *cour d'honneur* on the south end is filled with black-and-white-striped columns by Daniel Buren; though most Parisians have now gotten used to this unusual installation, when it was unveiled in 1987 it caused almost as much of a stir as Camille Desmoulins.

Rue St-Honoré, 1st arrond. Free admission to gardens and arcades, buildings closed to public. Gardens daily 7:30am–dusk. Métro: Palais Royal–Musée du Louvre.

Place Vendôme ★★ SQUARE   In 1686, Louis XIV decided the time had come to design a magnificent square, at the center of which would stand a statue of His Royal Highness. Though the statue is long gone, this is still one of the classiest squares in the city. The work of Jules Hardouin-Mansart, today this über-elegant octagonal ensemble of 17th-century buildings is the home of the original Ritz Hôtel, as well as the world's most glitzy jewelry makers, including Cartier, Van Cleef and Arpels, and Boucheron. The famous statue reigned over the square up until the Revolution, when it was melted down for scrap. When Napoleon took over, he decided it was the perfect place for a huge Roman-style column honoring his glorious army (yes, once again), this time documenting its victory at Austerlitz. A long spiral of bas-reliefs recounting the campaign of 1805 marches up the Colonne de la Grande Armée, which was crowned by a statue of the Emperor himself. The original statue did not survive the regime; a few decades later, Napoleon III replaced it with the existing copy.

Enter by rue de Castiglione, 1st arrond. Métro: Tuileries or Concorde.

Sainte-Chapelle ★★★ CHURCH   A wall of color greets visitors who enter this magnificent chapel. Stained-glass windows make up a large part of the walls of the upper level of the church, giving worshippers the impression of standing inside a jewel-encrusted crystal goblet. What isn't glass is elaborately carved and painted in gold leaf and rich colors: vaulting arches, delicate window casings, and an almost oriental wainscoting of arches and medallions. The 15 windows recount the story of the Bible, from Genesis to the Apocalypse, as well as the story of St-Louis, who was responsible for the chapel's construction. Back in the early 13th century, Louis IX (who was later canonized) spent 2 years bargaining with Emperor Badouin II of Constantinople for some of the holiest relics in Christendom: the Crown of Thorns and a piece of the Holy Cross. The relics were finally purchased for a princely sum, and Louis decided that they should be housed in an appropriately splendid chapel in the royal palace (the relics are now in the treasury of Notre-Dame; see p. 129). The record is not clear, but the architect may have been the illustrious Pierre de Montreuil, who worked on the cathedrals of St-Denis and Notre-Dame. Whoever it was was a speed-demon; the chapel was built in record time for the Middle Ages, from 1241 to 1248. He was also quite brilliant; he managed to support the structure with arches and buttresses in such a way that the walls of the upper chapel are almost entirely glass.

The lower chapel, which was meant for the servants, has a low, vaulted ceiling painted in blue and red and gold and covered with fleur-de-lis motifs. Up a small staircase is the upper chapel, clearly meant for the royals. This masterpiece suffered both fire and floods in the 17th century and was pillaged by zealous revolutionaries in the 18th. By the mid–19th century, the chapel was being used to store archives—2m (6½ ft.) of the bottom of each window was removed to install shelves. Fortunately, renewed interest in medieval art staved off plans for Ste-Chapelle's demolition, and eventually led to a conscientious restoration by a team that was advised by master restorer Viollet-le-Duc. The quality of the work on the windows is such that it is almost impossible to detect the difference between the original and the reconstructed stained glass (which makes up about one-third of what you see).

Sainte-Chapelle stages **concerts** from March to November at 7 and 8:30pm; tickets cost 16€ to 54€. You can take your chances and buy tickets at the door (although it may be a full house), but we recommend reserving in advance online at one of two websites: www.classictic.com or www.euromusic productions.fr (or by phone, ✆ **01-42-77-65-65**).

If you plan to visit the Conciergerie (p. 134), you can save money by buying a joint ticket: 15€ adults, 8.50€ ages 18 to 25.

Palais de Justice, 4 bd. du Palais, 1st arrond. www.monuments-nationaux.fr. ✆ **01-53-40-60-80**. 10€ adults, free for ages 17 and under and ages 18–25 from EU countries. Audioguide 5€. Oct–Mar daily 9am–5pm; Apr–Sept daily 9am–7pm. Métro: Cité, St-Michel, or Châtelet–Les Halles. RER: St-Michel.

St-Eustache ★ CHURCH A Gothic church with a Renaissance decor, St-Eustache is one of the largest in the city, at more than 105m long (344 ft.) and 43m wide (141 ft.). It was built from 1532 to 1640 along the plan of Notre-Dame; the intertwined arches of the ceiling give a similar sense of exalted elevation. These dimensions result in excellent acoustics for the church's huge 8,000-pipe organ, which is considered one of the finest in the city. The church's musical reputation stretches back centuries; Berlioz and

Famously called "the belly of Paris," **Les Halles** was the city's primary wholesale food market for 8 centuries. The smock-clad vendors, beef carcasses, and baskets of vegetables all belong to the past, as the market was relocated to the suburb of Rungis in the early '70s. In a fit of modernity, all the pretty 19th-century pavilions were torn down, and in their place a weird, partly underground shopping mall was constructed: the **Forum des Halles** (1–7 rue Pierre-Lescot, 1st arrond.). In 2010, the city embarked on a massive renovation program to overhaul the shopping center and the surrounding gardens, by building "the canopy," an immense, undulating sheet of glass and metal that floats over the Forum. Despite its multi-million price tag, most Parisians complain that it's unattractive, but it does house brand-new shops and restaurants (including Alain Ducasse's Champeaux brasserie; p. 86) and opens onto an immense garden that sweeps across lawns and kids' play areas over to 16th-century Eglise St. Eustache (p. 144)—a masterpiece of Gothic architecture. The underground will eventually get its makeover too, so some areas may be under construction. For info, visit www.parisleshalles.fr.

Liszt both conducted their works here, among others. Before the Revolution, Saint Eustache was a parish where both the nobility and working class came to worship—Cardinal Richelieu and Madame de Pompadour were baptized here, as was the playwright Molière. After the Revolution it was turned into a temple to agriculture, and, like many Parisian churches, its interior suffered mightily. It was subsequently restored and is currently undergoing another go-round. Work is progressing slowly and many chapels are still gloomy, but you can still admire the soaring nave and the overall effect of this graceful edifice. You can hear the organ and the choir in action Sunday at 5:30pm before (and during) the 6pm mass; other concerts are listed on the church's website or at www.fnacspectacles.com.

2 impasse St-Eustache, 1st arrond. www.st-eustache.org. ⓒ **01-42-36-31-05.** Free admission. Mon–Fri 9:30am–7pm; Sat–Sun 9am–7pm; Sun organ recitals 5:30pm. Métro: Les Halles.

St-Germain l'Auxerrois ★ CHURCH   This is a church with a checkered past. St-Germain was designated the royal church when the Valois moved in across the street at the Louvre in the 14th century, and kings, queens, and their entourages often attended mass here. Many of the artists who worked on the Louvre are buried here, including architects Le Vau and Soufflot. But its most infamous moment came at dawn on August 24, 1572, when the church's bells sounded the signal that began the Saint Bartholomew's Day massacre. Despite her erstwhile tolerance, Catherine de Medicis and her son Charles IX gave their blessing to a plot to slaughter the Huguenot (Protestant) leaders. The crowd murdered every Protestant in sight—between 2,000 and 4,000 were killed over the following 5 days.

The church has been rebuilt several times over the centuries, resulting in a mix of architectural styles. The 12th-century Romanesque tower hovers over a 15th-century Flamboyant Gothic porch embellished with human and animal figures. The vaulted interior is relatively simple and shelters some interesting works of art, among which are a monumental **sculpted wooden pew,** designed for the royal family in 1684 by Le Brun, and a 16th-century carved wood **retable** depicting scenes from the life of Christ.

2 place du Louvre, 1st arrond. www.saintgermainauxerrois.cef.fr. ℰ **01-42-60-13-96.** Free admission. Sept–June Tues–Sat 9am–7pm, Sun 9:30am–8:30pm; July–Aug Tues– Sun 9:30am–7pm. Métro: Louvre-Rivoli.

Opéra & Grands Boulevards (2nd & 9th Arrondissements)

The grandiose **Opéra Garnier** reigns over this bustling neighborhood, which teems with office workers, tourists, and shoppers scuttling in and around the Grands Magasins (Big Department Stores) on Boulevard Haussmann. There are more outstanding retail experiences here than cultural ones.

Musée Grévin ★ MUSEUM   This vast, kitsch cavern of wax figures— movie stars, historical figures, sports heroes, rock and rollers, notables from the political scene—is a fun place to take the kids. If you're not up on French history or pop culture, you might not recognize some of the faces, but don't worry, Marilyn Monroe, Brad Pitt, and Pope Francis are here, too. Stars appear in their natural habitats: chic brasseries, cocktail parties, and fashion shows. Historical tableaus feature such scenes as Joan of Arc being burned at the stake and Louis XIV holding court at Versailles. Also here: a light show in the renovated Palais des Mirages, a leftover from the Universal Exposition of 1900.

10 bd. Montmartre, 9th arrond. www.grevin-paris.com. ℰ **01-47-70-85-05.** Admission varies with the season, starting at 22€ adults, 18€ ages 15–17, 15€ ages 6–14, free 5 and under. Daily 10am–6:30pm (hours vary with seasons; check website for exact times). Métro: Grands Boulevards.

Opéra Garnier ★★ OPERA HOUSE   Flamboyant, extravagant, and baroque, this splendid example of Second Empire architectural excess, built by architect Charles Garnier between 1862 and 1875, sits on the underground lake that inspired Gaston Leroux's 1911 novel, *The Phantom of the Opera!* Corinthian columns, loggias, busts, and friezes cover the facade of the building, which is topped by a flattened gold dome. Seventy-three sculptors worked on the decoration, which includes portraits of composers, Greek gods, and symbolic representations of Music, Poetry, Drama, and Dance.

The interior is no less dramatic. The vast lobby, built in a spectrum of different colored marble, holds a spectacular double staircase that sweeps up to the different levels of the auditorium, as well as an array of glamorous antechambers, galleries, and ballrooms that make you wonder how the opera scenery could possibly compete. Mosaics, mirrors, gilt, and marble line these grand spaces, whose painted ceilings dance with fauns, gods, and nymphs. The largest room, the grand foyer, is drenched in gold leaf and hung with

Opéra Garnier National de Paris.

gigantic chandeliers, looking something like a real palace, which was, in fact, the effect Garnier was going for. The main event, of course, is the auditorium, which might seem a bit small, considering the size of the building. In fact, it holds not even 2,000 seats. The horseshoe shape of the seating area ensures that viewers see both the stage and each other—19th-century operagoers were equally concerned with what was on the stage and who was in the house. The beautiful ceiling was painted in 1964 with colorful images from various operas and ballets by Marc Chagall.

All of this (with the exception of the Chagall ceiling) sprang from the mind of a young, unknown architect named Charles Garnier, who won a competition launched when Napoleon III decided the time had come to build himself an opera house. Though the first stone was laid in 1862, work was held up by war, civil unrest, and a change in regime; the **Palais Garnier** was not inaugurated until 1875. Some contemporary critics found it a bit much (one called it "an overloaded sideboard"), but today it is generally acknowledged as a masterpiece of the architecture of the epoch.

You can visit the building on your own (for a fee; see ticket prices below), but there's so much history here and so many good stories, you might want to take advantage of the **guided visits in English** (14€ adults, 13€ children under 10; Wed, Sat, and Sun at 11:30am and 2:30pm; July–Aug and French school vacations daily 11:30am and 2:30pm). Or simply **buy tickets to a show;** consult the website to see what's on.

Corner of rue Scribe and rue Auber, 9th arrond. www.operadeparis.fr. ℂ **08-25-05-44-05.** Admission 11€ adults, 7€ students and ages 13–25, free children under 12. Oct to mid-July daily 10am–4:30pm, mid-July to Sept 10am–5:30pm. Métro: Opéra.

Musée de la Vie Romantique ★ MUSEUM   This quaint villa, with painted shutters and a fragrant rose garden, is where Romantic painter Ary Scheffer (1795–1858) once entertained such illustrious guests as Baronne Aurore Dupin (George Sand), Eugène Delacroix, Chopin, and Charles Dickens. Today, the tiny museum gives an inkling as to what life might have been like in the company of these iconic artists, with atmospheric period rooms, one of which is dedicated to George Sand with moving mementoes from her life—jewelry, trinkets paintings, and even a plaster cast of her right arm. In summer, the rose garden doubles as one of Paris's most charming tea rooms—a slice of countryside in the heart of what was once known as La Nouvelle Athènes (New Athens) after the Classical-style mansions that mushroomed in the early 19th century to house Paris's prestigious artist community.

16 rue Chaptal, 9th arrond. www.vie-romantique.paris.fr. ✆ **01-55-31-95-67.** Free admission to permanent collection except during certain temporary exhibits. Tues–Sun 10am–6pm. Métro: Saint-Georges, Pigalle, or Blanche.

Le Marais (3rd & 4th Arrondissements)

Home to royalty and aristocracy between the 14th and 17th centuries, the Marais still boasts remarkable architecture, some of it dating back to the Middle Ages. One of the few neighborhoods that was not knocked down during Baron Haussmann's urban overhaul, its narrow streets are lined with magnificent *hôtels particuliers* (such as mansions) as well as humbler homes from centuries past. The **Pompidou Center** is probably the biggest attraction, but the Marais also harbors a wealth of terrific smaller museums, as well as the delightful **Place des Vosges.** Remnants of the city's **historic Jewish quarter** can be found on rue des Rosiers, which has been invaded by clothing shops in recent years. Nowadays, the real Jewish neighborhood is in the 19th arrondissement.

Facade of the Centre Pompidou.

Centre Pompidou ★★ MUSEUM The bizarre architecture of this odd building provokes such strong emotions that it's easy to forget that there is something inside. Believe it or not, President Pompidou searched far and wide to find an architect. In 1971, an international design competition was held with entrants from 49 countries, and the winners were the Italo-British design team of Renzo Piano and Richard Rogers. Their concept was to put the support structure and transport systems on the outside of the building, thereby liberating space on the inside for a museum and cultural center. The result was a gridlike exoskeleton with a tubular escalator inching up one side, and huge multicolored pipes and shafts covering the other. To some, it's a milestone in contemporary architecture; to others, it's simply a horror. Either way, it's one of the most visited structures in France.

For the Pompidou is much more than an art museum. Its over 100,000 sq. m (1,076,390 sq. ft.) of floor space includes a vast **reference library,** a **cinema archive, bookshops,** and a **music research institute,** as well as a **photography** gallery, a **performance hall,** a **children's gallery,** and areas for educational activities.

The actual museum, the **Musée National d'Art Moderne,** is on the fourth and fifth floors. Getting there is half the fun as you glide up the exterior escalators. Since the collection is in constant rotation and **temporary exhibitions** are a huge draw, it's impossible to say what you are likely to see on your visit, but the emphasis is generally on works from the second half of the 20th century, with a good dose of surrealism, Dada, and other modern movements from the first half. This is not "pretty" art, but art that is designed to make you think. It might make you think about heading straight for the exit, but if nothing else, there are works here that will surprise you and get your juices flowing. Pieces range from relatively tame abstracts by **Picasso** and **Kandinsky** to **Andy Warhol**'s multiheaded portrait of Elizabeth Taylor ("Ten Lizes") to a felt-wrapped piano by **Joseph Beuys.** Video installations are often highlighted, as well as new artists.

Just outside of the front of the center is the **Atelier Brancusi,** where the sculptor's workshop has been reconstituted in its entirety; in his will, Brancusi left the workshop's contents to the museum on the condition that every sculpture and object be displayed exactly as it was found in his studio on the day of his death.

There's also a nonstop circus of comics, mimes, and other performances on the vast esplanade outside the building. Take note of the monumental sculpture/mobile by Alexander Calder, and do not miss the delightful **Stravinsky Fountain** around the side of the center; kids love watching its colorful mobile sculptures by Niki de Saint Phalle and Jean Tinguely.

Place Georges-Pompidou, 4th arrond. www.centrepompidou.fr. ✆ **01-44-78-12-33.** Admission 14€ adults, students 11€ ages 18–25, free 17 and under (and under 25s from the EU); admission may vary depending on exhibits. Wed–Mon 11am–10pm (until 11pm Thurs during temporary exhibitions). Métro: Hôtel de Ville. RER: Châtelet–Les Halles.

Gaîté Lyrique ★ CULTURAL INSTITUTION   One of the newer additions to the city's cultural scene, this gallery space/concert hall/educational center is devoted to exploring mixed-media and digital art forms. Set in an abandoned 19th-century theater (hence the name), the building has been restored and transformed to host rotating exhibits that range from music and multimedia performances to design, fashion, and architecture to new media— there's even an interactive room dedicated to video games.

3 bis rue Papin, 3rd arrond. www.gaite-lyrique.net. ✆ **01-53-01-52-00.** Tues–Sat 2–8pm, Sun noon–6pm. Prices vary depending on the event or exhibition. Métro: Réaumur-Sébastopol or Arts et Métiers.

Hôtel de Ville ★ HISTORIC SITE   No, it's not a hotel. This enormous neo-Renaissance wedding cake is Paris's city hall, and the only way to see the inside is to make friends with the mayor. Even if you can't get inside, you can feast on the lavish exterior, which includes 136 statues representing historic VIPs of Parisian history. Since the 14th century, this spot has been an administrative seat for the municipality; the building you see before you dates from 1873, but it is an accurate copy of an earlier Renaissance version that was burned down in 1870 during the Paris Commune. The vast square in front of the building, formerly called the place du Grève, was once used for municipal festivals and executions. It was also the stage for several important moments in the city's history, particularly during the Revolution: Louis XVI was forced to kiss the new French flag here, and Robespierre was shot in the jaw and arrested here during an attempted coup. Today the square is host to more peaceful activities: There's usually a merry-go-round or two to captivate the little ones, and in winter an ice-skating rink is set up. The Hôtel de Ville also hosts regular art exhibits on subjects linked to Paris's history (usually free). Access is through the back entrance on rue Lobau.

29 rue de Rivoli, 4th arrond. www.paris.fr. ℂ **01-42-76-63-01.** Free admission to exhibits. Métro: Hôtel-de-Ville.

Maison de Victor Hugo ★ MUSEUM   The life of Victor Hugo was as turbulent as some of his novels. Regularly visited by both tragedy and triumph, the author of *The Hunchback of Notre-Dame* lived in several apartments in Paris, including this one on the second floor of a corner house on the sumptuous place des Vosges. From 1832 to 1848, he lived here with his wife and four children, during which time he wrote *Ruy Blas;* wrote part of *Les Misérables;* met his lifelong mistress and muse, Juliette Drouet; was elected to the Academie Française; lost his 19-year-old daughter in a boating accident on the Seine; and entered the political arena. When Napoleon III seized power in 1851, this passionate advocate of free speech, universal suffrage, and social justice was made distinctly unwelcome, particularly after he declared the new king a traitor of France. Fearing for his life, Hugo left the country and lived in exile until 1870 when he triumphantly returned to France and was elected to the senate. By the time he died in 1885 he was a national hero; his funeral cortege through the streets of Paris is the stuff of legend, and his body was one of the first to be buried in the Panthéon (p. 177). The museum's collection charts this dramatic existence through the author's drawings, original manuscripts, notes, furniture, and personal objects, which are displayed in small rooms that re-create the ambience and the spirit of the original lodgings.

6 place des Vosges, 4th arrond. www.maisonsvictorhugo.paris.fr. ℂ **01-42-72-10-16.** Free admission to permanent collection except during certain temporary exhibits. Tues–Sun 10am–6pm. Métro: St-Paul, Bastille, or Chemin-Vert.

Musée Carnavalet ★★★ MUSEUM   *Note: The museum closed for extensive renovations in December 2016 and is expected to remain closed until 2019.* Paris has served as a backdrop to centuries' worth of dramatic

THE bridges OF PARIS

Despite its name (*neuf* means "new"), the **Pont Neuf** (Quai du Louvre to Quai de Conti) is the oldest bridge in Paris. The bridge was an instant hit when it was inaugurated by Henri IV in 1607 (its ample sidewalks, combined with the fact that it was the first bridge sans houses, made it a delight for pedestrians), and it still is. For a quiet picnic spot, take the stairs by the statue of Henri IV (in the center of the span) down to the **Square du Vert Galant.**

The **Pont des Arts** (Quai François Mitterrand to Quai de Conti) was originally constructed at the beginning of the 19th century. Delicately arching over the river, the iron pedestrian bridge is still the most romantic bridge in the city—with its splendid view of the Île de la Cité and its itinerant artists sketching along the railing—in spite of the fact that over-enthusiastic lovers attached so many locks to the railing that the barrier actually fell over and has now been replaced with plastic screens. It's best to avoid any symbolic gestures (like writing your names on a lock, attaching it to the railing, and throwing away the key) and opt for romantic selfies instead.

A modern way to get from the Left to the Right bank is via the **Passerelle Simone de Beauvoir** (Quai de Bercy to Quai François Mauriac). A graceful pedestrian passage, the bridge consists of two arching bands of oak and steel, which intertwine and cross the river without the support of a central pillar. The central lens-shaped structure was constructed by the Eiffel factory (founded by Gustave).

With its enormous pillars topped by gilded statuary, it's hard to miss the **Pont Alexandre III** (Cours de la Reine to Quai d'Orsay). Linking the vast esplanade of the Invalides with the glass-domed Grand Palais, this elegant bridge fits right in with its grand surroundings. The span was named after Czar Alexander III of Russia, and inaugurated at the opening of the Paris Exposition of 1900.

Incredibly, the small and lovely **Pont Marie** (Quai des Célestins to Quai d'Anjou–Ile St-Louis), composed of three gentle arches, was once loaded down by some 50 houses. The structure could not hold its charge, and during a flood in 1658, the Seine washed away two of its arches and 20 houses fell into the water. The tragedy, which claimed 60 lives, got city officials to thinking, and finally, in 1769, homesteading on bridges was outlawed.

events, from Roman takeovers to barbarian invasions, from coronations to decapitations to the birth of the modern French republic. These stories and others are told at this fascinating museum through objects, paintings, and interiors. The collection is displayed in two extraordinary 17th-century mansions—works of art in their own right. Starting with a prehistoric canoe from 4600 B.C. and continuing into the 20th century, the history of Paris is illustrated with items as diverse as Gallo-Roman figurines, Napoleon's toiletry kit, and an 18th-century portrait of Benjamin Franklin painted when he was the U.S. ambassador to France.

16 rue des Francs-Bourgeois, 3rd arrond. www.carnavalet.paris.fr. ℂ **01-44-59-58-58.** Free admission for permanent collection except during certain temporary exhibits. Tues–Sun 10am–6pm. Métro: St-Paul or Chemin Vert.

With one or two exceptions, all city museums are free (permanent collections only), all the time. That includes the following cultural cornucopias:

- Musée d'Art Moderne de la Ville de Paris (p. 159)
- Maison de Balzac (p. 159)
- Musée Bourdelle (p. 190)
- Musée Cognacq-Jay (p. 152)
- Petit Palais (p. 163)
- Maison de Victor Hugo (p. 150)
- Musée Zadkine (p. 180), except during temporary exhibits
- Musée de la Vie Romantique (p. 148)

You can also get into all national museums free of charge on the first Sunday of every month (seasonal restrictions may apply). Expect even bigger crowds than your usual Sunday. National museums include:

- Musée du Louvre (p. 138), October to March
- Musée National des Arts Asiatiques Guimet (p. 161)
- Musée National Eugène Delacroix (p. 180)
- Musée National du Moyen Age/ Thermes et Hôtel de Cluny (p. 177)
- Musée de l'Orangerie (p. 136)
- Musée d'Orsay (p. 185)
- Musée Rodin (p. 188)
- Picasso Paris (p. 154)

Musée Cognacq-Jay ★ MUSEUM   This bite-size museum offers a bite-sized taste of the finer side of 18th-century France. Its founder, Ernest Cognacq, led a rags-to-riches life: At 12 years old, he was selling odds and ends as an itinerant merchant, and by the end of his life he was the owner of a fabulously successful department store (the now-defunct La Samaritaine) with a prodigious private art collection. His rich assortment of 18th-century art and furniture make up the contents of this small museum, which is housed in a lovely *hôtel particulier* (mansion). The collection leans heavily toward the romantic side of the century, with many lesser works by famous artists like Chardin and Fragonard, but what's most impressive here is the furniture, like the bed *"à la polonaise"* draped in blue damask and framed in gilt, or the exquisite Louis XVI–era writing table with geometric wood inlay.

8 rue Elzévir, 3rd arrond. www.cognacq-jay.paris.fr. © **01-40-27-07-21.** Free admission to permanent collection except during certain temporary exhibits. Tues–Sun 10am–6pm. Métro: St-Paul or Chemin Vert.

Musée d'Art et Histoire du Judaïsme ★★ MUSEUM   Housed in the magnificent Hôtel de Saint Aignan, one of the many palatial 17th-century mansions that dot the Marais, this museum chronicles the art and history of the Jewish people in France and in Europe. It features a superb collection of objects of both artistic and cultural significance (a splendid Italian Renaissance torah ark, a German gold and silver Hanukkah menorah, a 17th-century Dutch illustrated Torah scroll, documents from the Dreyfus trial), which is interspersed with texts, drawings, and photos telling the story of the Jews and explaining the basics of both Ashkenazi and Sephardic traditions. You'll do a lot of reading here; documentation is translated in English, but if you're feeling lazy there's also an informative audioguide. The final rooms include a collection of works by Jewish artists, including Modigliani, Soutine, Lipchitz, and Chagall. Be prepared for airportlike security at the entrance.

71 rue du Temple, 3rd arrond. www.mahj.org. (☎) **01-53-01-86-60.** Admission 9€ adults, 6€ ages 18–25, free 17 and under. Mon–Fri 11am–6pm; Sun 10am–6pm. Métro: Rambuteau or Hôtel de Ville.

Musée de la Chasse et de la Nature ★ MUSEUM

If you can get over the fact that it's a museum dedicated to hunting, this small museum makes for a pleasant outing. You'll find the expected taxidermied animals, but they are discreetly presented among an elegant collection of paintings, tapestries, sculptures, and even contemporary art. Each room has a theme: For example, the blond wood-paneled Salle Cerf et Loup takes on the imagery of the stag and the wolf, illustrated in paintings by artists as disparate as Renaissance-era Lucas Cranach and 20th-century fauvist André Derain. The emphasis is not so much on the kill, as the symbolism behind the images: In the Middle Ages, the stag, which represented Christ, and the wolf, which represented the Devil, could coexist, a theme that is echoed in the 16th- and 17th-century tapestries that cover the walls. Once you've sauntered through rooms dedicated to dogs, birds, horses, and even unicorns, you will walk smack into the trophy room, where discretion is abandoned and hunting is blatantly celebrated in all its gory glory. Intricately inlaid rifles and the heads of various exotic animals will bring you face to face with the reality of this controversial sport (look out for the mounted head with moving eyes!). Still, there is something intriguing about this place; it reminds you that the relationship between humans and animals dates to well before there were naturalists and environmentalists, and if that relationship was filled with animosity and fear, it was also tinged with a sort of mystical respect.

62 rue des Archives, 3rd arrond. www.chassenature.org. (☎) **01-53-01-92-40.** Admission 8€ adults, 6€ ages 18–26 from EU countries, free 17 and under. Tues, Thurs–Sun 11am–6pm; Wed 11am–10pm. Métro: Rambuteau.

Couple overlooking the Seine.

Musée des Arts et Métiers ★★ MUSEUM   If you've read Umberto Eco's novel, you'll probably want to come here just to see Foucault's original pendulum swing in the church of St-Martin-des-Champs, but there are plenty of other reasons to spend a couple of hours at this temple of technology. The Musée harbors sterling examples of just about every discovery that made the mechanical world possible. True techies will linger over the many displays of gearboxes, steam engines, and other historic gizmos; the less technically inclined will probably prefer the first versions of telephones, movie cameras, and toasters. There are a lot of "firsts" here, like the first omnibus (a "high-speed" steam vehicle built in 1873), and the Blériot XI (the first plane to cross the English Channel), as well as the earliest examples of phonographs, light-bulbs, and tape decks. Those "new" antiques—the typewriters, record players, and VCRs on display in those old wooden cases—drive home the fact that the technological revolution is ongoing, and today's wonders will be tomorrow's curiosities.

60 rue Réaumur, 3rd arrond. www.arts-et-metiers.net. © **01-53-01-82-00.** Admission 6.50€ adults, 4.50€ students, free 17 and under. Tues–Wed and Fri–Sun 10am–6pm; Thurs 10am–9:30pm. Métro: Arts et Métiers.

Picasso Paris ★★★ MUSEUM   This shrine to all things Picasso is housed in the stunning Hôtel Salé, a 17th-century mansion built by salt-tax farmer Pierre Aubert, whose position gave the mansion its name—Salé means "salty." This unique institution valiantly strives to make sense of the incredibly diverse output of this prolific genius: Some 400 carefully selected paintings, sculptures, collages, and drawings are presented in a more or less chronological and thematic order, no small task when dealing with an artist who experimented with every style, from neoclassicism to surrealism to his own flamboyantly abstract inventions. Impressionist portraits ("Portrait of Gustave Coquiot," 1901), Cubist explorations ("Man with Guitar," 1911), mannerist allegories ("The Race," 1922), and deconstructionist forms ("Reclining Nude," 1932) make up only part of his oeuvre, which has been estimated to include some 50,000 works. Not only that, Picasso often worked in wildly different styles during the same period, sometimes treating the same subjects. For example, the rounded yet realistic lovers dancing in "La Danse des Villageois" painted in 1922, hang next to two forms in a blaze of color representing "The Kiss" painted in 1925. There's also a sampling of the somewhat disturbing portraits of the

Picasso Paris museum.

Lines at Paris's museums and other attractions keep growing, and visitor frustration levels are rising accordingly. Even smaller museums can have long lines during school holidays and special temporary exhibits. To avoid wasting precious hours standing in queues, buy your tickets ahead of time whenever possible, either online or at an **Fnac** store (www.fnac.fr). They may cost 1€ or 2€ more than at the door, but e-ticket in hand, you can generally breeze past everyone; just follow the signs marked *billet coupe-file*. A **Paris Passlib' card** (http://booking.parisinfo.com) will also get you to the front of the line at many, but not all, museums.

many women in his life, including portraits of Dora Maar and Marie-Thérèse, both painted in 1937. On the top floor is Picasso's private collection, which includes works by artists he admired like Courbet and Cézanne, as well as paintings by his friends, who included masters like Braque and Matisse.

All in all, what you see on the walls is less than 10% of the 5,000 works in the museum's collection; the presentation rotates every couple of years. Unless you enjoy waiting in long lines exposed to the elements, **buy your ticket in advance online;** you'll usually walk right in with your e-ticket.

5 rue de Thorigny, 3rd arrond. www.museepicassoparis.fr. ⓒ **01-85-56-00-36.** Admission 13€ adults, free 17 and under. Tues–Fri 10:30am–6pm; Sat–Sun 9:30am–6pm. Métro: St-Paul or Chemin Vert.

Place des Vosges ★★★ SQUARE   Possibly the prettiest square in the city, the Place des Vosges combines elegance, greenery, and quiet. Nowhere in Paris will you find such a unity of Renaissance-style architecture; the entire square is bordered by 17th-century brick town houses, each conforming to rules set down by Henri IV himself, under which runs arched arcades. In the center is a garden with a geometric arrangement of lush lawns, fountains, and trees. At the epicenter is a huge equestrian statue of Louis XIII, during whose reign (1610–43) the square enjoyed a golden age of festivals and tournaments. But it was a tournament in a previous century that proved pivotal to the creation of this square. In the 16th century, a royal palace called the Hôtel des Tournelles stood on this site. In 1559, an organized combat was held there, during which the current monarch, feisty Henri II, defeated several opponents. Feeling pleased with himself, he decided to fight Montgomery, the captain of his guard. A badly aimed lance resulted in Henri's untimely death; his wife, Catherine de Medici, was so distraught she had the palace demolished. His descendant, Henri IV, took advantage of the free space to construct a royal square. Over the centuries, a number of celebrities lived in the 36 houses, including Mme. de Sévigny and Victor Hugo (now the Maison de Victor Hugo; p. 150). Today the homes are for the rich, as are many of the chic boutiques under the arcades, but the park, the fountains, and the children's playground are for everyone.

4th arrond. Métro: St-Paul.

Champs-Élysées, Trocadéro & Western Paris (8th, 16th & 17th Arrondissements)

Decidedly posh, this is one of the wealthiest parts of the city in both per capita earnings and cultural institutions. While the **Champs-Élysées** is more glitz than glory, the surrounding neighborhoods offer high-end shops and restaurants as well as some terrific museums and concert halls. This is also where you will find grand architectural gestures, like the **Arc de Triomphe** and the **Place de la Concorde,** which bookend the Champs, and the **Grand Palais** and **Petit Palais,** leftovers from the legendary 1900 Universal Exposition.

Arc de Triomphe ★★★ MONUMENT   If there is one monument that symbolizes "La Gloire," or the glory of France, it is this giant triumphal arch. Crowning the Champs-Élysées, this mighty archway both celebrates the military victories of the French army and memorializes the sacrifices of its soldiers. Over time, it has become an icon of the Republic and a setting for some of its most emotional moments: the laying in state of the coffin of Victor Hugo in 1885, the burial in 1921 of the ashes of an unknown soldier who fought in World War I, and General de Gaulle's pregnant pause under the arch before striding down the Champs-Élysées before the cheering crowds after the Liberation in 1944.

It took a certain amount of chutzpah to come up with the idea to build such a shrine, and sure enough, it was Napoleon who instigated it. In 1806, still glowing after his stunning victory at Austerlitz, the Emperor decided to erect a monument to the Imperial Army, along the lines of a Roman triumphal arch. The architect chosen was Jean-François Chalgrin, who drew inspiration from Rome's Arch of Titus, though he abandoned the columns and made Napoleon's arch a whopping 50m (163 ft.) high and 45m (147 ft.) wide, the largest of its type on the planet. Unfortunately, the defeat at Waterloo put an end to the Empire before the arch was finished and construction came to an abrupt halt. It wasn't until 1823 that building got going again; it was finally finished in 1836 by Louis-Philippe.

The arch is covered with bas-reliefs and sculptures, the most famous of which is the enormous "Depart of the Volunteers" of 1792, better known as the Marseillaise, by François Rude, showing winged, female Liberty leading the charge of Revolutionary soldiers. Just above is one of the many smaller panels detailing Napoleonic battles—in this case, Aboukir—wherein the emperor trods victoriously over the Ottomans. At the base of the arch is the Tomb of the Unknown Soldier, over which a flame is relit every evening at 6:30pm. The inscription, which was added after WWI, reads ICI REPOSE UN SOLDAT FRANÇAIS MORT POUR LA PATRIE, 1914–1918 ("Here lies a French soldier who died for his country").

Don't even think about crossing the traffic circle; instead take the underpass near the Champs-Élysées Métro entrance. You can visit the area under the arch free of charge, but if you want to enjoy the view from the rooftop terrace, you have to pay. You also have to climb 284 stairs to get there (only the very young, the very old, and the handicapped get to use the elevator). Though you are not as high up the viewing platforms on the Eiffel Tower, the panorama is quite impressive. Directly below, 12 boulevards radiate from the star-shaped intersection (hence the moniker "Etoile"), and out front is the long sweep of the Champs-Élysées, ending at the obelisk of the Place de la Concorde, behind which lurks the Louvre. You can pick out many of the most famous monuments, including Sacré Coeur and the Eiffel Tower; to the west are the skyscrapers of La Défense, including the huge, hollowed-out Grande Arche, a modern version of the one you are standing on. The viewing terrace is closed in bad weather.

Place Charles de Gaulle, 8th arrond. www.monuments-nationaux.fr. ℂ **01-55-37-73-77.** Admission 12€ adults, 9€ ages 18–24, free 17 and under. Apr–Sept daily 10am–11pm; Oct–Mar daily 10am–10:30pm. Métro: Charles-de-Gaulle–Etoile.

Fondation Louis Vuitton ★ MUSEUM   Designed by mega-architect Frank Gehry, this stunning contemporary art museum is swathed in a mass of billowing "sails" of glass, giving the impression that it is about to sail off into the lush greenery of the Bois de Boulogne, a large park on the western edge of the city (p. 197). Once you've taken in the arty outside, you have two choices: (1) stand in line to see the sophisticated temporary collections of ultra-contemporary art, or (2) go explore the Bois de Boulogne's alleys, gardens, and lakes. If you choose the former, be sure to buy an online ticket in advance: You'll get a time slot, which will considerably reduce the time you spend in line. If you are not big on heady modern and conceptual art, you should probably stick to option number 2.

8 ave. du Mahatma Gandhi, Bois de Boulogne, 16th arrond. www.fondationlouis vuitton.fr. ℂ **01-40-69-96-00.** 14€ adults, 10€ ages 18–26, 5€ artists and children 3–17, free 2 and under. Mon, Wed–Thurs noon–7pm, Fri noon–11pm, Sat–Sun 11am–8pm. Métro: Les Sablons or Porte Maillot. Shuttle bus 1€ from Place Charles de Gaulle–Etoile, corner of ave. Friedland.

Galerie–Musée Baccarat ★ MUSEUM   The mansion of Marie-Laure de Noailles, an early-20th-century patron of the arts, is an ideal setting for this homage to crystal at its most luxurious. Before you enter the small museum section, take a peek at the **Cristal Room,** a sumptuous restaurant where Marie-Laure and her friends would feel right at home. While the collection rotates, you can be sure the exposition will include exquisite crystal glasses, vases, plates and other objects made by the house of Baccarat over the last 250 years. When you have finished gaping, have a seat in the lavish ballroom and watch a short film (in English on request) that will make you appreciate the amount of the time, effort, and skill that goes into creating these works of art and understand why a simple wine glass starts at over 100€. Speaking of which, when you go back downstairs, check out the boutique, which is almost as impressive as the museum (and doesn't cost 10€ to get into). Be sure to visit the bathrooms—probably the only ones in the city with chandeliers in the stalls.

11 place des États-Unis, 16th arrond. www.baccarat.com. ℰ **01-40-22-11-00.** Museum admission 10€ adults, 7€ students under 25, free 17 and under. Museum Mon, Wed–Sat 10am–6pm. Métro: Iéna or Boissière.

Grand Palais ★ HISTORIC SITE/MUSEUM   Built for the 1900 Universal Exhibition, this huge exhibition hall spans a total area of 72,000 sq. m (775,000 sq. ft.), with the biggest glass roof in Europe—an elegant lighting solution, since the building was constructed prior to electricity. After years of renovations, the Grand Palais is now as gorgeous as it was when it opened. It hosts a changing array of sporting and cultural events, as well as blockbuster temporary art exhibits (previous ones have included Rodin and Pissarro) in the adjacent gallery. These tend to be mob scenes, so it pays to buy tickets in advance if you are in town during a big show. The entrance to the big exhibits is usually at the side entrance, 3 ave. du Général Eisenhower.

Place Clemenceau, 8th arrond. www.grandpalais.fr. ℰ **01-44-13-17-17.** Opening hours and admission prices vary according to the exhibitions and events. Métro: Champs-Élysées–Clémenceau.

La Cité de l'Architecture et du Patrimoine ★ INSTITUTE/ MUSEUM   Created to promote French architecture and showcase evolving trends, this vast institution (located in the Palais de Chaillot), includes a museum, a research facility, and a top-notch school of architecture. On the ground floor, the enormous Galerie des Moulages, with its vaulting skylights, exhibits casts of the gems of French architecture from the 12th to the 18th centuries. Commissioned in the late 19th century as a way of documenting France's architectural heritage, the project turned out to be an invaluable tool when it came to restoring the ravages of two world wars. The cast of the beautiful Queen of Sheba, for example—the original of which graced the face of Reims cathedral—made it possible to create a faithful reproduction after the original was seriously damaged in World War I.

On the second floor, you'll dip into the cool waters of 20th- and 21st-century architecture, represented by intricate architectural models of structures like Piano and Rogers' Centre Pompidou (p. 148) and Rem Koolhaus's Maison Lemoine, a three-layer home built in Floriac, France, for a paralyzed man and his family. Don't miss clambering through a reconstruction of an apartment from Le Corbusier's Cité Radieuse, a shockingly (for the late 1940s) modern approach to urban housing.

1 place du Trocadéro, 16th arrond. www.citechaillot.fr. ℰ **01-58-51-52-00.** Admission 8€ adults, 6€ ages 18–25, free 17 and under. Wed and Fri–Mon 11am–7pm; Thurs 11am–9pm. Métro: Trocadéro.

La Madeleine ★ CHURCH   As you peer up the rue Royale from the Place de la Concorde, you'll see something that very closely resembles a Roman temple. It is in fact a church, one that owes its unusual form to its equally singular history. In 1763, architect Pierre Constant d'Ivry laid the first stone of a church that would include a neoclassical facade with multiple columns. He didn't get very far. First the architect died, and then the Revolution broke out, during which construction ground to a halt. No one knew what to do with the site until Napoleon finally strode onto the scene and declared that it would become the Temple de la Gloire, to honor the glorious victories of his army. He wanted something "solid" because he was sure that the monument would last "thousands of years." Unfortunately for him, military defeats and mounting debt would again delay construction until Napoleon decided that maybe it wouldn't be such a bad idea to make it a church after all—that way Rome would foot the bill. Once Napoleon was out of the picture for good, inertia took over the project again, and it wasn't until 1842, under the Restoration, that La Madeleine was finally consecrate.

The inside of the church is pretty dark, thanks to a lack of windows, but there are actually some interesting works of art here, if you can make them out in the gloom. On the left as you enter is François Rude's "Baptism of Christ"; farther on is James Pradier's sculpture "La Marriage de la Vierge."

Place de la Madeleine, 8th arrond. www.eglise-lamadeleine.com. (C) **01-44-51-69-00.** Free admission. Daily 9:30am–7pm. Métro: Madeleine.

Maison de Balzac ★ MUSEUM   Fleeing his creditors, in 1840, writer Honoré de Balzac rented this small house in what was then the village of Passy, where he lived for 7 years under an assumed name. He also worked like a demon: He was capable of writing for up to 20 hours a day for weeks at a time. The five rooms of Balzac's apartments are hung with paintings and portraits of his family and friends, including several of Madame Hanska, whom he finally married after 18 years of passionate correspondence. There are also a few manuscripts and personal objects, including his turquoise-encrusted cane, which was the talk of Paris, and his monogrammed coffee pot, which kept him going through the marathon work sessions. In his office is the little table where he wrote "The Human Comedy," "a witness," he wrote to Madame Hanska, "to my worries, my miseries, my distress, my joys, everything . . . my arm almost wore out its surface from taking the same path over and over again."

47 rue Raynouard, 16th arrond. http://maisondebalzac.paris.fr. (C) **01-55-74-41-80.** Admission free for permanent collection. Tues–Sun 10am–6pm. Métro: Passy or La Muette.

Musée d'Art Moderne de la Ville de Paris ★ MUSEUM   Housed in a wing of the massive Palais de Tokyo, this municipal modern-art museum covers ground similar to that of the Pompidou Center but on a smaller scale. Picasso, Rouault, Picabia—the big names are all there, but their works are often lesser-known, making the museum a fab spot for discovering significant paintings you may never have seen before. Highlights include a room dedicated to surrealism (the personal collection of André Breton) and a series of paintings by Delaunay and Léger. The contemporary section, from 1960 on, covers seriously abstract movements like Fluxus and Figuration. In recent years, the collection has acquired several new works from the 1980s on, but for the most recent cutting-edge ideas, you are probably better off at the Palais de Tokyo museum (p. 162) in the wing next door. There's also a huge room covered with brilliant wall murals by Raoul Dufy ("La Fée Electricité"), as well as another vast room with two enormous versions of "La Danse" by Matisse.

11 ave. du Président-Wilson, 16th arrond. www.mam.paris.fr. © **01-53-67-40-00.** Free admission to permanent collections. Tues–Sun 10am–6pm (until 10pm Thurs during temporary exhibitions). Métro: Iéna or Alma-Marceau.

Musée de l'Homme ★★ MUSEUM   The primitive art housed in this museum once inspired Picasso. Today, it is a state-of-the-art anthropology museum showcasing the richness of human culture and the evolution of mankind. In true existential Sartre fashion, this is where you come to reflect on the hard questions: What does it mean to be human? Where do we come from? And where are we headed—especially in the light of climatic change? The answer is there's no one answer, but it's great thinking about it as you work your way around the exhibits—everything from a Cro-Magnon skull to André Pierre Pinson's anatomical waxworks (fabulous, intricate examples of anatomy from the French Enlightenment and a gallery of 19th-c. busts designed to illustrate the diversity of human beings). The building itself is a showpiece. Set in the Passy wing of the Palais de Chaillot—built for the 1937 World Fair on the site of the former 1878 Trocadéro Palace—it is an Art Deco treasure filled with natural light, thanks to rows of floor-to-ceiling windows that look out onto the most famous icon of all, the Eiffel Tower. For the best views, head to **Café Lucy,** an ultra-modern cafeteria on the 2nd floor.

17 place du Trocadéro, 16th arrond. www.museedelhomme.fr. © **01-44-05-72-72.** Admission 10€ adults, 8€ students and children 13–25, free 12 and under. Wed–Mon 10am–6pm. Métro: Trocadéro.

Musée Jacquemart-André ★★★ MUSEUM   The love child of a couple of passionate art collectors, Nélie Jacquemart and Edouard André, this terrific, bite-size museum takes the form of a 19th-century mansion filled with fine art and decorative treasures, including Botticelli's "Virgin and Child." And because of its size, you can see a wide range of beautiful things here without wearing yourself to a frazzle.

The house itself is a work of art: At its inauguration in 1875, the marble Winter Garden with its spectacular double staircase was the talk of the town, and the awe-inspiring second floor—with works by masters like Bellini, Uccello, and Mantegna—is like walking into a felt-lined jewel box. An impressive assortment of Louis XV– and Louis XVI–era decorative objects are also in evidence, as are the paintings of Fragonard, Boucher, and Chardin. To honor the artists that influenced these French painters, the couple also amassed a number of 17th-century Dutch paintings, including a jaunty "Portrait of a Man" by Frans Hals, and Rembrandt's shadowy and powerful "Pilgrims at Emmaus," where the figure of Christ is backlit and it is only the look on his tablemate's face that reveals the identity of the mysterious guest.

Leave time to eat a light lunch or have tea in the Jacquemart-André's lovely dining room, where you can gaze up at a magnificent fresco by Tiepolo on the ceiling (see "The Top Tearooms," p. 125).

158 bd. Haussmann, 8th arrond. www.musee-jacquemart-andre.com. ✆ **01-45-62-11-59.** Admission 14€ adults, 11€ students and children 7–17, free 6 and under. Daily 10am–6pm (until 8.30pm on Thurs during temporary exhibitions). Métro: Miromesnil or St-Philippe-du-Roule.

Musée Marmottan Monet ★★ MUSEUM Boasting the world's largest collection of Monets, this museum offers an in-depth look at this prolific genius and some of his talented contemporaries. Among the dozens of Monet's canvases is the one that provided the name of an entire artistic movement. Pressed to give a name to this misty play of light on the water for the catalog for the 1874 exposition that included Cézanne, Pissarro, Renoir, and Degas, Monet apparently said, "Put 'impression.'" The painting, "Impression, Sunrise," certainly made one, as did the show—thereafter the group was referred to as the Impressionists. Monet never stopped being fascinated with the interaction of light and water, be it in a relatively traditional portrait of his wife and daughter against the stormy sea in "On the Beach at Trouville," or in an almost abstract blend of blues and grays in "Charring Cross Bridge." Monet was also interested in light's transformation; he often painted the same subject at different times of the day. One of his famous series on the Cathedral of Rouen is here: "Effect of the Sun at the End of the Day." Fans of the artist's endless water-lily series will not be disappointed; the collection includes dozens of paintings of his beloved garden in Giverny.

Paintings by Renoir, Sisley, Degas, Gauguin, and other contemporaries can also be seen in the light-filled rooms of this 19th-century mansion, which belonged to art collector Paul Marmottan. Upstairs is a room dedicated to the only female member of the group, Berthe Morisot, known for her intimate portraits and scenes of family life.

2 rue Louis-Boilly, 16th arrond. www.marmottan.fr. ✆ **01-44-96-50-33.** Admission 11€ adults, 7.50€ students under 25 and ages 8–18, free 7 and under. Tues–Wed and Fri–Sun 10am–6pm; Thurs 10am–9pm. Métro: La Muette. RER: Bouilainvilliers.

Musée National des Arts Asiatiques Guimet ★★ MUSEUM Founded in 1889 by collector and industrialist Emile Guimet, today this vast collection of Asian art is one of the largest and most complete in Europe. Here you'll find room after room of exquisite works from Afghanistan, India, Tibet, Nepal, China, Vietnam, Korea, Japan, and other Asian nations. You could spend an entire day here, or you could pick and choose regions of interest (displays are arranged geographically); the audioguide is a good bet for finding standouts and providing cultural context. Highlights include a marvelous Tibetan bronze sculpture ("Hevajra and Nairâtmya") of a multiheaded god embracing a ferocious goddess with eight faces and 16 arms; a blissfully serene stone figure of a 12th-century Cambodian king ("Jayavarman VII") who presided over a short-lived Khmer renaissance; and superb Chinese scroll paintings, including a magnificent 17th-century view of the Jingting mountains in autumn.

6 place d'Iéna, 16th arrond. www.guimet.fr. ℭ **01-56-52-53-00.** Admission to permanent collection 7.50€ adults, 5.50€ ages 18–25, free 17 and under (and under 26 from the EU). Wed–Mon 10am–6pm. Métro: Iéna.

Musée Nissim de Camondo ★★ MUSEUM   Having made a fortune in his business ventures, in 1914 Count Moïse de Camondo built a mansion in the style of the Petit Trianon at Versailles and furnished it with rare examples of 18th-century furniture, paintings, and art objects (like a series of six Aubusson tapestries illustrating the fables of La Fontaine and a pair of bronze vases covered with petrified wood that once belonged to Marie Antoinette). After the count's death in 1935, the house and everything in it was left to the state as a museum, named after the count's son, who was killed fighting in World War I. The family's troubles did not stop there—in 1945, the count's daughter and her family were deported and died at Auschwitz. This little-visited museum is a delight. The count's will stipulated that the house be left exactly "as is" when it was transformed into a museum; as a result you can wander through a fully equipped kitchen, a gigantic tiled bathroom, and salons filled with gilded mirrors, inlaid tables, and Beauvais tapestries—all in the same configuration as when Camondo lived there. Be sure to pick up a free English audioguide. Tickets can be combined with the Musée des Arts Décoratifs (p. 137; 13€).

63 rue de Monceau, 8th arrond. www.lesartsdecoratifs.fr. ℭ **01-53-89-06-40.** Admission 9€ adults, 6.50€ ages 18–25, free 17 and under. Wed–Sun 10am–5:30pm. Métro: Villiers.

Palais de Tokyo ★★ MUSEUM/PERFORMANCE SPACE   If you're traveling with cranky teenagers who've had enough of La Vieille France, or if you're also sick of endless rendezvous with history, this is the place to come for a blast of contemporary madness. This vast art space not only offers a rotating bundle of expositions, events, and other happenings but is also one of the only museums in Paris that stays open until midnight. While some might quibble about whether or not the works on display are really art, there's no denying that this place is a lot of fun. You'll find a completely different crowd here, one that is generally young and intense. There's no permanent collection, just continuous temporary exhibits, installations, and events, which include live performances and film screenings. The center, whose mission includes nurturing, promoting, and providing studio space for emerging artists, is one of the largest sites devoted to contemporary creativity in Europe. Check the website for what's on during your visit. In warm weather, you can eat on the splendid terrace of its chic, neo-Art-Deco brasserie, **Monsieur Bleu,** which has Eiffel Tower views.

13 ave. du Président-Wilson, 16th arrond. www.palaisdetokyo.com. ℭ **01-81-97-35-88.** Admission 12€ adults, 9€ ages 18–25, free 17 and under. Wed–Mon noon–midnight. Métro: Iéna.

Parc Monceau ★★ PARK/GARDENS   Located in a posh residential neighborhood and ringed by stately mansions, this small park is the brainchild of the duke of Chartres (the future Philippe Egalité), who commissioned a fanciful garden in 1769 filled with **"folies,"** faux romantic ruins, temples, and antiquities inspired by exotic far-away places. Don't be surprised to stumble upon a minaret, a windmill, or a mini-Egyptian pyramid here; the most famous *folie* is the **Naumachie,** a large oval pond surrounded in part by Corinthian columns. The park has had several makeovers over the centuries, but it is still essentially an English-style garden, complete with wooded glens and hillocks. There is a sizeable **playground** in the southwest corner, as well as a **merry-go-round** near the north entrance, where a **round pavilion** is surrounded by columns; the Duke of Chartres used to keep a small apartment on the second floor from which he could see the entire park.

35 bd. de Courcelles, 8th arrond. www.paris.fr. Free admission. 8am–sundown. Métro: Monceau or Villiers.

Petit Palais ★★ MUSEUM   The collection may not be exhaustive, and you may not see any world-famous works, but you will enjoy a wonderful mix of periods and artists at this small-ish municipal fine arts museum, whose chronology stretches from the ancient Greeks to World War I. The paintings of masters like Monet, Ingres, and Rubens are displayed here, as well as the Art Nouveau dining room of Hector Guimard, and the exquisite multilayered glass vases of Emile Gallé. Those interested in earlier works will find Greek vases, Italian Renaissance majolica, and a small collection of 16th-century astrolabes and gold-and-crystal traveling clocks. Intricately carved ivory panels and delicately sculpted wood sculptures (including a grinning, long-locked Saint Barbara who looks like she is about to burst out in a fit of the giggles) stand out in the small Medieval section, and a series of rooms dedicated to 17th-century Dutch painters like Steen and van Ostade is considered one of the best collections of its kind in France (after the Louvre). Refresh yourself after your visit at the cafe in the gorgeous inner courtyard.

Avenue Winston Churchill, 8th arrond. www.petitpalais.paris.fr. © **01-53-43-40-00.** Free admission to permanent collection. Tues–Sun 10am–6pm (until 9pm Fri during temporary exhibitions). Métro: Champs-Élysées–Clémenceau.

Place de la Concorde ★★★ SQUARE   Like an exclamation point at the end of the Champs-Élysées, the Place de la Concorde is a magnificent arrangement of fountains and statues, held together in the center by a 3,000-year-old Egyptian obelisk (a gift to France from Egypt in 1829). When it was inaugurated in 1763 during the reign of Louis XV, this vast plaza was on the outer edges of the city; today, though part of an urban landscape, it still gives the impression of open space. If it weren't for the cars hurtling around the obelisk like racers in the Grand Prix, this would be a delightful spot for a breath of fresh air (if you feel compelled to cross to the obelisk and you value your life, find the stoplight and cross there).

It's hard to believe that this magnificent square was once bathed in blood, but during the Revolution, it was a grisly stage for public executions: King Louis XVI and his wife, Marie-Antoinette, both bowed down to the guillotine here, as did many prominent figures of the Revolution, including Danton, Camille Desmoulins, and Robespierre. Once the monarchy was back in place, the plaza hosted less lethal public events like festivals and trade expositions. In 1835 the *place* was given its current look: Two immense fountains, copies of those in St-Peter's Square in Rome, play on either side of the obelisk; 18 sumptuous columns decorated with shells, mermaids, sea horses, and other sea creatures each hold two lamps; and eight statues representing the country's largest cities survey the scene from the edges of the action. On the west side are the famous **Marly Horses,** actually copies of the originals, which were suffering from erosion and have since been restored and housed in the Louvre. On the north side of the square are two palatial buildings that date from the square's 18th-century origins: On the east side is the **Hôtel de la Marine,** and on the west side is the **Hôtel Crillon,** where on February 6, 1778, a treaty was signed by Louis XVI and Benjamin Franklin, among others, wherein France officially recognized the United States as an independent country and became its ally.

8th arrond. Métro: Concorde.

Montmartre (18th Arrondissement)

There are few places in this city that will fill you with the urge to belt out sappy show tunes like the *butte* (hill) of Montmartre. Admiring the view from the esplanade in front of the oddly Byzantine **Basilique du Sacré-Coeur,** you'll feel like you have finally arrived in Paris, and that you now understand what all the fuss is about. Try to ignore the tour buses and crowds mobbing the church and the hideously touristy **place du Tertre** behind you and wander off into the warren of streets toward the **place des Abbesses,** or up **rue Lepic,** where you'll eventually stumble across the **Moulin de la Galette** and **Moulin du Radet,** the two surviving windmills (there were once 30 on this hill). We have a walking tour on p. 200 which will lead you to these less-touristed gems and others.

Basilique du Sacré-Coeur ★ CHURCH   Poised at the apex of the hill like a *grande dame* in crinolines, this odd-looking 19th-century basilica has become one of the city's most famous landmarks. After France's defeat in the Franco-Prussian War, prominent Catholics vowed to build a church consecrated to the Sacred Heart of Christ as a way of making up for whatever sins the French may have committed that had made God so angry at them. Since 1885, prayers for humanity have been continually chanted here (the church is a pilgrimage site, so dress and behave accordingly). This multidomed confection was inspired by the Byzantine churches of Turkey and Italy. Construction began in 1875, and the church was completed in 1914, though it wasn't consecrated until 1919 because of World War I. The white stone was chosen for

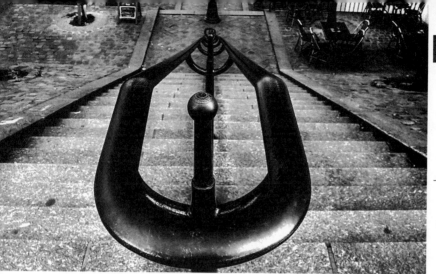

Stairs in Montmartre.

its self-cleaning capabilities: When it rains, it secretes a chalky substance that acts as a fresh coat of paint. The interior of the church includes a breathtaking mosaic ceiling, installed in the 1920s. Most visitors climb the 300 stairs to the dome, where the splendid view of the city extends over 48km (30 miles).

Parvis de la Basilique, 18th arrond. www.sacre-coeur-montmartre.com. ℂ **01-53-41-89-00.** Free admission to basilica, joint ticket to dome and crypt 8€ adults, 5€ ages 4–16, free under 4. Basilica and crypt daily 9:30am–8pm May–Sept, 9:30am–5pm Oct–Apr. Métro: Abbesses; take elevator to surface and follow signs to funicular.

Espace Dalí ★ MUSEUM This tiny museum dedicated to the works of surrealist Salvador Dali won't take more than 45 minutes to visit, but what a 45-minutes you'll spend! The space is littered with erotic engravings, dreamlike objects and whimsical furniture, not to mention Dali's theatrical sculptures (the most important assembly in France), including a spindly-legged Space Elephant, and several of his iconic soft watches, which seem to drip phantasmagorically to the floor. The man with the iconic moustache lived in Montmartre with his wife and muse Gala, in an apartment at 7 rue Becquerel. It was from here in 1956, following a commission for Dali to illustrate Cervantes' Don Quixote novel, that the Catalan staged one of the Butte's most memorable artistic moments: the filming of him creating the first engravings. Against a windmill backdrop, rose forth a knight on horseback, and Dali true to form used two rhinoceros' horns and bread dipped in ink to create the illustrations. You can see some engravings from the series alongside others from the Bible and Alice in Wonderland.

11 rue Poulbot, 18th. www.daliparis.com. ℂ **01-42-64-40-10.** Admission 12€ adults; ages 9–26 7€; free for children 8 and under. Daily 10am–6pm (until 8pm July–Aug). Métro: Anvers, Abbesses, or Lamarck-Caulincourt.

Musée de Montmartre ★★ MUSEUM   The main reason to visit this small museum is to get an inkling of what Montmartre really was like back in the days when Picasso, Toulouse-Lautrec, Van Gogh, et al., were painting and cavorting up here on the *butte.* While there are few examples of the artists' works here, there are plenty of photos, posters, and even films documenting the neighborhood's famous history, from the days when its importance was mainly religious to the glory days of the Paris Commune, and finally to the artistic boom in the 19th and 20th centuries. Next to an original poster of Jane Avril by Toulouse-Lautrec, for example, you'll see a photo of the real Jane Avril, as well as other Montmartre cabaret legends like Aristide Bruant and La Goulue. The few paintings and drawings by famed painters like Utrillo and Modigliani are supplemented by works by lesser-known Montmartrois, like Steinlen, Léandre, and de Belay. The 17th-century house that shelters the museum was at various times home of Auguste Renoir and Raoul Dufy, as well as Susan Valadon and her son, Maurice Utrillo, whose studio can now be visited. Surrounded by gardens and greenery, the site offers a lovely view of the last scrap of the Montmartre vineyard. English-language audioguides are a big help here.

12 rue Cortot, 18th arrond. www.museedemontmartre.fr. © **01-49-25-89-39.** Admission 9.50€ adults, 7.50€ ages 18–25, 5.50€ ages 10–17, free under 10. Daily 10am–6pm. Métro: Lamarck-Caulaincourt.

République, Bastille & Eastern Paris (11th & 12th Arrondissements)

While you can't really point to any major tourist attractions in this area, this part of town is seriously up-and-coming, and has great nightlife and clothing stores, not to mention a booming restaurant scene. There are also some important historical sites: The French Revolution was brewed in the workshops of the **Faubourg St-Antoine,** and was ignited at the **Place de la Bastille.** The former stomping grounds of the medieval Knights Templar, the recently remodeled **Place de la République** is a potent symbol of the French Republic.

La Promenade Plantée ★ WALKING TRAIL   Transformed from an unused train viaduct, this beautiful aerial garden walkway runs from the place de la Bastille to the Bois de Vincennes. The 4.5km (2.8-mile) pedestrian path traces flower gardens, tree bowers, rose trellises, and fountains and takes you over the 12th arrondissement, past the Gare de Lyon, and through the Reuilly Gardens. At ground level along Ave. Daumesnil, the brick archways now shelter the **Viaduct des Arts,** a series of galleries and workshops that show off the work of highly skilled artisans.

Enter by the staircase on Ave. Daumesnil just past the Opéra Bastille, 12th arrond. www.paris.fr.

Parc Zoologique de Paris ★★ ZOO This lush, ecologically correct animal reserve invites visitors to five regions of the world, from the plains of Sudan to Europe, via Guyana, Patagonia, and Madagascar. Going for quality instead of quantity, the zoo may not have room for elephants and bears, but it does introduce visitors to animals they might not be familiar with, like the fossa, a catlike carnivore from Madagascar, or the capybara, a giant South American rodent. There is also a good sampling of zoo favorites like lions, baboons, penguins, and a troupe of giraffes—if you are lucky you can get an up close look while the latter lunch in the giraffe house. The enclosures are well adapted to their inhabitants, so much so that at times it's hard to see them. But if you are patient you'll spy wolves peeking out of the foliage, or a bright red tomato frog gripping a vine. There are more than 1,000 animals in all, yet the zoo is human-sized—you can see the whole thing in a couple of hours. Don't miss the huge aviaries, one of which is home to a large flock of flamingos.

Parc de Vincennes, 12th arrond., www.parczoologiquedeparis.fr. (℗) **01-44-75-20-10.** 22€ adults, 17€ students 12–25, 14€ children 3–11, free 2 and under. Mid-Oct to mid-Mar Wed–Mon 10am–5pm, mid-Mar to mid-Oct Mon–Fri 10am–6pm, Sat–Sun and school holidays 9:30am–7:30pm.

Place de la Bastille ★ SQUARE The most notable thing about this giant plaza—aside from architect Carlos Ott's modern Opéra House, opened in 1989—is the building that's no longer there: the Bastille prison. Now an enormous traffic circle where cars careen around at warp speed, this was once the site of an ancient stone fortress that became a symbol for all that was wrong with the French monarchy. Over the centuries, kings and queens condemned rebellious citizens to stay inside these cold walls, sometimes with good reason, other times on a mere whim. By the time the Revolution started to boil, though, the prison was barely in use; when the angry mobs stormed the walls on July 14, 1789, there were only seven prisoners left to set free. Be that as it may, the destruction of the Bastille came to be seen as the ultimate revolutionary moment; July 14 is still celebrated as the birth of the Republic. Surprisingly, the giant bronze column in the center honors the victims of a different revolution, that of 1830.

12th arrond. Métro: Bastille.

Belleville, Canal St-Martin & La Villette (10th, 19th & 20th Arrondissements)

One of the most picturesque attractions in this area is the **Canal St-Martin** itself, which extends up to **La Villette,** a former industrial area that has been transformed into a gigantic park and cultural compound. Other intriguing outdoor attractions include the romantic **Père-Lachaise cemetery,** the resting place of France's most noteworthy notables, and the verdant **Buttes Chaumont park.** The Belleville neighborhood is home to one of the city's bustling Chinatowns, as well as many artists' studios.

6 **Cimetière du Père-Lachaise** ★★★ CEMETERY   Cemeteries are not usually on the top of anyone's must-see list, but this is no ordinary cemetery. Romantic and rambling as a 19th-century English garden, this hillside resting-place is wonderfully green, with huge leafy trees and narrow paths winding around the graves, which include just about every French literary or artistic giant you can imagine, plus several international stars. Proust, Apollonaire, Colette, Delacroix, Seurat, Modigliani, Bizet, and Rossini are all here, as well as Sarah Bernhardt, Isadora Duncan, and Simone Signoret and Yves Montand (buried side by side, of course). Though some are simple tombstones, many are miniature architectural marvels, embellished with exquisite marble and stone figures, or even phone-booth-size chapels, complete with stained-glass windows. Some of the standouts include:

o **Héloïse and Abélard:** These two legendary lovers actually existed, and their 12th-century remains were brought here in 1817, when the city built them this monument, which is covered by an openwork chapel taken from an abbey in southwestern France.

o **Molière and La Fontaine:** Although there was no romantic link, the celebrated playwright and noted fable writer were also brought here in 1817 and placed in nearby sarcophagi, both of which stand appropriately high on pillars. If the authenticity of the remains is in doubt, they still make a fitting memorial to these two brilliant talents.

o **Oscar Wilde:** This huge stone monument is topped with a winged figure that resembles an Aztec deity. It's an elegant homage to the brilliant writer, who died a pauper in Paris in 1900. For many years it was covered in lipstick kisses, which eroded the stone, hence today's protective see-through barrier.

Celebrity graves can be hard to find, so a map is essential. You can find one at the newsstand at the exit of Père Lachaise Métro or use the one in this book (p. 169). There are also good maps on the website, as well as the Paris

Long Live the Lizard King

Though the grave itself is unexceptional, the tomb of '60s rock star **Jim Morrison** is possibly the most visited, or at least the most hyped, in the cemetery. For years, fans made pilgrimages, leaving behind so much graffiti, litter, and mind-altering substances that families of those buried nearby began to complain, and the tomb was surrounded by a fence. Still, nothing can dispel the enduring attraction of the Morrison legend. In 1971, battling a variety of drug, alcohol, and legal problems, the singer/musician came to Paris, ostensibly with the goal of taking a break from performing and getting his life back on track. Four months later, he was found dead in a Parisian bathtub, at age 27. Since no autopsy was performed, the exact cause of his death was never known (although there was good reason to suspect a drug overdose), which has led to wild speculation on the part of his fans. Rumors still circulate that he was a target of the CIA, murdered by a witch, committed suicide, or that he faked his own death and is currently residing in India, Africa, or New Jersey under the name "Mr. Mojo Risin'."

Abélard & Héloïse **37**

Guillaume Apollinaire **5**

Pierre-Auguste
  Beaumarchais **30**

Hans Bellmer **24**

Sarah Bernhardt **9**

Georges Bizet **17**

Maria Callas **3**

Frédéric Chopin **36**

Colette **23**

Auguste Comte **34**

Jean Baptiste
  Camille Corot **11**

Honoré Daumier **10**

Jacques-Louis David **19**

Honoré de Balzac **16**

Eugène Delacroix **15**

Gustave Doré **14**

Isadora Duncan **6**

Paul Eluard **26**

Max Ernst **2**

Théodore Géricault **20**

Jean-Auguste-
  Dominique Ingres **13**

Jean La Fontaine **33**

René Lalique **12**

Lefebvre Masséna **29**

Amedeo Modigliani **28**

Molière **32**

Jim Morrison **35**

Alfred de Musset **21**

Edith Piaf **27**

Camille Pissarro **38**

Marcel Proust **4**

Gioacchio Antonio
  Rossini **22**

Rothschild family plot **39**

Henri de Saint-Simon **31**

Georges Seurat **18**

Simone Signoret &
  Yves Montand **8**

Gertrude Stein &
  Alice B. Toklas **25**

Oscar Wilde **1**

Richard Wright **7**

The Canal St-Martin

The Canal St-Martin is a pretty waterway that connects the river Seine, near Bastille, to the Canal de l'Ourcq, near the Villette in the 19th arrondissement. When Parisians talk about *le canal*, they are usually referring to the popular stretch of the quays Jemmapes and Valmy, which begins just above République and runs up by the Gare de l'Est. Inaugurated in 1825 with the aim of bringing fresh drinking water to the heart of the city, it narrowly escaped being entirely paved over in the 1970s. Finally listed a historic monument in 1993, today its tree-lined banks and high arched bridges make it a delightful place to stroll, especially on Sundays, when the east side is closed to cars. You can take a boat tour with **Paris Canal** (www.pariscanal.com; ✆ **01-42-40-96-97**) or **Canauxrama** (www.canauxrama. com; ✆ **01-42-39-15-00**).

municipal site: www.paris.fr (search for "Père Lachaise"). *Note:* Entry is via the gate opposite rue de la Roquette; the other entrances are generally closed.

16 rue de Repos, 20th arrond. www.pere-lachaise.com. Admission free. Mon–Fri 8am– 6pm; Sat–Sun 8:30am–6pm (closes at 5pm Nov to early Mar). Métro: Père-Lachaise or Philippe Auguste.

Cité des Sciences et de l'Industrie ★★ MUSEUM   This gigantic and terrific science and industry museum was built upon the site of the city's former 19th-century slaughterhouse auction room, which had closed in 1974 due to competition from the suburban Rungis food market, leaving the city with derelict land to fill. Today it includes a planetarium, a 3D movie theater, and a multimedia library, not to mention a real live submarine. The heart of the museum is its permanent collection, which flaunts huge floors of interactive exhibits and displays on subjects like sound, mathematics and human genes. There are also excellent temporary exhibits. On the ground floor, parents will be delighted to find the **Cité des Enfants** (separate admission, 12€ adults, 9€ under 25 or over 65, for a 1½-hr. session; see website for hours, reservations essential, particularly during French school vacations), which has separate programs for 2- to 7-year-olds and 5- to 12-year-olds. Kids get to explore the world around them in a series of hands-on activities and displays. If all this isn't enough, outside you can clamber into the **Argonaut** (access included with your ticket; must be over 3 to enter), a real submarine that was one of the stars of the French navy in the 1950s, or dip inside the gigantic metal sphere called the **Geode** (adults 12€, under 25 9€; www.lageode.fr), an IMAX-type movie theater showing large-screen films.

Parc de La Villette, 30 ave. Corentine-Cariou, 19th arrond. www.cite-sciences.fr. ✆ **01-40-05-80-00.** Varied ticket packages 12€ adults, 9€ under 25, free 2 and under. Tues–Sat 10am–6pm; Sun 10am–7pm. Métro: Porte de La Villette.

Musée de la Musique ★ MUSEUM   Located on the north end of the Parc de la Villette, and part of the striking Philharmonie de Paris concert complex (p. 239), this museum has a permanent collection of over a thousand instruments, sculptures, paintings, and other objects that recount the history of music in Europe from the 16th to 20th centuries. Pore over a beautiful and rare 17th-century guitar with ivory inlay, a clutch of Stradivarius violins, or a concert piano that Franz Liszt once played on. A separate section on music from around the world includes another 700 objects, mostly from Africa and Asia. As you wander about, you can listen to the instruments you look at on headphones, and you will probably come across live demonstrations by local musicians as well. The temporary exhibitions are always big hits here and include a program of top-notch concerts. The rest of the Philharmonie complex includes a library, a cutting-edge concert hall, and educational facilities.

In the Cité de la Musique, 221 ave. Jean-Jaurès, 19th arrond. http://philharmoniede-paris.fr. © **01-44-84-44-84.** Admission 7€ adults, 5.60€ ages 27–28, free for under 26. Tues–Sat noon–6pm; Sun 10am–6pm. Métro: Porte de Pantin.

Parc de la Villette ★★ PARK   This vast complex, which includes a park, museums, concert halls, and other cultural institutions (see above), was built on the site of the city's slaughterhouses, abandoned since the mid-1970s. Construction began in 1980, when Bernard Tschumi, a French-Swiss architect, was chosen to create an urban cultural park accessible to one and all. The park is certainly a success on the cultural end: It harbors **Cité de la Musique** and **Cité des Sciences et de l'Industrie**—two excellent museums—as well as the **Zénith** and **Cabaret Sauvage** concert halls, not to mention the spanking-new **Philharmonie de Paris** (p. 239). As far as the green spaces go—well, let me put it this way: If it is possible for a park to have a sense of humor, this one definitely has one. There are 11 themed gardens, around which are dotted

The Geode in the Parc de la Villette is a 3D-IMAX cinema.

25 red *"folies"*—oddball contemporary structures that sometimes house a drink stand or an information booth, and sometimes are just there for the heck of it. The gardens range from the sublime to the silly; a few are strictly reserved for children (who can bring along their parents).

From mid-July to mid-August the **Cinéma en Plein Air** takes place Tuesday to Sunday at sundown, presenting classic movies for free.

19th arrond. www.villette.com. ℂ **01-40-03-75-75.** Daily 6am–1am. Métro: Porte de Pantin or Porte de la Villette.

Parc des Buttes Chaumont ★ PARK   Up until 1860, this area was home to a deep limestone quarry, but thanks to Napoleon III, the gaping hole was turned into an unusual park, full of hills and dales, rocky bluffs, and cliffs. It took 3 years to make this romantic garden; over a thousand workers and a hundred horses dug, heaped, and blasted through the walls of the quarry to create green lawns, a cool grotto, cascades, streams, and even a small lake. By the opening of the 1867 World's Fair, the garden was ready for visitors. The surrounding area was, and still is, working-class; the Emperor built it to give this industrious neighborhood a green haven and a bit of fresh air. There are **pony rides** for the kids on weekends and Wednesdays (3–6pm; www.anima poney.com), plus a **puppet theater,** a **carousel,** and **two playgrounds.** The *guinguette*-style (open-air) bar/cafe—**Rosa Bonheur** (p. 107), named after the 19th-century feminist artist—is a bucolic spot for drinks and snacks, staying open even after the park has closed.

Rue Botzaris, 19th arrond. Open 7am–dusk. Métro: Botzaris or Buttes Chaumont.

THE LEFT BANK
Latin Quarter (5th & 13th Arrondissements)

For several hundred years, the students who flocked to this quarter spoke Latin in their classes at the **Sorbonne** (founded in the 13th c.). Today students still abound around the Sorbonne, and even though classes are taught in French, the name stuck. Intellectual pursuits aside, this youth-filled neighborhood is a lively one, with lots of cinemas and cafes. History is readily visible here, dating back to the Roman occupation: The **rue St-Jacques** and **boulevard Saint-Michel** mark the former Roman cardo, and you can explore the remains of the **Roman baths** at the **Cluny Museum** (p. 177).

Jardin des Plantes ★★ GARDEN   This delightful botanical garden, tucked between the Muséum National d'Histoire Naturelle (see below) and the Seine, is one of our favorite spots for a picnic and a stroll. Created in 1626 as a medicinal plant garden for King Louis XIII, in the 18th century, it became an internationally famed scientific institution thanks to naturalist, mathematician, and biologist Georges-Louis Leclerc, Count of Buffon, with the help of fellow-naturalist Louis-Jean-Marie Daubenton. Today the museums are still part academic institutions, but you don't need to be a student to appreciate these lush grounds.

Galerie de l'Evolution in the Natural History Museum, Jardin des Plantes.

The garden also harbors a small but well-kept zoo, the **Ménagerie, le Zoo du Jardin des Plantes** (www.mnhn.fr; ℂ **01-40-79-56-01;** 13€ adults, 9€ students 18–26 and children 4–16, free under 4; daily 9am–5pm, until 6pm in summer). Created in 1794, this is the oldest zoo in the world. Because of its size, the zoo showcases mostly smaller species; in particular, birds and reptiles. But there's also a healthy selection of mammals (240 to be exact), including rare species like red pandas, Przewalski horses, and even Florida pumas. If you're interested in tropical plantlife, don't miss the park's **Grandes Serres** (ℂ **01-40-79-56-01;** 7€ adults, 5€ children and students 4–25, free 3 and under; daily Oct–Mar 10am–5pm, Apr–Sept 10am–6pm)—four magnificent 19th-century greenhouses that take you on a botanical journey from the jungle to the desert via a prehistoric plant section and a special area on New Caledonia's unique vegetation (76% of its plants cannot be found anywhere else in the world). It's fascinating if you've got a green thumb, and a good bet on a cold day.

Rue Geoffroy-St-Hilaire, 5th arrond. www.jardindesplantes.net. ℂ **01-40-79-56-01.** Free admission to gardens; 8am–dusk. Métro: Gare d'Austerlitz.

Manufacture Nationale des Gobelins ★ TAPESTRY FACTORY TOUR   Back in the 17th century, Louis XIV purchased this famed tapestry factory with the aim of furnishing his new chateau (Versailles) with the most splendid tapestries around. France's most skilled workers created sumptuous carpets and wall-coverings using designs sketched by the top artists of the era. The workshop's reputation has survived the centuries, and the factory is still active, working with the same materials used in the time of Louis XIV (wool, cotton, silk). Still state-owned, today the factory operates under the auspices of the French Ministry of Culture, and produces modern tapestries to hang in some of France's grandest public spaces. This is definitely not a mass-market operation—these tapestries take several years to finish. Highly skilled workers (who study for 4 years at the on-site school) work from paintings by contemporary artists to create enormous works of art; during the tour you'll watch weavers in action at their giant looms. It is humbling to see how carefully and patiently the weavers work, tying tiny individual knots and/or passing shuttles of wool through a forest of warp and weft, all the while following an intricate

place des
États Unis

Boissiere

16e

av. Pierre Premier de Serbie
av. d'Iena

av. George V

av. Marceau

r. François Premier

av. Montaigne

av. Franklin D. Roosevelt

Franklin D. Roosevelt

av. des Champs-Élysées-Clemenceau

Champs Élysées-Clemenceau

Champs-Élysées

Concorde

place
Vendôme

r. Saint-Honoré

8e

cours Albert Premier

Grand Palais

Petit Palais

place de la
Concorde

de Rivoli

Tuileries

du
President Wilson

av. de New York

av. lena

Alma-
Marceau

Pont de
l'Alma

Seine

cours La Reine

Jardin des Tuileries

quai des Tuileries

Seine

Palais de
Chaillot

Jardins du
Trocadero

place de la
Résistance

quai Branly

r. de l'Université

quai d'Orsay

q. d'Orsay

Invalides

**Palais Bourbon/
Assemblée
Nationale**

quai Anatole France

**Musée
d'Orsay**

**7 Musée
d'Orsay**

**2
Musée du
Quai Branly**

Rapp

av. de la Bourdonnais

r. Saint-Dominique

esplanade
des
Invalides

place des
Invalides

Assemblée
Nationale

r. Saint-Dominique

Solférino

de

St-Germain

r. de l'Université

**1 Eiffel
Tower**

Champ de Mars-
Tour Eiffel

parc du Champ de Mars

r. de Grenelle

Bosquet

La Tour-
Maubourg

Tour-Maubourg

de La Motte-Picquet

**Hôtel des
Invalides**

4

Varenne

7e

Grenelle

Rue du Bac

av. de Suffren

École Militaire

Joffre

av. de Tourville

bd. de La Tour-Maubourg

Invalides

**5
Musée
Rodin**

de

Varenne

bd. Raspail

des

**École
Militaire**

place
Vauban

St-François
Xavier

r. de Babylone

Jardin
Catherine
Labouré

Sèvres-
Babylone

place
A. Deville

15e

Dupleix

pl.
Dupleix

La Motte-Picquet-
Grenelle

place
Cambronne

av. de Lowendal

av. de Suffren

av. de Ségur

Duquesne

de Breteuil

Ségur

r. de Sèvres

Vaneau

Rennes

r. d'Assas

r. Émile Zola

r. Frémicourt

Cambronne

bd. Garibaldi

Ségur

place de
Breteuil

Duroc

Vaugirard

St-Placide

de Rennes

Avenue
Émile Zola

place du
Commerce

Commerce

r. de la Croix Nivert

Sèvres-
Lecourbe

place Henri
Queuille

**HÔPITAL NECKER-
ENFANTS MALADES** ✚

Falguière

du

Notre-Dame-
des-Champs

bd. Raspail

Lecourbe

Pasteur

Volontaires

bd. de Vaugirard

Pasteur

6

Tour Montparnasse

**Gare
Montparnasse**

Montparnasse-
Bienvenüe

Vavin

Edgar Quinet

MONTPARNASSE

René Mouchotte

Gaîté

**CIMETIÈRE DU
MONTPARNASSE**

8

place de
Catalogne

r. Jean Zay

r. Froidevaux

Losserand

Château

av. du Maine

r. Daguerre

r. Liancourt

Raymond

Pernety

Didot

r. des Plantes

14e

Plaisance

r. d'Alésia

Mouton-
Duvernet

Cimetière du
Montparnasse **8**

Eiffel Tower **1**

Hôtel des Invalides/
Napoleon's Tomb **4**

Institut du Monde
Arabe **18**

Jardin des Plantes **19**

Jardin du Luxembourg **12**

Les Catacombes **14**

Manufacture Nationale
des Gobelins **21**

Musée Bourdelle **6**

Musée d'Orsay **7**

Musée des Egouts
de Paris **3**

Musée du Quai Branly **2**

Musée National
du Moyen Age/
Thermes de Cluny **15**

Musée National
Eugène Delacroix **10**

Musée Rodin **5**

Musée Zadkine **13**

Muséum National
d'Histoire Naturelle **20**

Panthéon **16**

St-Etienne-du-Mont **17**

St-Germain-des-Prés **9**

St-Sulpice **11**

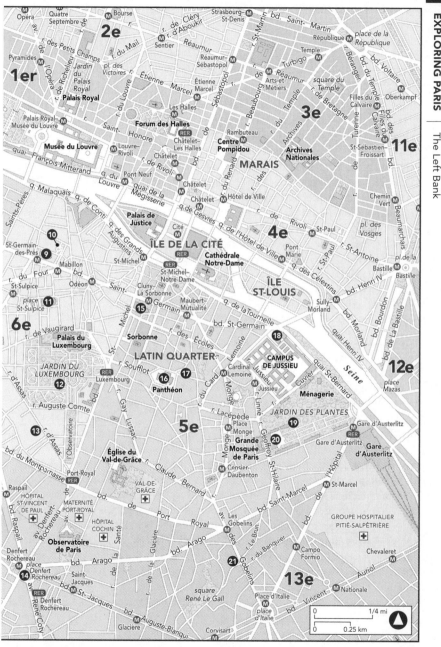

design scheme. To visit the ateliers, you must take a guided, 1-hour tour (in French; Tues–Wed 1–2pm; purchase tickets online or at Fnac stores: www. fnactickets.com; ℂ **08-92-68-36-22**); there is also a gallery that offers temporary shows on design themes.

42 ave. des Gobelins, 13th arrond. www.mobiliernational.culture.gouv.fr. ℂ **01-44-08-53-49.** Admission to temporary exhibits 8€ adults, 6€ students. Tues–Sun 11am–6pm. Tours 14€ adults, 10€ ages 13–25, 7€ ages 4–12. Tues–Wed 1pm. Closed Aug to mid-Sept. Métro: Gobelins.

Musée de l'Institut du Monde Arabe ★ MUSEUM   While it harbors a substantial collection, one of the biggest draws to this museum-library-research center is the building itself. Designed by architect Jean Nouvel in 1987, the south facade is covered by a metallic latticework echoing traditional Arab designs, with 30,000 light-sensitive diaphragms that open and close according to how bright it is outside. The airy museum space presents a collection that emphasizes the diversity of peoples and cultures in the Middle East, reminding us, among other things, that it was the birthplace of all three major Western religions. While intellectually stimulating, if art is what you are after, the Islamic Art section of the Louvre will be more satisfying. Still, there's a terrific view of the Seine and Notre-Dame from the rooftop restaurant, **Le Zyriab.**

1 rue des Fossés St-Bernard, 5th arrond. www.imarabe.org. ℂ **01-40-51-38-38.** Admission 8€, 4€ ages 12–26, free 11 and under. Tues–Fri 10am–6pm; Sat–Sun 10am–7pm. Métro: Jussieu, Cardinal Lemoine, Sully-Morland.

Muséum National d'Histoire Naturelle ★★ MUSEUM   This natural history museum was established in 1793, under the supervision of two celebrated naturalists, George Louis Lerclerc, Count of Buffon, and Louis Jean-Marie Daubenton. Originally (and still) an academic research institution, this temple to the natural sciences contains a series of separate museums, each with a different specialty. The biggest draw is no doubt the **Grande Galerie de l'Evolution,** where a sort of Noah's ark of animals snakes its way around a huge hall filled with displays that trace the evolution of life and man's relationship with nature. Another intriguing hall, the **Galerie de Minérologie et de Géologie,** includes a room full of giant crystals, and another with eye-popping precious stones from the Royal Treasury, as well as various minerals and even meteorites. For dinosaurs, saber-toothed tigers, ancient humans, and thousands of other fossilized skeletons, repair to the **Galeries de Paléontologie et d'Anatomie Comparée.** The Muséum's **Galerie des Enfants** (children's gallery) offers hands-on interactive displays for the little tykes. Except for the Grande Galerie, which has a joint ticket deal with the Galerie des Enfants, you'll have to pay for each Galerie separately.

36 rue Geoffrey, 5th arrond. www.mnhn.fr. ℂ **01-40-79-54-79.** Admission to each galerie 7€–11€ adults; free 26 and under. Wed–Mon 10am–6pm. Métro: Jussieu or Gare d'Austerlitz.

Musée National du Moyen Age/Thermes de Cluny (Musée de Cluny) ★★ MUSEUM   Ancient Roman baths and a 15th-century mansion set the stage for a terrific collection of medieval art and objects at this museum. Built somewhere between the 1st and 3rd centuries, the baths (visible from bd. St-Michel) are some of the best existing examples of Gallo-Roman architecture. They are attached to what was once the palatial home of a 15th-century abbot, whose last owner, Alexandre du Sommerard, amassed a vast array of medieval masterworks. When he died in 1842, his home was turned into a museum and his collection put on display. Sculptures, textiles, furniture, and ceramics are shown, as well as gold, ivory, and enamel work. There are several magnificent tapestries, but the biggest draw is the **"Lady and the Unicorn"** series, one of only two sets of complete unicorn tapestries in the world (the other is in New York City). In five of these late-15th-century tapestries, the lady, her unicorn, a lion, and various other symbolic representations of the animal and vegetable kingdoms illustrate the five senses, while in the sixth she stands before a tent bearing the inscription "To My Only Desire" while placing a necklace in a case held by her servant. The meaning of this last tapestry remains an enigma—but the mystery merely adds to its beauty.

Among the many sculptures displayed are the famous severed heads from the facade of Notre-Dame. Knocked off of their bodies during the furor of the Revolution, 21 of the heads of the Kings of Judah were found by chance in 1977 during repair work in the courtyard of a mansion in the 9th arrondissement. Other treasures include Flemish retables, Visigoth crowns, bejeweled chalices, stained-glass windows, and beautiful objects from daily life, like hair combs and game boards. Best to visit in the afternoon; school groups abound in the morning.

6 place Paul Painlevé, 5th arrond. www.musee-moyenage.fr. ✆ **01-53-73-78-00.** Admission 9€ adults, 7€ ages 18–24, free 17 and under; 1€ supplement during temporary exhibits. Wed–Mon 9:15am–5:45pm. Métro/RER: Cluny–La Sorbonne or St-Michel.

Panthéon ★★ CHURCH/MAUSOLEUM   High atop the "montagne" (actually a medium-size hill) of St-Geneviève, the dome of the Panthéon is one of the city's most visible landmarks. This erstwhile royal church has been transformed into a national mausoleum—the final resting place of luminaries such as Voltaire, Rousseau, Hugo, and Zola, as well as Marie and Pierre Curie, and—since 2015—four World War II heroes of the Résistance. Initially dedicated to St-Geneviève, the church was commissioned by a grateful Louis XV, who attributed his recovery from a serious illness to the saint. The work of architect Jacques-Germain Soufflot, who took his inspiration from the Pantheon in Rome, it must have been magnificent—the vast interior was clearly created with a higher power in mind. However, during the Revolution its sacred mission was diverted toward a new god—the Nation—and it was converted into a memorial and burial ground for Great Men of the Republic. This meant taking down the bells, walling up most of the windows, doing away with religious statuary and replacing it with works promoting patriotic virtues.

Frazzled parents take note: The Jardin de Luxembourg has loads of activities for kids who need to blow off steam. First off, an extra-large **playground** (1.50€ adults, 2.50€ under 12) is filled with swings and slides. Then there are the wonderful wooden **sailboats** (2.50€ per half-hour) to float in the main fountain, as well as an ancient **carousel** (2€, next to the playground). At the **marionette theater** (6€ each, parents and children; Wed, Sat, Sun, and school vacation days, shows usually start at 3:30pm; Sat–Sun additional shows at 11am; for schedule, visit www.marionnettesduluxembourg.fr), you can see Guignol himself (the French version of Punch) in a variety of puppet shows aimed at ages 2 to 6.

The desired effect was achieved—the enormous empty space, lined with huge paintings of great moments in French history, resembles a cavernous tomb. The star attraction in the nave is **Foucault's Pendulum** (named after the French physicist Léon Foucault, who invented it in 1851), a simple device—a heavy ball suspended on a long wire above markers—that proves the rotation of the Earth. And since major restoration work, visitors can once again climb the Panthéon's lofty dome (the highest spot in Paris until the Eiffel Tower was erected in 1889) to see the city unfurl in a higgledy-piggledy sprawl of gray rooftops. It's a breathtaking sight, spreading all the way out past the Eiffel Tower to the high-rises of Paris's out-of-town business district, La Defense.

Place du Panthéon, 5th arrond. www.paris-pantheon.fr. ℂ **01-44-32-18-00**. Admission 9€ adults, 6.50€ ages 18–25, free 17 and under (and under 26 from EU countries). Dome 2€ extra. Apr–Sept daily 10am–6:30pm; Oct–Mar daily 10am–6pm. Dome Apr–Oct only. Métro: Cardinal Lemoine. RER: Luxembourg.

St-Etienne-du-Mont ★★ CHURCH   One of the city's prettiest churches, this gem is a joyous mix of late Gothic and Renaissance styles. The 17th-century facade combines Gothic tradition with a dash of classical Rome; inside, the 16th-century chancel sports a magnificent **rood screen** (an intricately carved partition separating the nave from the chancel) with decorations inspired by the Italian Renaissance. Bookended by twin spiraling marble staircases, this rood screen is the only one left in the city. The entire church has been cleaned, making it easy to appreciate its riches, which include 16th- and 17th-century stained glass. A pilgrimage site, the church was once part of an abbey dedicated to St-Geneviève (Paris's patron saint), and stones from her original sarcophagus lie in an ornate shrine here. That's about all that is left of her—the saint's bones were burned during the Revolution, and her ashes were thrown in the Seine. The remains of two other great minds, Racine and Pascal, are buried here.

1 place St-Geneviève, 5th arrond. www.saintetiennedumont.fr. ℂ **01-43-54-11-79**. Free admission. Mon 6:30–7:30pm, Tues–Fri 8:45am–7:45pm (until 10pm Wed), Sat 8:45am–noon and 2–7:45pm, Sun 8:45am–12:15pm and 2:30–7:45pm. Métro: Cardinal Lemoine. RER: Luxembourg.

St-Germain-des-Prés & Luxembourg (6th Arrondissement)

In the 20th century, the St-Germain-des-Prés neighborhood became associated with writers like Jean-Paul Sartre, Simone de Beauvoir, Albert Camus, and the rest of the intellectual bohemian crowd that gathered at **Café de Flore** (p. 126) or **Les Deux Magots** (p. 127). But back in the 6th century, a mighty abbey was founded here that ruled over a big chunk of the Left Bank for almost 1,000 years. The French Revolution put a stop to that, and most of the original buildings were pulled down. You can still find remains of both epochs in this neighborhood, notably at the 10th-century church **St-Germain-des-Prés** and the surviving bookstores and publishing houses that surround it. After your tour, relax at the delightful **Jardin du Luxembourg** nearby.

Jardin du Luxembourg ★★★ GARDEN   Out of the many parks and gardens in Paris, this is our personal favorite. Rolling out like an Oriental carpet before the Italianate Palais du Luxembourg (the seat of the French Senate since 1958, not open to the public), this vast expanse of fountains, flowers, lush lawns, and shaded glens is the perfect setting for a leisurely stroll, a relaxed picnic, or a serious make-out session, depending on who you're with. At the center of everything is a fountain with a huge basin, where kids can sail toy wooden sailboats (2.50€ for a half-hour) and adults can sun themselves on the green metal chairs at the pond's edge. Sculptures abound: At every turn there is a god, goddess, artist, or monarch peering down at you from his or her pedestal—Vulcan, Venus, George Sand, or Anne de Bretagne, to name but a few. The most splendid waterworks is probably the **Medici Fountain** (most easily reached via the entrance at place Paul Claudel behind the Odéon), draped with lithe Roman gods sculptured by Auguste Ottin, and topped with the Medici coat of arms, in honor of the palace's first resident, Marie de Medicis.

Palais du Luxembourg.

In 1621, the Italian-born French queen, homesick for the Pitti Palace of her youth, bought up the grounds and existing buildings and had a Pitti-inspired palace built for herself as well as a smaller version of the sumptuous gardens. She moved in in 1625, only to be banished in 1630 for taking the wrong side against powerful Cardinal Richelieu. The palace passed on to various royals until the Revolution, when it was turned into a prison. American writer Thomas Paine was incarcerated there in 1793 after he fell out of favor with Robespierre; he narrowly escaped execution. On the plus side, the Revolutionaries increased the size of the garden and made it a public institution. The orchards of the neighboring charterhouse were annexed, the remnants of which can still be visited at the southwest corner of the gardens. There, visitors can see a horticulture school where pear trees have been trained into formal, geometric shapes, as well as beehives that are maintained by a local apiculture association. After the Revolution, the palace and grounds stayed in government hands up until today (the palace houses the French Senate), with the exception of the Orangerie, which now holds the **Musée du Luxembourg** (19 rue de Vaugirard, 6th arrond.; www.museeduluxembourg.fr; © **01-40-13-62-00;** admission and hours vary with exhibits; Métro: Odéon, RER: Luxembourg), which is only open during its excellent temporary exhibits.

Entry at Place Edmond Rostand, place André Honnorat, rue Guynemer, or rue de Vaugirard, 6th arrond. www.senat.fr/visite/jardin. © **01-42-34-20-00.** 8am–dusk. Métro: Odéon. RER: Luxembourg.

Musée National Eugène Delacroix ★ MUSEUM

Housed in what was once the painter's apartment and studio, this small museum is dedicated to Eugène Delacroix, one of the greatest artists of the Romantic period. Delacroix was old and sick when he moved here in 1857 to be closer to the church of St-Sulpice, where he was decorating a chapel. He managed to finish the paintings, 3 years before he died here, in 1863. "It takes great fortitude to be yourself," he once said, and he certainly had it: At his death, he left behind some 8,000 paintings, drawings, and pastels. Though none of his major works are in the museum, several smaller paintings decorate the walls, including the mysterious "Mary Magdalene in the Wilderness." Furniture, mementos, and other personal items are displayed, including the artist's palette and paint box. The museum is located on the exquisitely beautiful place de Furstenberg, a small, leafy square.

6 place de Furstenberg, 6th arrond. www.musee-delacroix.fr. © **01-44-41-86-50.** Admission 7€ adults, free for children 17 and under. Wed–Mon 9:30am–5:30pm (until 9pm on the 1st Thurs of the month). Métro: St-Germain-des-Prés or Mabillon.

Musée Zadkine ★★ MUSEUM

You could easily miss the alleyway that leads to this tiny museum in the small but luminous house where Ossip Zadkine lived and worked from 1928 to his death in 1967. A contemporary and neighbor of artists such as Brancusi, Lipchitz, Modigliani, and Picasso, this Russian-born sculptor is closely associated with the Cubist movement; his sober, elegant, "primitive" sculptures combine abstract geometry with deep humanity. Dozens of examples of his best works, like a superb 9-foot plaster sculpture of biblical Rebecca carrying a water pitcher, or a vaguely African head of a woman in limestone, are displayed in small, light-filled rooms. Be sure to visit the artist's workshop, tucked behind the tranquil garden. *Note:* Because of the museum's small size, during temporary exhibits you'll have to pay to enter even the permanent collection (which is usually free).

100 bis rue d'Assas, 6th arrond. www.zadkine.paris.fr. © **01-55-42-77-20.** Free admission to permanent collections. Tues–Sun 10am–6pm. Métro: Notre-Dame des Champs or Vavin.

St-Germain-des-Prés ★★ CHURCH

The origins of this church stretch back over a millennium. First established by King Childebert in 543 who constructed a basilica and monastery on the site, it was built, destroyed, and rebuilt several times over the centuries. Nothing remains of the original buildings, but the bell tower dates from the 10th century and is one of the oldest in France. Most of the rest of the church was built in the 11th and 12th centuries and is Romanesque in style. The church and its abbey became a major center of learning and power during the Middle Ages, remaining a force to be reckoned with up until the eve of the French Revolution. Once the monarchy toppled, however, all hell broke loose: The abbey was destroyed, the famous library burned, and the church vandalized. Restored in the 19th century, the buildings have regained some of their former glory, though the complex is a fraction of its original size.

The first thing you'll notice on entering is that much of the interior is painted in a range of greens and golds—one of the few Parisian churches to retain a sense of its original decor. The paint, however, is in a sorry state, so restoration work begun in 2016 may still be underway. There are several murals by 19th-century artist Hippolyte Flandrin over the archways in the nave. The heart of King Jean Casimir of Poland is buried here, as are the ashes of the body of René Descartes (his skull is in the collections of the Musée de l'Homme). On the left as you exit you can peek inside the **chapel of St-Symphorien,** where during the Revolution over 100 clergymen were imprisoned before being executed on the square in front of the church. The chapel was restored in the 1970s and decorated by contemporary artist Pierre Buraglio in 1992.

Classical music concerts are regularly held in the church on Thursday and Friday evenings. (Tickets and information are at www.fnactickets.com.) On the last Sunday of the month, afternoon organ recitals are free.

3 place St-Germain-des-Prés, 6th arrond. www.eglise-sgp.org. © **01-55-42-81-10.** Free admission. Daily 8am–7:45pm. Métro: St-Germain-des-Prés.

St-Sulpice ★★ CHURCH

The majestic facade of this enormous edifice looms over an entire neighborhood. Construction started in the 17th century over the remains of a medieval church; it took over a hundred years to build, and one of the towers was never finished. Inside, the cavernous interior seems to command you to be silent; several important works of art are tucked into the chapels that line the church. The most famous of them are **three master-pieces by Eugène Delacroix:** "Jacob Wrestling with the Angel," "Heliodorus Driven from the Temple," and "St-Michael Vanquishing the Devil" (on the right just after you enter the church). Jean-Baptiste Pigalle's statue of the "Virgin and Child" lights up the Chapelle de la Vierge at the farthest most point from the entrance. A bronze line runs north–south along the floor; this is part of a **gnomon,** an astronomical device set up in the 17th century to calculate the position of the sun in the sky. A small hole in one of the stained-glass windows creates a spot of light on the floor; every day at noon it hits the line in a different spot, climbing up to the top of an obelisk and lighting a gold disk at the winter equinox. Because of their size, churches were an ideal spot for this type of measurement, making for a rare collaboration between science and religion.

Place St-Sulpice, 6th arrond. http://pss75.fr/saint-sulpice-paris. (C) **01-42-34-59-98.** Free admission. Daily 7:30am–7:30pm. Métro: St-Sulpice.

Eiffel Tower & Les Invalides (7th Arrondissement)

The Iron Lady towers above this stately neighborhood stuffed with embassies and ministries, where the very buildings seem to insist that you stand up straight and pay attention. You'll see lots of elegant black cars with smoked glass cruising the streets, as well as many a tourist eyeing the **Eiffel Tower** or the golden dome of **Les Invalides,** and scurrying in and out of some of the city's best museums, like the **Musée du Quai Branly, Musée d'Orsay,** and **Musée Rodin.**

Eiffel Tower ★★★ MONUMENT   In his wildest dreams, Gustave Eiffel probably never imagined that the tower he built for the 1889 World's Fair would become the ultimate symbol of Paris, and for many, of France. Originally slated for demolition after its first 20 years, the Eiffel Tower has survived over a century and is one of the most visited sites in the nation. No fewer than 50 engineers and designers worked on the plans, which resulted in a remarkably solid structure that, despite its height (324m/1,063 ft., including the antenna) does not sway in the wind.

But while the engineers rejoiced, others howled. When the project for the tower was announced, a group of artists and writers, including Guy de Maupassant and Alexandre Dumas *fils,* published a manifesto that referred to it as an "odious column of bolted metal." Others were less diplomatic: Novelist Joris-Karl Huysmans called it a "hole-riddled suppository." Despite the objections, the tower was built—over 18,000 pieces of iron, held together with some 2.5 million rivets. In this low-tech era, building techniques involved a lot of elbow grease: The foundations, for example, were dug entirely by shovel, and the debris was hauled away in horse-drawn carts. Construction dragged on for 2 years, but finally, on March 31, 1889, Gustave Eiffel proudly led a group of dignitaries up the 1,665 steps to the top, where he unfurled the French flag for the inauguration.

Over 100 years later, the tower has become such an integral piece of the Parisian landscape that it's impossible to think of the city without it. Over

No need to go to the gym after marching up the 704 steps that lead you to the first and second floors of the Eiffel Tower. Not only will you burn calories, but you'll save money: At 7€ for adults, 5€ ages 12 to 24, and 3€ ages 4 to 11, this is the least expensive way to visit. Extra perks include an up-close view of the amazing metal structure and avoiding the long lines for the elevator. If you do decide to go to the top, you can buy supplementary tickets from the machines on the 2nd floor.

time, even the artists came around—the tower's silhouette can be found in the paintings of Seurat, Bonnard, Duffy, Chagall, and especially those of Robert Delaunay, who devoted an entire series of canvases to the subject. It has also inspired a range of stunts, from Pierre Labric riding a bicycle down the stairs from the first level in 1923, to Philippe Petit walking a 700m-long (2,296-ft.) tightrope from the Palais de Chaillot to the tower during the centennial celebration in 1989. Eiffel performed his own "stunts" toward the end of his career, using the tower as a laboratory for scientific experiments. By convincing the authorities of the tower's usefulness in studying meteorology, aerodynamics, and other subjects, Eiffel saved it from being torn down.

The most dramatic view of the tower itself is from the wide esplanade at the Palais de Chaillot (Métro: Trocadéro) across the Seine. From there it's a short walk through the gardens and across the Pont d'Alma to the base. Though several elevators whisk visitors skyward, they do take time to come back down, so be prepared for a wait. The first floor just had a makeover, with a new restaurant, displays and a bit of glass floor, so you can pretend you are walking on air. Personally, we think the view from the second level is the best; you're far enough up to see the entire city, yet close enough to clearly pick out the monuments. But if you are aching to get to the top, an airplanelike view awaits. The third level is, mercifully, enclosed, but thrill-seekers can climb up a few more stairs to the outside balcony (entirely protected with a grill). At the time of writing the base of the tower was set to be surrounded by 2 bulletproof glass walls as part of a plan to protect visitors and important monuments from terror attacks (as of the end of 2017). Don't be alarmed: It's precautionary and not the sign of an imminent danger, and you'll still be able to walk underneath for free once you've passed the security checks. The construction of the wall marks the beginning of a 15-year modernization plan that aims to improve access to the tower in general and provide shelter for visitors in bad weather. And of course, Paris wouldn't be Paris without the tower, so the monument will remain open throughout the work.

Champ de Mars, 7th arrond. www.tour-eiffel.fr. ⓒ **01-44-11-23-23.** Lift to 2nd floor 11€ adults, 8.50€ ages 12–24, 4€ ages 4–11; lift to 2nd and 3rd floors 17€ adults, 15€ ages 12–24, 8€ ages 4–11; stairs to 2nd floor 7€ adults, 5€ ages 12–24, 3€ ages 4–11. Free admission 3 and under. Mid-June to Aug daily 9am–midnight; Sept to mid-June daily 9:30am–11pm; Sept to mid-June stairs open only to 6:30pm. Métro: Trocadéro or Bir Hakeim. RER: Champ de Mars–Tour Eiffel.

Napoleon's Tomb at Hôtel des Invalides.

Hôtel des Invalides/Napoleon's Tomb ★★ MUSEUM   Military history rules at this grandiose complex, which houses a military museum, church, tomb, hospital, and military ministries, among other things. Over the entryway, LUDOVICUS MAGNUS is inscribed in huge letters, in homage to the builder of this vast edifice, otherwise known as Louis XIV. Determined to create a home for soldiers wounded in the line of duty, Louis commissioned architect Libéral Bruant to design a monumental structure with formal gardens on what was then the outskirts of the city. The first war veterans arrived in 1674—between 4,000 and 5,000 soldiers would eventually move in, creating a minicity with its own governor. An on-site hospital was constructed for the severely wounded, which is still in service today.

As you cross the main gate, you'll find yourself in a huge courtyard (102×207m, 335×207 ft.), the *cour d'honneur,* which was once the site of military parades. At the far end on the second story is a statue of "The Little Corporal" (Napoleon I) that once stood on top of the column in place Vendôme. The surrounding buildings house military administration offices and the recently renovated **Musée de l'Armée,** one of the world's largest military museums, with a vast collection of objects testifying to man's capacity for self-destruction. The most impressive section is **Arms and Armor,** a panoply of 13th- to 17th-century weaponry. Viking swords, Burgundian battle axes, 14th-century blunderbusses, Balkan *khandjars,* Browning machine guns, engraved Renaissance serpentines, musketoons, grenadiers—if it can kill, it's enshrined here. There is also a huge wing covering the exploits of everyone from **Louis XIV to Napoleon III,** another on the two **World Wars,** where the centennial of WWI (1914–18) is being honored in a series of galleries dedicated to the *Grand Guerre.* Also on-site is the **Musée des Plans et**

Reliefs, a somewhat dusty collection of scale models of fortresses and battlefields, and the **Musée de l'Ordre de la Libération,** which retraces the history of the Liberation (1940–45).

The **Eglise des Soldats** is actually the front half of the **Eglise du Dôme,** which was split in two when Napoleon's tomb was installed under the dome. The "Soldier's Church" is lovely and light-filled, decorated with magnificent chandeliers and a collection of flags of defeated enemies.

On the other side of the glass partition rests the Little Corporal himself. The **Tomb of Napoléon** lies under one of the most splendid domes in France. Designed by Hardouin-Mansart and constructed from 1679 to 1706, the interior soars 107m (351 ft.) up to a skylight, which illuminates a brilliantly colored cupola fresco by Charles de la Fosse. Ethereal light filters down to an opening in the center of the room, where you can look down on the huge porphyry sarcophagus, which holds the emperor's remains, encased in five successive coffins (one tin, one mahogany, two lead, and one ebony). Surrounding the sarcophagus are the tombs of two of Napoleon's brothers, his son, and several French military heroes. Don't blame the over-the-top setting on Napoleon; the decision to transfer his remains to Paris was made in 1840, almost 20 years after his death. Tens of thousands of people crowded the streets to pay their respects as the coffin was carried under the Arc de Triomphe and down the Champs-Élysées to Les Invalides, where it waited another 20 years until the spectacular tomb was finished.

Place des Invalides, 7th arrond. www.invalides.org. © **01-44-42-37-72.** Admission to all the museums, the church, and Napoleon's Tomb: 11€ adults, free for 17 and younger. Apr–Oct 10am–6pm; Nov–Mar 10am–5pm. Métro: Latour-Maubourg, Varenne, or Invalides. RER: Invalides.

Musée des Egouts de Paris ★ MUSEUM   If you want to get a better idea of Jean Valjean's underground ordeal in *Les Misérables,* take a trip through Paris's sewer museum. Though you won't actually get on a boat, you will be able to walk through a short stretch of the city's 2,400 km (1,490 miles) of sewers (don't worry, you'll be on a raised sidewalk on the side of the, uh, water), which should give you a pretty good idea of the different types of passageways and equipment that exist in this underground domain. There's also a film and a circuit of displays that explain the history of the city's water supply and waste disposal issues (this was no joke; for centuries, the lack of a proper sewage system helped spread diseases like the Black Plague), as well as technical aspects of this stinky world. Because it can on occasions be stinky, delicate noses should think twice before entering.

Pont de l'Alma, in front of 93 quai d'Orsay, 7th arrond. www.paris.fr. © **01-53-68-27-81.** Admission 4.40€ adults; 3.60€ students, and children 6–16; free 5 and under. May–Sept Sat–Wed 11am–6pm; Oct–Apr Sat–Wed 11am–5pm. Métro: Alma-Marceau. RER: Pont de l'Alma.

Musée d'Orsay ★★★ MUSEUM   What better setting for a world-class museum of 19th-century art than a beautiful example of Belle Epoque architecture? The magnificent Gare d'Orsay train station, built to coincide with the 1900 World's Fair, has been brilliantly transformed into an exposition space. The huge, airy central hall lets in lots of natural light, which has been artfully combined with artificial lighting to illuminate a collection of treasures that were once scattered among the Louvre and the Musée National d'Art Moderne.

The collection spans the years 1848 to 1914, a period that saw the birth of many artistic movements, such as the Barbizon School and Symbolism, but today it is best known for the emergence of Impressionism. Seeing them all together in one place makes it instantly obvious what a fertile time this was. All the superstars of the epoch are here, including Monet, Manet, Degas, Renoir, Cézanne, and Van Gogh.

The top floor is the home of the most famous Impressionist paintings, like Edouard Manet's masterpiece, "Le Déjeuner sur l'Herbe." Though Manet's composition of bathers and friends picnicking on the grass draws freely from those of Italian Renaissance masters, the painting shocked its 19th-century audience, which was horrified to see a naked lady lunching with two fully clothed men. Manet got into trouble again with his magnificent "Olympia," a seductive odalisque stretched out on a divan. There was nothing new about the subject; viewers were rattled by the unapologetic look in her eye—this is not an idealized nude, but a real woman, and a tough cookie, to boot.

The middle level is devoted to the post-Impressionists with works by artists like Gauguin, Seurat, Rousseau, and Van Gogh, like the latter's "Church at Auvers-sur-Oise," an ominous version of the church in a small town north of Paris where he moved after spending time in an asylum in Provence. This was

Musée d'Orsay.

one of some 70 paintings he produced in the 2 months leading up to his suicide.

A few other standouts:

○ **Renoir's "Dance at Le Moulin de la Galette, Montmartre":** The dappled light and the movement of the crowd in this joyous painting are such that you wonder if it's not going to suddenly waltz out of its frame. The blurred brushstrokes that created this effect rankled contemporary critics.

○ **Monet's "La Gare St-Lazare":** Here is another train station when steam engines were still pulling in on a regular basis. The metallic roof of the station frames an almost abstract mix of clouds and smoke; rather than a description of machines and mechanics, this painting is a modern study of light and color.

○ **Gauguin's "The White Horse":** The horse isn't even really white, but you don't care when you gaze at Gauguin's Tahitian version of paradise. Not everyone was charmed by the artist's use of vibrant color: The pharmacist who commissioned the painting refused it because the horse was too green.

Sculptures and decorative arts are also on display here, including a remarkable collection of Art Nouveau furniture and objects. Photo fans will appreciate the fine examples of early photography, including Félix Nadar's portrait of Charles Baudelaire; there are also some interesting works by nonphotographers like Edward Dégas and Emile Zola.

1 rue de la Légion d'Honneur, 7th arrond. www.musee-orsay.fr. © **01-40-49-48-14.** Admission 12€ adults, 9€ ages 18–25, free 17 and under. Tues–Wed and Fri–Sun 9:30am–6pm; Thurs 9:30am–9:45pm. Métro: Solférino. RER: Musée d'Orsay.

Musée du Quai Branly—Jacques Chirac ★★★ MUSEUM   Just a few blocks from the Eiffel Tower, this museum's wildly contemporary design has forever changed the architectural landscape of this rigidly elegant neighborhood. Its enormous central structure floats on a series of pillars, under which lays a lush garden, which is separated from the noisy boulevard out front by a huge glass wall. Looking up from the garden level, the museum looks a little like the hull of a container ship, with its rust-colored body and oddly stacked "boxes" sticking out from its sides. However you feel about the outside, you cannot help but be impressed by the inside: The vast space is filled with exquisite examples of the traditional arts of Africa, the Pacific Islands, Asia, and the Americas. Designed by architect Jean Nouvel, it makes an ideal showcase for a category of artwork that has too often been relegated to the sidelines of the museum world.

This magnificent collection is displayed in a way that invites visitors to admire the skill and artistry that went into the creation of these diverse objects. Delicately carved headrests from Papua New Guinea in the form of birds and crocodiles vie for attention with intricately painted masks from Indonesia. There's a selection of giant wooden flutes from Papua New Guinea, "magic stones" from the island nation of Vanuatu, Australian aboriginal paintings, an extensive Asian art section, and an African collection that includes embroidered silks from Morocco, geometric marriage cloths from Mali, and wooden masks from the Ivory Coast. The Americas collection includes rare Nazca pottery and Inca textiles, as well as an intriguing assortment of North American works, like Haitian voodoo objects, Sioux beaded tunics, and a huge totem pole from British Columbia. Though some documentation is translated in English, **audioguides** (5€) are a big help for non-French speakers.

37 quai Branly and 206 and 218 rue de Université, 7th arrond. www.quaibranly.fr. © **01-56-61-70-00.** Admission 10€ adults, free 17 and under. Mon–Wed and Sun 11am–7pm; Thurs–Sat 11am–9pm. Métro: Alma-Marceau. RER: Pont d'Alma.

Musée Rodin ★★★ MUSEUM   The grounds of this splendid museum are so lovely that many are willing to pay 4€ just to stroll around. Behind the Hôtel Biron, which houses the museum, is a formal garden with benches, fountains, and even a little cafe (no picnics allowed, unfortunately). Of course, it would be foolish not to go inside and drink in the some of the 6,600 sculptures of this excellent collection (don't worry, not all are on display), but it would be equally silly not to take the time to admire the large bronzes in the garden, which include some of Rodin's most famous works. Take, for example, "The Thinker." Erected in front of the Panthéon in 1906 during an intense political crisis, Rodin's first public sculpture soon became a Socialist symbol and was quickly transferred to the Hôtel Biron by the authorities, under the pretense that it blocked pedestrian traffic. Other important sculptures in the garden include the "Burghers of Calais," "Balzac," and the "Gates of Hell," a monumental composition that the sculptor worked on throughout his career.

Indoors, marble compositions prevail, although there are also works in terracotta, plaster, and bronze, as well as sketches and paintings on display. The most famous of the marble works is "The Kiss," which was originally meant to appear in the "Gates of Hell." In time, Rodin decided that the lovers were too happy for this grim composition, and he explored it as an independent work. The sculpture was inspired by the tragic story of Paolo and Francesca, in which a young woman falls in love with her husband's brother. Upon their first kiss, the husband discovers them and stabs them both. As usual with Rodin's works, the critics were shocked by the couple's overt sensuality, but not as shocked as they were by the large, impressionistic rendition of "Balzac," exhibited at the same salon, which critic Georges Rodenbach described as "less a statue than a strange monolith, a thousand-year-old menhir." There are hundreds of works here, many of them legendary, so don't be surprised if after a while your vision starts to blur. That'll be your cue to head outside and enjoy the garden.

79 rue de Varenne, 7th arrond. www.musee-rodin.fr. © **01-44-18-61-10.** Admission 10€ adults, 7€ ages 18–25, free 17 and under. Tues–Sun 10am–5:45pm. Métro: Varenne or St-Francois-Xavier.

Montparnasse (14th & 15th Arrondissements)

Even though its heart was ripped out in the early 1970s, when the original 19th-century train station was torn down and the Tour Montparnasse, an ugly skyscraper, was erected, this neighborhood still retains a redolent whiff of its artistic past. Back in the day, artists such as Picasso, Modigliani, and Man Ray hung out in cafes like **Le Dôme, La Coupole, La Rotonde,** and **Le Sélect,** as did a "Lost Generation" of English-speaking writers like Hemingway, Fitzgerald, Faulkner, and James Joyce. Today the cafes are mostly filled with rich tourists, but there are still quiet corners and even artists' studios.

Cimetière du Montparnasse ★ CEMETERY   This quiet cemetery is the final resting place of many French celebrities. A map to the left of the main gateway will direct you to the gravesite of its most famous couple, Simone de Beauvoir and Jean-Paul Sartre. Others resting here include Samuel Beckett, Guy de Maupassant, Pierre Larousse (famous for his dictionary), Capt. Alfred Dreyfus, auto tycoon André Citroën; sculptors Ossip Zadkine and Constantin Brancusi, actress Jean Seberg, composer Camille Saint-Saëns, photographer Man Ray, poet Charles Baudelaire, and American intellectual and activist Susan Sontag, who was interred here in 2005. You can download a map on the municipal website, www.paris.fr.

3 bd. Edgar-Quinet, 14th arrond. www.paris.fr. © **01-44-10-86-50.** Mon–Fri 8am–6pm; Sat 8:30am–6pm; Sun 9am–6pm. Métro: Edgar-Quinet.

Les Catacombes ★ CEMETERY/HISTORIC SITE   Definitely not for the faint of heart, the city's catacombs are filled with the remains of millions of ex-Parisians whose bones line the narrow passages of this mazelike series of tunnels. In the 18th century, the Cimetière des Innocents, a centuries-old, overpacked cemetery near Les Halles, had become so foul and disease-ridden that it was finally declared a health hazard and closed. The bones of its occupants were transferred to this former quarry, which were later joined by those of other similarly pestilential Parisian cemeteries. In 1814, the quarry stopped accepting new lodgers, and the quarry inspector had a novel idea. Rather than leaving just a hodgepodge of random bones, he organized them in neat stacks and geometric designs, punctuating the 2km (1¼ miles) with sculptures and pithy sayings carved into the rock. The one at the entrance sets the tone: STOP— HERE IS THE EMPIRE OF DEATH. The visit will be fascinating for some, terrifying for others; not a good idea for claustrophobes or small children. The lighting is appropriately eerie, so you should bring a flashlight if you really

Catacombes.

want to see. Explanations are in English, French, and Spanish. It's cool down here (around 54°F/12°C) and damp, so a jacket or sweatshirt and rubber-soled shoes are indispensable. **Audioguides** in English (5€) add interesting titbits of information to the visit.

1 ave. du Colonel Henri Rol-Tanguy, 14th arrond. www.catacombes.paris.fr. © **01-43-22-47-63.** Admission 12€ adults, 10€ ages 18–26, free 17 and under. Tues–Sun 10am–8:30pm (last entry 7:30pm). Métro and RER: Denfert-Rochereau.

Musée Bourdelle ★ MUSEUM   Recently renovated and expanded, this museum is a testament to the sculptor Antoine Bourdelle, whose work went far beyond the 10 years he spent as Rodin's assistant. A renowned teacher who influenced an entire generation of sculptors, including Alberto Giacometti and Aristide Maillol, Bourdelle was one of the pioneers of 20th-century monumental sculpture. Proud, muscular centaurs, gods, and goddesses stride across these rooms, as well as monuments to famous people. You can also visit the sculptor's studio. **Audioguides** in English (5€) are a big help here.

18 rue Antoine-Bourdelle, 15th arrond. www.bourdelle.paris.fr. © **01-49-54-73-73.** Free admission to the permanent collection. Tues–Sun 10am–6pm. Métro: Montparnasse-Bienvenüe.

ORGANIZED TOURS & CLASSES

If you've only got a couple of days and you just don't have the stamina to do the research, an organized tour can provide good background information on the city and help you get your bearings. Here are a few ideas for getting to know Paris in an easy and different way.

Boat Tours

The famed **Bateaux-Mouches** (www.bateaux-mouches.fr; © **01-42-25-96-10;** Métro: Alma-Marceau) cruises leave from Pont de l'Alma on the Right Bank of the Seine, and last for a little over 1 hour. They tend to be crowded and touristy, but can be a worthwhile way to enjoy the beauty of the sites along the Seine. Tickets cost 14€ for adults, 6€ for kids 4 to 11, free 3 and under; the recorded commentary is in French, English, and up to 3 other languages. There are also brunch, lunch and dinner cruises (starting at 50€–75€).

On the other side of the river, in front of the Eiffel Tower, the **Bateaux Parisiens** (www.bateauxparisiens.com; © **08-25-01-01-01;** 0.15€/min.; Métro: Bir Hakeim; RER: Champ de Mars Tour Eiffel) offers similar 1-hour tours (recorded commentary), but in smaller boats. Tickets cost 15€ for adults, 7€ children 3 to 12, free 2 and under. Bateaux Parisiens also runs a tour departing from Notre-Dame, but the service is a less regular. Gourmet lunch and dinner cruises start at 59€ and 69€.

A little less touristy, the **Vedettes du Pont Neuf** (www.vedettesdupontneuf.com; © **01-46-33-98-38;** Métro: Pont Neuf) runs hour-long cruises with live guides in French and English from the Square du Vert Galant at the tip of the Île de la Cité. Tickets cost 14€ for adults, 7€ children 4 to 12, free 3 and under; cheaper tickets can be bought online.

Canauxrama (www.canauxrama.com; ℰ **01-42-39-15-00;** Métro: Jaurés or Bastille) tours the picturesque Canal St-Martin. Boats leave from either the Bassin de la Villette or the Bassin de l'Arsenal (near the place de la Bastille) and tickets cost 18€, free for those 4 and under. The cruise takes about 2½ hours. The first part, which runs through a tunnel under the place de la Bastille, is eerie (in a fun way), and after you'll enjoy a lovely ride through locks and under pretty arched bridges. Tours daily from May to September; less frequent service the rest of the year.

Bus Tours

Yes, they're touristy, and yes, Paris is easy to navigate without an organized bus tour, but the city's hop-on, hop off buses are worth considering if (1) you're in a hurry and want to see all the main sights in 1 or 2 days, and (2) you don't want to use the public transport system. For the former, we suggest choosing the **Big Bus Paris** company (www.bigbustours.com; ℰ **01-53-95-39-53;** 1-day adult tickets 32€, 2-day adult ticket 36€, 16€ for children 4–12; prices are cheaper online), which has just two routes, one stopping at 10 top sites (including the Eiffel Tower and Notre-Dame), and the other covering Montmartre. The key to these tours is not actually hopping on and off (although you could, of course), but staying on board to see everything in one sweep—in 2¼ hours for the main tour and in 1¼ hours for Montmartre—leaving you with plenty of time for serendipitous exploring of your own. To avoid using public transport, we suggest **L'Open Tour** (www.paris.opentour. com; ℰ **01-42-66-56-56;** 1-day adult pass 33€, 2-day pass 37€, 3-day pass 41€, 17€ for children 4–11), which has over 75 stops spread over four routes that run from around 9am to 7pm (and 9:30pm in summer for night tours) just like normal buses. The advantage of this is that you will only be with like-minded visitors; the downside is that you may have a long wait between buses and therefore spend a lot of time standing in line rather than exploring. However, whichever tour you choose, multilingual audio guides are provided (you can switch them off if you just want to look at the city), and both sell tickets that can be combined with a river cruise (see websites for details).

Cycling Tours

Fat Tire Bike Tours (www.fattiretours.com/paris; ℰ **01-82-88-80-96,** or in North America 866/614-6218; Métro: Dupleix) offers a 3½-hour day- or night-tour of Paris by bike in English; adult tickets cost 34€, 32€ students and children 4 to 12. Kid-size bikes and toddler trailers are available, and the tour includes a break in a cafe in the Tuileries garden (where children can run around) so this is a good one to choose if you're travelling with your family. They also offer tours of Versailles and Monet's Garden in Giverny.

If you'd like to see Paris like a local, pick **Paris à Vélo, C'est Sympa** (22 rue Alphonse Baudin, 11th arrond.; www.parisvelosympa.com; ℰ **01-48-87-60-01;** Métro: Richard Lenoir): In addition to their "Heart of Paris" tour (which covers Notre-Dame, the Marais, and the Louvre area), they offer two themed 3-hour bike tours—Unusual Paris, and Paris Contrasts—both of which take you into areas tourists don't usually get to see. The first goes to the southern 13th and 14th arrondissements, home to cobbled lanes and artists' workshops; the second is to northern Paris, along the canals and onto futuristic Parc de la Villette. Adult tickets cost 35€, 29€ ages 12 to 25, 20€ 11 and under. They also rent bikes. Tours are in French and English.

Bike About Tours (www.bikeabouttours.com; ☎ 06-18-80-84-92) offers 3½-hour tours in small groups, led by friendly, knowledgeable, fluent-English speakers for 35€ per person (30€ students). All tours leave from the statue of Charlemagne in front of Notre-Dame at 10am (and 3pm during the summer) and cover all the main sights via the city's atmospheric back streets. They also include a pitstop in a Left Bank bakery (food not included) and a few quirky stop-offs, like at Jim Morrison's house and places where famous movies were shot. Bike rentals also available.

Hot-Air Balloon Tours

A unique way to see the city from above is by a hot-air balloon. Located in the Parc André Citroën in the 15th arrondissement, **Ballon de Paris** (www.ballondeparis.com; ☎ 01-44-26-20-00; Métro: Javel or Balard) has a hot-air balloon that reaches an altitude of 150m (492 ft.) but remains tethered to the ground. Tickets cost 12€ adults, 6€ ages 3 to 11, free 2 and under. Tours can be cancelled due to weather conditions; check website or call ahead to make sure the balloon is flying.

Walking Tours

Sight Seeker's Delight (www.sightseekersdelight.com; ☎ 07-63-07-09-68) offers a range of walking tours in English, including Paris Along the Seine, Tickle Your Tastebuds, and Secrets of the Night. Tours last from 2½ to 4 hours and prices vary between 30€ and 99€ per person (ages 4–10 half-price, 3 and under free).

Paris Walks (www.paris-walks.com; ☎ 01-48-09-21-40) organizes 2-hour walks of the city, based on either a theme or a neighborhood. Most of the walks cost 15€ for adults, 10€ ages 15–20, 8€ 14 and under; special small-group themed tours (chocolate, the Louvre, fashion) range from 20€ to 40€ per adult. Reservations are only necessary for special tours.

Paris Greeters (www.parisgreeters.fr) arranges free tours for one to six people with local volunteers. There's no catalog of specific tours; your walk is pretty much up to the greeter, who will choose a neighborhood. You register online and request a specific day and language; you'll then be contacted with the details of your tour.

Other Guided Tours

4 Roues Sous 1 Parapluie (www.4roues-sous-1parapluie.com; ☎ 01-58-59-27-82) offers chauffeur-driven themed rides around Paris in its colorful fleet of Citroën 2CV, the tiny, low-cost, and now classic French car that was jokingly referred to as "4 wheels under an umbrella." If there are three people in the car, prices start at 30€ per person for a 45-minute tour and 60€ per person for a 1½-hour tour; the price of the car is the same, it's simply a question of how you divvy up the bill.

Paris is a dream-come-true for shopaholics. **Chic Shopping Paris** (www.chicshoppingparis.com; © **09-77-19-77-85**, or in North America 573/355-9777) offers tours in English designed to give visitors a behind-the-scenes shopping experience. Themed tours include a Made in France tour, a Unique Boutique tour, and an Arts and Antiques tour of a flea market. Tours last 3½ to 4 hours and start at 100€ per person.

Cooking Classes

Several cooking schools in Paris offer short-term or 1-day courses. The most famous is **Le Cordon Bleu** (www.cordonbleu.edu; © **01-85-65-15-00**; Métro: Vaugirard)—this is where Julia Child mastered the art of French cooking. Well known for its professional cooking courses, it also offers short courses for lay food enthusiasts, with prices starting at 85€ for a 2-hour food and wine pairing demonstration and 115€ for macaroon-making lessons. Classes are translated into English and fill up fast; reserve ahead.

Less formal but equally enjoyable are the cooking classes offered by **La Cuisine Paris** (www.lacuisineparis.com; © **01-40-51-78-18**; Métro: Hôtel de Ville), a friendly school set up by a Franco-American team. It offers market tours and small classes by professional chefs in both French and English, including the popular French Macaron Class. Prices range from 69€ for 2 hours to 160€ for 5 hours.

Similarly, **Cook'n with Class** (www.cooknwithclass.com; © **01-42-57-22-84**; Métro: Simplon or Jules Joffrin) offers a range of individual and small-group classes, the most popular of which is the French Market class, where you learn to choose and cook the best produce from the market. Set up by a French chef, all classes are taught in English by professionals, and prices start at 130€ for 3-hour classes.

Language Classes

The **Alliance Française** (www.alliancefr.org; © **01-42-84-90-00**) has been offering quality French classes for over a century. Depending on how many hours and what kind of course you take, courses cost 133€ to 253€ per week for 1 to 3 weeks; rates go down when you attend more than 3 weeks.

ESPECIALLY FOR KIDS

Paris is not an especially kid-friendly city, but it's not kid-unfriendly, either. For one, Parisians generally like kids, as long as they are not running wild. If you visit in the summer, in addition to the suggestions below, just about any age child (including grown-up ones) will have a blast at **Paris Plage** or along the **newly reopened banks of the Seine, Les Berges,** between Musée d'Orsay and Pont d'Alma, and the **Rives de Seine,** between Bastille and Tuileries (see box, below). Here are some attractions that children may enjoy:

Bois de Boulogne (p. 197)
Bois de Vincennes (p. 198)
Centre Pompidou (p. 148)
Château de Vincennes (p. 198)
Cité des Sciences et de l'Industrie (p. 170)
Eiffel Tower (p. 182)
Gaîté Lyrique (p. 149)
Grévin (p. 146)
Jardin d'Acclimatation (p. 195)
Jardin des Plantes (p. 172)
Jardin des Tuileries (p. 135)
Jardin du Luxembourg (p. 179)
La Promenade Plantée (p. 166)
Les Dimanches au Galop (p. 253)
Musée des Arts et Métiers (p. 154)
Musée des Egouts de Paris (p. 185)
Muséum National d'Histoire Naturelle (p. 176)
Palais de Tokyo (p. 162)
Parc de la Villette (p. 171)
Parc des Buttes Chaumont (p. 172)
Parc Floral (p. 198)
Parc Zoologique de Paris (p. 167)

And here are some more ideas for kid entertainment, according to age group:

FOR TINY TOTS (0–5 YEARS OLD): There are nice **playgrounds** with safe equipment all over the city. For precise locations, visit http://en.parisinfo. com (search "playground"), ask at your hotel, or just follow the strollers. The Tuileries Gardens and the Luxembourg Gardens both have a large fountain where you can **rent wooden toy sailboats** (for around 3€) and push them around with a long stick. Most large gardens or parks in this book have a **merry-go-round;** visit www.offi.fr (search "manèges à Paris"). Kids will also love the activities in the Luxembourg Gardens (see box, p. 179).

FOR THE MIDDLE YEARS (6–9 YEARS OLD): This is when it's time to turn to attractions like **Grévin** (p. 146), the **Cité des Enfants** (p. 170), and the **Jardin d'Acclimatation** (p. 195), and if you are really desperate, there's always **Disneyland Paris** (p. 274). The **Parc Zoologique de Paris** (p. 167) is a good bet, as is another, smaller **zoo** at the Jardin des Plantes (the **Ménagerie,** p. 173). You might also consider going to one of the **municipal pools** (p. 199), which usually include a kiddie pool. The revamped Les Halles district conceals a new adventure playground, the **Jardin Nelson Mandela** (1 rue Pierre Lescot), with a trampoline and trees to climb.

Guignol, the Puppet Show Hero

Created by an itinerant merchant and tooth-puller in Lyon about 200 years ago, **Guignol**, the sly hero of traditional French puppet shows, is still packing houses all over the country. This valiant valet, who often finds himself in difficult situations due to his master's mischief, has an amazing way with children, who scream, hoot, and holler according to how Guignol's adventures unfold. There's lots of audience participation: The wide-eyed puppet will ask the children to help him find the robber/wolf/bad guy, and then will promptly head in the wrong direction as the kids desperately try to get him back on track. It's noisy, but good fun—even if you don't understand French, the stories are pretty easy to figure out. This is a great way to take part in an authentically French experience—though it might be a little overwhelming for sensitive souls under 3. Guignol puppet theaters can be found in the Jardin d'Acclimation, the Jardin du Luxembourg, the Parc Floral, Parc des Buttes-Chaumont, and on the Champs-Élysées.

FOR THE TWEENS (10–13 YEARS OLD): At this age, the scale can tip both ways, between "not another museum!" and actually getting interested in some of the cultural offerings. A few museums are particularly suited to this age, like the **Musée des Arts et Metiers** (p. 154), the **Gaîté Lyrique** (p. 149), and, in particular, the **Cité des Sciences et de l'Industrie. Boat** or **bike tours** (p. 196) also work for this crew.

Paris has one old-fashioned amusement park just off the Porte Maillot in the Bois de Boulogne:

Jardin d'Acclimatation ★ AMUSEMENT PARK/GARDEN You'll see plenty of grandmothers in fur coats at this elegant amusement park, which is adjacent to the swank suburb of Neuilly. There's a farm with some animals, but the main attraction here are the rides, which include bumper cars, merry-go-rounds, and small rollercoasters. As the rides (*manèges*) quickly add up (you pay as you go), you may want to point your offspring in the direction of the huge playground, which includes an area where kids can run around under giant sprinklers in the hot weather. In the same area, you'll find a puppet theater (Wed, Sat–Sun, and school holidays 3 and 4pm); Guignol's adventures are presented free of charge. To reach the park from Porte Maillot, take the *Petit Train* (little train; ticket 3.50€) from Allée de Longchamp at the entrance to the Bois de Boulogne.

Bois de Boulogne. www.jardindacclimatation.fr. ✆ **01-40-67-90-85.** Admission 3.50€ adults and children over 2, 1.50€ seniors, free 2 and under; attractions 3.50€ per ticket, 30€ book of 10 tickets. Mon–Fri 11am–5pm; Sat–Sun and school holidays 10am–6:30pm. Métro: Sablons or Porte Maillot.

ACTIVE PARIS

"Working out" is still a somewhat foreign concept in France, but that doesn't mean that you can't exercise. Though gyms are few and far between, pools are everywhere, and any enterprising sports enthusiast can easily find places to bike, rollerblade, or run.

In a bid to make Paris more environmentally and visitor-friendly, portions of the Seine's banks have been turned into pedestrian- and bike-only stretches. The first part covers the area between the Musée d'Orsay to the Pont d'Alma (known as **Les Berges,** or "the embankments"), and since April 2017, the quays between Bastille and the Tuilleries gardens have also been embellished with promenades, gardens, cultural spaces, cafes, sports facilities, and picnic areas along a stretch known as the **Rives de Seine.** This is great news for walkers, as it's now possible to stroll between Bastille and the Eiffel Tower (across bridges) without meeting a single car! You can also eat, drink, flirt at one of the bars, walk, or even take a tai chi class at various points along the route. There are kids' activities, too.

Meanwhile, another hugely successful riverside event is now into its second decade: **Paris Plage.** Every year from mid-July to mid-August, tons of sand is shipped in and dumped on the riverbanks to create a fun and funky "beach," complete with beach volleyball, tea dances, concerts, drink stands, and all sorts of excellent silliness. Success has been such that the beach can be found not only on the Voie Georges Pompidou (near the Hôtel de Ville, 4th arrond.) but also along edges of the Bassin de la Villette (19th arrond.), where you can rent paddleboats and canoes. The number of activities and events swells every season; for a complete rundown, visit the city's **Que Faire à Paris (What to Do in Paris)** website: **http://quefaire.paris.fr/parisplages.**

Cycling

You can **rent a bike** by the hour in the **Bois de Vincennes** at Lac Daumesnil or Lac des Minimes and in the **Bois de Boulogne** (in front of the Jardin d'Acclimatation or next to the Lac Inferieur [lower lake]). If you are up to the challenge of Parisian traffic and want to cycle around the city, you can try **Velib',** the city's wildly popular self-service bike program—just be sure you are armed with a chip-and-pin credit card or have picked up an Internet subscription for your stay (for details on how the system works, visit www.velib.fr and/or see p. 284). For longer-term rentals, try **Paris à Vélo, C'est Sympa** (www.parisvelo sympa.com), or **Bike About Tours** (www.bikeabouttours.com).

Ice-Skating Rinks

Two **indoor ice-skating rinks** are open to the public: **Patinoire Pailleron** (32 rue E. Pailleron, 19th arrond.; www.pailleron19.com; © **01-40-40-27-70;** Métro: Bolivar), open year-round, and **Patinoire Accorhotels Arena** (222 Quai de Bercy, 12th arrond.; www.accorhotelsarena.com/fr/arena/la-patinoire; © **01-58-70-16-75;** Métro: Bercy), open September to May. The latter has DJ–hosted soirées until midnight Fridays and Saturdays. In addition, every year, **outdoor rinks** are set up from December through February in public spaces; 2 of the best are found in front of the **Hôtel de Ville** and at **Trocadéro,** where you can fill-up on Eiffel Tower views as you glide. Both are free— you'll just have to pay a small fee for skate rental.

Parks

There are two huge parks on the outskirts of Paris where you can bike, run, and even watch horse races.

Bois de Boulogne ★★ PARK   In the 7th century, Dagobert, King of the Francs, used to go hunting in the woods that we now know as the Bois de Boulogne; it remained a hunting domain for the kings of France up until Louis XVI, who finally opened it up to the public. That was mighty grand of him, and we thank him for it—this lovely natural haven is just what stressed-out Parisians need. Thick stands of trees, broken up by grassy knolls, manicured gardens, and even a lake or two plus several posh restaurants are tucked into this verdant spread. There is even a nice spot for tiny urbanites to unwind: The **Jardin d'Acclimatation** (see above), a large children's garden/amusement park, is a delight for kids of all ages.

What you see today, however, is not what Dagobert saw. Once Louis XVI was beheaded, and the Revolution got underway, the park was ravaged. What was left of it was completely demolished during subsequent military campaigns: In 1814, it was occupied and pillaged by some 40,000 English and Russian soldiers. It wasn't until Napoleon III decided to remodel the entire city in the mid-1800s that the Bois de Boulogne was attended to. Inspired by the English public parks that he had visited during his years of exile, the Emperor gave the command to rebuild the park. Over 400,000 trees were planted, and dozens of chalets, pavilions, snack stands, and restaurants were built. A network of roads and trails was laid down totaling 95km (59 miles). Finally, the park was ready for the public, and the public was definitely ready for the park. Here are a few of its most popular areas:

o The **Parc de Bagatelle** is a park-within-a-park, with a lush **garden,** a small **château** that hosts concerts in the summer (check listing magazines for details), and a **rose garden** with over 1,000 varieties. New varieties are introduced every year in June, during an international rose competition. The version of the garden you see today was designed by Forestier, a friend of Monet, who was inspired by Impressionism, which is evident in the artfully placed clusters of flowers and plants.

o The **Pré Catelan** is most famous for its elegant and extremely pricey restaurant, but there are plenty of other reasons to come here. This green enclave includes lush lawns, playgrounds, and flowerbeds, as well as the **Jardin Shakespeare,** which attempts to re-create settings from the Bard's plays. Here you'll find the heaths of Macbeth, the Forest of Arden, and the pond where Ophelia meets her watery death.

o The **Jardin d'Acclimatation** is an old-fashioned amusement park, with lots of grassy areas and nifty playgrounds (p. 195).

In addition to walking, rollerblading, and cycling (**bike rentals** at the edge of the Lac Inferieur and at the Jardin d'Acclimatation), you can **rent a boat** on the lake, **go fishing** in some of the ponds, or take in a horse race at the

Longchamp and Auteuil hippodromes (www.france-galop.com). The spectacular **Fondation Louis Vuitton** (p. 157) is in the park, right next to the Jardin d'Acclimatation.

16th arrond. www.paris.fr. Métro: Porte d'Auteuil, Les Sablons, Porte Maillot, or Porte Dauphine.

Bois de Vincennes ★★ PARK   There aren't as many gardens and restaurants here as in its western counterpart, but there is more of a sense of wilderness in this vast patch of greenery on the eastern end of Paris. Endless paths and alleys wind through woods and open fields; this is a great place for a long bike ride or a hike. Not that there are just trees here—if rambling isn't your game, there are plenty of other things to do as well. For starters, there is the recently reopened **Parc Zoologique de Paris** (p. 167), a state-of-the-art zoo. Then there are the remains of a medieval castle, the Château de Vincennes (see below) and a large garden in the park, as well as theaters and a hippodrome for those who prefer to sit back and watch the action. In short, there are almost as many pleasures here as in the Bois de Boulogne, if not as much elegance.

Like the Bois de Boulogne, the Bois de Vincennes was once a royal hunting ground with a lodge built by Louis VII back in the 12th century. By the 13th century, it had grown into a castle, which Louis IX (St-Louis) became very fond of; it is said that he dispensed justice under one of the nearby oak trees. It wasn't until the 18th century, under Louis XV, that these woods were turned into a public park; unfortunately, after the Revolution, the army decided to use it as a training ground, and the castle became a prison (some of its more famous lodgers included the Marquis de Sade and the philosopher Denis Diderot). Needless to say, this did not do wonders for the landscaping. Finally, in the 19th century, Napoleon III made the park part of his urban renewal scheme, and it got the same thorough makeover as the Bois de Boulogne. Its troubles were not completely over, however. In 1944, the retreating German army left the chateau in ruins, but it has since been almost completely restored.

A few of the park's high points:

o The **Parc Zoologique de Paris** (aka the Paris Zoo): See p. 167.

o The **Parc Floral:** Created in 1969, this modern mix of **flower beds, ponds, picnic areas,** and **playgrounds** (including a few rides) is a very pleasant place to spend the afternoon, particularly between May and September when the open-air theater holds free music and theater performances. In July, the Paris Jazz Festival takes off for 3 weeks, and in most of August and September, the Festival Classique au Vert cooks up a great program of classical music. For the kids, **Guignol puppet shows** (www.guignolparcfloral.com; 2.80€ adults and children) play most Wednesdays, Saturdays, and Sundays at 3pm and 4pm, and every day during school holidays.

o The **Château de Vincennes:** It took 12 years to restore this former royal castle (the heart of France's monarchy until Louis XIV decided to move to Versailles in 1682) and the result—an ivory-colored compound with gracious, turreted ramparts—is truly beautiful. You can visit the imposing **castle keep,** a **gothic chapel** with 16th-century stained-glass windows, and the multi-turreted **ramparts,** on top of which you can take a stroll and pretend you are a knight on the lookout for enemy invaders. For the best views opt for a guided tour of the keep's upper floors, usually closed to the public (ave. de Paris, 12th arrond.; www.chateau-vincennes.fr; ℂ **01-48-08-31-20;** 9.50€ adults, 7.50€ 18–25, free 17 and under, and under 26s from EU countries; mid-Sept to mid-May 10am–5pm, mid-May to mid-Sept 10am–6pm; Métro: Château de Vincennes).

Like the Bois de Boulogne, the park has plenty of other outdoor activities. You can **rent bikes** in front of either of the two large lakes or on the esplanade by the château, or **rent boats** for rowing around the lake. There are several **playgrounds,** as well as a **farm** (La Ferme de Paris), where children can watch cows being milked and sheep being shorn. There is also a **hippodrome** here for thoroughbred racing fans (www.letrot.com).

Bois de Vincennes, 12th arrond. www.paris.fr. Admission free to main park. Metro: Porte Dorée or Château de Vincennes.

Public Pools

There are 39 public pools (*piscines,* pronounced "pee-*seen*") in Paris, and they are open to everyone. They are generally quite clean and always have lockers and dressing areas. The size of the pools varies—most are 25m (82 ft.), and a few, like the one at Les Halles, are 50m (164 ft.). The most unusual is the **Piscine Josephine Baker** (ℂ **01-56-61-96-50;** Métro: Quai de la Gare), a floating swimming pool docked on quai François Mauriac in the Seine (don't worry, the water is not from the river). The best way to find addresses and hours is to visit www.paris.fr/piscines. Entry to all municipal pools is 3€; you can buy a card for 10 entries for 24€. Swimming caps are obligatory, but you can purchase them from self-service machines at the pools.

Running

Today, *le footing,* as running is called, is considered pretty commonplace, though nowhere near as omnipresent as in London or New York. You can run anywhere, of course, but a few favored places are around the lakes in the **Bois de Boulogne** and the **Bois de Vincennes** (see above), the **Promenade Plantée** (p. 166), along the quays of the Seine, and the **Jardin du Luxembourg.**

Tennis

The French are huge tennis fans, and Parisians are no exception. Paris has some **43 public tennis courts,** all of which can be reserved online at the city's website (www.paris.fr/tennis). The courts in the **Jardin de Luxembourg** are particularly pleasant, as are those in the **Marais** (5–7 rue Neuve-Saint-Pierre, 4th arrond.; Métro: Saint Paul). The fee for an hour of play is 9€ in an open court and 17€ for covered courts. *Note:* You will need to bring your own tennis equipment.

WALKING TOURS OF PARIS

7

Paris is a walking city. You simply won't be able to fully appreciate the flavor of the place if you don't stroll through the streets, and absorb the sights, sounds, and even smells that make up its sensory identity. A mere city block can encompass several centuries' worth of history. Below are tours of two of the city's best areas for ambling about.

WALKING TOUR 1: **MONTMARTRE**

START:	**Place des Abbesses (Métro: Abbesses).**
FINISH:	**Sacré Coeur (Métro: Abbesses).**
TIME:	**About 1½ hours.**
BEST TIME:	**Weekdays, when there are fewer crowds and stores are open.**
WORST TIME:	**Weekends, when the area around Sacré Coeur looks like the Métro at rush hour.**

Montmartre has become forever linked with a certain mythic image of Paris: quaint cobblestoned streets, accordion serenades, and the Sacré Coeur hovering in the background. Or maybe it's the Moulin Rouge and can-can girls whooping it up on the place Blanche. Although the area just around the Sacré Coeur is probably the most tourist-clogged in the capital and the Moulin Rouge is a tour-bus trap, there's still magic on the Butte, and it's not hard to find. If legendary artists like Picasso and Utrillo are gone, new ones have taken their place, and they aren't the ones hawking portraits in the place du Tertre. In fact, within a couple blocks from the mobs on the *place,* there actually *are* quiet cobbled streets lined with lovely vine-trimmed houses and punctuated by cute cafes and shops.

1 Place des Abbesses

The first thing you'll notice when you are coming out of the Métro is the exit itself: This lovely Art Nouveau confection of smoked glass and metal is one of two surviving Métro entrances by Hector Guimard with a glass roof (the other is at Porte Dauphine in the 16th arrond.). Now, look around the

Montmartre Walking Tour

1 Place des Abbesses
2 Bateau Lavoir
3 Moulin de la Galette and the Moulin du Radet
4 Allée des Brouillards
5 Place Dalida
6 Clos Montmartre Vineyard
7 Au Lapin Agile
8 Musée de Montmartre
9 Rue St-Rustique
10 Place du Tertre
11 Sacré Coeur

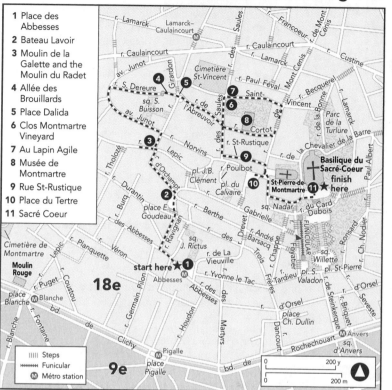

leafy plaza. Back in 1134, King Louis *Le Gros* (the Fat, otherwise known as Louis VI) founded an abbey up here, and this square is named after the various abbesses who ran it. As most of them came from wealthy, aristocratic families, they did not fare well during the French Revolution. In 1794, the 43rd abbess, Louise de Montmorency-Laval, who was 71 years old and both blind and deaf, was guillotined and the abbey was pillaged. Her crime? She was found guilty of "blindly and deafly plotting against the Revolution."

Walk west on rue des Abbesses to rue Ravignan, where you will make a right uphill. At the top of the short street is place Emile Goudeau. At No. 11 *bis*–No. 13 is the:

2 Bateau-Lavoir

This building started out as a piano factory but later was home to a virtual hall of fame of artists, actors, and poets, when they were all young and struggling. In 1889, this odd edifice—constructed on different levels to accommodate the steep slope it was built on—was split up into artists'

Abbesses Métro entrance.

studios. By 1904, a young man named Pablo Picasso was living and working there, as well as Kees Van Dongen, Juan Gris, and Amadeo Modigliani, not to mention the poets Max Jacob and Guillaume Apollinaire, among others. It was here that Picasso painted "Les Demoiselles d'Avignon" (even though he was nowhere near Provence), a painting that signaled the birth of Cubism. Unfortunately, this fertile artistic breeding ground, which was dubbed the **Bateau Lavoir,** or the Floating Laundry, by Jacob, burned down in 1970. All that's left of the original structure is one facade on the small plaza. The rest was rebuilt in 1978 and today still houses artists' studios. You can see a few vine-covered studios here.

Turn left on tiny rue d'Orchampt, a quiet cobbled street, which curves up to an intersection with rue Lepic. Take a short detour left down rue Lepic to the:

3 Moulin de la Galette & Moulin du Radet

There were once more than 30 windmills on Montmartre's slopes, which were covered in vineyards. Here are the last two that still exist: the **Moulin du Radet,** which is now a swank restaurant called the Moulin de la Galette, and—somewhat confusingly—the "real" **Moulin de la Galette,** of Renoir painting fame, located down the street at No. 75, also known as the Moulin Blute-Fin. Whatever its name, this old mill, which was owned by the same family of millers since the 17th century, was a witness to tragedy. In 1814, it had the misfortune of being attacked by a garrison of Cossacks, who were in town because the Allies (Germany, Prussia, and Russia, among a host of others) had come to Paris to stop French attacks on the rest of Europe and put Napoleon in his place. The miller tried valiantly to defend his property but ended up hacked to pieces and nailed to the blades of his windmill. Years later, the miller's son turned the farm into an outdoor music hall, the famous Moulin de la Galette depicted in a legendary painting by Renoir (you can see the painting at the Musée d'Orsay; p. 185). Other painters who frequented these bucolic dance parties included Toulouse-Lautrec, Van Gogh, and Utrillo. Today you won't get to dance here—the mill is private property and a

The actual distance on the walk described below is not long, but the terrain will make it seem a lot longer. Montmartre is up on a high hill (*butte*) overlooking the city, so be prepared for some steep ups and downs. Visitors with reduced mobility (or who are simply tired) might replace parts of this walk with the **Montmartrobus,** a bus that is part of the city bus system and makes a circuit of the Butte. The bus, which costs a regular Métro ticket, leaves place Pigalle every 15 minutes. For information and a map, visit www.ratp.fr.

prim little sign outside informs you that it is under electronic surveillance and protected by radar and guard dogs.

Return to rue Giradon and turn left, then left again on ave. Junot, walking past some of Montmartre's most elegant homes. Follow ave. Junot as it curves to the right, making a sharp right on rue Simon Dereure. The street ends at place Casadesus; climb the stairs to the footpath called:

4 Allée des Brouillards

This tranquil path leads past a number of massive houses, set back in large gardens, most of which are at least partially shielded from prying eyes by tall fences. The largest garden surrounds a white country manor known as the **Château des Brouillards,** or Fog Castle. Built in 1772 for a lawyer in the Parisian Parliament, this romantic dwelling most likely got its name from the mist that crept up from a nearby spring when the water contacted the cold morning air (real fog is a rare thing up here). Gérard de Nerval lived here in 1854, and surely this was the ideal writer's haven for this quintessential Romantic-era poet. Painter Pierre-Auguste Renoir lived and worked in one of the houses behind the Château; his son, filmmaker Jean Renoir, was born there.

Moulin du Radet.

Continue down the path to its end, at:

5 Place Dalida

This small crossroads is graced with a bust of one of Montmartre's most beloved residents, Yolanda Gigliotti, aka Dalida. This Egyptian-born singer, of Italian ancestry, was one of France's biggest stars, recording hundreds of hits and winning 70 gold records. The blonde bombshell moved to the Butte in 1962, where she lived out the rest of her stormy life in a four-story mansion that her fans dubbed "Sleeping Beauty's Castle." After a series of unfortunate love affairs, two of which ended with her partners' suicides, she took her own life in 1987. Her **statue** looks out on one of the most prototypical views of Montmartre, down rue de l'Abreuvoir: a cobbled lane leading up a hill with the Sacré Coeur in the background.

Walk up rue de l'Abreuvoir and turn left on rue des Saules:

6 Clos Montmartre Vineyard

As you make your way down rue des Saules, you will notice an unlikely vineyard on the right-hand side of the street. This is in fact the last of Montmartre's vineyards; for centuries, the Butte was covered with them. Back in the 16th century, winemaking was the primary industry in the area—though nobody ever bragged about the high quality of the product, which was mainly known for its diuretic virtues. A ditty about Montmartre wine went thus: "The wine of Montmartre—whoever drinks a pint, pisses a quarte." By the way, in those days, a "quarte" equaled 67 liters (70 quarts). Whatever its merits, this tiny vineyard still produces. Rare bottles of Clos Montmartre are auctioned off every year by the district and the proceeds benefit local public projects.

Continue down rue des Saules to the intersection with rue St-Vincent:

7 Au Lapin Agile

The story goes that a certain André Gill, a habitué of this rowdy corner cabaret—which was then called the Cabaret des Assassins—painted a sign for the place showing a rabbit (*lapin*) jumping out of a stock pot. The cabaret became known as the Lapin à Gill (Gill's rabbit), which in time mutated into Au Lapin Agile (the Agile Rabbit). The singer Aristide

Clos Montmartre Vineyard.

Bruant (immortalized in a poster by Toulouse-Lautrec) bought the inn in 1902, and asked Frédé, a local guitar legend, to run it. Under Frédé's guidance, the cabaret thrived, and the best and the brightest of the Montmartre scene was drawn to its doors, including Picasso, Verlaine, Renoir, Utrillo, and Apollinaire. Not everyone who came was a fan of modern art, however. The writer Roland Dorgelès had had enough of "Picasso's band" from the Bateau Lavoir and decided to play a trick on them: He tied a paintbrush to the end of Frédé's donkey, Lolo, and let him slop paint over a canvas. Dorgelès then entered the painting, which he titled "And the Sun Set Over the Adriatic," in the Salon des Independants, a major art show in Paris. The critics loved it—until they found out who really painted it, and a scandal ensued. Today Au Lapin Agile is still a cabaret, though a much calmer one, showcasing traditional French *chanson* (see box on p. 242). The shows are heavy on nostalgia and singalongs, but they can be good fun.

Turn right on rue St-Vincent, then right on rue Mont Cenis. Climb the stairs and turn right on rue Cortot:

8 Musée de Montmartre

At No. 12 rue Cortot lies the peaceful **Musée de Montmartre Jardins Renoir** (www.museedemontmartre.fr; ✆ **01-49-25-89-39;** p. 166), which offers an overview of the history of the neighborhood and is housed in the former residence of Rosimond, a famous 17th-century actor who was in Molière's troupe. In another century, Renoir painted here (this is where he created the "Bal du Moulin de la Galette"), as did Utrillo, who lived here with his mother, the model and painter Susan Valadon, and her lover André Utter.

Continue to the end of rue Cortot and turn left on rue des Saules; walk up to rue St-Rustique and turn left:

9 Rue St-Rustique

By now you'll have noticed the crowds thickening and a change in the atmosphere toward the Disneyesque. Trinket shops appear on every corner, and "artists" badger you to draw your portrait. Dive quickly into rue St-Rustique, a narrow channel of calm. Not only does the noise die down, but you'll be rewarded with an excellent photo op of the bulblike tops of Sacré Coeur sprouting above the end of the street. This is one of the oldest streets in Montmartre, with a medieval-style gutter in its center and no sidewalks.

Walk to the end of rue St-Rustique and turn right. On your right is the entrance to:

10 Place du Tertre

Now there's no avoiding it: the most tourist-drenched, mob-swamped spot in Paris. If you squint hard enough and use a tremendous amount of imagination, you'll see the lovely village square as it once was—but most likely you'll just be trampled by the crowds wandering around trying to figure out what all the fuss is about. Do not eat here, even if you are

---

Cinemacity—A Walking Tour App for Film Buffs

If you get misty-eyed watching Paris on the big screen, this is the app for you. Created by the Franco-German TV channel **Arte,** known for its cultural programming, this app offers walking tours to locations where movies were filmed, and even lets you watch the clip. You can also follow a "fictionalized" route, where you walk from one point to another to follow a story line. You can get the app in French, English, or German, and what's more, it's free. For more info and links to downloads, visit http://cinemacity.arte.tv.

---

starving—you will be taken for a ride. A quick walk down the hill toward the place des Abbesses will lead you to plenty of nice restaurants and cafes. You will probably be approached by people begging to do your portrait—these "artists" may do nice caricatures, but if you think you're looking at the next Picasso, you're kidding yourself.

Duck back out of place du Tertre and continue down rue du Mont Cenis until it curls around to the left and becomes rue Azaïs. Keep walking until you're in front of:

11 Sacré Coeur

After you've looked up at the gleaming white basilica and its odd, pseudo-Byzantine domes, turn around and admire the stunning view from the esplanade, or parvis, in front of the church; on a clear day you can see as far as 50km (31 miles). No matter how many people are standing around snapping pictures, it just won't ruin the beauty of this sight. Though you won't be able to see the Eiffel Tower (it's too far over on the right, though you can see it if you climb up the dome), you will take in a majestic panorama that includes the Pompidou Centre, St-Eustache, the Opéra, and the Louvre, not to mention distant hills and vales beyond the city. What you are mainly looking at here is eastern Paris, the more plebian side—an entirely appropriate view from this historically working-class, low-rent neighborhood. The view actually gets better as you walk down to the bottom-most level of the esplanade; from here you can also take in the lovely gardens below, which had a starring role in the ultimate Montmartre movie, *Amélie,* by Jean-Pierre Jeunet (2001).

WALKING TOUR 2: THE MARAIS

START:	**Village St-Paul (23–27 rue St-Paul, Métro: St-Paul).**
FINISH:	**Place des Vosges.**
TIME:	**1½ hours, not including time spent in shops, restaurants, or museums.**
BEST TIME:	**During the week, when the streets are full of life, and Sundays, when unlike other parts of the city, many shops and restaurants are open.**
WORST TIME:	**Saturdays, when most of the neighborhood is flooded with shoppers, and the Jewish quarter is completely shut down.**

The Marais Walking Tour

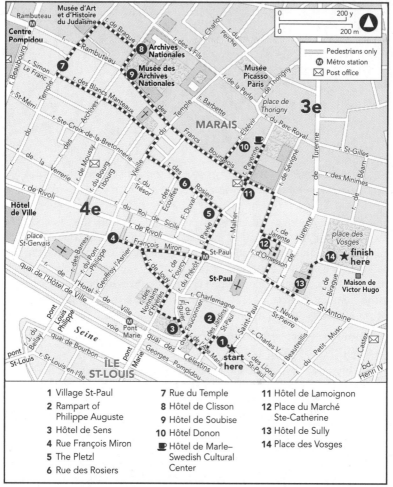

1 Village St-Paul	**7** Rue du Temple	**11** Hôtel de Lamoignon
2 Rampart of Philippe Auguste	**8** Hôtel de Clisson	**12** Place du Marché Ste-Catherine
3 Hôtel de Sens	**9** Hôtel de Soubise	**13** Hôtel de Sully
4 Rue François Miron	**10** Hôtel Donon	**14** Place des Vosges
5 The Pletzl	☕ Hôtel de Marle–Swedish Cultural Center	
6 Rue des Rosiers		

The Marais is one of the few areas that Baron Haussmann largely ignored when he was tearing up the rest of the city; for that reason, it still retains a medieval feel. Though very few buildings actually date from the Middle Ages, this warren of narrow streets and picturesque squares is layered with a rich history, which is apparent in the pleasing hodgepodge of architectural styles. The neighborhood's glory days date from the 16th and 17th centuries, when anyone who was anyone simply had to build a mansion or a palace here. Though the area fell from grace in the 18th and 19th centuries, many of the grand *hôtels particuliers* (private mansions) survived the slings and arrows of

Playing soccer by the walls of Philippe Auguste.

time and were reborn as museums and public archives when the neighborhood was restored in the latter half of the 20th century. Today, the Marais is a fascinating mix of hip gentrification and the remnants of a working-class neighborhood. It is at once the center of the city's gay life, as well as the historic Jewish quarter, even if a much larger community lives in the 19th arrondissement. Some of the city's best museums and boutiques are in the Marais, so you could easily spend an entire day here.

1 Village St-Paul

Many centuries ago, when the area was still mostly marshland (*marais* means "swamp"), there was a small hamlet on this spot. While the neighborhood has been transformed many times since, a small reminder of this village lives on, hidden behind an ordinary row of buildings on rue St-Paul. Pass through the entryway and you'll come into a kind of large interior courtyard that dates from the 14th century, when it was part of the gardens of Charles V's royal residence. At one point the houses and buildings that were built over and around the gardens were slated for demolition; a neighborhood committee saved them, and in the 1970s the village was restored and turned into a sort of antiques center, with stores and art galleries (see www.levillagesaintpaul.com and "Shopping," p. 215). The village hosts seasonal *déballages,* or outdoor arts and antiques fairs. Today the commercial emphasis has shifted from antiquities to design.

Exit the village on rue des Jardins St-Paul. On one side of this street is a playground that runs along a huge stone wall, the:

2 Rampart of Philippe Auguste

Before you is the best-preserved stretch of the city walls built by Philippe Auguste. Before leaving town on a crusade in 1190, Philippe decided the time had come to beef up security. The result was a mighty rampart that defined what was then the city limits. The wall in front of you once ran in a semicircle from the Seine, up to around rue Etienne Marcel, and curved over to protect the Louvre and back down to the Seine (a similar semicircle was built 20 years later on the Left Bank). Aside from this stretch, there are only small fragments here and there on both banks so you'll have to imagine the rest; you'll also have to imagine the towers and the six massive portals that once were the only land access into the city.

Turn left down rue des Jardins St-Paul and right on rue de l'Avé Maria. Just where it branches off to the right on rue du Figuier is:

3 Hôtel de Sens

Built between 1475 and 1519, this splendid fortress/mansion is a rare example of medieval urban architecture. When Paris came under the jurisdiction of the Bishop of Sens back in the 15th century, he promptly built himself a suitably fabulous home in the city. Later, Henri IV briefly used it to house his strong-minded wife, Queen Margot, whose many love affairs were causing him no end of headaches. The bishops stopped coming to the Hôtel de Sens altogether in 1622, preferring to rent it out. After the Revolution it served as a laundry operation, a jam factory, and a glass warehouse. By the time it was bought by the city in 1911 it was in a pitiful state; the building's restoration—which started in 1929—wouldn't be completed until 1961. The Hôtel now houses the **Bibliothèque Forney,** a library dedicated to the decorative arts. Take a minute to admire the turrets and towers in the courtyard (visible from the street).

Follow the side of the building down rue du Figuier and turn left onto the path that leads around to the back of the Hôtel, where there are pretty French gardens. The path leads to rue des Nonnains d'Hyères, where you'll turn right, then walk left on rue de Jouy to where it intersects with:

4 Rue François Miron

Walk left down rue François Miron to the corner of rue Cloche Perce. You will notice two multistoried half-timbered houses: the **Maison à l'Enseigne du Faucheur** (No. 11) and

Hôtel de Sens.

the **Maison à l'Enseigne du Mouton** (No. 13). Pre-Haussmann, houses like these were once all over the city; now they are extremely rare. These two date from the 14th century, though after 1607 the crisscrossed wood facades of all such houses were covered with a layer of plaster in accordance with a law that aimed to reduce the risk of fire. When these houses were restored in the 1960s, the plaster was removed and the wood was once again revealed.

Double back and continue down rue François Miron until it ends at the St-Paul Métro station. Cross the rue de Rivoli and continue left up rue Pavée to:

5 The Pletzl

You are now entering the city's oldest Jewish quarter, once called the *Pletzl* ("little place" in Yiddish), where there has been a Jewish presence since the 13th century. This community swelled and shrank over the centuries, in line with various edicts and expulsions, but the largest influx was in the 1880s, when tens of thousands of Eastern European Jews, fleeing poverty and persecution back home, settled in France. The Pletzl was hit hard during the infamous roundups of 1942, when police came and emptied apartment buildings and even schools of their Jewish occupants and sent them off to Nazi concentration camps. Though the neighborhood is slowly being eaten up by the advancing gentrification in the area, and chic shops butt up against kosher butchers, there's still a small community here, and a fairly traditional one at that. At No. 10 is the unusual **Synagogue de la rue Pavée,** which was designed by Hector Guimard, the Art Nouveau master who created the famous Métro entrances. This is the only existing religious edifice by Guimard, whose wife was Jewish (they fled to the U.S. during World War II). In 1940, on Yom Kippur, the Germans dynamited the synagogue; it was eventually restored and is now a national monument (open for religious services only).

Continue up rue Pavée to where it crosses:

6 Rue des Rosiers

Rumor has it that this street got its name from the rose bushes that once lined its edges, back in the days when it ran along the exterior of the city walls. Up until recently, it was the main artery of the Jewish quarter; today, all that's left are a few kosher restaurants and a bookstore or two. There's still great falafel to be found here (**L'As du Fallafel;** p. 92); if you happen to be in the area around lunchtime, you might get handed a free sample from one of the competing restaurants.

Turn left on rue des Rosiers and continue to the end, where you'll turn right on rue Vieille du Temple. You are now in the thick of the trendier (and gay) part of the neighborhood, which is filled with fun restaurants and boutiques. Take the first left at rue des Blancs Manteaux and follow this pretty street all the way to where it ends at:

7 Rue du Temple

By the time you hit this street you'll notice that the neighborhood has changed from trendy to workaday; rue du Temple is lined with jewelry and clothing wholesalers. But this street—which back in medieval times led to the stalwart fortress of the Knights Templar—also harbors some lovely examples of 17th-century *hôtels particuliers* (private mansions). Turn right and walk to No. 71, the **Hôtel de St-Aignan,** otherwise known as the **Musée d'Art et d'Histoire du Judaïsme** (p. 152). Even if you don't visit the museum, you can peek into the courtyard during opening hours. This exercise in 17th-century grandeur includes a sneaky architectural lie: One of the three facades facing the courtyard, which seems to be the front of an enormous building, is really just a facade. Despite the presence of carefully curtained windows, on the other side of the wall is merely another wall, yet another chunk of Philippe Auguste's ramparts.

Continue up to rue de Braque and turn right. Walk to the end where the street intersects with rue des Archives. Across the street is the:

8 Hôtel de Clisson

The vaulted archway is what is left of the **Hôtel de Clisson,** a magnificent mansion that was built in 1380 and for centuries housed some of the grandest of the grand, including dukes of Guise, who hung out there for 135 years. Well, it may have been good enough for them, but by 1700, when the François de Rohan, the Prince of Soubise got his hands on it, he decided the time had come for a change (see below).

Turn right and walk down rue des Archives to rue des Francs Bourgeois and turn left. First thing you'll see on your left is the sumptuous gateway to the:

9 Hôtel de Soubise

The enormous *cour d'honneur,* a huge horseshoe-shaped courtyard, is edged with open galleries holding 56 pairs of double columns. These lead to a largely 17th-century palace, which now holds the National Archives. This jaw-dropping sight was the creation of architect Pierre Alexis Delamair, who was hired by the Prince of Soubise to build on to the courtyard and overhaul the building. Later the prince's son, the future Cardinal de Rohan, asked Delamair to build him his own palace next door, the adjoining **Hôtel de Rohan-Strasbourg** (more archives are stashed here, not open to the public). A part of the Hôtel de Soubise houses the **Musée des Archives Nationale** (60 rue des Francs-Bourgeois, 3rd arrond.; www. archives-nationales.culture.gouv.fr; *©* **01-40-27-60-96;** admission to permanent collection 3€ adults, free under 26; Mon and Wed–Fri 10am–5:30pm, Sat–Sun 2–5:30pm), which displays tantalizing items from the vast National Archives, as well as temporary expositions. For example, you can see the **Serment de Jeu de Paume,** a document that signaled the birth of the French Republic, and **Marie Antoinette's last letter.** You can also visit the **apartments of the Prince and Princess of Soubise.** Though just a few rooms, they retain the sumptuous decor of the period and give a sense of how the other half lived in the 18th century. You will most likely have the rooms to yourself, giving the odd impression that you have somehow stumbled into a private château.

Hôtel de Soubise.

Continue down rue des Francs Bourgeois and window-shop (or just plain shop) in the stylish boutiques that line this street. Turn left onto rue Elzevir, and head to the:

10 Hôtel Donon

This sumptuous 16th-century mansion houses the **Musée Cognacq-Jay** (p. 152), a small but fabulous museum dedicated to 18th-century art. It's free, so even if you don't have time for a leisurely museum visit, you can wander into its courtyard (a good place for admiring its beautiful exterior) or zip quickly through its lavish rooms, filled with paintings and knickknacks, without guilt. Originally built in 1575, the *hôtel* got its name from its first owner, Médéric de Donon, Controller General of the Royal Estates. From 1640 onwards, however, it passed into the hands of other wealthy families who made their own improvements and extensions—not all of them good: By the early 20th century, the building had (like many other Marais mansions) become commercial premises, with one area containing a grubby garage. Fortunately, it was acquired by the City of Paris in 1974, and restored to its former glory, so today you can easily imagine how it would have looked in old Médéric's day. Architecturally, the building is typical of other 16th-century Marais *hotels*—symmetrical design, with wings set around a rectangular courtyard—but it stands out for its stonework, which is much less ornate than that of other grand mansions in the Marais. Not that *that* detracts from its beauty: Stand in the courtyard and you'll find its straight, simple lines simply breathtaking.

Go back and turn left back onto rue des Francs Bourgeois, then left again to the intersection with rue Payenne for a short detour to the right, about a half a block down:

Take a Break ☕

The Hôtel de Marle is the home of the **Institut Suédois** (Swedish Institute; 11 rue Payenne, 3rd arrond.; ⓒ **01-44-78-80-11**; https://paris.si.se; Tues–Sun noon–6pm), which has a lovely **cafe** with tables in the courtyard in the summer. Nibble a vanilla-scented *kanelbulle* while you take in the exterior of this 16th-century mansion, which at one point was the home of Yolande de Polastron, a close friend of Marie Antoinette. If you still need a rest, sprawl out on a bench in the Square Georges Cain, a small leafy park just across the street.

Walk back down rue Payenne, cross rue des Francs Bourgeois, and walk another half-block down rue Pavée (the extension of rue Payenne) to:

11 Hôtel de Lamoignon

Built in 1584 for Diane de France, the legitimized daughter of one of Henri II's extramarital encounters, this massive mansion was acquired by a famous family of magistrates (the Lamoignons) in the 17th century. You'll have no problem getting into the courtyard here (the building now houses the **Library of the History of the City of Paris**), where you can get a good look at the facade. The dog's heads, arrows, quivers, and other hunting imagery carved into the stonework are references to the first owner's namesake, Diana, goddess of the hunt. A later Lamoignon, Guillaume, who was the first president of the Parisian Parliament, turned his home into a meeting place for the leading lights of the epoch—Madame de Sévigné, Racine, and Bourdaloue were regulars at his parties. The building became a library in the 1960s.

Go back up to rue des Francs Bourgeois and turn right. Turn right again on rue de Sévigné and left on rue de Jarente to:

12 Place du Marché Ste-Catherine

Though there's no longer an open-air market here, as the name suggests, this shaded plaza is still a lovely oasis of green and quiet in this busy neighborhood. There are no cars allowed on the square, and the cafes on its edges all have outdoor seating in nice weather.

Continue to rue St-Antoine and turn left without crossing the street to No. 62:

13 Hôtel de Sully

The most splendiferous of the many splendiferous mansions in the Marais, the **Hôtel de Sully** was built by a rich 17th-century businessman, a certain Mesme-Gallet. While his version was quite sumptuous, the mansion really came to life when it was bought by the Duc de Sully, who hired architect François Le Vau to give it a makeover. After his death, like so many mansions in the Marais, the palacelike edifice was sold, divided, and built upon; in 1827 it was a boardinghouse for young girls, and up until the end of World War II it was still disfigured by shops and outbuildings. Using the original plans and contemporary drawings and etchings, the building was completely restored in the 1970s to Le Vau's version;

you can now stroll through the courtyard and admire the sculpted exterior in its virtually pristine state. Though the building is closed to the public, you can traipse through the front courtyard to a second one with a peaceful **garden** filled with sparrows.

Go through the archway in the back of the garden to the:

14 **Place des Vosges**
Officially inaugurated in 1612, this exquisite **Renaissance square,** bordered by 36 virtually identical stone and brick town houses, was the idea of King Henri IV, who unfortunately didn't live to see it finished. After a stroll under the

Detail of sculpture at Hôtel de Sully.

arcades, which run below the town houses, take a seat on a bench in the square and admire the tall trees and elegant symmetry of the landscaping, as well as the huge **statue** in the middle of Louis XIII astride his horse. This statue is a 19th-century replacement for the original, which was melted down during the Revolution. The square has seen a number of illustrious tenants over the centuries: Madame de Sévigné was born at No. 1 *bis,* the 19th-century actress Rachel lived at No. 9, and poet Théophile Gautier and novelist Alphonse Daudet both lived at No. 10. The most famous inhabitant, no doubt, was Victor Hugo, who lived at No. 6 from 1832 to 1848; his house is now the free-to-visit **Maison de Victor Hugo** (p. 150).

SHOPPING

Vuitton, Chanel, Baccarat—the names of famous French luxury brands roll around the tongue like rich chocolate. But while it's fun to window-shop at Cartier, few of us can actually afford to buy anything there. Guess what? Neither can most Parisians. And yet they manage to look terrifically put together. What's their secret? We'll attempt to shed some light on this puzzling mystery; the shops below will give you a point of departure for your Parisian shopping adventure.

8

Paris has always been the capital of *luxe*. As early as the 16th century, the city was known as the place to go for luxury goods, and over the centuries an entire industry grew up around the whims and whimsies of the French aristocracy. To keep up appearances, nobles spent outrageous amounts of money on sumptuous clothing, opulent homes, and lavish dinner parties for dozens of similarly well-heeled aristocrats. By the 18th century, thousands of merchants and artisans were working full-time to fill the voluminous orders of some 150 grand families, not to mention Louis XIV and his court in Versailles. So it's no wonder that even today, the high and mighty, or just plain rich, come here to deck themselves out in the best of the best.

Yet there is so much more shopping to explore than those big-box luxury stores on the Champs-Élysées. There are small boutiques by up-and-coming designers, lesser-known but fab chocolate stores, and hip yet inexpensive French chain stores where you can throw together a look in minutes. Paris is shopaholic heaven, if you know where to go to find your *bonheur* (happiness).

SHOPPING BY AREA

In Paris, each neighborhood has its own personality, and each personality imposes itself on one or two main shopping streets. To preserve your sanity, and shoe leather, aim for the areas with the highest concentration of your kind of store.

The Right Bank
LOUVRE & ÎLE DE LA CITÉ (1ST ARRONDISSEMENT)
The east side of this arrondissement includes the subterranean shopping mall **Forum des Halles** (covered by the recently added and marvelously modern canopy), which is a short stroll from a major shopping strip on the **rue de Rivoli**. Both feature a wide

Passage Jouffroy.

range of affordable international clothing chains. As you move west, the atmosphere shifts dramatically. The arcades of the **Palais Royal** have recently been taken over by fashionable labels like Stella McCartney. Farther on, chic **rue St-Honoré** is lined with pricey, sophisticated stores. As you head farther west, the prices go through the roof at **Place Vendôme,** which probably has the city's highest density of gemstones per square meter. Even if you are too shy to enter Chaumet or Boucheron, you can happily drool over the window displays.

OPÉRA & GRANDS BOULEVARDS (2ND & 9TH ARRONDISSEMENTS)

Boulevard Haussmann cuts through this neighborhood like a steamship's wake, drawing hordes of shoppers toward the city's two most famous department stores, **Galeries Lafayette** and **Printemps.** These two behemoths have spawned an entire neighborhood full of inexpensive shops just north of the boulevard on **rue de Provence, rue de Mogador,** and **rue Caumartin.** To the south and east of the boulevard lies a maze of **19th-century covered shopping arcades** (see "Arcades," below), as well as a **market street** lined with enticing **food stores,** rue de Montorgueil.

THE MARAIS (3RD & 4TH ARRONDISSEMENTS)

The success of the hip boutiques on the **rue des Francs-Bourgeois** has been such that stylish clothing stores have been cropping up on all the streets around it, even crowding out the kosher restaurants on **rue des Rosiers,** the historic Jewish quarter. Not as pricey as the luxury boutiques to the west, these stores have stylish duds at vaguely attainable prices (and they are open on Sun, a rarity in this city). **Rues de Bretagne** and **Charlot** in the northern Marais are a hotbed of independent French designers.

CHAMPS-ÉLYSÉES, TROCADÉRO & WESTERN PARIS (8TH, 16TH & 17TH ARRONDISSEMENTS)

Rue du Faubourg St-Honoré is dotted with dozens of chic boutiques, but it pales in comparison to ultra-exclusive **avenue Montaigne.** Paris's most glamorous shopping street is lined with unspeakably fancy shops, where you float from Dior to Chanel and everything in between. Teens, tourists, and other young things flock to the neighboring **Champs-Élysées** to crowd into hot mass-market flagships. High-end food shops (Hédiard, Fauchon) live in the area around the **Madeleine.**

MONTMARTRE (18TH ARRONDISSEMENT)

The winding streets that fan out around Montmartre's **place des Abbesses** are filled with small, fairly affordable design, fashion, jewelry, and food shops. Wander along **rue des Abbesses,** down **rue Houdon,** and up **rue des Martyrs** and discover hidden treasures. If you are looking for adventure and serious bargains, head east to the working-class Barbès neighborhood, where on **Boulevard Rochechouart,** you'll find Tati, a huge discount department store.

RÉPUBLIQUE, BASTILLE & EASTERN PARIS (11TH & 12TH ARRONDISSEMENTS)

As **rue du Faubourg St-Antoine** heads east from the place de la Bastille, you'll find a number of chain stores. The choices get more interesting in and around **rue de Charonne,** home to offbeat, youth-oriented clothing and goodies. A great place to window-shop is the **Viaduc des Arts,** which runs along avenue Daumesnil: a collection of about 30 specialist craft stores occupying a series of vaulted arches under the **Promenade Plantée** (p. 166).

BELLEVILLE, CANAL ST-MARTIN & LA VILLETTE (10TH, 19TH & 20TH ARRONDISSEMENTS)

The **Canal St-Martin** is a bastion of local bohemian charm, and you can find interesting shops along neighboring streets like **rue de Marseille, rue Beaurepaire,** the **quai de Valmy,** and **quai de Jemmapes.** Belleville may not have trendy boutiques, but it's a nice place to explore specialty shops from the city's various immigrant communities.

Taxes, *Detaxe* & Refunds

Most items purchased in stores (aside from certain categories like food and tickets to performances) are subject to a 20% Value Added Tax (VAT), which is included in the price you pay (and not tacked on at the end like in the U.S.). The good news is that non–E.U. residents who are over 15 and stay in France less than 6 months can get a refund of VAT (TVA in French) if they spend over 175€ in a single shop on the same day. Ask the retailer for a *bordereau de vente à l'exportation* (export sales invoice), which will have a bar code. Both you and the shopkeeper sign the slip, and you then choose how you will be reimbursed (credit on card, bank transfer, or cash). Once you get to the airport, scan the code in one of the new "Pablo" terminals (if your airport doesn't have one, just go to the *"detaxe"* counter). If you chose to be reimbursed by credit to your bank account or credit card, that will happen automatically once you scan the slip. If you chose cash, you'll need to go to the *"detaxe"* counter, where you'll be refunded on the spot. For more info, visit the **Paris Tourist Office** website (www.parisinfo.com), and search for "tax-free shopping" for a complete rundown.

arcades: 19TH-CENTURY SHOPPING MALLS

Paris is filled with covered arcades, primarily in the 2nd arrondissement. These lovely iron and glass galleries are 19th-century antecedents of today's shopping malls—each one is lined with shops, tearooms, and even the occasional hotel—and range in ambience from slightly seedy to ultra hip.

Built in 1825, the city's longest arcade, **Passage Choiseul** (40 rue des Petits Champs, 2nd arrond.; Métro: Pyramides), runs from rue des Petits Champs to rue de Saint Augustin and shelters everything from bargain shoe shops to used book stores to art galleries. The **Passage des Panoramas** (11 bd. Montmartre, 2nd arrond.; Métro: Grands Boulevards) intersects with several other short arcades (**Feydeau, Montmartre, Saint-Marc,** and **Variétés**), making an interesting warren of bookshops, collectors' shops (stamps, coins, postcards, engravings), and increasingly, trendy restaurants, including Canard & Champagne (p. 97). Across the street is the entrance to **Passage Jouffroy** (10 bd.

Montmartre, 9th arrond.; Métro: Grands Boulevards), which is lined with collectors' shops featuring figurines, dollhouses, and cinema memorabilia. Pricier gifts are to be found at **Passage Verdeau** (across the street from the back end of Jouffroy, 31 bis rue du Faubourg Montmartre, 9th arrond.; Métro: Grands Boulevards), a particularly atmospheric arcade with stores selling rare books, antique engravings, and vintage photos.

Farther south, near the Palais Royal, is the chic **Galerie Vivienne** (4 rue des Petits Champs, 2nd arrond.; www.galerie-vivienne.com; Métro: Bourse), a beautifully restored arcade with a mosaic tile floor and neoclassical arches. Stores here sell high-end clothes, handbags, textiles, and objets d'art. Legrand Filles et Fils (p. 232) has tons of fine bottles of wine, as well as a wine school and cafe. Toward Les Halles is the very stylish **Passage du Grand Cerf** (10 rue Dussoubs, 2nd arrond.; Métro: Etienne Marcel), which is filled with flashy designer jewelry, clothing stores, and interior design agencies.

The Left Bank

LATIN QUARTER (5TH & 13TH ARRONDISSEMENTS)

Chain stores have taken over a large chunk of the **Boulevard St-Michel,** which used to be known for its cafes and bookstores. There are a few survivors, though, like the massive Gibert Joseph, which has several outposts on the Boul' Miche selling books, stationery, and more. Food enthusiasts will enjoy the delicious goodies on sale in the shops at the southern end of **rue Mouffetard.**

ST-GERMAIN-DES-PRÉS & LUXEMBOURG (6TH ARRONDISSEMENT)

Even if it's technically in the 7th arrondissement, the shopping nerve center of this smart neighborhood is **Le Bon Marché,** the city's most stylish department store. Radiating eastward is a network of streets with oodles of delightful shops, ranging from bargain-oriented **rue St-Placide** to chain stores and shoe heaven on **rue de Rennes** to designer labels and cute boutiques on **rue St-Sulpice, rue du Cherche Midi,** and **rue du Vieux Colombier.** Down toward the Seine, **rue Bonaparte** and **rue Jacob** tempt with classy, if pricey, offerings, and you can stop in at the legendary La Hune bookstore just off **Boulevard St-Germain** for a taste of the neighborhood's intellectual past.

EIFFEL TOWER & NEARBY (7TH ARRONDISSEMENT)

Most of this area is more focused on culture and architecture than fashion, but along its eastern edge, around the **rue du Bac** and **rue du Grenelle,** you'll find hopelessly expensive designer shops. The market street of **rue Cler** has dozens of charming bakeries, charcuteries, and fruit sellers.

MONTPARNASSE & NEARBY (14TH & 15TH ARRONDISSEMENTS)

An ugly shopping center in the Tour Montparnasse complex is filled with the usual chain stores and a reduced version of Galeries Lafayette (see below), but the more interesting shopping draw here is farther south on **rue d'Alesia,** which is lined with outlet stores (*déstock*) selling surplus and discounted wares, including designer labels like Sonia Rykiel. **Rue Daguerre** is a lovely market street filled with food shops that is as cute as rue Cler but less famous (you'll hear a lot more French here). Farther south in the 15th, **rue de Commerce** buzzes with shops and restaurants.

DEPARTMENT STORES
Les Grands Magasins

Known as the *grands magasins* ("big stores"), the great Parisian department stores were born in the late 19th century and have become landmarks.

BHV ★★ Here's a department store that even men will love. Sure, it has acres of clothes and perfumes, but it's mostly known for what it has in its basement: **hardware, electronics, gadgets,** and other items for *bricoleurs* (do-it-yourselfers) of all nationalities. There are also terrific **kitchen, hobby,** and **decoration** sections upstairs. The practical side of this store spawned several ministores, all on streets surrounding the mother ship. There's **BHV L'Homme** (36 rue de la Verrerie) for men's clothing, **BHV Solex** (40 rue de la Verrerie) for electric bikes, and **BHV La Niche** (42 rue de la Verrerie) for pets. 52 rue de Rivoli, 4th arrond. www.bhv. fr. ✆ **09-77-40-14-00.** Métro: Hôtel de Ville.

Galeries Lafayette's stained-glass cupola is classified as a historic monument.

For shoppers, Paris is most definitely not a 24-hour city. In general, shops are open from 9 or 10am to 7pm. Many larger stores and most department stores stay open late (that is, 9pm) one night during the week (called a *nocturne*), and most supermarkets are open until at least 8pm, often 9pm. Many shops are closed on Monday, and most are closed on Sunday, which is still considered a day of rest in this country. This is great for family get-togethers, but hard on working shoppers, who have only Saturday to get to the stores. Don't shop on Saturday if you can avoid it; the crowds are annoying, to say the least. If you do want to shop on a Sunday, head to the **Marais,** one of the only areas where boutiques stay open, or the **Carousel du Louvre,** a chic shopping mall below the Louvre museum.

The French tradition of closing for lunch is quickly vanishing in Paris (although it is still very common elsewhere in France). However, smaller, family-run operations still sometimes close between noon and 2pm.

Final note: Many shops close down completely for 2 or 3 weeks during July or August, when a mass vacation exodus empties out major portions of the city.

Galeries Lafayette ★★   This grandest of the *grand magasins* was a humble haberdasher shop when it was opened in 1895. Success inspired architectural excess, like the sumptuous Belle Epoque dome under which fashionable goodies are displayed. I prefer Galeries Lafayette to its more glamorous rival next door (see Printemps, below). It's a bit less expensive and so huge you can usually find just what you're looking for. There's everything from luxury labels to kids' stuff to stationery. A separate building's just for men (**Lafayette Homme**) and another across the street has housewares as well as a wine and gourmet shop (**Lafayette Maison**). 40 bd. Haussmann, 9th arrond. www.galerieslafayette.com. ℂ **01-42-82-34-56.** Métro: Chaussée d'Antin-Lafayette.

Le Bon Marché ★★★   Founded by an enterprising milliner in the mid-1800s, this was the one of the world's first department stores. Despite its name (*bon marché* means "affordable"), this is the most expensive of Paris's grand magasins. It is also the most stylish, with beautiful displays and fabulous clothes of every imaginable designer label, both upscale and mid-range. Right next door is their humongous designer supermarket, **La Grande Epicerie** (see "Specialty Groceries," later in this chapter). 24 rue de Sèvres, 7th arrond. www.lebonmarche.com. ℂ **01-44-39-80-00.** Métro: Sèvres–Babylone.

Printemps ★★   The glistening domes of this 19th-century building bring to mind a grand hotel on the French Riviera. *Printemps* means "spring," which is certainly eternal in this elegant store. Split into four sections (women's fashions, menswear, housewares, and beauty), four of the seven floors of women's fashion are devoted to designer labels. If you can't handle the crowds inside, you can always enjoy the famed *vitrines,* or **window displays,** which are usually very creative and original. Better yet, ride to the top of

Printemps Beauté/Maison and enjoy the splendid **panoramic view;** there's even a cafe for lunch. 64 bd. Haussmann, 9th arrond. www.printemps.com. *(C)* **01-42-82-50-00.** Métro: Havre-Caumartin or St-Lazare.

MARKETS: FOOD & FLEA
Food Markets

Marchés (open-air or covered markets) are small universes unto themselves where nothing substantial has changed for centuries. The fishmonger trumpeting the wonders of this morning's catch probably doesn't sound a whole lot different than his ancestor in the Middle Ages (although their dress has changed), and housewives no doubt assessed the goods in the stalls with the same pitiless stares that they do today. Certainly the hygiene and organization have improved and there are no more jugglers or bear baiters to entertain the crowds, but the essence of the experience remains the same—a noisy, bustling, joyous chaos where you can buy fresh, honest food.

Even if you don't have access to cooking facilities, *marchés* are great places to pick up picnic goodies or just a mid-morning nosh; along with fruit and vegetable vendors, you'll find bakeries, *charcuteries* (sort of like a deli, but better), and other small stands selling homemade jams, honey, or desserts. Some of the covered markets have small cafes inside—these are ideal for sitting down and soaking up the atmosphere.

A few marché rules: Unless you see evidence to the contrary, don't pick up your own fruits and vegetables with your hands. Wait until the vendor serves you and point. Also, don't be surprised if the line in front of the stand is an amorphous blob of people; this is the French way. Surprisingly, fistfights are rare; somehow everyone seems to be aware of who came before them, and if they aren't, no one seems to care.

There are *marchés* in every arrondissement in the city. Below is a selective list; you can find hours and locations of all on the municipal website (https://meslieux.paris.fr/marches), or just ask at your hotel for the one closest.

o **Marché d'Aligre:** One of the city's largest; aka Marché Beauvau (place d'Aligre, 12th arrond.; outdoor market Tues–Fri 7:30am–1:30pm, Sat–Sun 7:30am–2pm, covered market Tues–Sat 9am–1pm and 4–7:30pm, Sun 9am–1:30pm; Métro: Ledru Rollin or Gare de Lyon)

o **Marché Bastille** (bd. Richard Lenoir btw. rue Amelot and rue St-Sabin, 11th arrond.; Thurs and Sun 7am–2:30pm; Métro: Bastille)

o **Marché Batignolles** Organic (bd. Batignolles btw. rue de Rome and Place Clichy, 17th arrond.; Sat 9am–3pm; Métro: Rome)

o **Marché Cours de Vincennes** (cour de Vincennes, 12th arrond.; Wed 7am–2.30pm and Sat 7am–3pm; Métro/RER: Nation)

o **Marché Edgar Quinet** (bd. Edgar Quinet, near Gare Montparnasse, 14th arrond.; Wed and Sat 7am–2:30pm; Métro: Edgar Quinet)

o **Marché Grenelle** (bd. Grenelle, btw. rue Lourmel and rue du Commerce, 15th arrond.; Wed and Sun 7am–2:30pm; Métro: Dupleix)

- **Marché Monge** (place Monge, 5th arrond.; Wed, Fri, and Sun 7am–2:30pm; Métro: place Monge)
- **Marché Raspail** (bd. Raspail btw. rue de Cherche-Midi and rue de Rennes, 6th arrond.; Tues and Fri, 7am–2:30pm; **organic** Sun 9am–3pm; Métro: Rennes)
- **Marché Saxe-Breteuil** (ave. du Saxe near place de Breteuil, 7th arrond.; Thurs and Sat 7am–2:30pm; Métro: Ségur)

Antiques Fairs & Brocantes

You've probably heard of the famous *marché aux puces,* or **flea market,** at Clignancourt (see below), and if you're an inveterate browser, it's probably worth the visit. But the better deals are to be had at the *brocantes,* antiques or jumble sales, held periodically around the city. Though most of what you will find at these sales is sold by professional *brocanteurs* who scout estate sales and other insider sources, your selection will be much wider and the chances of your finding a postwar ceramic pastis pitcher or heirloom lace curtains at affordable prices are much higher than at some of the more overpopulated flea markets. To find out where and when the *brocantes* are happening, visit http://quefaire.paris.fr/brocantes or look in the **special supplements** of *Le Parisien* (Sun) or *Le Figaro* (Wed, the supplement is called *Figaroscope*).

Flea Markets

Marché aux Puces de la Porte de Vanves ★★   This weekend event sprawls along two streets and is the best flea market in Paris—dealers swear by it. There's little in terms of formal antiques and furniture. It's better for old

Shopping for antiques at Marché aux Puces de Paris St-Ouen.

linens, vintage Hermès scarves, toys, ephemera, costume jewelry, perfume bottles, and bad art. Sadly, dealers tend up the prices when they hear a foreign accent. Get there early—the best stuff goes fast. Open Saturday and Sunday, 7am to 2pm. Ave. Georges-Lafenestre, 14th arrond. www.pucesdevanves.fr. No phone. Métro: Porte de Vanves.

Marché aux Puces de Paris St-Ouen–Clignancourt ★   Engulfing the Porte de Clignancourt area at the northern edge of the city, this claims to be the largest antiques market in the world. Split into 15 specialty markets, this sprawling mini-city is visited by thousands of visitors each weekend (also open Mon). Although it was once a bargain-hunter's dream, prices now often rival those of regular antiques dealers. Still, hardcore browsers will get a kick wandering through the serpentine alleyways of this Parisian medina, and may turn up a treasure. *Note:* Beware of pickpockets. Also to avoid the tatty markets surrounding Les Puces, get off at Métro Garibaldi. Porte de Clignancourt, 18th arrond. www.marcheauxpuces-saintouen.com. ✆ **01-40-11-77-36.** Sat 9am–6pm, Sun 10am–6pm, Mon 10am–5pm. Métro: Porte de Clignancourt or Garibaldi.

RECOMMENDED STORES
Antiques & Collectibles

Atomes ★   There's a bit of everything in this shop: old, new and somewhere in between. Vintage and reproduction vintage decorative objects, clothing, jewelry and house wares mix with modern creations. 65 rue du Montparnasse, 14th arrond. ✆ **01-43-22-70-13.** Métro: Edgar Quinet.

L'Objet qui Parle ★★   This delightful and quirky shop sells a jumble of vintage finds, including framed butterflies, teapots, furniture, chandeliers, hunting trophies, religious paraphernalia, and old lace. Great for souvenir shopping. 86 rue des Martyrs, 18th arrond. ✆ **06-09-67-05-30.** Métro: Abbesses.

Village St-Paul ★★   When you pass through an archway on rue St-Paul, you come upon a lovely villagelike enclosure, the remnant of a centuries-old hamlet that was swallowed up by the city. Today, it's a village of antiques dealers and design shops, selling everything from old bistro chairs and vintage lingerie to Brazilian eco-furniture and Iranian kilim rugs. Check the website for their periodic antiques fairs. www.levillagesaintpaul.com. No phone. Métro: St-Paul.

Beauty & Perfume

At the airport, you'll be assaulted with **duty-free shops** carrying loads of tax-free perfume; another colony of similar shops is near the Opéra. But don't be afraid to go elsewhere because you will most likely get the same tax rebate no matter where you go (as long as you spend more than 175€; see box on taxes, p. 217). Discounts can also be found at two huge perfume chains: the ubiquitous **Marionnaud** (www.marionnaud.fr) and the user-friendly **Sephora** (www.sephora.fr). If you would like to bring home something more original, try one of the shops listed below.

Detaille 1905 ★ Founded by the Countess of Presle in 1905, this handsome old store offers its own elegant line of eau de toilette and other beauty products for both men and women, such as its signature *Baume Automobile*, developed by the Countess when she realized (even back then) what pollution can do to your skin. These unique products can only be purchased at the wood-paneled boutique or ordered by phone or online through the shop's website. 10 rue St-Lazare, 9th arrond. www.detaille.com. ✆ **01-48-78-68-50.** Métro: Notre Dame de Lorette.

The Different Company ★★ There is indeed something different about this perfume company. For one, this is an independent operation, founded in 2000, that makes its own unique fragrances with mostly natural materials. Signature scents include Osmanthus, Sel de Vétiver, and Rose Poivrée. 10 rue Ferdinand Duval, 4th arrond. www.thedifferentcompany.com. ✆ **01-42-78-19-34.** Métro: St-Paul.

Editions de Parfums Fréderic Malle ★★ A superb range of original fragrances have been developed in this chic temple to the nose, which was established by master perfumer Fréderic Malle in 2000. Sample his wares in special "smelling columns," round, phone-booth-like tubes where you can experience aromas like Noir Epices and Lipstick Rose. It has stores in two other locations: 140 avenue Victor Hugo in the 16th arrondissement, 13 rue des Francs Bourgeois in the 4th, and 21 rue du Mont Thabor in the 1st. 37 rue de Grenelle, 7th arrond. www.fredericmalle.com. ✆ **01-42-22-76-40.** Métro: Rue du Bac.

Make Up Forever ★★ Why not come back from Paris with a whole new look? This French cosmetics company, which trains professional makeup artists, also runs a boutique in the Marais where you can not only buy pro-quality products for the same price as regular name brands, but also have a **makeup lesson** (25 min. for 25€; 60 min. for 60€; call to reserve ahead). A second location is at 5 rue de la Boétie in the 8th arrondissement. 5 rue des Francs Bourgeois, 4th arrond. www.makeupforever.fr. ✆ **01-42-71-23-19.** Métro: St-Paul.

Books
ENGLISH BOOKSTORES
Paris's English-language bookshops tend to double as cultural meeting places. Those that have survived the ongoing bookshop crisis are good places to pick up English-language newsletters, chat in English, and attend readings (sometimes by famous authors).

The Abbey Bookshop ★ Canadians will be happy to find a cozy store that specializes in Canadian authors, as well as other English-language literature. You'll have to squeeze in between the piles of books, but this is a relaxed, welcoming place with good readings and events, including hikes in nearby forests. 29 rue de la Parcheminerie, 5th arrond. www.facebook.com/abbeybookshop. ✆ **01-46-33-16-24.** Métro: St-Michel.

Born in Baltimore in 1887, **Sylvia Beach** fell in love with Paris early in life and moved there for good at the end of World War I. A few years later, with the encouragement of her companion, bookshop owner Adrienne Monier, Beach opened **Shakespeare and Company,** a bookstore and lending library specializing in English and American books. For the next 20 years, the shop at 8 rue Dupuytren served as an unofficial welcome center for American and English visitors, particularly literary ones, and specifically those who would later come to be known as members of **"The Lost Generation":** T. S. Eliot, Ezra Pound, F. Scott Fitzgerald, Gertrude Stein, and Ernest Hemingway. But the one who made the biggest impression, literally, was James Joyce. After his novel *Ulysses* was banned in both the U.S. and England and no publisher would touch the manuscript, Beach cou-rageously published it herself. In February 1922, after endless proofs and corrections by the author, the 1,000 copies arrived in the store, all of which were snapped up instantaneously. Later, the book became a modern classic, making a mint for its publisher, Random House. Beach never saw a penny but claimed that she didn't mind because she'd have done anything for Joyce and his art. In 1941, during the Nazi occupation of Paris, the contents of the entire bookstore "vanished" overnight (hidden in a vacant apartment in the same building) to avoid confiscation by the Germans. The books were saved, but Beach spent 6 months in an internment camp. After the war, she returned to Paris, but the bookshop's doors never reopened. The store's memory lives on, however, in its more recent incarnation at 37 rue de la Bûcherie (see Shakespeare and Company, above).

Berkeley Books of Paris ★ This offshoot of the San Francisco Book Company (see below) is yet another quirky used book store, describing itself as a "bastion of free thinkers." They offer lots of readings, art exhibits and mini-concerts; check their Facebook page for info. 8 rue Casimir Delavigne, 6th arrond. www.berkeleybooksofparis.org. ✆ 01-46-34-85-73. Métro: Odéon.

Galignani ★★★ The oldest English-language bookstore in Paris, this old-fashioned shop has thrived since 1810. Owned by the literary Gagliani family, whose ancestor used one of the first printing presses back in 1520, the store is filled with a terrific range of both French and English books, with a special emphasis on French classics, modern fiction, sociology, and fine arts. 224 rue de Rivoli, 1st arrond. www.galignani.com. ✆ **01-42-60-76-07.** Métro: Tuileries.

San Francisco Book Company ★★ This centrally located shop has a good stock of used books, including hardback classics, paperback airplane reading, and rare and out-of-print editions. 17 rue Monsieur Le Prince, 6th arrond. www.sfparis.com. ✆ **01-43-29-15-70.** Métro: Odéon.

Shakespeare and Company ★★ This venerable literary shrine is so popular with tourists that you may have to wait to get in because of the store's limited capacity. Run by George Whitman for some 60 years before he passed away in 2011 at 98, it's helmed today by his daughter, Sylvia, who was named

Sylvia Whitman, owner of Shakespeare and Company.

after Sylvia Beach (who founded the original bookshop in 1919; see box below). Many legendary writers (Allen Ginsberg and Henry Miller, to name a couple) have stopped in over the decades for a cup of tea; many an aspiring author has camped out in one of the back rooms. Check the website for readings and events. 37 rue de la Bûcherie, 5th arrond. www.shakespeareandcompany. com. ✆ **01-43-25-40-93.** Métro/RER: St-Michel–Notre-Dame.

WH Smith ★   If a wide selection is what you're after, a visit to the Paris branch of this English chain might be in order. Along with its huge range of English-language books and magazines, it hosts readings by famous authors, and harbors a lovely Twinings tearoom upstairs. 248 rue de Rivoli, 1st arrond. www.whsmith.fr. ✆ **01-44-77-88-99.** Métro: Concorde.

FRENCH BOOKSTORES

Gibert Joseph ★★   Wander the endless aisles of this book-lovers' haven, which sells both French and English books, as well as French comics ("BDs"), maps, and just about anything else on the printed page. There are six stores to choose from (all right next to each other), selling used books, new books, DVDs, art supplies, and stationery. 26–34 bd. St-Michel, 6th arrond. www. gibertjoseph.com. ✆ **01-44-41-88-88.** Métro: Cluny–La Sorbonne.

Les Mots à la Bouche ★   This is Paris's largest, best-stocked gay bookstore. You can find French- and English-language books as well as gay-info magazines such as *Têtu.* 6 rue Ste-Croix-la-Bretonnerie, 4th arrond. www.mots bouche.com. ✆ **01-42-78-88-30.** Métro: Hôtel-de-Ville.

Librarie La Hune ★   This mythic bookstore has been catering to existentialists and other intellectuals since 1949. Excellent selection, mostly in

French. 18 rue de l'Abbaye, 6th arrond. www.la-hune.com. ℃ **01-42-01-43-55.** Métro: St-Germain-des-Prés.

Clothing & Shoes

Abou d'Abi Bazar ★★   Here's a store with mostly casual clothes, multiple brands, and rotating collections—in other words, great one-stop boutique shopping. There are two other locations: 33 rue de Temple in the Marais, and 15 rue Soufflot, near the Panthéon in the 5th. 59 rue des Francs Bourgeois 4th arrond. www.aboudabibazar.com. ℃ **01-40-33-24-59.** Métro: Rambuteau.

agnès b. ★   This designer's relaxed but elegant urban fashion has been winning over Parisians, and the rest of the planet, since the '70s. Guys can wander over to see her menswear collection around the corner at **agnès b. homme** (1 rue Dieu, 10th arrond.). A dozen other locations are scattered around the city (including in the Galeries Lafayette); see website for addresses. 13 rue de Marseille, 10th arrond. www.agnesb.com. ℃ **01-42-06-66-58.** Métro: Jacques Bonsergent.

Antoine & Lili ★★   Hot pink is the signature color at this wacky store, where the gaily painted walls are hung with colorful objects from around the world. Clothes are innovative and fresh, yet wearable, and come in a range of bright colors. There are five Parisian branches (see website). 95 quai de Valmy, 10th arrond. www.antoineetlili.com. ℃ **01-40-37-41-55.** Métro: Jacques Bonsergent.

Azzedine Alaïa ★★   Alaïa, who became the darling of French fashion in the 1970s, designs beautiful, body-hugging clothing. If you can't afford the current collection, try the **outlet shop** around the corner at 18 rue de la Verrerie (℃ **01-42-72-83-19;** closed at lunchtime), where last season's leftovers are sold at serious discounts. 7 rue Moussy, 4th arrond. www.alaia. fr. ℃ **01-42-72-30-69.** Métro: Hôtel-de-Ville.

Comptoir des Cotonniers ★   Yes, it's a chain, but it's an elegant one, with streamlined clothing that works well both in the office and on casual outings. There are dozens of locations all over town. 12 place St-Sulpice, 6th arrond. www.comptoirdes cotonniers.com. ℃ **01-46-33-42-37.** Métro: St-Sulpice.

French Trotters ★   Airy and spacious, this Marais emporium is the flagship store for this temple of urban chic.

Taking a shopping break.

affordable FASHION: A QUICK GUIDE TO THE CHAINS

Several European chain stores sell fashionable clothing at remarkably low prices. Fresh and fun, these stores have loads of colorful, mod clothing—but don't expect high quality. The following stores have branches throughout the city:

Caroll A little more upscale and conservative, with a good selection of moderately priced clothing for working women who want something more feminine than a power suit. www.caroll.com.

Mango Colors at this Spanish chain tend to favor a Mediterranean complexion, a nice change from the Nordic hues at other stores. www.mango.com.

Promod A French chain with great clothes in wearable colors. The look is young, but not adolescent. www.promod.com.

Zara Another Spanish outfit, Zara stocks both work and play clothes for the young and trendy. Great for basics like T-shirts and turtlenecks. www.zara.com.

While the original store (which is still open at 30 rue de Charonne, 11th arrond.) featured both hot local French labels and the store's own brand of relaxed *branchitude* (hipness), this one sells all that plus housewares, books, and stationery. Terrific styles for both men and women. 128 rue Vieille du Temple, 3rd arrond. www.frenchtrotters.fr. ℂ **01-44-61-00-14.** Métro: Saint Sébastien-Froissart or Files du Calvaire.

Vicxite.A ★ You'll find fun, contemporary clothing by young designers here in bright patterns and unusual combinations at accessible prices. They have a second store at 52 rue des Batignolles in the 17th. 47 rue des Abbesses, 18th arrond. ℂ **01-42-55-31-68.** Métro: Abbesses.

Zadig & Voltaire ★ I don't know what the philosopher would make of this trendy young French brand, but Voltaire might have appreciated its rock 'n' roll spirit. Perfectly worn jeans, comfy cashmeres, biker boots, and more, for men, women, and children. Dozens of branches around Paris. 3 rue du Vieux Colombier, 6th arrond. www.zadig-et-voltaire.com. ℂ **01-45-48-39-37.** Métro: St-Sulpice.

CHILDREN'S CLOTHING

Botoù ★★ If you're looking for something funky for your children's feet, this is where to head. These cool and colorful shoes will make your kids look like they live in this fun and hip neighborhood (SoPi), with everything from goldfish-print sneakers to chick-yellow ankle boots. 20 rue Milton, 9th arrond. www.botou.com. ℂ **09-83-82-06-58.** Métro: Notre-Dame-de-Lorette.

Du Pareil au Même ★ Covering everything from baby needs to early adolescence, the style at this inexpensive chain store (found all over the city) is fun and original, with lots of bright colors, cute logos, and appliqués. 27 rue Saint Antoine, 4th arrond. www.dpam.com. ℂ **01-42-77-74-26.** Métro: Bastille or St Paul.

Marie Puce ★★ You can dress everyone—from babies to teens—here. Marie offers easy elegance—especially for tots who need to dress up (at least a little) but can't stand frills. Much of the clothing here is 100% made in France. 60 rue du Cherche Midi, 6th arrond. www.mariepuce.com. ℂ **01-45-48-30-09.** Métro: Sèvres-Babylone or St-Placide.

LINGERIE

Judging from the sheer number of lingerie stores in even the smallest towns in France, French women must put aside a large portion of their budgets for underwear purchases. And for good reason—French lingerie is exquisite and worth the splurge.

Fifi Chachnil ★★★ A boudoir-boutique tucked into a courtyard, this is where young French movie stars go to find retro-sexy-fun-posh underthings with a decidedly girly feel. Prices are steep, but the experience and the lingerie are unique. It has one other pink and fluffy boutique: 34 rue de Grenelle in the 7th. 68 rue Jean-Jacques Rousseau, in the courtyard, 1st arrond. www.fifichachnil.com. ℂ **01-42-21-19-93.** Métro/RER: Les Halles.

Orcanta ★★ This is a chain with a great selection of name brands (such as Lise Charmel, Chantal Thomas, and Huit), and there is usually at least a rack or two of discounted items. More locations on the website. 60 rue St-Placide, 6th arrond. www.orcanta.fr. ℂ **01-45-44-94-44.** Métro: St-Placide.

VINTAGE CLOTHING

Most Parisian vintage shops sell designer clothing. You may find treasures, but you'll pay for them. For the truly cheap, try the *brocantes* and flea markets.

Didier Ludot ★ An homage to the haute couture of yesteryear. Fancy frocks created between 1900 and 1980 line this swank boutique, which is more of an antiques shop than a clothing store. 24 galerie de Montpensier, in the arcades of the Palais Royal, 1st arrond. www.didierludot.fr. ℂ **01-42-96-06-56.** Métro: Palais-Royal–Musée du Louvre.

Free'p'Star ★ Terrific finds are in the offing for vintage hunters at this trendy store in the heart of the Marais, which specializes in funky fashions from yesteryear. Some of it's tatty, but there are real bargains to be had. Other addresses are 52 and 61 rue de la Verrerie, also in the 4th arrondissement. 20 rue de Rivoli, 4th arrond. www.freepstar.com. ℂ **01-42-77-63-43.** Métro: St Paul.

Kiliwatch ★★ This hip emporium is a true vintage store, featuring everything from torn jeans and Day-Glo dresses to leather jackets and high fashion. Books and knickknacks, too. 64 rue Tiquetonne, 2nd arrond. http://kiliwatch.paris. ℂ **01-42-21-17-37.** Métro: Etienne-Marcel.

Food & Drink
CHOCOLATE

A La Mère de Famille ★ Founded in 1761, this piece of Parisian history (rumor has it the original owner hid the mother superior of the nearby convent from raging revolutionaries during the Terror) has committed its soul to candies and chocolates à l'ancienne. You'll find classic chocolates as well as old-fashioned bonbons like *berlingots,* lemon drops, caramels, and jellied fruits. There are nine other locations. 35 rue du Faubourg Montmartre, 9th arrond. www.lameredefamille.com. ℂ **01-47-70-83-69.** Métro: Grands Boulevards.

François Pralus ★★★ Pralus owns a cacao plantation in Madagascar, ensuring the extraordinary quality of every bean that goes into his chocolate, which comes in "crus" (vintages), rather like wine. Choose between 18 lip-smacking types, each wrapped in colorful paper like exquisite parcels. Be sure to try the *barre infernale*—melt-in-your-mouth bars of dark chocolate–encased praline. A second boutique is at 44 rue Cler in the 7th arrondissement. 35 rue Rambuteau, 4th arrond. www.chocolats-pralus.com. ℂ **01-57-40-84-55.** Métro: Rambuteau.

Patrick Roger ★★ Is that a life-sized chocolate orangutan in the window? Oh yes it is. Not only is Patrick Roger a master *chocolatier,* but he is also a sculptor who uses his medium (chocolate) to convey his message. This year elephants have tickled his creative fancy, but in the past he's tackled subjects as challenging as a 13-ft tall chocolate version of Rodin's *Balzac.* He his six Parisian shop (see website for locations). 108 bd. St-Germain, 6th arrond. www.patrickroger.com. ℂ **09-63-64-50-21.** Métro: Odéon.

Via Chocolat ★★ Here is an opportunity to sample the works of dozens of different master *chocolatiers.* Specializing in "chocolate d'auteur," this "cho'room" features chocolate delights by selected local artisans. You can buy a box with a mix of auteurs or choose your own bars and bonbons. 5 rue Jean Baptiste Pigalle, 9th arrond. www.viachocolat.com. ℂ **01-45-26-12-73.** Métro: Trinité.

SPECIALTY GROCERIES

Fauchon ★ Some find it overhyped and overpriced, but others think it's heaven on earth. Founded in 1886, this tearoom-*cum*-luxury-food-emporium has been wowing the crowds for more than a century, and the crowds are certainly still coming. Today you can find Fauchon everywhere from Hamburg to Ho Chi Min City. The multi-storied, multi-function establishment includes a restaurant, a *pâtissier,* a *boulangerie,* a gourmet delicatessen, and a wine cellar. 30 place de la Madeleine, 8th arrond. www.fauchon.com. ℂ **01-70-39-38-00.** Métro: Madeleine.

La Grande Epicerie de Paris ★★ This huge gourmet grocery mecca, an outgrowth of Le Bon Marché department store (see above), stocks every gourmet substance you could possibly imagine, and many that you couldn't. Sculpted sugar cubes, designer mineral waters, truffled balsamic vinegar, pink salt from the Himalayas—need we go on? It also has an excellent (if expensive) takeout department if you are looking for picnic items. 38 rue de Sèvres, 7th arrond. www.lagrandeepicerie.fr. ℂ **01-44-39-81-00.** Métro: Sèvres-Babylone.

Maille ★ True, you can find Maille gourmet mustard all over the place, but you can only get it hand-pumped here in the official boutique. Pumped fresh

In the name of fair competition, the French government has traditionally put controls on sales. Two times a year, around the second week in January and the second week in July (official dates are pasted a couple of weeks in advance on advertisements and store websites), retailers are allowed to go hog wild and slash prices as far as they want. Recently, free-market forces have loosened the laws, and smaller sales with less drastic reductions can happen year-round. Moreover, there are now lots of Internet *vente privés*, or pre-sales, for customers with store fidelity cards. The result is that while many still breathlessly await the two big seasonal sales, opening day is both mobbed and anticlimactic. Not only is a lot of the good stuff already gone, but the initial reductions are minimal. If you must go, the best time is the second or third week, when the crowds have thinned and the stores start really cutting their prices (sales go on for at least 5 weeks). Unless you're a dedicated masochist, don't try to shop on a weekend during sale season; you'll be trampled on and risk asphyxiation in crowded, stuffy stores.

into a genuine stoneware pot and sealed with a cork, it has an altogether different taste, and it is delicious. Choose from mustard made with a dash of Chablis, Chardonnay, Sauternes, or splurge on Chablis with truffle bits. 6 place de la Madeleine, 8th arrond. www.maille.com. ℂ **01-40-15-06-00.** Métro: Madeleine.

Comptoir des Abbayes ★★★ *Ora et labora* (pray and work) is the guiding rule for monks and nuns in France's many monasteries, who produce handmade, unique goodies to eat and drink, as well as traditional handicrafts. Usually, you'd need to trek into the mountains to buy their wares, but thanks to this boutique, you can nab a bottle of artisanal chartreuse, a jar of tomato jam, or hand-made beeswax candles right in the middle of Paris. A specialty: home herb teas and remedies recommended by none other than Hildegarde von Bingen, the 12th-century German saint. 23 rue des Petits Champs, 1st arrond. www.comptoir-des-abbayes.fr. ℂ **01-42-96-11-24.** Métro: Pyramides.

WINES

Wine in France is stunningly cheap. In Paris you can buy a bottle of something extremely pleasant for as little as 5€ or 6€. But before you start planning to stock your wine cellar back home, consider this sad truth: Most non–E.U. countries won't let you bring back much more than a bottle or two. Wine stores abound, and even the most humble of them are generally staffed by knowledgeable wine-lovers who will be glad to help you find the perfect bottle to celebrate your Parisian adventure.

Cave des Abbesses ★ This small wine shop/wine bar has been serving knowing residents of Montmartre for almost 20 years. Not only will the staff help you muddle through excellent vintages, you can also sample a few while you're there and nibble on cheese and charcuterie (open until 10:30pm). 43 rue des Abbesses, 18th arrond. www.cavesbourdin.fr. ℂ **01-42-52-81-54.** Métro: Abbesses.

Legrand Filles et Fils ★★   More than just a wine store, this is a place where you can learn everything there is to know about the sacred grape. Not only does this store have a dedicated, knowledgeable staff and a huge stock of wines, but it also hosts wine tastings and wine classes, and sells wine books, paraphernalia, and glasses. Located in the glamorous Passage Vivienne (see the "Arcades" box, above). 1 rue de la Banque, 2nd arrond. www.caves-legrand.com. ℂ **01-42-60-07-12.** Métro: Bourse.

Les Domaines Qui Montent ★★★   French wine-drinkers know that you'll get the best prices when you buy direct at a vineyard. In an attempt to make these prices available to urbanites, this association of some 150 wine producers offers a vast selection of *vins du producteur,* wines that come from small independent vineyards where the emphasis is on quality and *terroir,* not quantity. Prices are very good, and if you come by at lunchtime you can open a bottle and eat a meal at their *table d'hôte* (16€ for two courses). They have two other locations: 136 bd. Voltaire in the 11th, and 2 place Lili Boulanger in the 9th. 22 rue Cardinet, 17th arrond. www.lesdomainesquimontent.com. ℂ **01-42-27-63-96.** Métro: Courcelles or Wagram.

Gifts & Souvenirs

Colette ★★   What can you say about a store that sells both Gucci scarves and Andy Warhol figurines? This shopping phenomenon offers both high style and high concept—if it's utterly cool and happening, they sell it, including Saint Laurent jeans, arty photography, pinky rings, and designer toothpaste. 213 rue St-Honoré, 1st arrond. www.colette.fr. ℂ **01-55-35-33-90.** Métro: Tuileries.

Fnac ★   A huge chain that sells a compelling combination of books, music, and electronics, Fnac (pronounced "fnack") has branches all over the city. Since electronics stores are few and far between in Paris, this is an ideal spot to drop in if you need something for your computer, iPod, or digital camera. 136 rue de Rennes, 6th arrond. www.fnac.com. ℂ **08-25-02-00-20** (.18€ per min). Métro: St-Placide.

La Tuile à Loup ★★   Dedicated to promoting (and selling) authentic handicrafts from the provinces of France, this cozy shop has a stock that includes handwoven baskets, cutlery, woodcarvings, and pottery. It has a particularly good collection of ceramics, in both traditional styles and works by contemporary artists. 35 rue Daubenton, 5th arrond. www.latuilealoup.com. ℂ **01-47-07-28-90.** Métro: Censier-Daubenton.

Tout S'arrange ★   Who says the French don't have a sense of humor? This tiny boutique is filled with unique, off-the-wall gifts that will make you smile. Goofy masks, bicycle sunglasses, peanut-shell figurines, and oodles of handmade jewelry and bags that appeal to the kid in everyone. 27 rue Delambre, 14th arrond. www.toutsarrange.fr. ℂ **01-43-26-44-68.** Métro: Edgar Quinet.

Housewares, Kitchen & Decoration

La Bovida ★★★   Founded in 1921, this renown professional kitchen supplier only recently opened its doors to the public, and you can now browse the aisles at their venerable store near Les Halles. Top-quality ergonomic zesters, icing bags, pepper mills, coffee sets, corkscrews, whip cream siphons, table-ware, sauté pans—they're all here and then some, and at competitive prices. 36 rue de Montmartre, 1st arrond. www.mybovida.com. ✆ **01-42-36-09-99.** Métro/RER: Les Halles.

La Maison Ivre ★★   Linens and beautiful handmade pottery from all over France, especially Provençal ceramics, including ovenware, bowls, platters, plates, pitchers, mugs, and vases. The beautiful tea towels, placemats, and tablecloths here make great gifts and pack easily. 38 rue Jacob, 6th arrond. www.maison-ivre.com. ✆ **01-42-60-01-85.** Métro: St-Germain-des-Prés.

La Vaissellerie ★   With four locations in the city center, this is the most convenient choice for discount china and ceramics. These small stores are so chockfull of cute gift items that their wares generally spill out onto the side-walk. In addition to china, it offers piles of salt shakers, cheese knives, and all sorts of utensils you never knew you needed (like champagne corks) as well as magnets, shopping bags, and so on. Other locations listed on the website. 85 rue de Rennes, 6th arrond. www.lavaissellerie.fr. ✆ **01-42-22-61-49.** Métro: St-Sulpice.

Plastiques ★★   Who knew plastic could be so much fun? This colorful shop is loaded with plastic dishes, lampshades, toothbrush holders, and all sorts of other gift ideas in all the colors of the rainbow. A couple doors down on the corner of rue d'Assas is their second shop, which has a fabulous range of designer plasticized tablecloths and *toile ciré* (oilcloth), which come in various table sizes or by the meter. 103 rue de Rennes, 6th arrond. www.plastiques-paris.fr. ✆ **01-45-48-75-88.** Métro: St-Sulpice or Rennes.

Jewelry & Accessories

Bijoux Blues ★★   Handcrafted, unique jewelry at reasonable prices made in an atelier in the Marais—who could ask for more? Made of Austrian and bohemian crystals, natural and semiprecious stones, pearls, and coral, the designs are fun and funky, yet elegant. Pieces can be custom-designed. 30 rue St-Paul, 4th arrond. www.bijouxblues.com. ✆ **01-48-04-00-64.** Métro: St-Paul.

Bijoux Burma ★   Pretend you are a princess with these excellent copies of the kind of spectacular pieces you could never afford. Famous for their quality synthetic jewels, which are set in gold, silver, or vermeil, these are some of the best fakes around. All six branches are strategically placed in the fanciest shopping neighborhoods. 50 rue François 1er, 8th arrond. www.bijoux-burma.com. ✆ **01-47-23-70-93.** Métro: Franklin-D-Roosevelt.

White Bird ★★   If you are looking for a unique engagement ring or pres-ent for your sweetheart, this is a good bet. This low-key store offers a terrific selection of jewelry made by talented, independent craftspeople and design-ers. There's a second store at 7 blvd. des Filles du Calvaire. 38 rue du Mont Thabor, 1st arrond. www.whitebirdjewellery.com. ✆ **01-58-62-25-86.** Métro: Concorde.

Stationery

Gibert Joseph ★   One of the largest selections of everything from elegant fountain pens to creamy pastels can be found at this multi-leveled store. Mostly geared toward student needs, this is a good place to find both the practical and the pretty at reasonable prices. 30 bd. St-Michel, 6th arrond. www.gibertjoseph.com. ℂ **01-44-41-88-88.** Métro: Cluny–La Sorbonne.

L'Art du Papier ★★   This delightful stationery store has a fab selection of colored papers and envelopes, as well as ink-stamps, sealing wax, and the essentials for hobbies like calligraphy and "le scrapbooking." There are three other locations: 16 rue Daunou in the 2nd, 197 bd. Voltaire in the 11th, and 17 ave. de Villiers in the 17th. 48 rue Vavin, 6th arrond. www.art-du-papier.fr. ℂ **01-43-26-10-12.** Métro: Vavin.

Toys & Games

Jeux Descartes ★   The name of this store is a play on words: *jeu de cartes* means "card games," and Descartes was, you know, that philosopher guy. It is full of every possible card, board, puzzle and role-playing game you could imagine. Most are in French, but some are in English. 52 rue des Ecoles, 5th arrond. www.jeux-descartes.fr. ℂ **01-43-26-79-83.** Métro: Cluny-La Sorbonne.

Tikibou ★★   One of the oldest in Paris (founded in 1884), this human-sized establishment is a marvelous example of the quintessential French toy store. Wooden toys, scale models, figurines, music boxes, musical instruments, dolls, board games, stuffed animals, costumes—in short, everything that delights and enchants and doesn't need batteries. There's a second store at 33 blvd. Edgar Quinet, close to the Montparnasse train station. 20 ave. Félix Faure 15th arrond. www.tikibou.com. ℂ **01-45-58-17-44.** Métro: Félix Faure.

ENTERTAINMENT & NIGHTLIFE

P aris blooms at night. Its magnificent monuments and buildings become even more beautiful when they're cloaked in their evening illuminations. The already glowing Eiffel Tower bursts out in twinkling lights for the first 10 minutes of every hour. While simply walking around town can be an excellent night out, the city is also a treasure trove of rich nightlife offerings. There are bars and clubs from chic to shaggy, sublime theater and dance performances, top-class orchestras, and scores of cinemas and art-house cinemas.

While Paris isn't a 24-hour town like some international capitals, and many neighborhoods may seem pretty quiet after sundown, there are still plenty of places to go if you are ready for a night out. So whether you're planning to hit the most happening clubs or happy with a 3€ beer in a student bar in the Latin Quarter, we're here to help you find your way. Below is a biased selection of some of the better ways to spend your Parisian evenings; the end of the chapter is dedicated to sports fans in search of a game/race/match.

GETTING TICKETS Many hotels will help you get tickets, and most venues have a reservation link online, but the easiest way to buy tickets is at **Fnac,** the giant bookstore/music chain that has one of the most comprehensive box offices in the city (follow the signs to the "Billeterie"). You can also **order your tickets online** in English at www.fnactickets.com or **by phone** at ✆ **08-92-68-36-22** (.40€ per min.). **Ticketmaster.fr** offers a similar service.

Discount hunters can stand in line at one of the city's three **half-price ticket booths,** all run by **Le Kiosque Théâtre** (www.kiosque theatre.com). There's one in front of the Montparnasse train station, another on the west side of the Madeleine (facing 15 place de la Madeleine, exit rue Tronchet from the Madeleine Métro stop), and a third in the center of Place des Ternes (17th arrond.) The first two are open from Tuesday to Saturday (12:30–7.30pm), and Sun (12:30–3:45pm), while Ternes' is open just Tuesday to Saturday (12:30–2:30pm, 3–7:30pm). Half-price tickets for same-day performances go on sale here at 12:30pm. Don't dawdle—by noon the line is long. There are also plenty of ticket discounts at **BilletRé-duc,** www.billetreduc.com (in French).

THEATER

Paris has hundreds of theaters, most of which have something going on almost every night. The obvious catch here is, almost all of it is in French. Even if you can't spit out much more than *bonjour* and *merci*, fear not, you have options. There are a few English-language shows like the hit "How To Become a Parisian in One Hour" (see "Belly Laughs in English," below), or you can opt for one of the many avant-garde offerings at theaters like Théâtre de Chaillot or Théâtre de la Ville, where shows that combine dance, theater, and images don't really need translation. Ticket prices, particularly for the large, state-funded theaters, are remarkably low. For example, the most expensive seats are 41€ at the Odéon and 42€ at the Comédie-Française.

Comédie-Française ★★ In 1680, Louis XIV announced the birth of a company of actors, chosen by himself, with the aim of "making theater productions more perfect." Some 300 years later, it is still considered by many the crème de la crème of the French theater scene. In addition to the gorgeous just-restored main theater (**Salle Richelieu**), the company presents its offerings in its two other theaters: the medium-size **Théâtre du Vieux Colombier** (21 rue du Vieux Colombier, 6th arrond.; Métro: St-Sulpice or Sèvres–Babylone) and the smaller **Studio-Théâtre** (Galerie du Carrousel du Louvre, under the Pyramid, 99 rue de Rivoli, 1st arrond.; Métro: Palais Royal–Musée du Louvre). Place Colette, 1st arrond. www.comedie-francaise.fr. © **01-44-58-15-15.** Métro: Palais-Royal–Musée du Louvre.

Odéon, Théâtre de l'Europe ★ Less venerable and more modern, this grand theater presents both new plays and old classics, but even the classics usually get a modern twist. There are lots of cutting-edge, contemporary pieces here, including several from other European countries (hence the moniker "Théâtre de l'Europe"). Foreign productions are supertitled, which can be a plus if you can read French. The Odéon's second space, **Ateliers Berthier** (1 rue André Suarès, 17th arrond.; Métro: Porte de Clichy) presents smaller-scale productions, as well as theater for young actors. Place de l'Odéon, 6th arrond. www.theatre-odeon.eu. © **01-44-85-40-40.** Métro: Odéon.

Finding Out What's On

Paper magazine listings are dwindling, but for up-to-the-minute dates and schedules for what's happening in music, theater, dance, and film, you can still pick up the weekly *l'Officiel des Spectacles* (1€), a comprehensive listing of weekly events. also has a weekly pull-out listings guide, complete with reviews. Both come out on Wednesdays and are available at any newsstand.

Online, *Pariscope* has excellent listings (www.pariscope.fr), as do *l'Officiel des Spectacles* (www.offi.fr) and *Télérama* (www.telerama.fr). All three sites are in French only. By the way, if you see a sign at a theater or on an events website that says *location*, that means "box office," not location.

Paris is the nation's dance capital, and most of the country's best companies are based here, including the phenomenal **Ballet de l'Opéra de Paris** (see "Opéra de Paris," below). Top French choreographers like Angelin Preljoçaj, Blanca Li, and José Montalvo produce here, as well as other European stars like Sidi Larbi Cherkaoui and Mats Ek. Two of the biggest dance venues are **Théâtre de Chaillot** or **Théâtre de la Ville** (see above). For some reason, dance is often grouped with classical music in magazine and website listings.

LANDMARK MULTIUSE VENUES

La Seine Musicale ★★★   The latest addition to Parisian music scene resembles a futuristic cruise ship in the middle of the Seine. Open as of April 2017, this architectural marvel sits on an island in the river next to the western suburb of Boulogne Billancourt. The complex includes recording studios, restaurants, a garden, and two top-notch concert spaces: one dedicated to classical music, and the other for dance, pop music, musical comedies, and other cultural events. The magnificent classical music hall is encased in a huge globe-shaped structure protected by an enormous photovoltaic sail that slowly rotates around the globe, screening it from the sun and producing solar energy. It's a bit of a trek to get here, but it will be a concert experience you won't forget in a hurry. Ile de Seguin, Boulogne-Billancourt. www.laseinemusicale.com. ✆ 01-74-34-53-53. Métro: Pont de Sèvres, then a 10-min walk.

Théâtre de la Ville ★★   *Note: The theater will be closed for renovations until 2019, this season's productions will take place at other venues.* It's hard to say which lineup is the most impressive here: theater (new and recent authors), dance (modern dance companies, such as Anne Teresa De Keersmaeker and Lucinda Childs), or music (mostly young stars of the classical music scene). A lot of international productions stop by here on tour. There's also a separate World Music series. 2 place du Châtelet, 4th arrond. www.theatredelaville-paris.com. ✆ **01-42-74-22-77.** Métro: Châtelet.

Théâtre du Châtelet ★★   *Note: The theater will be closed for renovations until 2019, this season's productions will take place at other venues.* Specializing in all that is big and splashy, this lovely 19th-century theater hosts visiting international orchestras, divas, and ballet companies, as well as revivals of musical-theater classics (usually in their original language; "Singing in the Rain" is on tap for Nov 2017 through Jan 2018 at the Grand Palais). 1 place du Châtelet, 1st arrond. www.chatelet-theatre.com. ✆ **01-40-28-28-40.** Métro: Châtelet.

Théâtre National de Chaillot ★★   Dance and theater are on equal footing at this beautiful Art Deco theater in the Palais de Chaillot, where contemporary choreographers and theater directors share a jam-packed program.

9

ENTERTAINMENT & NIGHTLIFE

Landmark Multiuse Venues

There is a lot of blurring of lines here between the two disciplines; dance programs often include video and text, and theater productions often incorporate the abstract. *Tip:* One of the best views of the Eiffel Tower can be seen from the theater's lobby, which has a bar and restaurant. 1 place du Trocadéro, 16th arrond. www.theatre-chaillot.fr. ☎ **01-53-65-30-00.** Métro: Trocadéro.

OPERA & CLASSICAL MUSIC

Opéra Comique/Salle Favart ★★ For a lighter take on opera, try this architectural puff pastry filled with operettas and (French) musicals. Created in 1714 for theatrical performances that included songs, the Opéra Comique endured several fires before finally settling down in a beautiful 19th-century theater complete with huge chandeliers. An excellent opportunity to enjoy both history and music in a splendid setting. 5 rue Favart, 2nd arrond. www.opera-comique. com. ☎ **01-80-05-68-60.** Métro: Richelieu–Drouot or Quatre-Septembre.

Opéra de Paris ★★★ This mighty operation includes both the **Palais Garnier** (place de l'Opéra, 9th arrond., an attraction in itself; p. 146) and the **Opéra Bastille** (place de la Bastille, 12th arrond.), a slate-colored behemoth that has loomed over the place de la Bastille since 1989, when the national opera company decided it needed a new home. Not wanting to abandon the Palais Garnier, the company decided to split its energies between the two venues. In theory, more operas are performed at the Bastille, which has more space and top-notch acoustics. The Garnier, home of the **Ballet de l'Opèra de Paris,** focuses more on dance, but the reality is you can see either at both. The opera program sticks pretty much to the classics (although the productions

The Opéra Bastille was inaugurated in 1989 for the bicentennial of the Revolution.

The beautiful ceiling at the Palais Garnier, home of the Ballet de l'Opèra de Paris.

themselves can be cutting edge), while the ballet offerings are becoming more adventurous. www.operadeparis.fr. 𝄞 **08-92-89-90-90** (.35€ per min.); from outside France 𝄞 01-71-25-24-23.

Philharmonie de Paris ★★★ Hovering over La Villette like a visiting spaceship, this mega venue seats 2,400 spectators and serves as the new home of the Orchestre de Paris. Yet another creation of über-architect Jean Nouvel (this time in partnership with Harold Marshall and with input from Yasuhisa Toyota), this silvery apparition also encompasses a music museum and other performance spaces in the adjacent **Philharmonie 2** building (the former Cité de la Musique), as well as a nifty cafe and restaurant. In keeping with La Villette's policy of making culture accessible to one and all, the season includes symphonic and choral concerts, as well as performances specially designed for young people, families, and audiences that don't usually find themselves in concert halls. As for the Philharmonie 2 complex, it offers a wide range of music options, from classical to contemporary to jazz, and a good dose of the offbeat and unexpected, like a silent film accompanied by the music of Philip Glass, or a weekend of dance and music dedicated to African women. Young musicians and rising stars are highlighted; small orchestras and chamber musicians also show up on the program. 221 ave. Jean-Jaurès, 19th arrond. www.philharmoniede paris.com. 𝄞 **01-44-84-44-84.** Métro: Porte de Pantin.

CABARET

At the end of the 19th century, cabarets and music halls opened in Montmartre, frequented by oddballs and artists, as well as bourgeois, aristocrats, and demi-mondaines looking for a good time. These nightclubs offered an offbeat reflection of the times, where singers like Aristide Bruand would sing about the life of the destitute and sharp political satire would share the stage with cheeky dancing girls dancing that new step, the can-can. Those days are long gone. Although some visitors feel they simply haven't enjoyed the true Paris experience without seeing a show at the Moulin Rouge or the Lido, there is nothing particularly Parisian, or even French, about them anymore. Today's audiences are more likely to arrive in tour buses than touring cars, and contemporary shows are more Vegas than Paris. What you will see here is a lot of scenic razzmatazz and many sublime female bodies, mostly *torse nue* (topless). If you still want to see one of these shows, do yourself a favor and have dinner somewhere else. The food in these establishments is expensive for the quality. (The following theaters have strict dress codes as well, so be sure to inquire about them when making reservations.)

Chez Michou ★★ If you are looking for a wacky and joyously tacky alternative to the standard girls-with-feathers cabaret show, this is the place to go. There are girls here, of a sort—this is Paris's most famous drag show. Michou, the venerable master of ceremonies, presents a bevy of cross-dressed beauties who lip-sync in a range of terrific costumes; some imitate celebrities ranging from Céline Dion to Grace Jones. 80 rue des Martyrs, 18th arrond. www. michou.com. © **01-46-06-16-04.** 45€–78€ show only at bar; 60€–95€ show only seated; 115€–145€ dinner package. Métro: Pigalle.

The Crazy Horse ★★ Don't come here expecting to see can-can. This temple to "The Art of the Nude" presents an erotic dance show with artistic aspirations. The current show, "Désirs," was created with the help of renowned choreographer Philippe Découflé. Be advised that unlike the other shows, this one is known for what the girls aren't wearing. Lighting effects are plentiful, music is mostly modern, and the performers, who slither, swagger, and lip-sync with panache, have names like Ero Tikka and Zora Moonshine. Note that aside from drinks and hors d'oeuvre platters, there is no dining on-site; dinner packages include a meal at a nearby restaurant. 12 ave. George V, 8th arrond. www.lecrazyhorseparis.com. © **01-47-23-32-32.** Show standing at the bar 40€–50€ ages 18–20; 65€–85€ 21 and over; 85€–165€ show seated; show plus dinner packages start at 160€. Métro: George V or Alma Marceau.

Lido de Paris ★ For the full-on glamour gala, head for the Lido. Head-dresses and high heels are of such dimensions that the dancers can't do much dancing, but you're probably not coming here for prima ballerina turns. The latest show, Paris Merveilles, conceived by Franco Dragone of Cirque du Soleil fame, includes 200 kg of feathers, 300 projectors, and of course, the famed Bluebell Girls. Unlike some of the other cabarets, the music is live here, and the food is of a higher caliber. A few lunchtime shows are offered. 116 ave. des Champs-Élysées, 8th arrond. www.lido.fr. © **01-40-76-56-10.** 70€–165€ show only; 170€ show with lunch; 170€–400€ show with dinner. Métro: George V.

Belly Laughs in English

English-language shows are rare, and comics even more so, but a couple of long-standing gigs in town are worth a detour. At press time, the best place to go for a giggle was **"How to Become a Parisian in One Hour"** (at Théâtre des Nouveautés; reservations at www.olivier giraud.com), a one-person show written by Olivier Giraud, a Frenchman who spent several years in the U.S. More humor is on tap at **SoGymnase,** Paris's only English-language comedy club, on the fourth floor of the Théâtre du Gymnase Marie Bell (38 ave. Bonne Nouvelle, 10th arrond.; www. sogymnase.com; © **01-42-46-79-79**), Fridays 8pm, Saturdays at 9:30pm.

With few exceptions, the major concert halls and theaters are in action between September and June, taking off the summer months. Since the city virtually empties out as Parisians storm the beaches during the annual vacation exodus, many smaller venues and dance clubs also close their doors. On the upside, Paris sees several wonderful summer music festivals, including **Jazz à La Villette** (www.jazzalavillette.com), an international jazz blowout that takes place in the Parc de la Villette in August and September, and the **Festival Chopin** (www.frederic-chopin.com), a tribute to the master at the Parc de la Bagatelle in the Bois de Boulogne in June and July. But if you have your heart set on opera or theater, you're better off visiting during the colder weather.

Moulin Rouge ★   When it opened in 1889, the Moulin Rouge was the talk of the town, and its huge dance floor, multiple mirrors, and floral garden inspired painters like Toulouse-Lautrec. In later decades legendary French singers like Charles Trenet and Charles Aznavour regularly wowed the crowds. Times have changed. Today's Moulin Rouge relies heavily on lip-syncing and prerecorded music, backed up by dozens of be-feathered Doriss Girls, long-legged ladies that prance about the stage. Be prepared for plenty of glitz and not a whole lot else. 82 bd. Clichy, place Blanche, 18th arrond. www.moulinrouge.fr. ✆ **01-53-09-82-82.** 87€–210€ show alone; 190€–420€ show with dinner. Métro: Blanche.

Paradis Latin ★   This cabaret may be a bit less glitzy than the others, but it makes more of an attempt to harken back to the cabarets of yesteryear,

The Moulin Rouge.

Chanson: The Next Generation

You've all heard it, the tremulous voice, the monotonous tunes, the intense sincerity of it all—yes, that's *chanson*, those peculiarly melody-challenged songs that Edith Piaf sang. If you don't understand the words, it's hard to understand why so many French people get all misty-eyed when they listen to it. But that's just it; with chanson, it's the words that count. Each song is a poem set to music, in fact some lyrics are the works of famous French authors. In recent years, a new generation of young singers/writers have been coming up with their own poetic versions of the trials and tribulations of life, and their heroes are not so much Piaf and Aznavour as Leonard Cohen and Bob Dylan. The biggest venue for chanson these days is the newly reborn **Les Trois Baudets** (64 bd. de Clichy, 18th arrond.; www.lestroisbaudets.com; ✆ **01-42-62-33-33**), but the following two other venues also specialize in this quintessentially French style:

○ **Théâtre des 2 Anes** (100 bd. de Clichy, 18th arrond.; www.2anes.com; ✆ **01-46-06-10-64;** Métro: Blanche). Depending on the night, it could be humor or singing here, but it will always be with an ironic edge.

○ **Au Lapin Agile** (48 bis rue Custine, 18th arrond.; www.au-lapin-agile.com; ✆ **01-46-06-85-87;** Métro: Lamarck-Caulaincourt). This legendary spot was once the hangout of then unknown artists and poets like Picasso, Utrillo, and Apollonaire. Despite being a tourist destination, the shows here are nostalgic and heartfelt, with the audience often joining in.

which featured live and sometimes talented performers. You'll see a variety of acts, as well as the obligatory topless beauties in feathered costumes and a rollicking can-can. There is a fair amount of audience interaction, and a good portion of the show is translated in English. The metallic armature holding up the roof was designed by Gustave Eiffel. There are some lunchtime shows. 28 rue du Cardinal Lemoine, 5th arrond. www.paradislatin.com. ✆ **01-43-25-28-28.** 65€–90€ show only; 120€ lunch and show; 130€–190€ dinner and show. Métro: Cardinal Lemoine.

MOVIES

With over 400 movie screens and between 450 and 500 films on offer every week, Paris merits its title as cinephile capital of the world. Close to 100 are art-house cinemas, which specialize in rare films, old classics and independent works. Many of the mainstream movies shown in the big chain movie theaters are dubbed in French (v.f., or *version française*); if you want to see a mainstream English-language film, make sure you find one in v.o. You can find listings of both mainstream and art house theaters in *l'Officiel du Spectacle,* or on the Internet at Allocine (www.allocine.fr).

Some of the most famous art houses include **Le Champo, Reflet Medecis, Action Ecoles,** and **Accatone,** all in the Latin Quarter. The most scandalous is **Studio 28** (10 rue Tholozé, 18th arrond.; www.cinema-studio28.fr; ℂ **01-46-06-36-07;** Métro: Blanche or Abbesses), where Luis Buñuel's polemical 1930 movie, *L'Age d'Or,* was censored after only two showings here. The newest addition to the art-house scene is the recently reborn **Louxor** (170 bd. Magenta, 10th arrond.; www.cinemalouxor.fr; ℂ **01-44-63-96-96;** Métro: Barbès-Rochechouart), a gorgeous neo-Egyptian 1920s movie palace that had been abused and abandoned until the city finally took it over and restored it.

In addition to regular movie theaters, two giant **cinema archives** have their own theaters and programs. The first, in a wacky building designed by Frank Gehry, is the **Cinémathèque Française** (51 rue de Bercy, 12th arrond.; www. cinematheque.fr; ℂ **01-71-19-33-33;** Métro: Bercy), home to a cinema, library, museum, and research center. The other is the **Forum des Images** (Forum des Halles, Porte St-Eustache, 1st arrond.; www.forumdesimages.fr; ℂ **01-44-76-63-00;** Métro: Châtelet–Les Halles), which is funded by the City of Paris, and has a bank of over 7,500 films, including thousands that feature Paris as either the subject or the setting. A new addition to the cinema archive world is the **Fondation Jérôme Seydoux-Pathé** (75 ave. des Gobelins, 13th arrond; www.fondation-jeromeseydoux-pathe.com; ℂ **01-83-79-18-96;** Métro: Place d'Italie), which specializes in film history and regularly screens silent films accompanied by live pianists.

LIVE ROCK, JAZZ & MORE

Paris has a wide range of places to hear live music, from tiny medieval basements to huge modern concert venues. Whatever your musical tastes you are bound to enjoy your outing: Not only do many of the world's greatest musicians swing through the city on a regular basis, but you can't beat the walk to the nightclub/bar/theater with the lights of Paris twinkling in the background.

Live Music
JAZZ CLUBS

Paris has been a fan of jazz from its beginnings, and many legendary performers like Sidney Bechet and Kenny Clark made the city their home. Still a haven for jazz musicians and fans of all stripes, Paris boasts dozens of places to duck into and listen to a good set or two. Here are some of the best.

Baiser Salé ★★ On a street lined with famous jazz clubs, this one holds its own with a lineup that shows off jazz in all its diversity. Some of the biggest Franco-African jazz stars, like Richard Bona and Angelique Kidjo, got their start here, and the program still highlights the best in African, Caribbean, and Asian, as well as French jazz. There are regular jam sessions on Sundays and Mondays. 58 rue des Lombards, 1st arrond. www.lebaisersale.com. ℂ **01-42-33-37-71.** Cover free to 25€, depending on the act. Métro: Châtelet.

Caveau de la Huchette ★ This temple of swing has seen business boom since it was recreated in a short scene in the hit film "La La Land." Legends like Count Basie and Lionel Hampton once graced this basement club, and some excellent jazz musicians still play here. The first part of the evening (starting at 9:30pm) is for enjoying the music. After that there's swing and Lindy Hop. 5 rue de la Huchette, 5th arrond. www.caveaudelahuchette.fr. ℂ **01-43-26-65-05.** Cover 13€ Sun–Thurs; 15€ Fri–Sat; students 24 and under 10€. Métro/RER: St-Michel.

Le Duc des Lombards ★★ This is one of the most famous jazz clubs in Paris, where famous names come to play in a small, intimate space. That said, it's a relatively low-key place and tickets aren't too hard to get—but good seats are (they are not numbered), so get here early if you want to sit up front. Light meals are served; see website for concert-dinner packages. The club hosts free jam sessions on Fridays and Saturdays after midnight. 42 rue des Lombards, 1st arrond. www.ducdeslombards.com. ℂ **01-42-33-22-88.** Cover free– 50€; dining options are available. Métro: Châtelet.

Le Sunset/Le Sunside ★★ Yet another famous jazz club on the rue des Lombards, what sets this one off is its split personality. Le Sunset Jazz, created in 1983, is dedicated to electric jazz and international music, whereas Le Sunside, launched in 2001, is devoted to acoustic jazz for the most part. Some of the hottest names in French jazz appear here regularly (Jacky Terrasson and Didier Lockwood, to name a couple) along with a new crop of international stars like Kyle Eastwood. 60 rue des Lombards, 1st arrond. www.sunset-sunside. com. ℂ **01-40-26-46-60.** Tickets free–32€. Métro: Châtelet.

New Morning.

New Morning ★★★ Big names and hot acts? Look no further. This place has terrific lineups, including virtuosos like bassist Avishai Cohen, pop-soul masters like Roy Ayers and Joan Armatrading, as well as a long list of young upstarts and world music stars. This relatively large club (the room holds 300) fills up quick, and it's no wonder: This is one of the best jazz venues in town, but the top ticket price is only around 30€. 7 rue des Petites-Ecuries, 10th arrond. www.newmorning.com. No phone. Cover free–30€. Métro: Château-d'Eau.

CONCERT VENUES

Cabaret Sauvage ★★ Is it a cool club or a circus tent? The answer is not clear at this unusual space where you are just as likely to encounter Brazilian samba, electro funk, or trapeze artists. Blues bands from the Balkans and Vietnamese jazz musicians share the calendar with avant-garde circus acts and Algerian acrobats. Although this big-top cabaret is essentially a performance space with an accent on world music and dance, it also hosts themed dance parties, where you can boogie to jungle and techno, as well as raï, mambo, samba, and so forth. Parc de la Villette, entrance at 59 bd. Mac Donald, 19th arrond. www.cabaretsauvage.com. ℰ **01-42-09-03-09.** Métro: Porte de la Villette.

La Cigale ★★ This 19th-century music hall draws some of the biggest artists working in music today—everything from indie rock to hip-hop and jazz. Balcony seating is available for those who arrive early, and there's plenty of open floor space for those who want to dance. 120 boulevard de Rochechouart, 18th arrond. www.lacigale.fr. ℰ **01-49-25-89-99.** Métro: Pigalle or Anvers.

Olympia ★★★ For French musicians, playing the Olympia is a little like reaching the golden heaven of the Greek gods. Legends like Georges Brassens, Edith Piaf, Louis Armstrong, and Aretha Franklin have all appeared at this cavernous hall, which draws French and international pop, rock, and jazz stars like Juliette Greco, Diana Krall, and Sting. 28 bd. des Capucines, 9th arrond. www.olympiahall.com. ℰ **08-92-68-33-68** (.34€ per min). Métro: Opéra or Madeleine.

LIVE MUSIC BARS

L'Alimentation Générale ★★ This bar/restaurant/music space was created in the spirit of an *alimentation génerale,* a little corner grocery store that stays open late and sells a little bit of everything. Its ambience is comfortable and slightly kitsch, its programming eclectic, including a good dose of world music. DJs or live bands play here practically every night, and the cover charge ranges from nothing to 10€ (drink included). You can nibble on pizzas and other Italian delicacies at the onsite restaurant. 64 rue Jean-Pierre Timbaud, 11th arrond. www.alimentation-generale.net. ℰ **01-43-55-42-50.** Métro: Parmentier.

L'International ★ Here's a no-brainer for a fun night out that won't hurt your pocketbook: two to three bands and a DJ set in a relaxed (albeit tiny) setting for free. On the eclectic agenda is a string of folk, rock, electro, you-name-it bands playing to hip indie crowds. Beer is cheap and there are periodic after-show parties until 4am. Happy hour from 7pm–9pm. 5/7 rue Moret, 11th arrond. www.linternational.fr. ℰ **09-80-53-76-41.** Métro: Ménilmontant.

Many of Paris's most beautiful churches and cathedrals, including Notre-Dame, St-Eustache, and Ste-Chapelle, host organ and other classical music concerts. Not only is the setting delightful, but the acoustics are generally otherworldly. While there is no ticket central for these artistic houses of God, concerts are usually listed in the weekly-listings magazines and websites (*Pariscope, l'Officiel des Spectacles*) under classical music. Most churches print monthly music schedules, which they display near the entrance to the sanctuary (and sometimes post on their websites). Ticket prices are reasonable; you shouldn't pay more than 25€.

Supersonic ★ A temple to the independent spirit, Supersonic is free and promotes unknown stars of tomorrow. There's an industrial ambience here; this is not the place to wear those new suede boots you just bought in the Marais. Live bands play 7 days a week, and dance parties roll on 'til dawn on Friday and Saturday nights (after the bands). 9 rue Biscornet, 12th arrond. www. supersonic-club.fr. ℂ **01-46-28-12-90.** Métro: Bastille.

CATEGORY-DEFYING VENUES

An increasing number of venues are so multifunctional they defy any attempt to fit them under the usual headings. Sure, you can enjoy music and dance in these places, but you can also go to a screening, check out a poetry lounge, visit an art expo, happen in on a lecture/demonstration, and of course, eat, drink, and be merry. Many are all-day affairs, where the activities change as the sun goes down, others are purely for night owls. With so many variables, checking the venue's program online is the best way to find out what's on during your stay.

La Bellevilloise ★★ This 19th-century building was the home of the city's first workers' cooperative, offering cultural activities and meeting spaces to the downtrodden. Today, the structure has been transformed, but the mission is still a cultural one. Dedicated to "light, night, and creativity," the lofty space has been divvied up into art galleries, performance spaces, a concert hall, a club, and a restaurant with a lovely outdoor terrace where you can have a drink. The program ranges from film festivals to fashion shows, with a good dose of contemporary music. On the weekends, daytime activities include workshops, specialty markets, and tea dances. 19–21 rue Boyer, 20th arrond. www.labellevilloise.com. ℂ **01-46-36-07-07.** Métro: Gambetta.

Le Carreau du Temple ★★ A recent addition to the growing list of multitasking cultural centers rising from the ashes of neglected historic buildings, this former covered market spent several sorry decades as a used clothing bazaar. Today, after a several-million-euro facelift, the city-owned and -operated venue features sports facilities, rehearsal rooms, concert halls, and other spaces where artists, musicians, actors, and fashion mavens can strut their stuff. This means you can see theater, music or dance, watch fashion shows, work out, or enjoy a film—programming is eclectic. 4 rue Eugène Spuller, 3rd arrond. www.carreaudutemple.eu. © **01-83-81-93-30.** Métro: Temple or République.

Le Centquatre ★★★   What was once the municipal morgue is now a vast space dedicated to all things artistic and fun. There is food for both the spirit and the stomach here: theater, dance, music, visual arts, as well as a gourmet grocery, cafes, and restaurants. Along with concerts and dance parties for grown-ups, there are activities for families and little ones (musical events, art workshops, and so forth). If that's not enough, you can also shop for bargains in the Emmaüs shop (a charitable organization that sells wonderful used knickknacks and furniture) or browse at the bookstore. 5 rue Curial, 19th arrond. www.104.fr. © **01-53-35-50-00.** Métro: Riquet.

Point Ephemere ★   Describing itself as a "center for artistic dynamics," this converted warehouse on the banks of the Canal St-Martin prides itself on nurturing up-and-coming artists, musicians, dancers, and filmmakers, and offers residencies to a chosen few who work in on-premise studios. The packed program includes lots of *soirées,* or dance parties, with an emphasis on electronic music, though experimental rock is represented, too. Dance concerts, art expositions, and discussion forums are also on the agenda. Tickets for most events are in the 10€ to 22€ range. A suitably downscale-hip quayside **bar and restaurant** opens up to an outdoor terrace in nice weather. 200 quai Valmy, 10th arrond. www.pointephemere.org. © **01-40-34-02-48.** Métro: Jean Jaurès.

THE BAR SCENE

For a city that does not seem to have a particularly feisty nightlife at first sight, Paris has an astounding assortment of bars. There are cafes galore, of course, but a cafe is not necessarily a bar. Though both serve alcoholic beverages, cafes offer a laid-back place to sip at any time of day or night, whereas anything that calls itself a bar usually has an edgier feel and gets going after dark. Two recent developments may be responsible for the per-capital barstool increase: First, France has finally discovered cocktails and is putting its culinary talent to work behind the bar. Second, there is a new fondness for beer, a beverage that has often been treated with scorn and dismay in this wine-drinking country. Artisanal brewpubs are cropping up all around town. Bars, be they beer-, wine-, or cocktail-oriented, generally stay open until around 2am.

Bars & Cafes

Andy Wahloo ★★   After a decade or so of hosting the happening crowd in an ambience of North African kitsch, this ultra-cool bar has had a makeover—now it is sleek and sophisticated, with a decor that gives a nod to the 1950s. In keeping with the times, the bartenders outdo themselves working up clever cocktails. 69 rue des Gravilliers, 3rd arrond. www.andywahloo-bar.com. © **01-42-71-20-38.** Métro: Arts et Métiers.

Au Folies ★★ This ancient cafe features period details, swirls of aging neon, and spindly tables spilling out on the sidewalk—in short, it's easy to understand why it's a Belleville institution. Open all day, it comes to life at night when the neon switches on and the crowds come pouring in. 8 rue de Belleville, 20th arrond. www.aux-folies-belleville.fr. © **06-28-55-89-40.** Métro: Belleville.

Café Charbon ★ This turn-of-the-20th-century beauty (it was once a dance hall) welcomes hordes of happy night-birds under its arched ceilings; the door in the back leads to the nightclub, **Le Nouveau Casino,** where live bands and DJs shake it up until the wee hours. You can come here any time of day, for coffee, a drink, or a good meal. 109 rue Oberkampf, 11th arrond. http://nouveaucasino.fr. © **01-43-57-55-13.** Métro: Parmentier or Ménilmontant.

Le Perchoir ★★★ Take in a fabulous view of eastern Paris from this rooftop bar, which has been so successful it has spawned a passel of other high-altitude nightspots on top of buildings in the Marais, Buttes Chaumont, and other hip parts of the city (check website for locations). Sip a cocktail on an outdoor sofa and gaze at the Sacré-Coeur, or flirt at the tented bar; if you want to sit down, come early before the crowd arrives. 14 rue Crespin du Gast, 11th arrond. www.leperchoir.tv. © **01-48-06-18-48.** Métro: Ménilmontant.

Outland Bar ★★ An outgrowth of the current Parisian fascination with craft beers, this spacious new "American style" brew pub offers 12 artisanal beers on tap, eight of which hail from the terrific Outland brewery, located in a nearby suburb. The low-key atmosphere includes hanging sausages and hams, which are sliced and served along with other tapaslike fare to accompany beers with names like "Clearly Hoppy" and "Shameless." 6 rue Emile Lepeu, 11th arrond. www.outland-beer.com. © **01-46-59-04-28.** Métro: Charonne.

Experimental Cocktail Club ★ A sophisticated spot to spot stars, this bar is known, not surprisingly, for its gourmet cocktails. It has the feel of a retro speakeasy. 37 rue St-Sauveur, 2nd arrond. www.facebook.com/eccparis/. © **01-45-08-88-09.** Métro: Sentier.

La Palette ★ Cézanne, Picasso and Braque once hung out in this Olde Worlde Left Bank bar, and you'll still find a spattering of artists, students, and gallery owners today. The front room's where the regulars prop themselves up; the beautiful back room is where the romantics go to sip wine amid original frescos and old mirrors. 43 rue de Seine, 6th arrond. www.cafelapaletteparis.com. © **01-43-26-68-15.** Métro: St-Germain-des-Prés.

Grand Marché Stalingrad ★★ This huge, round 18th-century pavilion (formerly known as "La Rotonde") sits at the southern end of the Bassin de La Villette on place Stalingrad. It originally served as a giant tollbooth (a *barrière d'octroi*), when "foreign" merchants were obliged to pay a tax to sell their goods in Paris. Today, it houses an art gallery, a restaurant, a wine and beer bar (**Le Refuge**), a small club, and on warm days, a delightful terrace where you can sip in the sun. 6–8 place de la Bataille de Stalingrad, 19th arrond. www.larotonde.com. © **01-80-48-33-40.** Métro: Stalingrad or Jaurès.

The Bar Scene ENTERTAINMENT & NIGHTLIFE

With its frescoes in the back room, La Palette is a magnet for art students.

Le Bar du Plaza Athénée ★★★ Knock yourself out and order a shockingly expensive drink at this classy, historic joint, which simply drips with glamour and fabulousness. The bar (and the entire hotel) just had an in-depth overhaul, and its latest iteration sports a transparent bar and extra-posh cocktails. Hotel Plaza-Athénée, 25 ave. Montaigne, 8th arrond. www.dorchestercollec tion.com. © **01-53-67-66-00.** Métro: Alma-Marceau.

Le China ★ This sleek bar and restaurant evokes 1930s Shanghai with its dim lighting, red walls, and deep leather Chesterfield couches. The restaurant serves pricey gourmet Chinese cuisine, while the long zinc bar (the longest in Paris) on the ground floor invites you to order a cocktail. Downstairs is another bar, with live jazz and pop music. 50 rue de Charenton, 12th arrond. www. lechina.eu. © **01-43-46-08-09.** Métro: Ledru Rollin.

Wine Bars

Wine fans can lose their heads in this city, not because they drink too much, but because there are so many tempting wine bars out there to choose from. Not only can you sample all sorts of delightful fruits of the vine at a *bar à vin,* but you can usually nibble something salty and delicious (generally cheese or charcuterie) to complement what's in the glass.

5e Cru ★ Offering a multitude of the best and brightest French wines, this trendy spot also tickles the taste buds with a terrific lunch menu. At night, it serves up cheese and charcuterie platters as well as frequent themed wine tastings. 7 rue du Cardinal Lemoine, 5th arrond. www.5ecru.com. © **01-40-46-86-34.** Métro: Jussieu.

Jéroboam ★ Here's a fab spot for those looking to develop their palate: On one side you'll find a wine shop with over 350 types of *vin;* on the other is a low-key restaurant serving great food. The fun bit? An automatic wine-dispensing machine in the resto allowing self-sampling mini-glasses of a choice of 25 delicious wines for a euro or two per "shot." 10 rue Saint-Sébastien, 11th arrond. www.jeroboam-baravin.com. ✆ **09-84-05-94-75.** Métro: Saint-Sébastien–Froissart.

Le Baron Rouge ★★ This neighborhood institution spills out on a corner that it shares with the sprawling Marché d'Aligre. It has only a few tables, so most people stand at the counter or outside, glass in hand, especially during market hours. Huge vats of wine are stacked up inside, and you can fill up if you bring a bottle. In season, platters of oysters are served to accompany your wine; otherwise, the menu is limited to cheese and charcuterie. It's a little rough and tumble getting in your drink order at the bar, but that's half the fun. 1 rue Théophile Roussel, 12th arrond. ✆ **01-43-43-14-32.** Métro: Ledru-Rollin.

Les Caves Populaires ★★ A neighborhood wine bar where locals come to shoot the breeze. The waiters are friendly, the decor understated, and the wine and cheese and sausage platters cheap. Coming here is a good excuse to explore the offbeat Batignolles neighborhood, a mix of artsy types, old-timers, and students. 22 rue des Dames, 17th arrond. ✆ **01-53-04-08-32.** Métro: Place de Clichy.

DANCE CLUBS

Like in any big city, Parisian clubs are divided into different scenes: Some places are more "see and be seen," while others tend to focus less on what you're wearing and more on the music being played. Certain locations stay popular for years, but most will wax and wane in their level of coolness. Also, the French love their fashion, so dressing to impress is obligatory—sneakers will rarely get you past the line outside. Most clubs don't really get going until at least 11pm, if not later. *Note:* Many of the clubs listed below don't have websites, but are very present on Facebook.

Batofar ★★ For over 15 years, this bright red boat has been the site of music, dancing, and general good times. Docked on the quai François Mauriac, just in front of the imposing François Mitterand National Library, this multifunctional floating venue includes a dance club, bar, restaurant, and a terrace for cocktail hour and low-key soirees. From May to September a "beach" is even set up on the riverbank, where you can eat, drink, and continue to be merry. But the main event here is the dance club, and on good nights you'll see hundreds of gyrating dancers moving in rhythm to house, garage, techno, and live jazz music. Facing 11 quai François Mauriac, 13th arrond. www.batofar.org. ✆ **01-53-60-37-85.** Métro: Quai de la Gare.

Chez Moune ★ If you want to stomp around in your best dancing shoes while pumping your fist in the air, Chez Moune is the place to do it. A former lesbian cabaret that dates from the 1930s, this fun club is filled with young *branché* (hip) Parisians dancing their hearts out. What's more, there is often no cover. The music pounds (mostly electro and house), the walls glitter (mirror tiles everywhere), and the beat goes on and on. 54 rue Jean-Baptiste Pigalle, 9th arrond. ✆ **09-67-50-28-44.** Métro: Pigalle.

Batofar barge.

Concrete ★★ A whiff of Berlin floats above the dancing crowd at this barge-based, floating club known for its top techno talent. And like its Germanic club cousins, this one has managed to get a permit to stay open 24 hours on the weekends, making it possible to literally rock around the clock. A slew of dance parties, live performers, and guest DJs play non-stop from Friday to Sunday. Wear something cool; the bouncers are picky. 69 Port de la Rapée, 12th arrond. No telephone. www.concreteparis.fr. Métro: Gare de Lyon.

Favela Chic ★★ It's always Rio at this Brazilian hotspot where patrons dance to bossa jazz, samba rap, and tropical electro into the wee hours of the night. The floor may be crowded, and the conditions may get saunalike, but the music is great and bartenders make the best mojitos in town. Regular themed party nights with guest DJs. There's a restaurant here, too. 18 rue du Faubourg du Temple, 11th arrond. www.favelachic.com. ⓒ **01-40-21-38-14.** Métro: République.

Machine du Moulin Rouge ★★ A heck of a lot more hip than its historic next-door neighbor, this three-story club has dance floors, concert space, and bars—basically, everything you need for a rollicking night out. The music-savvy crowds come for electronic everything: rock, funk, pop, dubstep, glitch, drum'n'bass, house—not to mention live music by rising stars. Themed soiree nights are hosted by various labels and radio stations. 90 bd. de Clichy, 18th arrond. www.lamachinedumoulinrouge.com. ⓒ **01-53-41-88-89.** Métro: Blanche.

Rex Club ★ Set in the bowels of the huge movie theater of the same name, this is one of the old stalwarts of the Parisian rock and roll scene. The space recalls the big techno-grunge clubs of London, complete with an international mood-altered crowd. The music here is usually deep and dark, bass-heavy house, and other electronica. 5 bd. Poissonnière, 2nd arrond. www.rexclub.com. ℃ **01-42-36-10-96.** Métro: Bonne Nouvelle.

Showcase ★   This unusual club is actually under a bridge. Seriously. Set in an old boat hangar beneath the Pont Alexandre III, it has incredible views of the Seine and atmospheric spaces lined with original stone walls and archways. Music-wise, expect high-quality electro, techno, hip-hop and house. Port des Champs-Élysées under the Pont Alexandre III. www.showcase.fr. No phone. Métro: Invalides.

Social Club ★★   This club is so hip that you actually don't dress up (or rather, you try to make it look like you are not dressing up); the vibe is alternative and the mood is chill. Thursdays are for G-House, Fridays are gay-friendly, and Saturdays are dedicated to diversity; i.e., a mix of trap, house, hip-hop, techno, and more. 142 rue de Montmartre, 2nd arrond. www.parissocial-club.com. No telephone. Métro: Bourse or Grands Boulevards.

THE GAY & LESBIAN SCENE

Paris has a vibrant gay nightlife scene, primarily centered around the Marais. Gay dance clubs come and go so fast that even the magazines devoted to them, like *Qweek* (www.qweek.fr)—distributed free in the gay bars and bookstores—have a hard time keeping up. *Têtu* magazine (www.tetu.com), sold at most newsstands, has special nightlife inserts for gay bars and clubs.

Gay & Lesbian Bars & Clubs

Banana Café ★★   A popular night spot, Banana is known for its party-hardy atmosphere as well as its go-go boys, who do their go-go thing every night of the week. In addition to the usual nightly frolicking, there are themed parties, tea dances, and drag nights. 13 rue de la Ferronnerie, 1st arrond. www.facebook.com/bananacafeparis. ℃ **01-42-33-35-31.** Métro/RER: Châtelet.

La Champmeslé ★   This low-key and colorful dive bar is one of the Marais's stalwart lesbian hangouts. The nights tend to start off quietly, but don't be fooled: Several potent mojitos later, and there's dancing on the bar and loud music until 4am. 4 rue Chabanais, 2nd arrond. ℃ **01-42-96-85-20.** Métro: Pyramides.

Le Raidd ★   This wild, trendy place offers hunky bartenders, a spacious dance floor, go-go dancers, and male strippers who take it all off under an open shower. On weekends you'll have to get past the *selectionneur* at the door who decides who's cool enough to enter. 23 rue du Temple, 4th arrond. www.raiddbar.com. ℃ **01-42-77-04-88.** Métro: Hôtel-de-Ville or Rambuteau.

Le 3w Kafe ★★   The most popular lesbian bar in the Marais, this is a good place to come to find company. Downstairs, a DJ spins on weekends, when there's dancing. Men can only enter the premises if accompanied by a woman. 8 rue des Ecouffes, 4th arrond. ℰ **01-48-87-39-26.** Métro: St. Paul.

Les Souffleurs ★★★ The challenge is finding this cozy bar, tucked into a corner of the Marais. Known for its relaxing ambiance and elegant décor, there's an open-minded ethos here that makes it a favorite nightspot. Though the clientele is mostly young and masculine, women and trans are welcome. Weekends the energy level cranks up with DJs and dance parties. 7 rue del a Verrerie, 4th arrond. ℰ **01-44-78-04-92.** Métro: Hôtel de Ville.

Open Café ★ Relaxed and diverse, this cafe-bar has a busy sidewalk terrace that is usually full both day and night. Everyone from humble tourists to sharp-looking businessmen to TV stars hangs out here. 17 rue des Archives, 4th arrond. www.opencafe.fr. ℰ **01-42-72-26-18.** Métro: Hôtel-de-Ville.

SPECTATOR SPORTS

For inveterate sports fans who need a good dose of athletic adrenaline, Paris can supply an ample fix. The French go crazy for soccer, rugby, tennis, and horse racing, among other sports.

Horse Racing

Paris boasts an army of avid horse-racing fans who get to the city's eight racetracks whenever possible. Info on races is available in newspapers like *L'Equipe,* sold at Paris kiosks, and online at www.france-galop.com.

The epicenter of Paris horse racing is the **Hippodrome de Longchamp,** in the Bois de Boulogne, 16e (ℰ **01-44-30-75-00;** RER or Métro: Porte Maillot, and then a free shuttle bus on race days; otherwise, bus 244). Established in 1855 during the autocratic and pleasure-loving reign of Napoleon III, it's the most prestigious track, boasts the greatest number of promising thoroughbreds, and awards the largest purse in France. The most important events at Longchamp are the **Grand Prix de Paris** in July and the **Qatar Prix de l'Arc de Triomphe** in early October. *Note:* Longchamp is closed for refurbishment until spring 2018.

Another racing venue is the **Hippodrome d'Auteuil,** also in the Bois de Boulogne (ℰ **01-40-71-47-47;** Métro: Porte Auteuil), known for its steeplechases and obstacle courses. On Sundays in April and May, both host **Les Dimanches au Galop,** a day-long racing fiesta that includes races by both professionals and amateurs, shows, games, and of course, pony rides, all free of charge. Visit www.dimanchesaugalop.com for details.

Soccer (Football)

Known throughout France as *le football,* or just *le foot,* soccer is one of France's most popular national sports. The Paris team is *Paris Saint-Germain,* also known as *PSG.* They play their home matches at the **Parc des Princes,** 24 rue du Commandant Guilbaud, 16e (www.leparcdesprinces.fr;

Métro: Porte de Saint-Cloud), a stadium with a capacity of almost 49,000 spectators. The season runs September to May; tickets start at 12€ and go through the roof. *Note:* A small but nasty segment of PSG fans can get violent at games, particularly when the match is against a rival team like Marseilles. National games, played at the **Stade de France** (see above) are generally much calmer.

Tennis

France's version of Wimbledon, the **French Open** (or as it's known here, **Roland Garros;** www.rolandgarros.com), takes place over 2 weeks between late May and early June in the Roland Garros Stadium in the 16th arrond. (Métro: Porte d'Auteuil). Tickets should be purchased well in advance for this world-scale tennis event; tickets can be purchased online.

DAY TRIPS FROM PARIS

P arisians generally feel that their capital is the center of the universe. They may be correct, if only geographically speaking. Paris is at the heart of the region of *Ile-de-France* (the Island of France) and is encircled by seven suburban *départements* commonly and regally referred to as the *petite* and *grande couronnes*. These "crowns" are dotted with cultural and historic treasures, from majestic palaces to picturesque artistic villages, and are only a short journey from the city.

Paris has no lack of intriguing day-trip destinations. Your main problem will be deciding which one(s) to visit. If you've never been there, your first choice should probably be the château and gardens of **Versailles**. They're close by, easily accessible by train, and truly not to be missed. **Chartres** would be our second choice, for its breathtaking Gothic cathedral, its winding streets, and half-timbered houses, which will give you a taste of something completely different from Paris. After that, it's a toss-up. If castles are your game, **Fontainebleau** and **Vaux-le-Vicomte** should be high on your list. Fans of Claude Monet love exploring the gardens at **Giverny,** and families with kids in tow tend to pick **Disneyland Paris.**

All of these destinations are reachable by train from Paris. Train tickets do not require reservations and can be bought the day of an excursion at the departing train or subway station. You can find more information about the train schedule of suburban trains at www.transilien.com. For Chartres and Vernon/Giverny, you can also check www.voyages-sncf.com.

VERSAILLES ★★★

21km (13 miles) SW of Paris, 71km (44 miles) NE of Chartres

The grandeur of the Château of Versailles is hard to imagine until you are standing in front of it. Immediately, you start to get an idea of the power (and ego) of the man who was behind it, King Louis XIV. One of the largest castles in Europe, it is also forever associated with another, less fortunate king, Louis XVI, and his wife, Queen Marie Antoinette, who were both forced to flee when the

French Revolution arrived at their sumptuous doorstep. The palace's extraordinary gardens, designed by the legendary landscape architect André Le Nôtre, are almost worth the visit on their own.

Don't feel you have to see everything. For many, a visit to the palace is enough culture, and a nice relaxing stroll/picnic/nap in the park is a great way to finish off the day. To escape the hordes (and they're intense at Versailles), my favorite spot is Marie Antoinette's Estate, where—hidden from the palace—you'll get a more bucolic taste of life during the Ancien Régime, thanks to the quaint garden, the pretty Trianons (mini-palaces), hamlet, and other small buildings. You won't be alone, but you won't be elbow-to-elbow with crowds.

Essentials

GETTING THERE   Take the **RER C** (www.transilien.fr; about 40 min. from the Champs de Mars; Pont d'Alma, Invalides, St-Michel, Musée d'Orsay or St-Michel stations) to **Versailles-Château–Rive Gauche.** Make sure the final destination for your train is Versailles-Château–Rive Gauche and *not* Versailles Chantier, which actually runs in the opposite direction, touring all around Paris before arriving at Versailles, which will add an hour or so to your journey. Assuming you've taken the right train, it's about a 5-minute walk from the Versailles Rive Gauche train station to the chateau—don't worry, you can't miss it. For a little more (4.35€ adults, 2.15€ ages 4–10), you can also take the **SNCF** Transilien suburban train (www.transilien.fr; 40 min.) from the Gare St-Lazare station to **Versailles–Rive Droite,** and then walk about 10 minutes to the chateau (around 50 min. total).

Unless you have a **Paris Visite** or other pass that includes zones 1–4, you'll need to buy a special ticket for the RER C (one-way fare 3.55€ adults, 1.75€ 4–10, free under 4); a regular Métro ticket will not suffice. You can buy a ticket from any Métro or RER station; the fare includes a free transfer to the Métro.

TICKETS   If you are made of tough stuff and want to see everything in a day, you can buy the all-inclusive **Château Passeport,** which grants you access to the main chateau, the gardens, the Trianon palaces, the Marie Antoinette Estate and the temporary exhibitions (Nov–Mar 20€ adults; from Apr– Oct the price, 27€, includes Les Grandes Eaux; free 17 and under and under 26 from the EU). If you'd like to make an overnight of it, consider the **2-day Passport** (Nov–Mar 25€ adults, Apr–Oct adults 30€), which offers the same entries plus discounts around town. If you have limited time and energy, you can buy a **ticket to just the Palace** (18€, free 17 and under) or **just the Trianons and Marie Antoinette's Estate** (12€). From April to October, the under-18 crowd (who get in free) will likely have to buy a ticket to get into the gardens (9.50€). You can avoid some of the long lines at the entrance by purchasing your tickets online. A **Paris Museum Pass** (p. 135) will get you into everything except Les Grandes Eaux musicales (Apr–Oct; see above), so

Ile-de-France

you'll have to buy a separate ticket to get into the gardens when the fountain shows are playing (9.50€; see below).

Important note: Tuesdays is by far the busiest day of the week at Versailles (because that's when the Louvre is usually closed). Most any other day of the week will be (slightly) less crowded.

VISITOR INFORMATION Château de Versailles, www.chateau versailles.fr; ✆ **01-30-83-78-00. Palace:** Apr–Oct Tues–Sun 9am–6:30pm; Nov–Mar 9am–5:30pm. **Marie Antoinette's Estate:** Apr–Oct Tues–Sun noon–6:30pm; Nov–Mar Tues–Sun noon–5:30pm. **Garden and park:** Apr–Oct daily 8am–8:30pm; Nov–Mar daily 8am–6pm. **Versailles Tourist Office:** 2 bis ave. de Paris; www.versailles-tourisme.com; ✆ **01-39-24-88-88.**

EVENING SHOWS Spectacular **fountain night shows** are held from mid-June to mid-September (26€ adults, 22€ ages 6–17), where you stroll around the gardens and enjoy illuminated fountains, music, and fireworks. During the same period, you can walk through the Hall of Mirrors and the

Fountain of Apollo in the gardens of Versailles Palace.

royal apartments accompanied by musicians and dancers in baroque period costumes in the **Royal Serenade** (24€ adults, 21€ ages 6–17), giving you a taste of what it was like back in the day. You can buy **combination tickets** for the two events (42€ adults, 35€ ages 6–17).

Big names in classical music, theater, and dance fill the stage at the magnificent **Opéra Royal** in the palace; reserve well in advance and expect royal ticket prices (55€–400€).

DAYTIME SHOWS From April to October on weekends and Tuesdays, **"Les Grandes Eaux Musicales"** (depending on your ticket, this could be included; otherwise 9.50€ adults, 8€ ages 6–17) play throughout the gardens closest to the castle. This consists of fountains playing to Baroque music. While pleasant, you won't miss anything essential if your ticket does not offer you entrance to this part of the gardens (the rest of the park is accessible from side entrances and is free of charge).

Tickets: You can purchase tickets to all shows mentioned above at the chateau, at www.chateauversailles-spectacles.fr (✆ **01-30-83-78-89**), or from a Fnac store (www.fnactickets.com; ✆ **08-92-68-36-22**; .40€ per min).

Les Grandes Ecuries: The **Académie de Spectacle Equestre** is housed in the **royal stables,** situated immediately opposite the chateau. Both the school and its shows are directed by Bartabas, whose equestrian theater company, Zingaro, has garnered world fame. Visitors can watch hour-long riding demonstrations by the students and their mounts on Sundays and certain weekdays at 10am; tickets cost 8€ to 10€. On some weekend afternoons, a more elaborate "equestrian ballet" is on offer; tickets to those shows are 16€ to 25€. After the shows, visitors can tour the stables. For additional information and schedule, see www.bartabas.fr.

The Chateau of Versailles

Back in the 17th century, after having been badly burned by a nasty uprising called Le Fronde, Louis XIV decided to move his court from Paris to Versailles, a safe distance from the intrigues of the capital. He also decided to have the court move in with him, where he could keep a close eye on them and nip any new plots or conspiracies in the bud. This required a new abode

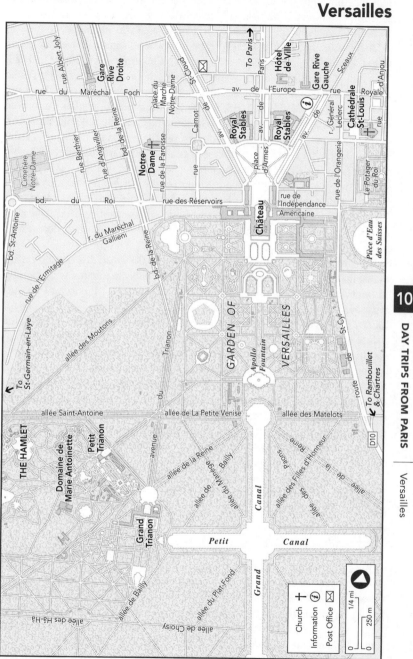

that was not only big enough to house his court (anywhere from 3,000 to 10,000 people would be palace guests on any given day), but also one that would be grand enough to let the world know who was in charge.

There was already a chateau on the site when Louis came to town; his father, Louis XIII, had built a small castle, "a hunting lodge," there in 1623. This humble dwelling simply would not do for the so-called "Sun King," who brought in a flotilla of architects, artists, and gardeners to enlarge the castle and give it a new look. In 1668, the King's architect, Louis Le Vau, began work on the enormous "envelope," which literally wrapped the old castle in a second building. From the front, you can see the remnants of the old castle; the buildings that surround the recessed central courtyard (called the **Marble Court**) are what's left of that structure.

Meanwhile, legendary garden designer André Le Notre was carving out formal gardens and a huge park out of what had been marshy countryside. Thousands of trees were planted, and harmonious geometric designs were achieved with flower beds, hedges, canals, and pebbled pathways dotted with sculptures and fountains.

Construction, which involved as many as 36,000 workers, ground on for years; in 1682 the King and his court moved in, but construction went on right through the rest of his reign and into that of Louis XV. Louis XVI and his wife, Marie Antoinette, made few changes, but history made a gigantic one for them: On October 6, 1789, an angry mob of hungry Parisians marched on the palace and the royal couple was eventually forced to return to Paris. Versailles would never again be a royal residence.

The palace was ransacked during the Revolution, and in the years after it fell far from its original state of grace. Napoleon and Louis XVIII did what they could to bring the sleeping giant back, but by the early 1800s, during the reign of Louis-Philippe, the castle was slated for demolition. Fortunately for us, this forward-thinking king decided to invest his own money to save Versailles, and in 1837 the vast structure was made into a national museum. Little by little, precious furniture and art objects were retrieved or re-created; paintings, wall decorations, and ceilings were restored. Restoration is ongoing, so be prepared for the unexpected. Even if a few areas are closed, the place is so huge that should you can still tour yourself into a 17th-century stupor.

Touring the Palace

The rooms in the "envelope," or the newer part of the building, were designed to impress, which they do. They include a series of rooms called the **Grand Apartments,** used primarily for ceremonial events (a daily occurrence), the **Queen's Apartments,** and the **Galerie des Glaces.** These, along with the **King's Apartments** and the **Chapel,** are must-sees. If you have the fortitude, you can take a **guided visit** to the royal family's private apartments (an additional 7€; some in English) to get a more intimate look at castle life.

Each room in the **Grand Apartments ★★★** is dedicated to a different planet (that circles around the sun, as in Sun King), and each has a fabulous

The Hall of Mirrors in Versailles Palace.

painting on the ceiling depicting the god or goddess associated with said heavenly sphere. The first and probably the most staggering, painting-wise, is in the **Salon d'Hercule ★★**. It holds an enormous canvas by Paolo Veronese, "Christ at Supper with Simon," as well as a splendid, divinity-bedecked ceiling portraying Hercules being welcomed by the gods of Olympus by Antoine Lemoyne. At 480 sq. m (5,166 sq. ft.), it is one of the largest paintings in France. The **Salon d'Apollon ★**, not surprisingly, was the throne room, where the Sun King would receive ambassadors and other heads of state.

The ornate **Salon de Guerre ★** and **Salon de Paix ★** bookend the most famous room in the place, the recently restored **Galerie des Glaces (the Hall of Mirrors) ★★★**. Louis XIV commanded his painter-in-chief, Charles Le Brun, to paint the 12m-high (40-ft.) ceiling of this 73m-long (240-ft.) gallery with representations of his accomplishments. This masterwork is illuminated by light from the 17 windows that overlook the garden, which are matched on the opposite wall by 17 mirrored panels. Add to that a few enormous crystal chandeliers, and the effect is dazzling. This splendid setting was the scene of a historic event in a more recent century: In 1919, World War I officially ended when the Treaty of Versailles was signed here.

The **Queen's Apartments ★★** include a gorgeous bedroom with silk hangings printed with lilacs and peacock feathers, which looks exactly as it did in 1789, when the Queen, Marie Antoinette, was forced to flee revolutionary mobs through a secret door (barely visible in the wall near her bed). The **King's Apartments ★★★** are even more splendiferous, though in a very different style: Here the ceilings have been left blank white, which brings out the elaborate white and gold decoration on the walls. The **King's Bedroom ★★★**, hung from top to bottom with gold brocade, is fitted with a banister that separated the King from the 100 or so people who would watch him wake up in the morning.

You should also make sure to see the **Chapel ★★★**, a masterpiece of light and harmony by Jules Hardouin Mansart, where the kings attended mass. This lofty space (the ceiling is more than 25m/82 ft. high) reflects both Gothic and baroque styles, combining a vaulted roof, stained glass, and gargoyles with columns and balustrades typical of the early 18th century.

Touring the Domaine de Marie Antoinette

Northwest of the fountain lies the **Domaine de Marie Antoinette ★★★** (if you don't have a Château passport or museum pass you'll pay a separate ticket to get in). It was here that the young queen sought refuge from the strict protocol and infighting at the castle. Her husband gave her the **Petit Trianon ★★**, a small manor that Louis XV used for his trysts, which she transformed into a stylish haven. When the queen had finished decorating the manor in the latest fashions, she set to work creating an entire world around it, including a splendid **English garden ★**, several lovely pavilions, a jewel-like **theater ★★**, and even a small **hamlet ★**, complete with a working farm and a dairy, where she and her friends would play cards and gossip, or just go for a stroll in the "country." Although the **Grand Trianon ★** is not really linked to the story of Marie Antoinette, it is worth a brief visit. Built by Louis XIV as a retreat for himself and his family, this small marble palace consists of two large wings connected by an open columned terrace from which there is a delightful **view ★** of the gardens. The furniture and decor dates mostly from the Napoleonic era, but throughout the 20th century it was used for official state receptions and as a residence for notable guests such as John and Jackie Kennedy, General de Gaulle, and Queen Elizabeth II.

Touring the Gardens & Park

The entire 800-hectare (2,000-acre) park is laid out according to a precise symmetrical plan. From the terrace behind the castle, there is an astounding **view ★★★** that runs past two parterres, down a central lawn (the Tapis Vert), down the **Grand Canal ★★** and seemingly on into infinity. Le Nôtre's masterpiece is the ultimate example of French-style gardens; geometric, logical, and in perfect harmony—a reflection of the divine order of the cosmos. Given that the Sun King was the star of this particular cosmos, a solar theme is reflected in the statues and fountains along the main axis of the perspective; the most magnificent of these is the **Apollo Fountain ★★★**, where the sun god emerges from the waves at dawn on his chariot. On the sides of the main axis, near the castle, are a set of six groves, or **bosquets ★**, leafy minigardens that are hidden by walls of shrubbery; some were used as small outdoor ballrooms for festivities, others for intimate rendezvous out of reach of the prying eyes of the court. Today, you can **picnic, bike ride** (bikes can be rented next to the restaurant), or even **row a boat** on a sunny day.

Place d'Armes. www.chateauversailles.fr. ✆ **01-30-83-78-00.** Palace 18€ adults, free 17 and under. Marie Antoinette's Estate 12€ adults, everything free for children 17 and under. For hours, see above.

CHARTRES ★★★

97km (58 miles) SW of Paris, 76km (47 miles) NW of Orléans

You'll spot it long before you see the actual town: the spire of the cathedral of Chartres rising above a sea of wheat fields. About an hour from Paris, this stunning church and its inspiring stain-glassed windows are easy to tour and still have enough time to wander through the narrow streets of the ancient (and beautiful) town.

Essentials

GETTING THERE From Paris's Gare Montparnasse, **trains** run directly to Chartres, taking about an hour. Tickets cost 16€ one-way; for more information and reservations, see www.voyages-sncf.com or call ✆ **36-35.** If **driving,** take A10/A11 southwest and follow signs to Le Mans and Chartres. (The Chartres exit is marked.)

VISITOR INFORMATION The **Office de Tourisme** in the Maison du Saumon, 8 rue de la Poissonerie (www.chartres-tourisme.com; ✆ **02-37-18-26-26**).

Exploring the Cathedral

This magnificent UNESCO-protected Gothic cathedral, with its carved portals and three-tiered flying buttresses, would be a stunning sight even without its legendary **stained-glass windows**—though the world would be a drearier place. For these ancient glass panels are truly glorious: a kaleidoscope of colors so deep, so rich, and so bright, it's hard to believe they are some 700 years old. Meant as teaching devices more than artwork, the windows functioned as a sort of enormous cartoon, telling the story of Christ through pictures to a mostly illiterate populace. From its beginnings, pilgrims came from far and near to see a piece of cloth that believers say was worn by the Virgin Mary during Christ's birth. The **relic** is still here, but these days it's primarily a different sort of pilgrim that is drawn to Chartres: More than 1.5 million tourists come here every year to admire the magnificent edifice.

A Romanesque church stood on this spot until 1194, when a fire burnt it virtually to the ground. All that remained were the towers, the Royal Portal, and a few remnants of stained glass. The locals were so horrified that they sprung to action; in a matter of only 3 decades a new cathedral was erected, which accounts for its remarkably unified

Cathedral of Our Lady of Chartres.

For more than 3 decades, Malcolm Miller has been studying the cathedral and giving **guided tours in English.** His rare blend of scholarship, enthusiasm, and humor will help you understand and appreciate what you are looking at. From Easter through October, his 75-minute tour begins at noon Monday through Saturday (10€). From May through September, there is a second tour by his colleague, Anne Marie Woods, at 2:45pm. No need to reserve; a sign at the meeting point inside at the entrance to the cathedral's gift shop indicates that day's tour schedule. You can also rent an **audioguide** (in English) for 6.20€.

Gothic architecture. This was one of the first churches to use buttresses as a building support, allowing the architect (whose name has been lost) to build its walls at twice the height of the standard Romanesque cathedrals and make space for its famous windows. The new cathedral was dedicated in 1260 and has miraculously survived the centuries with relatively little damage. The French Revolution somehow spared the cathedral. During World War I and World War II, the precious windows were carefully dismounted piece by piece and stored in a safe place in the countryside.

Before you enter the church, take in the **facade ★★**, a remarkable assemblage of religious art and architecture. The base of the two towers dates from the early 12th century (before the fire). The tower to your right (the **Old Tower,** or South Tower) is topped by its original sober Romanesque spire; that on your left (**New Tower,** or North Tower) was blessed with an elaborate Gothic spire by Jehan de Beauce in the early 1500s, when the original burned down. Below is the **Royal Portal ★★★**, a masterpiece of Romanesque art. Swarming with kings, queens, prophets, and priests, this sculpted entryway tells the story of the life of Christ. The rigid bodies of the figures contrast with their lifelike faces; it is said that Rodin spent hours here contemplating this stonework spectacle. You can **climb to the top of the New Tower** to take in the **view ★**; just remember to wear rubber-soled shoes—the 300 steps are a little slippery after all these centuries.

Once inside the cathedral, you'll really understand what all the fuss is about. The dimness is pierced by the radiant colors of the **stained-glass windows ★★★**, which shine down from all sides. Three windows on the west side of the building, as well as the beautiful rose window to the south called **Notre Dame de la Belle Verière ★**, date from the earlier 12th-century structure; the rest, with the exception of a few modern panels, are of 13th-century origins. The scenes depicted in glass read from bottom to top and recount stories from the Bible as well as the lives of the saints. You will soon find yourself wondering how in the world medieval artists, with such low-tech materials, managed to create such vivid colors. The blues, in particular, seem to be divinely inspired. In fact, scientists have finally pierced at least part of the mystery: The blue was made with sodium and silica compounds that made the color stand up to the centuries better than glass made with other colors.

Chartres Cathedral

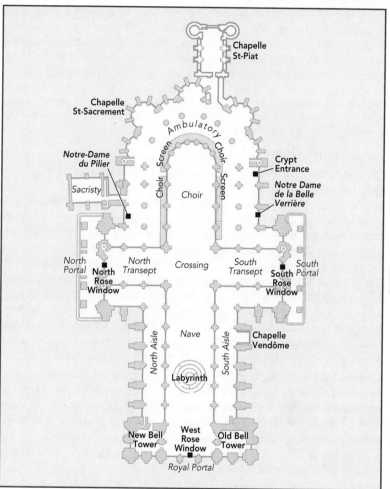

Chapelle
St-Piat

Chapelle
St-Sacrement

Ambulatory

Notre-Dame
du Pilier

Choir Screen

Choir Screen

Crypt
Entrance

Notre Dame
de la Belle
Verrière

Sacristy

Choir

North
Portal

North
Rose
Window

North
Transept

Crossing

South
Transept

South
Rose
Window

South
Portal

North Aisle

Nave

South Aisle

Chapelle
Vendôme

Labyrinth

New Bell
Tower

West
Rose
Window

Old Bell
Tower

Royal Portal

10

DAY TRIPS FROM PARIS | Chartres

Another indoor marvel is the **chancel enclosure ★★★**, which separates the chancel (the area behind the altar) from the ambulatory (the walkway that runs around the outer chapels). Started in 1514 by Jehan de Beauce, this intricately sculpted wall depicts dozens of saints and other religious superstars in yet another recounting of the lives of the Virgin and Christ. Back in the ambulatory is the Chapel of the Martyrs, where the cathedral's cherished **relic** resides: a piece of cloth that the Virgin Mary supposedly wore at the birth of Christ, which was a gift of Charles the Bald in 876.

Chartres also harbors a rare **labyrinth ★**, which is traced on the floor of the cathedral near the nave. A large circle, divided into four parts, is entirely filled

265

by a winding path that leads to the center. In the Middle Ages, these labyrinths represented the symbolic path that one must follow to get from earth to God; pilgrims would follow the path while praying, as if they were making a pilgrimage to Jerusalem. *Note:* The cathedral asks that visitors not talk or wander around during mass, which is generally held in the late morning and early evening. You are welcome to sit in on services, of course.

16 Cloître Notre-Dame. www.cathedrale-chartres.org. ℂ **02-37-21-75-02.** General admission to the cathedral is free, admission to the towers 5.50€ adults, 4.50€ adults 18–25, free 17 and under. Cathedral open daily 8:30am–7:30pm. Towers open Jan–Apr and Nov–Dec Mon–Sat 9:30am–12:30pm and 2–5pm, Sun 2–5pm; May–Nov Mon–Sat 9:30am–12:30pm and 2–6pm, Sun 2–6pm.

Exploring the Old Town

Give yourself a little time to explore the medieval cobbled streets of the **Vieux Quartier (Old Town)** ★★. There are several gabled houses in the narrow lanes near the cathedral, including the colorful facades of **rue Chantault,** one of which is 8 centuries old. Seek out **rue du Bourg,** where you'll find the famous **Salmon House** (which houses the tourist office) and some lovely sculptures (including a certain fish). In the lower town, you can stroll along the picturesque **Eure River** with its stone bridges and ancient washhouses. If you go on a Saturday or Wednesday morning, there is a covered farmer's market in **place Billard** (until 1pm), the perfect place to grab some supplies for a casual picnic in the park behind the cathedral or along the river. Between April and November, also look out for **Chartres en Lumières,** a fabulous sound-and-light show (www.chartresenlumieres.com; free; dusk–1am), which turns the cathedral's facade into a beautiful, rippling screen of color.

Centre International du Vitrail ★ Get the stained-glass back story at this international center devoted to the glory of this luminous art form. The permanent collection focuses on ancient stained glass, while the temporary shows highlight contemporary works. The center also offers workshops, classes and training programs for both professionals and amateurs.

5 rue du Cardinal Pie. www.centre-vitrail.org. ℂ **02-37-21-65-72.** Mon–Fri 9:30am–12:30pm and 1:30–6pm, Sat 10am–12:30pm and 2:30–6pm, Sun and holidays 2:30–6pm Admission 7€ adults, 5.50€ students, ages 14–18 and students, free 13 and under.

GIVERNY ★★

74km (46 miles) NW of Paris

For this trip, a lot depends on the weather. If you luck out and the sun is shining, it's worth the shlep by train or car to bask in the glory of this stunning garden, which bears the artistic stamp of its genius creator, Claude Monet. The painter and his family moved to this tiny town in 1883, and Monet liked it so much he spent the rest of his life here, painting views of the dreamlike garden that he created out of the grassy slope behind his house. Today, the

Fondation Claude Monet à Giverny (84 rue Claude Monet, Giverny; www. fondation-monet.com; ℂ **02-32-51-28-21**) is open to the public, and for a small fee, you too can wander about the brilliant flower beds, lush bowers, and water-lily ponds that inspired this Impressionist master. Once you are done with the garden, you can sample the bucolic joys of the village, which manages to stay charming despite the seasonal tourist infestation. You can also take in one of the excellent temporary exhibits at the **Musée des Impressionismes** (see box, below). On the other hand, if it is raining or truly dreary out, you'll be better off staying in town and getting your Monet fix at the **Musée Marmottan Monet** (p. 161) and/or visit the water lilies at the **Orangerie** (p. 136).

Essentials

GETTING THERE   Trains (SNCF; for schedules, visit www.voyages-sncf. com) leave every hour or two from the Gare St-Lazare train station to Vernon, the closest stop to Giverny, which is about 7km (4½ miles) away. The trip takes around 45 minutes and costs 15€ one-way. From Vernon you can either take a shuttle bus (8€ round-trip) or rent a bike at the station (L'Arrivé de Giverny; ℂ **02-32-21-16-01;** 14€ for the day) and pedal there on the marked bike path.

If you're **driving,** take the Autoroute A14 to the A13 toward Rouen. Take exit 16 for Vernon and follow the D181 across the Seine into the town. From Vernon take the D5 to Giverny. Expect it to take about an hour; try to avoid weekends.

TICKETS   Unless you can get there at opening time, try to buy your tickets to the gardens in advance. Not only will you avoid standing in the extremely slow-moving line at the ticket booth, but you will have the right to use the special entrance for the *billet coupe-file* (cut-in-front-of-the-line ticket) and walk right in. You can buy your tickets online at the Fondation Claude Monet site (see above), at a Fnac ticket office, or on the Fnac site (in English, www.fnactickets.com). Tickets are 9.50€ for adults (1€ more via FNAC), 5.50€ for ages 7 to 17 and students, and free for children 6 and under.

VISITOR INFORMATION The **Maison du Tourisme Normandie Giverny** is located close to the Fondation Monet at 80 rue Claude Monet (www.normandie-giverny.fr; ℂ **02-32-64-45-01**).

Monet's house in Giverny.

While you won't see any original paintings at the Fondation Monet, you will see plenty of Impressionist art at the **Musée des Impressionismes** (99 rue Claude Monet; www.mdig.fr; ℘ **02-32-51-94-65;** 7€ adults, 4.50€ ages 12–18, 3€ ages 7–11, free 6 and under; Apr to Oct 10am–6pm, closed Nov–Mar). Housed in a sleek modern building with yet another lovely garden, this airy museum offers temporary exhibits that explore the high points of the movement, both in France and abroad.

Exploring Giverny

When you enter this kingdom of color, you'll quickly realize that Monet wasn't just a brilliant painter, he was also a gifted gardener. His dual talents complemented each other completely; by the end of his life, the garden was just as much a work of art as the paintings, or perhaps they *were* the paintings. If you have already visited the Orangerie in Paris and seen Monet's magical "Nympheas," or water lilies, spread across huge canvases in two oval-shaped rooms, in a way you have already visited this garden; they were painted here, with the aim of faithfully re-creating the feeling you would have if you were looking at the same flowers at Giverny.

There are actually two gardens here: The first and closest to the house is the **Clos Normand ★★**, an ostensibly French-style garden that is a glorious riot of color. Gladioli, larkspur, phlox, daisies, and asters, among other flowers, clamor for your attention; irises brighten the small lawn. In the midst of it all is **Monet's house ★**, where you can see where he lived and admire his **Japanese print collection.**

The painter's most famous works, the endless water-lily series, were born in the **Water Garden ★★★**, farther down the slope. Here, Monet's intention was to build a garden that resembled those in the Japanese prints he collected, including a **Japanese bridge ★** that figures prominently in several of his canvases. Today the garden looks much as it did when Monet was immortalizing it. Willows weep quietly into the ponds; heather, ferns, azaleas, and rhododendrons carpet the banks; and frogs croak amongst the water lilies. This garden was a sanctuary for the painter, who came here to explore one of his favorite subjects: the complex interplay of water and light.

Be advised that it will be virtually impossible to experience the gardens as Monet did—more or less alone. This is an extremely popular outing for both individuals and tour groups, so your best bet is to come on a slow day like Monday or Wednesday, and/or to arrive at the opening or after 3pm, when the groups have left. You can't picnic in the gardens, but you can lunch at the **Restaurant Baudy** in the village, an old inn where many an Impressionist used to stay when they would come to visit Claude (81 rue Claude Monet; www. restaurantbaudy.com; ℘ **02-32-21-10-03**).

84 rue Claude-Monet. www.fondation-monet.com. ℘ **02-32-51-28-21.** Admission 9.50€ adults, 5.50€ students and ages 7–17, free for children 6 and under. Apr–Oct daily 9:30am–6pm. Closed Nov–Mar.

VAUX-LE-VICOMTE ★★★

47km (29 miles) SE of Paris; 24km (15 miles) NE of Fontainebleau

This jewel of a castle comes with a story that reads like a Hollywood screenplay. Nicolas Fouquet, the chateau's original owner, was a brilliant finance minister and lover of arts and leisure. In the early 1700s he was the toast of Paris; his penchant for pleasure and beauty drew France's top artists and intellectuals to his gorgeous home in the country. Unfortunately, Fouquet underestimated the jealousy of his superiors, in particular the young king, Louis XIV.

A messy financial scandal gave his enemies an excellent opportunity to topple the much-admired minister; his fortunes took a precipitous fall one fateful night in the summer of 1661. As Voltaire put it: "On August 17, at six in the evening, Nicolas Fouquet was the King of France; at two in the morning, he was nobody." Oblivious to the fact that the king was already fed up with his penchant for stealing the spotlight, Fouquet organized a stupendous party in his honor. He pulled out all the stops: There was a sumptuous meal, a play written and performed by Molière, and a fireworks display—no one had seen anything like it. Three weeks later, Fouquet was arrested on trumped-up charges of embezzlement. The king seized the castle, confiscated its contents, and hired its artists and architects to work on Versailles. Though writers like Madame de Sévigné and La Fontaine pleaded with the king on Fouquet's behalf, the once-untouchable financial minister spent the rest of his life in prison.

Essentials

ARRIVING   Though it's close to Paris, Vaux-le-Vicomte is not easy to reach by mass transit. By **car,** take the A4 east to the N104 south to Vert Saint-Denis, then the D82 east to Vaux-le-Vicomte (its GPS coordinates are Maincy, D215 road, 48.568727000, 2.713580000). Trains run once an hour from Gare de l'Est to Verneuil l'Etang (direction Provins; 35 min.; 8.40€ adults, 4.20€, children 4–10), but the shuttle bus ("Chateaubus") only runs from the train station to Vaux-le-Vicomte certain times of the day (consult the schedule on the website; 10€ adults round-trip [25€ during candlelit evenings; see box, below], 5€ students and children 6–16, free ages 5 and under; cash only).

Vaux by Candlelight

To give you just an inkling of what Vaux looked like on the evening of the famous party Fouquet threw for Louis XIV back in 1661, visit the castle when it's illuminated by candlelight. On Saturday nights from May to early October, some 2,000 candles illuminate your evening visit. From 5pm until midnight, you can visit the castle's interior, stroll in the gardens, and enjoy a fireworks display with classical music (20€ adults, 18€ students, 16€ ages 6–17, free 5 and under). Top it off with a meal in the chateau's **cafeteria** (main courses around 14€), or the gourmet garden restaurant, **Les Charmilles** (fixed-price menu from 50€).

There are also **trains** from Gare de Lyon to Melun (30 min; 8.20€ adults, 4.10€ children 4–10), but then you must take a taxi from the station 8 km (5 miles) to Vaux-le-Vicomte (15€–18€ each way). From April to October there are also **day tour packages** including transport from the center of Paris and visits to both Vaux-le-Vicomte and Fontainebleau (www.pariscityvision.com; from 75€ per adult).

Note: Vaux-le-Vicomte is only open from the end of March through early November and a few weekends during the Christmas holidays (dates online).

VISITOR INFORMATION   The nearest **tourist office** is in Melun at 26 place St-Jean (www.melun-tourisme.fr; ℭ **01-64-52-64-52**).

Touring the Chateau

Though his reaction was extreme, Louis XIV's jealousy is not too hard to understand when you are standing in front of Vaux-le-Vicomte; the edifice is the epitome of 17th-century elegance. The castle was eventually released to Fouquet's widow and has remained in private hands ever since. The ancestors of the current owners, Jean-Charles and Alexandre de Vogüé, bought the palace in 1875, when they started a much-needed restoration program to restore Vaux to its original splendor. The chateau is now entirely restored and filled with splendid tapestries, carpets, and art objects.

One of its most impressive rooms remains unfinished: the oval **Grand Salon ★★**, which Fouquet never got a chance to paint or furnish. Here, you actually don't miss all the decorative trimmings; the bare white pilasters and detailed carvings have a classical beauty that stands on its own. For something more ornate, the lavish ensemble of chandeliers, brocade, and painted ceiling (by Le Brun) that is the **King's bedroom ★★** was a model for the King's Apartments in

Costumed guide at Vaux-le-Vicomte.

Versailles. The **Salon des Muses ★** also gets a fabulous ceiling by Le Brun, as well as several fine tapestries covering its walls. To help imagine what Fouquet's dinner parties were like, take a stroll through the elaborately decorated **Salle à Manger ★** (dining room), where a table is set with stacks of rare fruits and gold candlesticks, and a sideboard displays a set of extraordinary majolica. You can see life on the other side of the banquet table downstairs in the **kitchen,** with its more humble servants' dining area.

The **gardens ★★★** are almost as spectacular as the chateau. The carefully calculated geometry of the flower beds and alleyways makes this a study in harmony, even if you couldn't call them exactly

The King's Office at Vaux-le-Vicomte.

natural. Nature is lurking close by, however—the entire ensemble is surrounded by seemingly endless kilometers of forest. Just behind the castle are two enormous beds of boxwood that have been trimmed into elaborate designs; Le Nôtre took his inspiration from the patterns in Turkish carpets. The far end of the gardens is crossed by a large **canal,** which you don't even see until you are just about on top of it. There you will also find a series of grottos, each sheltering a statue of a different river god. Finally, from the last basin, turn around and take in the lovely **view** ★★ of the gardens with the chateau rising in the background.

77950 Maincy. www.vaux-le-vicomte.com. ✆ **01-64-14-41-90.** Admission 16€ adults, 14€ students, 10€ ages 6–17, free children 5 and under. Mar to mid-Nov daily 10am–7pm. Closed mid-Nov to Feb, except for certain days during the Christmas holidays.

FONTAINEBLEAU ★★★

60km (37 miles) S of Paris, 74km (46 miles) NE of Orléans

Napoleon called it "the house of the centuries; the true home of kings," and he had a point: Fontainebleau was a royal residence for over 700 years. Elegant and dignified, this grand chateau carries the architectural imprint of many a monarch. Surrounded by dense forest and verdant countryside, a trip here is a relaxing green interlude to your Parisian trip.

GETTING THERE **Trains** to Fontainebleau leave from the Gare de Lyon (schedules and info at www.transilien.fr). The trip takes 40 minutes and costs 8.85€ for adults and 4.40€ for ages 4 to 10 one-way. Get off the train at Fontainebleau–Avon and take the local bus (line 1) direction Lilas, to the Chateau stop; the fare is 2€ one-way; you can also use a regular metro ticket. The buses come frequently and are timed to arrive at the arrival of the train from Paris. If you're **driving,** take A6 south from Paris, exit Fontainebleau.

VISITOR INFORMATION The **Office de Tourisme** is at 4 rue Royale, Fontainebleau (www.fontainebleau-tourisme.com; ℰ **01-60-74-99-99**), opposite the main entrance to the chateau.

Exploring Fontainebleau

Though kings were already living here by the 12th century (Philippe August and Saint Louis both spent a good deal of time at the castle), it was during the Renaissance that Fontainebleau really took on its regal allure. In 1528, inveterate castle-builder King François I decided to completely rebuild Fontainebleau and make it into a palace that would rival the marvels of Rome. He tore down everything but the core of the medieval castle and hired an army of architects and artisans to construct a new one around it. He also brought in two renowned Italian artists, Il Rosso and Primaticcio, to decorate his new home. Their style of work came to be known as the School of Fontainebleau, which was characterized by the use of stucco (moldings and picture frames) and frescoes that depicted various allegories and myths. This school was highly influenced by the Mannerist style of Michelangelo, Raphael, and Parmigianino.

François I was also an art collector: His vast accumulation of Renaissance treasures included Da Vinci's "Mona Lisa" and "The Virgin of the Rock," both of which once hung here. After François' death his descendants continued work on the castle, but it wasn't until the 17th century and the arrival of Henri IV on the scene that there were any major transformations. Henri added several wings and a courtyard (the **Cour des Offices** ★★), and made major changes to the decor, inviting a new clutch of artists, who established a second School of Fontainebleau. This time, the artists were of French and Flemish origins (Ambrose Dubois, Martin Fréminet, and others) and used oil paint and canvas instead of frescoes. Louis XIV, preferring Versailles, didn't bother much with Fontainebleau, but Louis XV and Louis XVI found the palace very much to their liking and added their own decorative flourishes. Napoleon was also very fond of this palace and made a lasting imprint on the castle's interior. No doubt, Fontainebleau made an imprint on the Emperor as well: On April 20, 1814, he abdicated here, before being sent off to exile on the island of Elba.

Hiking Along Trails Left by French Kings

The Forest of Fontainebleau is riddled with *sentiers* (hiking trails) made by French kings and their entourages who went hunting in the forest. A "Guide des Sentiers" is available at the tourist information center (see above; you can also download trail maps from its website). Bike paths also cut through the forest. You can rent bikes at **A La Petite Reine,** 14 rue de la Paroisse, in the center of town, a few blocks from the chateau (www.alapetitereine.com; ℰ **01-60-74-57-57**). The cost of a bike is 8€ per hour, 15€ for a full day.

Chateau de Fontainebleau.

Touring the Chateau

Most of what you'll want to see (and what is described below) is in the **Grands Appartements.** The **Petits Appartements,** a series of rooms that were Napoleon's private residence, can only be seen on a guided tour and requires an extra ticket—though they're very much worth the effort if you have time.

Your first encounter with the chateau will take place in the **Cour du Cheval Blanc ★★★** at the entrance to the palace. It was in this grand square, which is surrounded by wings of the castle on three sides, that Napoleon said adieu to his faithful imperial guards. "Continue to serve France," he pleaded, "Her welfare was my only concern." The main building before you dates from François I's era; the sumptuous **horseshoe staircase ★★** was added by Henri II. On the left as you enter is the **Chapelle de la Trinité ★.** When he was 7, Louis XIII climbed up the scaffolding to watch Martin Fréminet, his art instructor, paint the glorious ceiling. This is where Louis XV married Polish princess Marie Leczinska and where the future Napoleon III was baptized. Linking the chapel with the royal apartments is the **Gallery of François I ★★★**, a stunning example of Renaissance art and decoration. Overseen by Il Rossi, a team of highly skilled artists covered the walls with exceptional frescoes, moldings, and *boiseries* (carved woodwork). The paintings, which are full of mythological figures, pay tribute to the glory of the monarchy and the wisdom of the King's rule. Throughout the gallery (and elsewhere in the castle) you will see the salamander, François' official symbol.

The other major must-see is the **Salle de Bal ★★★**. This 30m (98-ft.) long ballroom is a feast of light and color; the frescoes by Primaticcio and Nicolo dell'Abate have been completely restored, and their rich hues radiate as if they were painted yesterday. Huge windows let in light from both sides of this long room; the monumental fireplace at the far end was designed by 16th-century architect Philibert Delorme.

The **Royal Apartments ★★** have been decorated and redecorated by successive monarchs. Louis XIII was born in the **Salon Louis XIII ★**, a fact that is symbolized in the ceiling mural showing Love riding a dolphin. Though several different queens slept in the **Chambre de l'Impératrice ★★**, its current set-up reflects the epoch of Empress Josephine (Napoleon's first wife). The sumptuous bed, crowned in gilded walnut and covered in embroidered silk, was made for Marie Antoinette in 1787. The queen would never see it; the Revolution exploded before she could arrange a visit to the chateau. Napoleon transformed the Kings' bedroom into the **Salle du Trône** ★, or Throne Room. Since several centuries of kings, from Henri IV to Louis XVI, slept here, the decor is a mashup of styles: The throne is Empire, the folding chairs are Louis XVI, and the ceiling murals date from the 17th and 18th centuries.

You can learn more about the Emperor at the **Musée Napoléon 1er** ★, located in the Louis XV wing, where you'll see historic memorabilia and artwork relating to his reign, like the tent he slept in during military campaigns and a remarkable mechanical desk. Separate from the Musée Napoléon, and at the price of an additional ticket for a guided tour, you can visit the **Petits Appartements,** which date from Louis XV but were redecorated in Empire style for Napoleon and his Empress (first Josephine, then Marie-Louise).

Touring the Gardens

The formal gardens must have been beautiful when André Le Nôtre put his hand to them in the 17th century, but today, though well-kempt, they look a little arid. More lush is the **Garden of Diane** ★, a quiet spot of green on the north side of the castle created during the time of François I, which centers around a statue of the goddess surrounded by four dogs. The **English Garden** ★, complete with an artificial stream and lush groves of tall trees, was added by Napoleon. The vast **Carp Pond** ★, which extends directly from the south side of the **Cour de la Fontaine,** has a small island in the center with a small pavilion where an afternoon snack would be served to the royal residents. Surrounding the gardens and its park is the enormous **Fontainebleau Forest** ★★, which, if you have the time, is definitely worth the visit (see box, below).

77300 Fontainebleau. www.chateaudefontainebleau.fr. ✆ **01-60-71-50-70.** Chateau 11€ adults, 9€ students 18–25; castle entry plus guided tour of the *petits appartements* 14€–16€ depending on length of visit; all admissions free 17 and under. Apr–Sept Wed–Mon 9:30am–6pm; Oct–Mar Wed–Mon 9:30am–5pm.

DISNEYLAND PARIS ★

41km (25 miles) E of Paris

It might not be particularly French, but there's no denying that this is a fun place to visit—especially if you're traveling with kids. There are two parks here, **Disneyland Paris** and **Disney Studios;** depending on your stamina, you can do them both in a day.

Essentials

GETTING THERE By far the easiest way to get to the parks from central Paris is by **RER A** (RATP; www.ratp.fr; 45 min.; 7.60€ adults, 3.80€ ages 4–10 one-way). Alight at any of its downtown stations and take it all the way to its terminus at Marne-la-Vallée–Chessy (just make sure that this is the terminus—the RER A has multiple destinations). When you get out, you'll be a 5-minute walk from the entrance. By **car,** head east on the A4 and take the Parcs Disney exit. By train, from outside Paris, you could arrive by **TGV** (the French railway's high-speed train); see www.voyages-sncf.com. From Paris's Roissy-Charles de Gaulle (CDG) and Orly airports, you could also catch the **Magic Shuttle** (http://magicalshuttle.co.uk; 23€ adults, 10€ children 3–10, free 2 and under), a direct shuttle to the parks and Disney hotels.

VISITOR INFORMATION   **Disneyland Paris Guest Relations Office,** located in City Hall on Main Street, U.S.A. (www.disneylandparis.com; ✆ **08-25-30-05-00;** .15€ per min). For general tourist information for the region, visit the **Centre d'Acceuil Regionale de Tourisme** between the train station and Disney Village (www.visitparisregion.com; ✆ **01-60-43-33-33**).

ADMISSION   Admission varies depending on the season. In peak season, a 1-day, 1-park ticket (for either the main park or Walt Disney Studios) costs 69€ adults, 62€ children 3–11, and free for children 2 and under; a 2-day park-hopper ticket is 140€ adults, 126€ kids; and a 3-day park-hopper ticket is 174€ adults, 159€ kids. Special offers run throughout the year, some that include transportation to and from Paris; check the website for details.

HOURS   Hours vary throughout the year, but most frequently they are 10am to 7pm. Check the website for exact hours during your stay.

Exploring Disney

This giant resort is comprised of two parks: the classic **Disneyland,** complete with "It's a Small World" and Space Mountain, and **Disney Studios,** which has thrill rides and exhibits themed around Disney animation techniques and films. (Disneyland is a better choice for the under-7 crowd.). Yes, there's also a golf course, a spa and tennis courts, and **Disney Village** here, with its boutiques, restaurants, a discotheque, a cinema, and an IMAX theater. But for the purposes of this guide, we'll just stick with the parks.

The "Mad Hatter" entertains Disney crowds during a parade.

Disneyland Park

Isn't it comforting that some things never change? Here you are in France, and yet there is Frontierland, Adventureland, and Fantasyland, just the way you remember them back home. Okay, not exactly. For one thing, everyone's speaking French. And Bulgarian, Hindi, and Farsi. The success of this resort is its international appeal. When you enter the park, you'll step right into **Main Street USA,** that utopian rendition of early-20th-century

America, complete with horse and buggies and barbershop quartets. Here you'll find the **information center** as well as a train that leaves from Main Street Station. The train, which does a circuit around the park, will whisk you off to **Frontierland,** where you'll find Big Thunder Mountain, Phantom Manor, a paddlewheel steamboat, and the Lucky Nugget saloon. Next is a chug through **Adventureland,** with old favorites like the Swiss Family Robinson treehouse and the Pirates of the Caribbean, as well as Indiana Jones and the Temple of Doom. Onward toward **Fantasyland,** with Sleeping Beauty's Castle (Le Château de Belle au Bois Dormant), whizzing teacups, flying Dumbos, and "It's a Small World." Last stop: **Discoveryland,** home of Space Mountain and Buzz Lightyear Laser Blast. There are parades every afternoon on Main Street, and a spectacular light and fountain show, Disney Dreams, around closing time.

Disney Studios

Though the primary draw here, of course, is Disneyland Park, Disney Studios makes a decent alternative for older kids who have already done Disney and are up for something different. Along with films, stunt shows, and parades, the park offers an introduction to the wonders of movie making at **Disney Animation Studios** and the **Back Lot,** with its special effects and stunt shows.

Naturally, there are fun rides here, too, like the **Tower of Terror** (based on the *Twilight Zone* TV show), **Crush's Coaster,** and the **Rock 'n Rollercoaster** (featuring Aerosmith tunes). The latest addition is **Ratatouille,** a 3D ride where you get a mouse's-eye view of the restaurant kitchen in the movie of the same name. Smaller visitors will appreciate **Toy Story Playland,** where they can speed around on the **RC Racer** or try the **Toy Soldiers Parachute Drop.**

PLANNING YOUR TRIP TO PARIS

E ven if all roads do not lead to it, getting to Paris is a pretty straightforward affair. But once you arrive, you'll need to know how to get around and how to take care of practical matters. Below we supply all the nitty-gritty details you need to have a comfortable, safe, and affordable stay in Paris.

GETTING THERE

By Plane

Paris has two international airports: **Aéroport d'Orly,** 18km (11 miles) south of the city (mostly European flights), and **Aéroport Roissy-Charles-de-Gaulle** (CDG; mostly long-haul carriers), 30km (19 miles) northeast. The contact information for both airports is www.parisaeroport.fr; ℂ **00-33-1-70-36-39-50** from abroad, **39-50** or 08-92-56-39-50 from France (.35€ per min.).

If you are taking Ryanair or another discount airline that arrives at **Beauvais airport** (see below), be advised that that airport is located about 80km (50 miles) from Paris.

ROISSY-CHARLES-DE-GAULLE (CDG) AIRPORT CDG has three terminals that are some distance apart from one another. A free train called the **CDGVAL** connects all three to the two train stations.

The quickest way into central Paris from the airport is the fast **RER B** (www.ratp.fr) suburban trains, which leave every 10 to 15 minutes between 4:50am and 11:50pm. It takes about 40 minutes to get to Paris, and RER B stops at several central Métro stations, including Châtelet-Les-Halles and Saint-Michel–Notre-Dame. A single ticket, which can be bought at the machines in the stations at the terminals, costs 9.75€.

Le Bus Direct operates three routes from the airport to the center of Paris (www.lebusdirect.com; ℂ **08-10-81-20-01;** .12€ per min.): The first (line 2) stops at Port Maillot, Charles de Gaulle–Etoile, and Trocadéro, with a terminus at the Eiffel Tower; the second (line 3) links CDG to Orly airport; while the third stops at Gare de Lyon with a terminus at Gare Montparnasse. There are good Métro connections from all stops. Depending on the route, a one-way trip costs 12€ to 21€ adults and children ages 4 and over (children 3 and under travel free), and e-tickets can be bought in advance online (valid for 1 year from purchase); trips take about an hour and 10 minutes, depending on traffic. Buses leave every 30 minutes between roughly 6am and 11pm. The **Roissybus** (www.ratp.fr; ℂ 34-24 from France only) departs every 20 minutes from the airport daily from 6am to 12:30am and costs 11.50€ for the 70-minute ride. The bus leaves you in the center of Paris, at the corner of rue Scribe and rue Auber, near the Opéra.

There is now a flat rate for a **taxi** from Roissy into the city (50€ Right Bank, 55€ Left Bank), not including supplements (1€ per item of luggage, 20% extra 5pm–10am and Sun and bank holidays). Taxi stands can be found outside each of the airport's terminals. Alternatively, Uber functions in France, with flat rates of 45€–50€ in an uberX car (www.uber.com; also see p. 286).

ORLY AIRPORT Orly has two terminals: Orly Sud and Orly Ouest. To get to the center of Paris, take the 8-minute monorail **OrlyVal** to the RER station "Antony" to get **RER B** into the center. Combined travel time is about 40 minutes. Trains run between 6am and 11:30pm, and the one-way fare for the OrlyVal plus the RER B is 12.05€ adults and 6€ children 4 to 10; free under 4.

Le Bus Direct operates one route (line 1) from the airport to the center of Paris (www.lebusdirect.com; ℂ 08-10-81-20-01; .12€ per min.), leaving from both Orly terminals every 20 minutes between 6am and 11:30pm, stopping at Gare Montparnasse, the Eiffel Tower, Trocadéro, and Charles de Gaulle–Etoile. The fare is 12€ one-way for adults, 7€ children ages 4–11 (free for kids 3 and under). E-tickets can be bought in advance online (valid for 1 year from purchase). Depending on the traffic, the journey takes about an hour. The **Orlybus** (www.ratp.fr), which leaves every 15 minutes between 6am and 12:30am, links the airport with Place Denfert-Rochereau, a 30-minute trip that costs 8€ for both adults and children.

There is a flat rate for a **taxi** from Orly to central Paris (Left Bank 30€, Right Bank 35€) not including supplements (1€ per item of luggage, and 20% extra 5pm–10am and Sun and bank holidays). Or try the international taxi app Uber, which offers a flat rate of 35€ for the Left Bank and 40€ for the Right Bank in an uberX car (www.uber.com; also see p. 286).

BEAUVAIS AIRPORT Beauvais airport (www.aeroportbeauvais.com; ℂ 08-92-68-20-66; .45€ per min.) is located around 80km (50 miles) from Paris and is served by budget airlines such as Ryanair and Wizz Air. Buses leave about 20 minutes after each flight has landed and, depending on the traffic, take about 1 hour and 15 minutes to get to Porte Maillot on the western edge of Paris. To return to Beauvais, you need to be at the bus station at least 3 hours before the departure of your flight. A one-way ticket costs 17€ (15.90€ if you purchase it online in advance).

By Train

One of best ways to get around France and Europe is by train. The French railway agency, the **SNCF, Societé Nationale des Chemins de Fer Français** (www.voyages-sncf.com), has a vast network that connects most major cities and quite a few smaller towns, though you will often have to pass through Paris to get from one place to another. For reservations, visit the SNCF website.

The SNCF connects to railways in neighboring countries, including the U.K. The **Eurostar** (www.eurostar.com), which passes under the channel for a nerve-wracking 20 minutes, will get you from Paris's Gare du Nord to St. Pancras Station, London, in just 2¼ hours. If London is your destination, know that even though the regular ticket price can be high (around 200€ one-way!), there are scads of discounts available on the website, especially if you purchase in advance. Brussels is only an hour and a quarter away on the high-speed **Thalys** train, and tickets range anywhere from 29€ to 142€ depending on what deal you get. Visit the site (www.thalys.com) for high-speed trains to Brussels, Amsterdam, and Cologne. For rail passes that you can use throughout Europe, visit **Rail Europe** (www.raileurope.com).

Paris has six major train stations: **Gare d'Austerlitz** (13th arrond.), **Gare de Lyon** (12th arrond.), **Gare Montparnasse** (14th arrond.), **Gare St-Lazare** (8th arrond.), **Gare de l'Est** (10th arrond.), and **Gare du Nord** (10th arrond.). Stations can be reached by bus or Métro. *Warning:* As in many cities, stations and surrounding areas can be seedy and are frequented by pickpockets. Be alert, especially at night.

By Bus

Cheapest of all, and the most time-consuming, is the bus. For travel within Europe, contact **Eurolines** (www.eurolines.com), a consortium of dozens of different bus lines with routes that span the continent (Seville to Zurich, anyone?). Most long-haul buses arrive at the **Eurolines France** station on the eastern edge of the city, 23 ave. du Général-de-Gaulle, Bagnolet; Métro: Gallieni.

By Car

We wouldn't recommend driving in Paris to our worst enemy, but renting a car and driving around France can be a lovely way to see the country. All of the major car-rental companies have offices here (see below), but you'll often get better deals if you reserve before you leave home. **AutoEurope** (www.autoeurope.com) is an excellent source for discounted rentals. Even better may be **AutoSlash.com** which applies discount codes to rentals from all of the major multinational firms, which can mean big savings. It also monitors prices, so if a rate drops, it re-books you automatically. You pay for the rental at the counter, not in advance.

Before you step on the gas, at the very least, try to get a list of international road signs; your car rental agency should have one. Driving in France is not substantially different from driving in most English-speaking countries (although British travelers will have to get used to driving on the "wrong" side of the road). However, you'll have to get used to French drivers, who tend to zoom around with what the more timid among us would call reckless abandon. Truthfully, since the installation of radar a few years ago, drivers have become much more well-behaved; you, too, should pay attention to speed limits or risk a steep fine. The two biggest driving differences: *priorité à droite,* which means priority is always given to vehicles approaching from the right at intersections, unless otherwise indicated; and the fondness for **roundabouts.** Rule number one regarding the latter: The person getting into the roundabout does *not* have priority. Rule number two: Be sure to take a look at the sign posted *before* the roundabout that indicates which exit goes in what direction so that you'll be prepared when it's time to get off. The good news is that if you miss your turnoff, you can just circle around until you figure out where it is.

By Ferry from England or Ireland

Ferry travel to France appears to be in its waning days, since more and more travelers are opting for low-cost flights or a much speedier passage through the Channel Tunnel. In England the two leading operators of ferries are **P&O Ferries** (www.poferries.com; ✆ **03-66-74-03-25**), which runs ferries from Dover to Calais, and **Brittany Ferries** (www.brittanyferries.com; ✆ **08-25-828-828;** .15€ per min.), which runs ferries from Portsmouth to Caen, Cherbourg, St-Malo, or Le Havre. **Irish Ferries** (www.irishferries.com; ✆ **01-70-72-03-26**) operates an overnight ferry from Cherbourg to Rosslare or Dublin. Call or check websites for times, prices, and points of departure/arrival.

GETTING AROUND

Finding an Address

The river Seine divides Paris into the **Rive Droite (Right Bank)** to the north and the **Rive Gauche (Left Bank)** to the south. You can figure out which is which if you face west. (Figuring out which way is west is another problem.) Paris is divided into 20 municipal districts called **arrondissements,** which spiral out clockwise starting with the 1st, which is the geographical center of the city. It's not easy to figure out without a map, so we strongly suggest that you invest in some version of "Paris par Arrondissement," a small book of maps showing the streets, Métro, and bus routes that costs around 7€. Our personal favorite is "Paris Pratique par Arrondissment," which has a bus and metro map for each arrondissement, and shows where the Velib' stands are. And there are, of course, dozens of good map apps for Paris if you prefer using your phone—though Wi-Fi doesn't always work as well as it should in public spaces.

By Public Transport

For everything you ever wanted to know about the city's public transport, visit the **RATP** (www.ratp.fr; ✆ **34-24** in France). Paris and its suburbs are divided into five travel zones, but you'll probably only be concerned with zones 1 and 2, which cover the city itself.

RATP tickets are valid on the Métro, bus, tram and RER. You can buy tickets at the window (if you are lucky—ticket booths are an endangered species) or from machines at most Métro entrances. The machines take coins and chip-enabled credit cards only. So if you don't have one of those, you can also buy tickets from some cafes that have a TABAC sign outside. A **single ticket** costs 1.90€ and a *carnet* of 10 tickets costs 14.50€. Children 4 to 9 years old pay half-price; kids under 4 ride free. A special transit pass for tourists called **Paris Visite** offers unlimited travel in zones on bus, Métro, and RER, and discounts on some attractions, but aside from the ease of having an unlimited pass to jump on and off buses and Métros, its usefulness is limited. Remember, Paris is a relatively small city, and you'll probably end up walking a lot. In the end a cheaper *carnet* of 10 tickets does the trick just fine. Not only that, unlike a pass, a *carnet* can be shared with your fellow travelers. Next, there is the cost (high): A 1-day adult pass for zones 1 to 3 costs 11.65€, a 2-day pass 18.95€, a 3-day pass 25.85€, and a 5-day pass 37.25€. It is also possible to buy even more expensive passes for zones 1 to 5, which will also get you to both Versailles and the airport.

However, if a transit pass if what you are after, there are other options that serve the same purpose and are less expensive, even if they don't include Paris Visite's minimal discounts to some attractions. First there is the slightly cheaper 1-day **Mobilis** ticket, which offers unlimited travel in zones 1 up to 5; a pass for zones 1 and 2 costs 7.30€. Travelers under 26 can buy a **Ticket Jeunes,** a 1-day ticket that can be used on a Saturday, Sunday, or bank holiday and provides unlimited travel in zones 1 to 3 for 4€ or zones 1 to 5 for 8.70€. If you're staying for a week or longer and will be doing a lot of buzzing around, it may be worth getting the **Navigo Découverte** (www.navigo.fr), a swipe card that you can buy at certain Métro or train stations for 5€. You must provide a passport photo, but once you have the card it offers unlimited travel in the relevant zones. The weekly tariff (which runs Mon–Sun) for zones 1 to 5 is 22.15€. That includes going to and from the airport, and transport for day trips such as Versailles or Fontainebleau, so it could quickly pay off. If your trip fits into a Mon–Sun schedule, this 7-day card is substantially cheaper than a 5-day Paris Visite card.

BY MÉTRO (SUBWAY)

The city's first Métro, or subway, was at the apex of high tech when it was inaugurated on July 19, 1900, and over a century later, it still functions very well. Its biggest problem is not actually technical, but political: Subway workers are fond of strikes (*grèves*) and periodically instigate slowdowns or complete shutdowns of a few lines. Usually, strikes are merely annoying and most of the time your route will not be affected, though your trip might take a little longer than normal. If you see the euphemism "Movement Social" on the TV monitor as you enter the station, read the message carefully to see if your line is involved (low groans and cursing by ticket holders are also good indicators of strike activity).

Strikes aside, the Métro is usually efficient and civilized, especially if you avoid rush hour (7:30–9:30am and 6–8pm). It's generally safe at night, and you don't need to worry about taking it at 3am because you can't. Alas, when people dolefully talk about "The Last Métro," they're usually not discussing a movie by François Truffaut. Instead, they're referring to a fact of Parisian life: Your evening out must be carefully timed so that you can run to the station before the trains shut down between midnight and 1am. To ease your pain, the transit authority has recently added an extra hour on weekends, so now the Métro closes around 2am on Friday, Saturday, and pre-holiday evenings. The suburban trains (the RER, see below) close down around the same time (without the weekend bonus hour).

Most Métro lines ramble across the city in anything but a straight line, connecting at strategic points where you can transfer from one to the other. A map is essential (pick one up at any ticket window, or take a look at the one on the inside back cover of this book); for a good app, download the one by the RATP, or ViaNavigo, which covers the whole Paris region. The key is to know both the number of the line and its final destination. So if you are on the no. 1 line (direction La Défense) and you want to transfer at the enormous Châtelet station to get to St-Michel, at Châtelet you'll need to doggedly follow the signs to the no. 4, direction Mairie de Montrouge.

BY RER

Your only underground express choice is the **RER** (pronounced "ehr-euh-ehr"), the suburban trains that dash through the city making limited stops. The down sides are (a) they don't run as often as the Métro, (b) they're a lot less pleasant, and (c) they're hard to figure out since they run on a different track system and the same lines can have multiple final destinations. *Important:* Make sure to hold on to your ticket because you'll need it to get out of the turnstile on the way out. To check your destinations, check the departure boards (or screens) on the quays: The stops served by the next train are either listed or lit up.

BY BUS

Thanks to a new network of dedicated bus lanes, buses can be an efficient way to get around town, and you'll get a scenic tour to boot. The majority start running around 6am and stop anywhere from 9:30pm to midnight; service is reduced on Sundays and holidays. You can use Métro tickets on the buses or you can buy tickets directly from the driver (2€). Alas, you can't re-use a ticket you've used on the Métro on the bus, even if you're within the 2-hour time limit. You can, however, re-use the same ticket you've used on the bus on a tram (and vice versa). Tickets need to be validated in the machine next to the driver's cabin.

"Ride a bike around Paris," you ask. "Are you nuts?" Yes and no. True, you have to have a bit of the daredevil in you to take to the streets on a bicycle in this traffic-crazed city, but since July 2007, when the City of Paris inaugurated a wildly successful system of low-cost bike rentals called Velib' (vel-*leeb*), it's really hard to resist the temptation to do so. Quite simply it's fun to check out these high-tech, sexy-looking bikes and take them for a spin, dropping them off at bike stands with no fuss and no muss.

Here's how it works: You buy a 1- or 7-day subscription (1.70€ or 8€, respectively) from the machine at one of the futuristic-looking bike stands, which gives you the right to as many half-hour rides as you'd like for 1 or 7 days. If you want to go over a half-hour, you can either check in your bike, wait 5 minutes, and check it out again, or you can pay 1€ for your extra half-hour, 2€ for the half-hour after that one and 4€ for the third half-hour on. Everything is meticulously explained in English on the website (www.velib.fr), and there's even a number you can call for English-speaking assistance (© **01-30-79-79-30**). There's one big catch, however—to use the machines you must have a credit or debit card with a chip in it. This can be a problem for North American tourists, so we advise either getting a TravelEx "cash passport" with money on it (www.travelex.com) or just **buy your subscription online ahead of time** (make sure you have your secret code to punch in on the stand). Helmets are not provided, so if you're feeling queasy about launching into traffic, bring one along. There are few bike lanes so far, but new ones are being added. **Note:** Cyclists no longer always have the right to ride in the bus lanes; check for road signs. **One more tip:** Before you ride, get a map of the city that shows where the bike stands are or download the app on the Velib' site so you don't waste precious time looking for a place to check in or check out.

Inside the bus, the next stop is usually written on an electronic panel on the ceiling of the bus. Press the red button when you want to get off.

After the bus and Métro services stop running, head for the **Noctilien** night bus (www.transilien.com/static/noctilien). The 47 lines crisscross the city and head out to the suburbs every half-hour or so from 12:30 to 5:30am. Tickets cost the same as for the regular bus (see above).

BY TRAM

Over the past decade, Paris has added eight new tramway lines, with extensions and new lines in progress. These tramway lines connect Paris with its suburbs; within Paris they run along the outer circle of boulevards that trace the city limits. Tickets are the same price as the Métro.

By Bicycle

Cycling in Paris has been revolutionized by the hugely successful **Velib'** bike rental scheme launched in 2007 (the name comes from *vélo,* meaning "bicycle," and *liberté,* meaning "freedom"). It takes a little effort for a tourist to sign up, but it's worth it to see Paris on two wheels (see box below).

Alternatively, you can rent a bike from **Paris à vélo, c'est sympa!,** 22 rue Alphonse Baudin (www.parisvelosympa.com; *©* **01-48-87-60-01;** Métro: St-Sébastien-Froissart or Richard Lenoir). Rentals for a regular bicycle cost 12€ for half a day and 15€ for a full day, but they do require a safety deposit of at least 250€, depending on the type of bike you rent. If you're feeling extra lazy, there are also electric bikes from 20€ for half a day.

A Word About Driving in Paris

Don't. Even if you are a Formula 1 racecar driver with years of experience, you'll be alternately outraged and infuriated by the aggressive tactics of your fellow drivers and the inevitable *bouchons* (literally, a bottle stopper or cork), or jams, that tie up traffic and turn a simple jaunt into a harrowing nightmare. To make matters worse, it's easy to believe that the street and direction signs were cunningly placed by a sadistic madman who gets kicks out of watching hapless drivers take wrong turns. No matter how carefully you try to follow the signs pointing toward, say, Trocadéro, you'll suddenly find yourself on an outer boulevard headed for Versailles.

Your troubles are not over once you get to your destination, because then you will have to park, which is a whole other trauma. Spots are elusive, to say the least, and you'll probably find yourself touring the neighborhood for at least 20 minutes until you find one. By then you'll have figured out why it is that Parisians park on the sidewalks: Often, there's nowhere else to park.

One final hurdle: feeding the **parking meter.** All parking is *payant*—that is, you must pay. And you can't use coins in the *horodateur* (parking meter) anymore—you must either pay with a chip-enabled credit card or buy a "Paris Carte" parking card at a *tabac*, or smoke shop. This card is inserted directly into the meter, which will print out a ticket that you must put on your dashboard; parking in the most central arrondissements (1 to 11) costs 4€ per hour; in the outer arrondissements (12 to 20) it's 2.40€ per hour. What's more, you can't stay in the same spot for more than 2 hours. Mercifully, on Sundays and from 8pm to 9am the rest of the week, all street parking is free. If you are not up to the challenge, try one of the many **underground parking lots,** indicated by a sign with a white "P" on a blue background; parking in one of these is between 2.60€–4€ per hour, and you can stay all day (you don't need a card here).

If, despite this rant, you still feel compelled to rent a car and drive around the city, or are forced to do so due to extenuating circumstances, at the very least get your hands on a basic explanation of international street signs (this should be available at your car-rental agency) and a good street map. Try to do your driving on a Sunday, when most Parisians head for the country (but forget about Saturday, when they all do their shopping). Finally, try to keep your cool, because no matter how sure you are that you are following the rules of the road, at some point, someone in another car will curse you. Good luck—you're going to need it.

The Velib' bike-rental system now has a four-wheeled cousin: **Autolib'** (www.autolib.eu; ✆ **01-58-34-44-10**). The concept is the same: a short-term self-service rental, but this time, you get to tool around in a spiffy electric car. There are hundreds of rental stations in Paris and the surrounding area. To register, you can go to one of the Autolib' subscription kiosks if you have a credit card with a chip; if not, go to the Autolib' information center (5 rue Edouard VII, 9th arrond.) with your driver's license (plus—for non-European drivers—your international driving license), a valid form of ID, and a credit card. The easiest option, though, is to **register online.** A 1-day subscription is free, but you pay 9€ per half-hour. A year is 120€ plus 6€ per half-hour. You are given a badge that you then pass over the sensor at a rental station to unlock the car. Unplug it from the charger and drive away. One of the best things about Autolib', however, is parking when you are done. Instead of going insane looking for a spot (see above), just use the GPS to find an Autolib' station and plug in the Bluecar. For information about other car-rental companies, please refer to the "By Car" section of "Getting There," earlier in this chapter.

By Boat

The **Batobus** (www.batobus.com; ✆ **08-25-05-01-01;** .15€ per min.) is a fleet of boats that operates along the Seine, stopping at such points of interest as the Eiffel Tower, the Musée d'Orsay, the Louvre, Notre-Dame, and the Hôtel de Ville. Much like the hop-on-hop-off buses (see "Bus Tours," p. 191), these boats are more about sightseeing and less about getting quickly from place to place, though they will get you up and down the Seine. Unlike the Bateaux-Mouches (p. 190), the Batobus does not provide a recorded commentary. The only fare option available is a day pass valid for either 1 or 2 days, each allowing as many entrances and exits as you want. A 1-day pass costs 17€ for adults and 8€ for children 15 and under; a 2-day pass costs 19€ for adults and 10€ for children 15 and under. Boats operate daily minutes starting at 10am; boats come by every 25 to 40 minutes, depending on the season. Last call is anywhere from 5pm during the week in the winter to 9:30pm in the summer, see the website for exact intervals and closing hours.

By Taxi

This is the most expensive way to get around and not necessarily the most efficient. Merely hailing a cab can be an ordeal: You can hail them in the street, but not all will stop (only hail those with a full green or white light), or look for a taxi stand, which resembles a bus stop and usually sports a blue TAXI sign. Once inside, you'll have to pray that your driver is skilled in dodging Parisian traffic, which is horrendous. Sooner or later you'll find yourself stuck in a jam, watching the meter tick, and cursing yourself for not having taken the Métro.

Australian Citizens The **Australian Customs Service** (www.customs.gov.au; ℭ **131-881** in Australia, or 612/9313-3010 from abroad) has complete customs information on its website under "Individuals and Travellers." The duty-free allowance in Australia is A$900 or, for those 17 or younger, A$450. Those over 18 can bring home up to 2.25 liters of alcoholic beverages.

Canadian Citizens For a clear summary of Canadian rules, visit the website of the **Canada Border Services Agency** (www.cbsa-asfc.gc.ca; ℭ **800/461-9999** in Canada, or 204/983-3500 from abroad). Canada allows its citizens a C$800 exemption. You can also bring back up to 1.5 liters of wine, 1.14 liters of other alcoholic beverage, or up to 8.5 liters of beer.

New Zealand Citizens The answers to most questions regarding customs can be found on the website of the **New Zealand Customs Service** under "Customs charges, duties and allowances" (www.customs.govt.nz; ℭ **0800/4-CUS-TOMS,** 0800/428-786, or 649/927-8036 from outside New Zealand). The duty-free allowance for New Zealand is

NZ$700. You are allowed to bring back 4.5 liters of wine or beer, and not more than 1.25 liters of spirits.

U.K. Citizens When returning to the U.K. from an E.U. country such as France, you can bring in an unlimited amount of most goods. There is no limit on what you can bring back from an E.U. country, as long as the items are for personal use (this includes gifts) and you have already paid the duty and tax. For information, contact **HM Revenue Customs** (www.gov.uk/duty-free-goods; ℭ **44/300-200-3700**).

U.S. Citizens For specifics on what you can bring back and the corresponding fees, click on "Know Before You Visit" at **www.cbp.gov**. Or, contact the **U.S. Customs & Border Protection** (CBP; ℭ **877/227-5511** in the U.S. or 202/325-8000 from outside the U.S.). Returning U.S. citizens who have been away for 48 hours or more are allowed to bring back, once every 30 days, $800 worth of merchandise duty-free. Included in your allowance is 1 duty-free liter of alcoholic beverage; after that, it depends what state you live in, so check with your state customs office for amounts.

Calculating fares is a complicated business. When you get in, the meter should read 2.60€. Then, the basic rates for Paris *intramuros* ranges from 1.06€ to 1.56€ per kilometer, depending on the day of the week and the hour. There's a minimum fare of 7€; if you have more than four people in your party, you'll also be charged 4€ for each additional passenger. You'll also be charged 1€ for each suitcase you put in the trunk. The saving grace here is that the distances are usually not huge, and barring excessive traffic, your average crosstown fare should fall between 15€ and 25€ for two without baggage. Tipping is not obligatory, but rounding up or a .50€ to 1€ tip is customary.

It's often easier to call a cab then to hail one on the street: Contact **Les Taxis Bleus** (www.taxis-bleus.com; ℭ **36-09**; .35€ per min.) or **Taxi G7** (www.taxisg7.fr; ℭ **36-07**; .15€ per min.). Avoid minicabs or unlicensed taxis.

Changing the taxi landscape in France (much to the disdain of regular taxi drivers) is **Uber** (www.uber.com). Just download the smart phone app and enter your credit-card details. Once you're logged on, you enter your location and your destination. No money changes hands, and the cost of your journey is precalculated according to its "real" distance, so you're not penalized if you have to make a detour. While you wait, the screen shows the whereabouts of your taxi in real time, as well as the car's number plate, the driver's name, and his/her photo. When traveling abroad (especially if you're a woman), it's reassuring to know who will be driving your taxi, and for central Paris, you rarely have to wait more than 5 minutes for an Uber to arrive. Generally speaking, Uber is cheaper than standard taxis as well.

On Foot

If you have the time and the energy, the best mode of transport in this small and walkable city is your own two feet. You can cross the center of town (say from the Place St-Michel to Les Halles) in about 20 minutes. This is the best way to see and experience the city, and take in all the little details that make it all so wonderful. You could spend an afternoon exploring one small neighborhood, or try one of the walking tours in chapter 7.

[FastFACTS] PARIS

Area Codes The country code for France is 33 and the area code for Paris is 01.

Business Hours Opening hours in Paris are erratic. Most museums close 1 day a week (usually Mon or Tues) and some national holidays. Museum hours tend to be from 9:30am to 6pm. Generally, **offices** are open Monday to Friday from 9am to 6pm, but don't count on it—always call first. **Banks** tend to be open from 9am to 5pm Monday to Friday, but some branches are open on Saturday instead of Monday. **Large stores** are open from around 10am to 6 or 7pm. Some **small stores** have a lunch break that can last for up to 2 hours, from noon onward, but this is becoming increasingly rare. Most shops, except those in the

Marais or on the Champs-Élysées, are closed on Sunday. Restaurants are typically closed on Sundays and/or Mondays, and many businesses across the city are closed in August.

Cellphones The three letters that define much of the world's wireless capabilities are **GSM** (Global System for Mobile Communications), a big, seamless network that makes for easy cross-border mobile phone use throughout Europe and dozens of other countries worldwide. You can use your mobile phone in France provided it is GSM and tri-band or quad-band; just confirm this with your operator before you leave.

Using your phone abroad can be expensive, and you usually have to pay to receive calls, so it's a good idea to get your phone

"unlocked" before you leave. Then you can buy a SIM card from one of the three main French providers: **Bouygues Télécom** (www.bouyguestelecom.fr), **Orange** (www.orange.fr), or **SFR** (www.sfr.fr). A temporary SIM card (carte prepayée) costs anywhere from 4€ to 40€, depending on the number of minutes bundled with it. Alternatively, if your phone isn't unlocked, you could buy a cheap mobile phone in Paris. To top-up your phone credit, buy a prepaid card from tabacs, supermarkets, and mobile phone outlets. Prices range from 5€ to 100€.

A final strategy? Use Skype for phone calls. Make sure you have the app before you get to Europe and then use it whenever you have a signal for ridiculously inexpensive phone calls.

Customs What you can bring into France: Citizens of E.U. countries can bring in any amount of goods as long as the goods are intended for their personal use and not for resale. Non–E.U. citizens are entitled to 200 cigarettes, 100 small cigars, 50 cigars, or 250g of tobacco duty-free. You can also bring in 4 liters of alcoholic beverages less than 22% alcohol and 1 liter of spirits more than 22% alcohol.

Dentists & Doctors
Doctors are listed in the **Pages Jaunes** (French equivalent of the Yellow Pages; www.pagesjaunes.fr) under "Médecins." The standard fee for a consultation with a general practitioner (*médecin generaliste*) is 23€. **SOS Médecins** (✆ **36-24** or 01-47-07-77-77) makes house calls that cost around 90€ to 130€ (prices quoted are for people without French social security). Download a list of English-speaking dentists and doctors in Paris on the U.S. Embassy website: http://photos.state.gov/libraries/france/5/acs/paris-doctors.pdf. You can also reach U.S. Citizens Services by phone at ✆ **01-43-12-22-22.** See also "Emergencies" and "Health," below.

Disabled Travelers I suppose you could blame it on its centuries-old streets, but Paris has only recently started making a concerted effort to become accessible for people with disabilities. While the city still won't win any prizes for accessibility

(tortuous sidewalks, few ramps at public facilities, endless stairways in Métro stations), there has been slow and steady progress, with over 60 wheelchair-accessible bus lines, several RER stations, and stations on the Métro line 14. Access to all tram lines is flush with the ground, though you might have to navigate a curb to get to the station. To find the closest accessible stations, maps, and more, visit www.infomobi.com (in English) or call ✆ **09-70-81-83-85** (in French). Many museums are now accessible; visit their websites for details. Several art museums even offer tactile visits for the blind. Many hotels with three or more stars (under the French national rating system, not ours) have at least one handicap-accessible room. Hotels that are particularly sensitive to the subject may bear the "Tourisme & Handicaps" label. The **Paris Tourist Office** (www.parisinfo.com) has a good listing of accessible hotels on its site, as well as plenty of other info and links for disabled travelers. Click "Practical Paris" and then "Visiting Paris with a Disability."

Drinking Laws Supermarkets, grocery stores, and cafes sell alcoholic beverages. The legal drinking age is 18. Wine and liquor are sold every day of the week, year-round. Cafes generally open around 6am and serve until closing (midnight–2am). Bars and nightclubs

usually stay open until 2am (sometimes 5am), but they must stop serving alcohol 1½ hours before closing.

The law regarding drunk driving is tough. A motorist is considered legally intoxicated if his or her blood-alcohol limit exceeds .05%. If it is between .05% and .08%, the driver faces a fine of 750€. Over .08% and it could cost 4,500€ or up to 2 years in jail.

Driving Rules The French drive on the right side of the road. At junctions where there are no signposts indicating the right of way, cars coming from the right have priority. When entering a roundabout (*rond point*), you do not have priority; once you are on, be sure to signal when you are about to turn off.

Electricity Electricity in France runs on 220 volts AC (60 cycles). Adapters or transformers are needed to fit sockets, which you can buy in branches of Darty, FNAC, or BHV. Make sure your appliance can handle 220 volts; otherwise, you risk frying it. If it can't, be sure to use a transformer.

Embassies & Consulates If you have a passport, immigration, legal, or other problem, contact your consulate. Call before you go—they often keep odd hours and observe both French and home-country holidays.

The Embassy of **Australia** at 4 rue Jean-Rey, 15e (www.france.embassy.gov.au; ✆ **01-40-59-33-00;**

Métro: Bir Hakeim) is open Monday to Friday 9am to 5pm except public holidays. The Consular section is open Monday to Friday from 9am to noon and 2 to 4pm.

The Embassy of **Canada** at 35 ave. Montaigne, 8e (www.canadainternational.gc.ca/france; $\mathcal{C}$ **01-44-43-29-00;** Métro: Franklin-D-Roosevelt or Alma-Marceau) is open Monday to Friday 9am to noon.

The Embassy of **Ireland** at 4 rue Rude, 16e (www.dfa.ie/irish-embassy/france; $\mathcal{C}$ **01-44-17-67-00;** Métro: Argentine) is open Monday to Friday 9:30 to 5:30; consular and passport services 9:30am to noon.

The Embassy of **New Zealand** at 103 rue de Grenelle, 7e (www.nzembassy.com/france; $\mathcal{C}$ **01-45-01-43-43;** Métro: Solferino) is open Monday to Friday 9am to 1pm and 2pm to 5pm.

The Embassy of the **United Kingdom** at 35 rue du Faubourg St-Honoré, 8e (www.gov.uk/government/world/france; $\mathcal{C}$ **01-44-51-31-00;** Métro: Concorde or Madeleine) is open Monday to Friday 9:30am to 1pm and 2:30 to 5pm.

The Embassy of the **United States,** 2 ave. Gabriel, 8e (http://fr.usembassy.gov; $\mathcal{C}$ **01-43-12-22-22;** Métro: Concorde) is open Monday to Friday 9am to 6pm. Appointment required for passport and other services; you can schedule online on the website.

Emergencies In an emergency, call $\mathcal{C}$ **112,** or the fire brigade (*Sapeurs-Pompiers;* $\mathcal{C}$ **18**), who are trained to deal with all kinds of medical emergencies, not just fires. For a medical emergency and/or ambulance, call $\mathcal{C}$ **15.** For the police, call $\mathcal{C}$ **17.**

Etiquette & Customs
Parisians like pleasantries and take manners seriously: Say *bonjour, madame/monsieur,* when entering an establishment and *au revoir* when you depart. Always say *pardon* when you accidentally bump into someone. With strangers, people who are older than you, and professional contacts, use *vous* rather than *tu* (*vous* is the polite form of the pronoun you).

Health For travel abroad, non–E.U. nationals should consider buying medical travel insurance. For U.S. citizens, Medicare and Medicaid do not provide coverage for medical costs incurred abroad, so check what medical services your health insurance covers before leaving home. That said, medical costs are a fraction of what they are in the U.S. (for example, a visit to a GP costs 23€), so you may even decide to do a little medical tourism (be sure to bring your prescriptions). U.K. nationals will need a **European Health Insurance Card (EHIC)** to receive free or reduced-cost medical care during a visit to a European Union (E.U.) country, Iceland, Liechtenstein, Norway, or Switzerland (go to www.nhs.uk/ehic).

If you suffer from a chronic illness, consult your doctor before your departure. Pack prescription medications in your carry-on luggage and carry them in their original containers, with pharmacy labels—otherwise they won't make it through airport security. Carry the generic name of prescription medicines, in case a local pharmacist is unfamiliar with the brand name.

For further tips on travel and health concerns, and a list of local English-speaking doctors, contact the **International Association for Medical Assistance to Travelers (IAMAT;** www.iamat.org; $\mathcal{C}$ **716/754-4883** in the U.S., or 416/652-0137 in Canada). You can also download a list of English-speaking dentists and doctors in Paris at the U.S. Citizens Services page on the U.S. embassy website (http://fr.usembassy.gov) and click "Resources for US Citizens." See also "Dentists & Doctors," "Emergencies," "Hospitals," and "Pharmacies" in this section.

Holidays Major holidays are New Year's Day (Jan 1), Easter Sunday and Monday (late Mar/Apr), May Day (May 1), VE Day (May 8), Ascension Thursday (40 days after Easter), Pentecost/Whit Sunday and Whit Monday (7th Sun and Mon after Easter), Bastille Day (July 14), Assumption Day (Aug 15), All Saints Day (Nov 1), Armistice Day (Nov 11), and Christmas Day (Dec 25).

Hospitals In my experience, French public hospitals are very good. Most Parisian hospitals have 24-hour emergency rooms, and some have a specialty (Hôpital Necker is the best children's hospital, for example). For addresses and information on all Paris' public hospitals, visit www.aphp.fr.

Two private hospitals in nearby suburbs have English-speaking staff and operate 24 hours daily (and cost much more than the public ones): the **American Hospital of Paris** (63 bd. Victor Hugo, 92200 Neuilly-sur-Seine; www.american-hospital.org; ℰ **01-46-41-25-25;** Métro: Pont de Levallois; 15 min. walk from station; bus: 43, 82, 93, 163, 164, and 174); and the **Institute Hospitalier Franco-Britannique** (3 rue Barbès or 4 rue Kleber, Levallois; www.ihfb.org/en; ℰ **01-47-59-59-59;** Métro: Anatole-France).

Hotlines **S.O.S. Help** is a hotline for English-speaking callers in crisis (www.soshelpline.org; ℰ **01-46-21-46-46;** open daily 3–11pm).

Internet & Wi-Fi Many Parisian hotels and cafes have Internet access, and Wi-Fi (pronounced *wee-fee* here) is becoming increasingly common in cafes and public spaces. Cybercafes open and close so quickly it

is hard to list them, but the two huge **Milk** locations (in Les Halles and Montparnasse) seem to be reliably open 24/7 (www.milklub.com).

Language English is increasingly common in Paris, particularly in tourist areas, but you'll get much better service (or at least a shadow of a smile) if you attempt to use a few French words like "bonjour" and "merci." For handy French words and phrases, as well as food and menu terms, refer to chapter 12, "Useful Terms & Phrases."

LGBTQ Travelers France is known for being a particularly tolerant country when it comes to gays and lesbians, which made the acrimonious blather surrounding the legalization of same-sex marriage in 2013 all the more upsetting. "Gay Paree" boasts a large gay population, and had an openly gay mayor, Bertrand Delanoë, for over a decade. The center of gay and lesbian life is in the Marais. The annual Gay Pride March takes place on the last Sunday in June. Information and resources can be found in Paris's largest, best-stocked gay bookstore, **Les Mots à la Bouche**, 6 rue Ste-Croix de la Bretonnerie, 4th arrond. (www.mots bouche.com; ℰ **01-42-78-88-30;** Métro: Hôtel-de-Ville), which carries publications in

both French and English. **Tétu** (www.tetu.com) is a national magazine dedicated to gay life; to find listings and events, try **Qweek** (www.qweek.fr), a website focused on Paris.

Lost & Found If you left something in the bus, Métro, or RER less than 5 days ago, call the the **Bureau des Objets Trouvés** (http://scope.ratp.fr/ quand-un-objet-a-ete-perdu-sur-le-reseau-ratp; 36 rue des Morillons, 15e; ℰ **32-46;** .80€ per min.) If it has been 5 days or more, you'll need to visit the office in person.

Mail There are post offices (**La Poste;** www.laposte.fr; ℰ **36-31**) in every arrondissement. Most are open Monday to Friday 9am to 7pm, Saturday 9am to 1pm; the Louvre post office (16 rue Etienne Marcel; Métro: Louvre-Rivoli) is open daily midnight to 6am and 8am to midnight. Stamps are also sold in *tabacs* (tobacconists).

Medical Requirements Unless you are arriving from an area of the world known to be suffering from an epidemic, especially cholera or yellow fever, inoculations or vaccinations are not required for entry in France.

Money & Costs Frommer's lists exact prices in the

THE VALUE OF THE EURO VS. OTHER POPULAR CURRENCIES

Euro (€)	US$	C$	UK£	A$	NZ$
1	1.07	1.40	0.85	1.40	1.46

WHAT THINGS COST IN PARIS

	EURO €
Taxi from the airport to downtown Paris (Orly or CDG)	35.00–55.00
Métro ticket	1.90
Double room, expensive	350.00–800.00
Double room, moderate	150.00–350.00
Double room, inexpensive	100.00–150.00
Three-course dinner for one without wine, moderate	28.00–35.00
Glass of beer, 25cl	3.50–6.00
Espresso	1.00–3.00
1 liter of premium gas	1.45–1.65
Admission to most museums	10.00–15.00

local currency. The currency conversions quoted above were correct at press time. However, rates fluctuate, so before departing consult a currency exchange website such as www.oanda.com or www.xe.com to check up-to-the-minute rates.

ATMs are widely available in Paris, but if you're venturing into rural France, it's always good to have cash in your pocket. Be sure you know your personal identification number (PIN) and daily withdrawal limit before you depart. Many banks impose a fee when you withdraw money abroad, and that fee can be higher for international transactions than for domestic ones. In addition, the bank from which you withdraw cash may charge its own fee. For currency exchanges, always use a bank (you'll get a better exchange rate that way).

Visa is the most common credit card in France, but with the exception of American Express, which is sometimes refused, international credit cards are widely accepted. Foreign credit cards, particularly those without an embedded chip, do not always work in machines. Check for hidden fees when using your card abroad—some bank charges can be up to 3% of the purchase price. Use the following number to report any lost or stolen credit card: ℂ **08-92-70-57-05** (.35€ per min). For a specific card, call: **American Express** (www.americanexpress.com; ℂ **01-47-77-72-00**); **MasterCard** (www.mastercard.com; ℂ **08-00-90-13-87**); or **Visa** (www.visaeurope.com; ℂ **08-00-90-11-79**). There are still shops, restaurants, and bars, often family run, that don't accept credit or debit cards, so it's always good to both check in advance and have cash on you.

Travelers' checks are no longer accepted in many stores and restaurants. A better solution would be to buy a **MasterCard Cash Passport** (www.cashpassport.com), a prepaid,

reloadable currency card with a chip and a PIN number that works like a debit card.

Newspapers & Magazines English-language newspapers are available at kiosks across the city; the most widely available is the *International New York Times* (www.inyt.com), the former *International Herald-Tribune*. **WH Smith** (248 rue de Rivoli; www.whsmith.fr; ℂ **01-44-77-88-99**) has a good selection of English-language press.

Passports Citizens of New Zealand, Australia, Canada, and the United States need a valid passport to enter France. The passport is valid for a stay of 90 days. All children must have their own passports. For the moment, citizens of the UK need a valid passport to enter France but there is no time limit to how long they can stay. This rule may change, however, as the UK is leaving the European Union.

Allow plenty of time before your trip to apply for

a passport; processing normally takes 3 weeks but can take longer during busy periods (especially spring). Keep in mind that if you need a passport in a hurry, you'll pay a higher processing fee.

Pharmacies You'll spot French *pharmacies* by looking for the green neon cross above the door. If your local pharmacy is closed, there should be a sign on the door indicating the nearest one open. Pharmacists give basic medical advice and can take your blood pressure. *Parapharmacies* sell medical products and toiletries, but they don't dispense prescriptions. Both the **Pharmacie du Drugstore des Champs-Elysées** (133 ave. des Champs-Élysées; www.pharmacie-drugstore-champselysees.com; Ⓒ 01-47-20-39-25; Métro/RER: Charles de Gaulle Etoile) and the **Pharmacie Européene** (6 place de Clichy; Ⓒ 01-48-74-65-18; Métro: Place de Clichy) are open 24 hours daily. See also "Emergencies" and "Health," above.

Police In an emergency, call Ⓒ **17** for the police, or **112,** the European Union–wide toll-free emergency number. The Préfecture de Police has stations all over Paris. To find the nearest one, call Ⓒ **17** or go to www.prefecturedepolice.interieur.gouv.fr/English. See also "Emergencies," above.

Safety In general, Paris is a safe city and it is safe to use the Métro late at night.

However, certain Métro stations (and the areas around them) are best avoided at night: Châtelet-Les Halles, Gare du Nord, Barbès Rochechouart, and Strasbourg St-Denis. The RER can get scary late at night; try to find alternative transport to and from the airport (such as buses or taxis) late at night or early in the morning.

The most common crime problem in Paris is pickpockets. They prey on tourists around popular attractions such as the Louvre, the Eiffel Tower, Notre-Dame, St-Michel, Centre Pompidou, Versailles, and Sacré Coeur, in the major department stores, and on the Métro. Take precautions and be vigilant at all times: Don't take more money with you than necessary, keep your passport in a concealed pouch or leave it at your hotel, and ensure that your bag is firmly closed at all times. Also, around the major sites it is quite common to be approached by a young Roma girl or boy and asked if you speak English. It's best to avoid these situations, and, in any incident that might occur, by shaking your head and walking away.

In cafes, bars, and restaurants, it's best not to leave your bag under the table or on the back of your chair. Keep it between your legs or on your lap to avoid it being stolen. Never leave valuables in a car.

In times of heightened security concerns, the government mobilizes police

and armed forces, so don't be surprised to see soldiers strolling around transport hubs and carrying automatic weapons. Also see "Terrorism," below.

Paris is a cosmopolitan city and most nonwhite travelers won't experience any problems, outside of some unpleasant stares. Although there is a significant level of discrimination against West and North African immigrants, harassment of African-American and Asian tourists is exceedingly rare. **S.O.S. Racisme** (51 ave. de Flandre, 19th arrond.; www.sos-racisme.org; Ⓒ **01-40-35-36-55**) offers legal advice to victims of prejudice and will even intervene to help with the police.

Female travelers should not expect any more hassle than in other major cities and the same precautions apply. French men tend to stare a lot, but it's generally harmless. Avoid walking around the less safe neighborhoods (Barbès Rochechouart, Strasbourg St-Denis, Châtelet-Les-Halles) alone at night and never get into an unmarked taxi. If you are approached in the street or on the Métro, it's best to avoid entering into conversation and walk away.

Senior Travel Many discounts are available to seniors—men and women over 60. Although they often seem to apply only to residents of E.U. countries, it pays to announce at the ticket window of a museum or monument that you are 60 years old or more. You may not receive a discount, but it doesn't hurt to ask. "Senior," incidentally, is pronounced *seenyore* in France. Senior citizens do not get a discount for traveling on public transport in Paris, but there are senior discounts on national trains. Check out www.voyages-sncf.com for details.

Smoking Smoking is now banned inside all public places, including cafes, restaurants, bars, and nightclubs; it is still rife on cafe terraces, however.

Student Travel Student discounts are less common in France than in other countries, simply because young people under 26 are usually offered reduced rates. Some discounts only apply to residents of E.U. countries, who will need to prove this with a passport or driver's license, but if you're not from the E.U. it's worth carrying an ID to prove your age and announcing it when buying tickets. Look out for the **Ticket Jeunes** when using the Métro. It can be used on a Saturday, Sunday, or bank holiday, and provides unlimited travel in zones 1 to 3 for 4€ (see "By Public Transport," earlier in this chapter). SNCF also offer 25% off for under-26-year-olds traveling on national trains (www.voyages-sncf.com).

Taxes As a member of the European Union, France routinely imposes a value-added tax (VAT in English; *TVA* in French) on most goods. The standard VAT is 20% and is already included in virtually all prices for consumer goods and services (you'll know for sure when you see TTC, which means *toutes taxes comprises*, "all taxes included"). If you're over 16 and not an E.U. resident, you can get a VAT refund if you're spending less than 6 months in France, you purchase goods worth at least 175€ at a single shop on the same day, you are transporting the good yourself, and the shop offers *vente en détaxe* (duty-free sales or tax-free shopping). Give them your passport and ask for a *bordereau de vente à l'exportation* (export sales invoice), which must have a barcode. Both you and the shopkeeper sign the slip, and you choose how you want to be reimbursed (credit on card, bank transfer, or cash). Once you get to the airport, scan the code in one of the new "Pablo" terminals (if your airport doesn't have one, just go to the "detaxe" counter). If your reimbursement is a credit to your bank account or credit card, it will be sent automatically once you scan the slip. If you chose cash, you'll need to go to the "detaxe" counter. If all of this is too confusing, download the flyer in English on the French customs website, www.douane.gouv.fr (it's a little tricky to find: Click "Particulier," "Détaxe," and then "conditions d'éligibilité" and scroll down to the bottom of the page) or search for "duty free" at the tourist office: www.parisinfo.com.

Telephones As of 2016, there are no more public telephone booths in France. If you want to pay for a call from phone that is not your own, you can still use a prepaid card with a code. Called a *carte* téléphonique *à code,* or a *carte prépayé,* they are sold at newsstands, smoke shops, or cafes where you see a TABAC sign. This is not always the cheapest or most practical way to make a call, so it may make more sense to investigate mobile phone options (see "Cell Phones" above).

The country code for France is 33. To make a local or long-distance call within France, dial the 10-digit number of the person or place you're calling. Mobile numbers begin with 06. Numbers beginning with 0 800, 0 805, and 0 809 are free in France; other numbers beginning with 8 are not. Many public service numbers are now four digits, and some are toll-free.

To make international calls from Paris, first dial 00 and then the country code (U.S. and Canada 1, U.K. 44, Ireland 353, Australia 61, New Zealand 64). Next dial the area code and number. For example, if you want to call the British Embassy in Washington, D.C., you would dial ✆ **001 202/588-6500.**

Terrorism France has reinforced its domestic security measures following the terror attacks of 2015 and 2017. But don't let the fear of terrorism dissuade you from traveling here. Just be vigilant and follow the advice of the local authorities. When you enter a new place, familiarize yourself with the emergency exits. If you see something untoward, or notice an abandoned bag or package on public transport, get off the train/bus/tram or move away, and alert either a member of staff or the **police** (© **17** or 112). Elsewhere, if you see anything suspicious, call the police or go to the nearest police station. In the unlikely event that you find yourself in danger, the words to remember are "escape, hide, alert." Move away from the danger, help others to move away, and alert the people around you. If you need to hide, turn off both the ring and vibration mode on your telephone. If you see security forces, do not run toward them or make sudden movements, and keep your hands up or open.

Time France is on Central European Time, which is 1 hour ahead of Greenwich Mean Time. French daylight saving time lasts from the last Sunday in March to the last Sunday in October. France uses the 24-hour

clock. So 13h is 1pm, 14h15 is 2:15pm, and so on.

Tipping By law, all bills in cafes, bars, and restaurants say *service compris*, which means the service charge is included. Waiters are paid a living wage and do not expect tips. However, they certainly won't mind if you leave one, and if you are planning on frequenting a certain cafe, it's a good investment to leave a euro or two after a meal. Taxi drivers usually appreciate a 5% to 10% tip, or for the fare to be rounded up to the next euro. The French give their hairdressers a tip of about 15%, and if you go to the theater, you're expected to tip the usher 1€ or 2€.

Toilets Paris is full of grey-colored street-toilet kiosks, which are a little daunting to the uninitiated, but free, and are automatically washed and disinfected after each use. If you're in dire need, you can duck into a cafe or brasserie to use the toilet, but expect to make a small purchase if you do so. In older establishments, you can still find Turkish toilets, otherwise known as squat toilets (holes in the ground). Fortunately, they are a dying breed.

Visas E.U. nationals don't need a visa to enter France. Nor do U.S., Canadian, Australian, New Zealand, or South African citizens for trips of up to 3 months. If non–E.U. citizens wish to stay longer than 3 months, they must apply to a French embassy or consulate for a long-term visa.

Visitor Information
The **Office du Tourisme et des Congrès** (www.parisinfo.com; 25 rue des Pyramides, 1er; © **01-49-52-42-63**) is open every day from 9am to 7pm from May to October (except May 1); from November to April it's open from 10am to 7pm. There are several other offices around Paris: **Anvers** (72 bd. Rochechouart, 9e; daily 10am–6pm except major holidays); **Gare du Nord** (18 rue de Dunkerque, 10e; daily 8am–6pm except major holidays); **Gare de l'Est** (place du 11-novembre-1918, 10e; Mon–Sat 8am–7pm except major holidays); and **Paris Rendezvous** (29 rue de Rivoli, 4e; Mon–Sat 10:30am–6:30pm).

Water Drinking water is safe, if not particularly tasty. To order tap water in a restaurant ask for *une carafe d'eau*.

USEFUL TERMS & PHRASES

I t is often amazing how a word or two of halting French will change your hosts' disposition in their home country. At the very least, try to learn a few numbers, basic greetings, and—above all—the life-raft phrase, *Parlez-vous anglais?* (Do you speak English?). Many Parisians speak passable English and will use it liberally if you demonstrate the basic courtesy of greeting them in their language. *Bonne chance!*

THE BASIC COURTESIES

English	French	Pronunciation
Yes/No	Oui/Non	**Wee/Noh**
Okay	D'accord	*Dah-core*
Please	S'il vous plaît	**Seel voo *play***
Thank you	Merci	*Mair-see*
You're welcome	De rien	**Duh ree-*ehn***
Hello (during daylight)	Bonjour	**Bohn-*jhoor***
Good evening	Bonsoir	**Bohn-*swahr***
Goodbye	Au revoir	**O ruh-*vwahr***
What's your name?	Comment vous appellez-vous?	**Kuh-*mahn* voo za-pell-ay-*voo*?**
My name is	Je m'appelle	**Jhuh ma-*pell***
How are you?	Comment allez-vous?	***Kuh*-mahn tahl-ay-*voo*?**
So-so	Comme ci, comme ça	**Kum-*see*, kum-*sah***
I'm sorry/excuse me	Pardon	**Pahr-*dohn***

GETTING AROUND & STREET SMARTS

English	French	Pronunciation
Do you speak English?	Parlez-vous anglais?	**Par-lay-voo ahn-*glay*?**
I don't speak French	Je ne parle pas français	**Jhuh ne parl pah frahn-*say***
I don't understand	Je ne comprends pas	**Jhuh ne kohm-*prahn* pah**
Could you speak more loudly/ more slowly?	Pouvez-vous parler plus fort/plus lentement?	**Poo-vay voo par-*lay* ploo for/ ploo lan-te-*ment*?**

English	French	Pronunciation
What is it?	Qu'est-ce que c'est?	Kess kuh say?
What time is it?	Qu'elle heure est-il?	Kel uhr eh-teel?
What?	Quoi?	Kwah?
How? or What did you say?	Comment?	Ko-mahn?
When?	Quand?	Kahn?
Where is?	Où est?	Ooh eh?
Who?	Qui?	Kee?
Why?	Pourquoi?	Poor-kwah?
here/there	ici/là	ee-see/lah
left/right	à gauche/à droite	a gohsh/a drwaht
straight ahead	tout droit	too drwah
Fill the tank (of a car)	Le plein, s'il vous plaît	Luh plen, seel-voo-play please
I want to get off at	Je voudrais descendre à	Jhe voo-dray day-sen drah-ah
airport	aéroport	air-o-por
bank	banque	bahnk
bridge	pont	pohn
bus station	gare routière	gar roo-tee-air
bus stop	arrêt de bus	ah-ray duh boohs
by means of a car	en voiture	ahn vwa-tur
cashier	caisse	kess
cathedral	cathédrale	ka-tay-dral
church	église	ay-gleez
driver's license	permis de conduire	per-mee deh con-dweer
elevator	ascenseur	ah-sahn-seuhr
entrance (to a port building or a city)	porte	port
exit (from a building or a freeway)	sortie	sor-tee
gasoline	carburant/essence	car-bur-ahn/eh-sahns
hospital	hôpital	oh-pee-tahl
luggage storage	consigne	kohn-seen-yuh
museum	musée	mu-zay
no smoking	défense de fumer	day-fahns de fu-may
one-day pass	ticket journalier	tee-kay jhoor-nall-ee-ay
one-way ticket	aller simple	ah-lay sam-pluh
police	police	po-leece
round-trip ticket	aller-retour	ah-lay re-toor
store	magasin	ma-ga-zehn
street	rue	roo
ticket	billet	bee-yay
toilets	les toilettes/les WC	lay twa-lets/les vay-say

NECESSITIES

English	French	Pronunciation
I'd like	Je voudrais	Jhe voo-*dray*
a room	une chambre	ewn *shahm*-bruh
the key	la clé (la clef)	la clay
How much does it cost?	C'est combien?/Ça coûte combien?	Say comb-bee-*ehn*?/Sah coot comb-bee-*ehn*?
That's expensive	C'est cher/chère	Say share
Do you take credit cards?	Est-ce que vous acceptez les cartes de credit?	Es-kuh voo zaksep-tay lay kart duh creh-*dee*?
I'd like to buy	Je voudrais acheter	Jhe voo-dray ahsh-*tay*
aspirin	aspirines	ahs-peer-*een*
condoms	préservatifs	pray-ser-va-*teef*
a gift	un cadeau	uh kah-*doe*
a hat	un chapeau	uh shah-*poh*
a map of the city	un plan de ville	uh plahn de *veel*
a newspaper	un journal	uh zhoor-*nahl*
a postcard	une carte postale	ewn carte pos-*tahl*
a road map	une carte routière	ewn cart roo-tee-*air*
some soap	du savon	dew sah-*vohn*
a stamp	un timbre	uh *tam*-bruh

NUMBERS & ORDINALS

English	French	Pronunciation
zero	zéro	*zare*-oh
one	un	oon
two	deux	duh
three	trois	twah
four	quatre	kaht-*ruh*
five	cinq	sank
six	six	seess
seven	sept	set
eight	huit	wheat
nine	neuf	noof
ten	dix	deess
eleven	onze	ohnz
twelve	douze	dooz
thirteen	treize	trehz
fourteen	quatorze	kah-*torz*
fifteen	quinze	kanz
sixteen	seize	sez
seventeen	dix-sept	deez-*set*
eighteen	dix-huit	deez-*wheat*
nineteen	dix-neuf	deez-*noof*
twenty	vingt	vehn

English	French	Pronunciation
thirty	trente	**trahnt**
forty	quarante	**ka-rahnt**
fifty	cinquante	**sang-kahnt**
one hundred	cent	**sahn**
one thousand	mille	**meel**
first	premier	**preh-mee-ay**
second	deuxième	**duhz-zee-em**
third	troisième	**twa-zee-em**
fourth	quatrième	**kaht-ree-em**
fifth	cinquième	**sank-ee-em**
sixth	sixième	**sees-ee-em**
seventh	septième	**set-ee-em**
eighth	huitième	**wheat-ee-em**
ninth	neuvième	**neuv-ee-em**
tenth	dixième	**dees-ee-em**

THE CALENDAR, DAYS & SEASONS

English	French	Pronunciation
January	Janvier	**jhan-vee-ay**
February	Février	**feh-vree-ay**
March	Mars	**marce**
April	Avril	**a-vreel**
May	Mai	**meh**
June	Juin	**jhwehn**
July	Juillet	**jhwee-ay**
August	Août	**oot**
September	Septembre	**sep-tahm-bruh**
October	Octobre	**ok-toh-bruh**
November	Novembre	**no-vahm-bruh**
December	Decembre	**day-sahm-bruh**
Sunday	Dimanche	**dee-mahnsh**
Monday	Lundi	**luhn-dee**
Tuesday	Mardi	**mahr-dee**
Wednesday	Mercredi	**mair-kruh-dee**
Thursday	Jeudi	**jheu-dee**
Friday	Vendredi	**vawn-druh-dee**
Saturday	Samedi	**sahm-dee**
yesterday	hier	**ee-air**
today	aujourd'hui	**o-jhord-dwee**
this morning/this afternoon	ce matin/cet après-midi	**suh ma-tan/set ah-preh-mee-dee**
tonight	ce soir	**suh swahr**
tomorrow	demain	**de-man**
summer	été	**aytt-ay**

English	French	Pronunciation
fall	automne	aw-*tonne*
winter	hiver	iv-*erre*
spring	printemps	prehn-*tawm*

BASIC MENU TERMS

Note: No need to get intimidated when ordering in French. Simply preface the French-language menu item with the phrase *"Je voudrais"* (jhe voo-*dray*), which means, "I would like. . . ." *Bon appétit!*

MEATS

English	French	Pronunciation
beef	boeuf	buhf
beef stew	pot au feu	poht o *fhe*
chicken	poulet	*poo*-lay
dumplings of chicken, veal, or fish (often pike)	quenelles	ke-*nelle*
duck breast	magret de canard	maa-*gray* duh can-*ar*
preserved duck	confit de canard	con-*fee* duh can-*ar*
fattened goose or duck liver	foie gras	fwah grah
ham	jambon	jham-bohn
kidneys	rognons	row-nyon
leg of lamb	gigot d'agneau	*jhi*-goh dahnyoh
lamb	agneau	lahn-*nyo*
lamb chop	cotelette d'agneau	koh-te-*let* dahn-*nyo*
liver	foie	fwah
pork	porc	pohr
potted and shredded pork	rillettes de porc	ree-*yet* duh pohr
rabbit	lapin	lah-*pan*
dried sausage	saucisson	soh-see-*sohn*
snails	escargots	ess-car-*goh*
steak	bifteck	beef-*tek*
steak with pepper sauce	steak au poivre	stake o *pwah*-vruh
sweetbreads	ris de veau	day *ree* duh voh
veal	veau	voh
veal stew with white sauce	blanquette de veau	blahn-*ket* duh voh

FISH/SEAFOOD

English	French	Pronunciation
fish	poisson	pwoss-*ohn*
herring	hareng	ahr-*rahn*
lobster	homard	oh-*mahr*
monkfish	lotte	loht
mussels	moules	*moohl*

English	French	Pronunciation
oysters	huîtres	**hoo-*ee*-truhs**
pike	brochet	**broh-*chay***
sea bass	bar	**bar**
sea bream	dorade	**dor-*ahde***
shrimp	crevettes	**kreh-*vette***
smoked salmon	saumon fumé	**soh-*mohn* fu-may**
trout	truite	**tru-eet**
tuna	thon	**tohn**

SIDES/APPETIZERS

English	French	Pronunciation
bread	pain	**pan**
butter	beurre	**bhuhr**
fries	frites	**freet**
green beans	haricots verts	***ah*-ri-co ver**
rice	riz	**ree**
salad	salade	**sa-*lahd***
vegetables	légumes	**lay-*goom***

BEVERAGES

English	French	Pronunciation
beer	bière	**bee-*aire***
coffee (espresso)	café	**ka-*fay***
coffee (decaf)	décaféiné/déca	**day-kah-fay-nay/day-ca**
coffee (with milk)	café crème/café au lait	**ka-fay krem/ka-fay o-*lay***
coffee (long, with hot water)	allongé	**al-on-djhay**
milk	lait	***lay***
orange juice	jus d'orange	**zhoo dor-*ahnjhe***
soda	soda	**so-*da***
tap water	eau du robinet	**oh doo rob-in-ay**
tea	thé	***tay***
tea (herbal)	tisane	**tee-*zahn***
tea (w/lemon)	thé au citron	**tay o see-*tran***
water	eau	**oh**
wine (red)	vin rouge	**vhin *rooj***
wine (white)	vin blanc	**vhin *blahn***

SPICES/CONDIMENTS

English	French	Pronunciation
mayonnaise	mayonnaise	**may-o-*nayse***
mustard	moutarde	**moo-*tard***
olive oil	huile d'olive	**weele dol-*eeve***

English	French	Pronunciation
pepper	poivre	*pwah*-vruh
salt	sel	*sel*
sugar	sucre	*sook*-ruh
vinegar	vinaigre	vin-*aigre*

Index

See also Accommodations and Restaurant indexes, below.

General Index

5e Cru, 249

A

The Abbey Bookshop, 224
Abou d'Abi Bazar, 227
Académie Française, 14
Accatone, 242
accessibility, 288
  of accommodations, 50
  in Louvre, 141
accommodations. *See also*
  Accommodations index
  accessibility, 50
  aparthotels, 79
  bed-and-breakfasts, 78
  Belleville, Canal St-Martin, and
    La Villette (10th, 19th, 20th
    arrondissements), 63–64
  best of, 5–6
  best rates, 44
  Champs-Élysées, Trocadéro,
    and western Paris (8th, 16th,
    17th arrondissements), 54–56
  Eiffel Tower (7th
    arrondissement), 73–75
  French star system, 45
  high and low seasons, 45
  Latin Quarter (5th & 13th
    arrondissements), 64, 68–70
  Louvre and Ile de la Cité (1st
    arrondissement), 46–47
  Marais (3rd & 4th
    arrondissements), 47, 50–52
  Montmartre (18th
    arrondissement), 58–61
  Montparnasse (14th & 15th
    arrondissements), 75–77
  Opéra and Grands Boulevards
    (2nd & 9th arrondissements),
    56–58
  Palace hotels, 57
  République, Bastille, and
    eastern Paris (11th & 12th
    arrondissements), 61–63
  short-term rentals, 77–78
  single rooms, 46
  St-Germain-des-Prés and
    Luxembourg (6th
    arrondissement), 70–73
  what to expect, 43–44
  when to reserve, 45
  Wi-Fi in, 54
Action Ecoles, 242
addresses, finding, 280
agnès b., 227
air travel, 277–278
A La Mère de Famille, 229–230
Allée des Brouillards, 203

amenities in hotels, 43–44
antiques and collectibles
  shopping, 223
antiques fairs, 222
Antoine & Lili, 227
aparthotels, 79
apéritif, 2
Apollo Fountain, 262
Arc de Triomphe, 3, 156–157
  history of Paris, 17
  neighborhood of, 36
  one-day itinerary, 27
  two-day itinerary, 29
arcades, 218
architectural landmarks, best of,
  3–4
area codes, 287
Arènes de Lutèce, 11
arrondissements, 33, 280
Arte (Cinemacity app), 206
Ateliers Berthier, 236
Atomes, 223
attractions
  Belleville, Canal St-Martin,
    and northeast Paris (10th,
    19th, 20th arrondissements),
    167–172
  Champs-Élysées, Trocadéro,
    and western Paris (8th, 16th,
    17th arrondissements), 156–
    164
  Eiffel Tower (7th
    arrondissement), 182–188
  for kids, 193–195
  Latin Quarter (5th & 13th
    arrondissements), 172–178
  Louvre and Ile de la Cité (1st
    arrondissement), 129–146
  Marais (3rd & 4th
    arrondissements), 148–155
  Montmartre (18th
    arrondissement), 164–166
  Montparnasse (14th & 15th
    arrondissements), 188–190
  Opéra and Grands Boulevards
    (2nd & 9th arrondissements),
    146–148
  République, Bastille, and
    eastern Paris (11th & 12th
    arrondissements), 166–167
  St-Germain-des-Prés and
    Luxembourg (6th
    arrondissement), 179–182
Au Lapin Agile, 204–205, 242
Australian Customs Service, 286
authentic experiences, best of,
  2–3
Autolib,' 285
Azzedine Alaïa, 227

B

Baiser Salé, 243
Ballet de l'Opéra de Paris, 237,
  238
Banana Café, 252
Barbarian invasions of Paris, 11
Barbés, neighborhood of, 38

bars
  cafes, compared, 247
  LGBT bars and clubs, 252–253
  list of, 247–249
  live music, 245–246
  wine bars, 249–250
Basilica of St-Denis, 11
Basilique du Sacré Coeur. *See*
  Sacré Coeur
Bastille. *See* Bastille opera house;
  Place de la Bastille
Bastille opera house, 38
Bateau-Lavoir, 201–202
Batofar, 250
Beach, Sylvia, 225
beauty and perfume shopping,
  223–224
Beauvais airport, 278
bed-and-breakfasts, 78
Belle Epoque, 18–19
Belleville, 8
Belleville, Canal St-Martin, and La
  Villette (10th, 19th, 20th
  arrondissements)
  accommodations, 63–64
  attractions, 167–172
  neighborhood of, 39
  restaurants, 105–108
  shopping, 217
Berkeley Books of Paris, 225
BHV, 219
Bibliothèque Forney, 209
Bibliothèque National François
  Mitterrand, 21
Bijoux Blues, 233
Bijoux Burma, 233
bike riding, 3, 196
  in Fontainebleau, 272
  tours, 191–192
  Velib,' 3, 22, 32, 283–284
boat tours, 190–191, 285
Bois de Boulogne, 9, 197–198
  history of Paris, 18
  neighborhood of, 37
Bois de Vincennes, 39, 198–199
bookstores, 224–227
Botoù, 228
Boulevard St-Michel
  history of Paris, 20
  neighborhood of, 40
Bourse, neighborhood of, 35
bread, 116
breakfast in hotels, 44
bridges, 151
brocantes (antiques fairs), 222
bus tours, 8, 191
buses
  into Paris, 279
  within Paris, 282–283
business hours, 287
Buttes Chaumont, 18

C

cabaret, 239–242
Cabaret Sauvage, 171, 245
cafes
  bars, compared, 247
  best of, 126–128
  list of, 247–249

Canada Border Services Agency, 286
Canal de l'Ourcq, 17
Canal St-Martin, 170. *See also* Belleville, Canal St-Martin, and La Villette (10th, 19th, 20th arrondissements)
cancellations on hotels, 45
candlelight tours of Vaux-le-Vicomte, 269
Capetian dynasty, 12–13
Carnavalet, neighborhood of, 36
Carolingian dynasty, 11–12
Caroll, 228
Carousel du Louvre, neighborhood of, 34
Carp Pond, 274
cars
    driving tips, 279–280, 284, 288
    renting, 285
Cathedral of Notre-Dame. *See* Notre-Dame
Cave des Abbesses, 231
Caveau de la Huchette, 244
cellphones, 287
Centre International du Vitrail, 266
Centre Pompidou, 4, 148–149
    history of Paris, 20
    neighborhood of, 36
chain stores, 228
Chambre de l'Impératrice, 273
Champs de Mars
    family itinerary, 30
    neighborhood of, 41
Champs-Élysées
    history of Paris, 20
    one-day itinerary, 27
    romantic itinerary, 32
    two-day itinerary, 29
Champs-Élysées, Trocadéro, and western Paris (8th, 16th, 17th arrondissements)
    accommodations, 54–56
    attractions, 156–164
    neighborhood of, 36–37
    restaurants, 93–96
    shopping, 216–217
chanson, 242
Chapel (at Versailles), 262
Chapelle de la Trinité, 273
Charles X, 17–18
Chartres day trip, 263–266
    arrival information, 263
    cathedral tours, 263–266
    Old Town tours, 266
    visitor information, 263
Chartres en Lumières, 266
Château de Vincennes, 9, 198–199
Château des Brouillards, 203
Château of Versailles
    history of Paris, 15
    Versailles day trip, 258–260
cheap attractions. *See* free & cheap attractions
Chez Michou, 240
Chez Moune, 250
children. *See* kids

Chinatown, 112
chocolate, 229–230
churches, music in, 246
Cimetiére du Montparnasse, 42, 189
Cimetiére du Père-Lachaise. *See* Père-Lachaise cemetery
cinema archives, 243
Cinéma en Plein Air, 172
Cinemacity app, 206
Cinémathèque Française, 243
Cité de l'Architecture, neighborhood of, 37
Cité des Enfants, 170
Cité des Sciences et de l'Industrie, 170
city layout, 33
classes
    cooking, 193
    language, 193
classical music venues, 238–239
Clos Montmartre Vineyard, 204
Clos Normand, 268
clothing stores, 227–229
coffee, terminology, 127
Colette, 232
College de France, 14
Comédie-Française, 236
Comptoir des Abbayes, 231
Comptoir des Cotonniers, 227
concerts
    in churches, 246
    free, 7
Conciergerie, 34, 134
Concrete, 251
consulates, 288–289
cooking classes, 193
"Coronation of Napoléon," 141
costs, typical, 290–291
Cour Carrée, 15
Cour de la Fontaine, 274
Cour des Offices, 272
Cour du Cheval Blanc, 273
Cours des Femmes, 134
The Crazy Horse, 240
Cristal Room, 157
crown jewels, 140
Crown of Thorns, 133
Crypte Archéologique du Parvis Notre-Dame, 135
currency values, 290
customs rules, 286, 288

D
"Dance at Le Moulin de la Galette, Montmartre," 187
dance clubs, 250–252
dance performances, 237
day trips
    Chartres, 263–266
    Disneyland Paris, 274–276
    Fontainebleau, 271–274
    Giverny, 266–268
    trains for, 255
    Vaux-le-Vicomte, 269–271
    Versailles, 255–262
dentists, 288
department stores, 219–221
Detaille 1905, 224

Didier Ludot, 229
The Different Company, 224
dining. *See* restaurants
Disney Studios, 276
Disneyland Paris, 274–276
doctors, 288
Domaine de Marie Antoinette, 262
drinking laws, 288
drinking water, 294
driving tips, 279–280, 284, 288
Du Pareil au Même, 228

E
eastern Paris. *See* République, Bastille, and eastern Paris (11th & 12th arrondissements)
Ecole Militaire, neighborhood of, 41
Editons de Parfums Fréderic Malle, 224
Eglise des Soldats, 185
Eglise du Dôme, 185
Eiffel Tower, 2, 4, 182–183
    family itinerary, 30
    history of Paris, 19
    one-day itinerary, 23
    two-day itinerary, 27
    walking up, 183
Eiffel Tower and nearby (7th arrondissement)
    accommodations, 73–75
    attractions, 182–188
    neighborhood of, 41–42
    restaurants, 118–122
    shopping, 219
electricity, 288
embassies, 288–289
emergencies, 289
English Garden, 274
English-language shows, 240
Enlightenment, 16–17
entertainment and nightlife, 235–254
    bars and cafes, 247–249
    cabaret, 239–242
    dance clubs, 250–252
    dance performances, 237
    LGBT bars and clubs, 252–253
    live music, 243–247
    movies, 242–243
    multiuse venues, 237–238
    opera and classical music, 238–239
    schedule listings, 236
    spectator sports, 253–254
    theater, 236
    tickets, 235
    wine bars, 249–250
Espace Dalí, 165
etiquette, 289
Eure River, 266

F
families
    especially for kids, 193–195
    itinerary for, 30–31
    kids in restaurants, 98
    Luxembourg Gardens, 178

farmer's markets, 3
FastPass system, 276
Fauchon, 230
Favela Chic, 251
ferries, 280
Festival Chopin, 241
Feydeau, 218
Fifi Chachnil, 229
flea markets, 222–223
Fnac, 232
Fondation Claude Monet à Giverny, 267
Fondation Jérôme Seydoux-Pathé, 243
Fondation Louis Vuitton, 4, 157, 198
Fontainebleau
  arrival information, 271
  chateau tours, 273–274
  day trip, 271–274
  garden tours, 274
  history of Paris, 14
  visitor information, 272
Fontainebleau Forest, 274
food. See restaurants
food and drink shopping, 229–232
food markets, 221–222
football (soccer), 253–254
Forum des Halles, 145
  history of Paris, 20
  neighborhood of, 34
Forum des Images, 243
Foucault's Pendulum, 178
François Pralus, 230
free & cheap attractions, best of, 7–8
Free'p'Star, 229
French Revolution, 16–17
French terms and phrases, 295–301
French Trotters, 227–228

G

Gaîté Lyrique, 149
Galerie des Glaces (Hall of Mirrors), 260, 261
Galerie Vivienne, 218
Galerie–Musée Baccarat, 157–158
Galeries Lafayette, 220
Galignani, 225
Gallery of François I, 273
Gallery of the Kings of Judah and Israel, 132
Gallo-Roman baths, 11
Garden of Diane, 274
gardens
  best of, 9
  Fontainebleau day trip, 274
  Versailles day trip, 262
Gare de Lyon, neighborhood of, 39
gargoyles, 137
Gibert Joseph, 226, 234
gift and souvenir stores, 232
Giverny, 9
  arrival information, 267
  day trip, 266–268

tickets, 267
visitor information, 267
Grand Apartments, 260
Grand Canal, 262
Grand Magasins, neighborhood of, 35
Grand Palais, 19, 158
Grand Salon, 270
Grande Carrée, 136
Grandes Serres, 173
Grands Appartements, 273
Grands Boulevards. See Opéra and Grands Boulevards (2nd & 9th arrondissements)
Grévin, 31
guided tours, 192–193
Guignol (puppet show), 195, 198

H

healthcare, 289
Hèloïse and Abélard, 168
Hidalgo, Anne, 22
hiking in Fontainebleau, 272
history of Paris, 10–21
  Barbarian invasions, 11
  Capetian dynasty, 12–13
  Commune to Belle Epoque, 18–19
  Enlightenment to Revolution, 16–17
  Louis XIV, 15–16
  medieval glory, 13
  Merovingian & Carolingian dynasties, 11–12
  Napolean Bonaparte, 17
  postwar era, 20–21
  prehistoric Paris, 10
  Renaissance, 14
  restoration and urban renewal, 17–18
  Roman rule, 10–11
  World Wars, 19–20
HM Revenue Customs, 286
holidays, 289
horse racing, 253
hospitals, 290
hot-air balloon tours, 192
Hôtel Crillon, 164
Hôtel de Clisson, 211
Hôtel de la Marine, 164
Hôtel de Lamoignon, 213
Hôtel de Rohan-Strasbourg, 211
Hôtel de Sens, 209
Hôtel de Soubise, 211
Hôtel de St-Aignan, 211
Hôtel de Sully, 213–214
Hôtel de Ville, 12, 14, 150
Hôtel des Invalides, 184–185
Hôtel Donon, 212
hotels. See accommodations
hotlines, 290
housewares stores, 232–233
"How to Become a Parisian in One Hour," 240
Hugo, Victor, 150, 214

I

ice skating, 9, 196
Ile de la Cité, 2. See also Louvre and Ile de la Cité (1st arrondissement)
  history of Paris, 10
  one-day itinerary, 26
Ile St-Louis, 15
immunizations, 290
Institut du Monde Arabe
  history of Paris, 21
  neighborhood of, 40
Institut Suédois, 213
Internet access, availability of, 54, 290
itineraries
  for families, 30–31
  iconic Paris in one day, 23–27
  iconic Paris in three days, 29–30
  iconic Paris in two days, 27–29
  for romantics, 31–32

J

Japanese restaurants, 89
Jardin d'Acclimatation, 9, 195, 197
Jardin des Plantes, 8, 172–173
  family itinerary, 31
  neighborhood of, 40
Jardin des Tuileries. See Tuileries Garden
Jardin du Luxembourg. See Luxembourg Gardens
Jardin Nelson Mandela, 194
Jardin Shakespeare, 197
Jardins du Trocadéro, neighborhood of, 37
Jazz à La Villette, 241
jazz clubs, 243–245
Jéroboam, 249–250
Jeux Descartes, 234
jewelry stores, 233
Joyce, James, 225

K

kids. See also families
  attractions for, 193–195
  clothing stores, 228–229
  Luxembourg Gardens, activities in, 178
  in restaurants, 98
Kiliwatch, 229
King's Apartments, 260, 261
King's Bedroom, 261, 270

L

La Bellevilloise, 246
La Bovida, 232–233
La Champmeslé, 252
La Cigale, 245
La Cité de l'Architecture et du Patrimoine, 158
La Coupole, 19, 189
"La Gare St-Lazare," 187
La Grande Epicerie de Paris, 230

La Madeleine, 3, 158–159
La Maison Ivre, 233
La Promenade Plantée, 166
La Rotonde, 189
La Seine Musicale, 237
La Tuile à Loup, 232
La Vaissellerie, 233
La Villette. See Belleville, Canal
  St-Martin, and La Villette (10th,
  19th, 20th arrondissements)
"Lady and the Unicorn," 177
Lafayette Homme, 220
Lafayette Maison, 220
L'Alimentation Générale, 245
landmarks. See architectural
  landmarks
language classes, 193
language usage, 290, 295–301
L'Art du Papier, 234
Latin Quarter (5th & 13th
  arrondissements), 8
  accommodations, 64, 68–70
  attractions, 172–178
  family itinerary, 30
  neighborhood of, 39–40
  restaurants, 108–114
  two-day itinerary, 28
Le 3w Kafe, 252–253
Le Baron Rouge, 250
Le Bon Marché, 220
Le Carreau du Temple, 246–247
Le Caveau de la Huchette,
  neighborhood of, 40
Le Centquatre, 247
Le Champo, 242
Le Dôme, 19, 189
Le Duc des Lombards, 244
Le Raidd, 252
Le Relais de l'Entrecôte, 30
Le Select, 19, 189
Le Sunset, 244
Le Sunside, 244
Left Bank, 33
  accommodations, 64–77
  addresses, finding, 280
  attractions, 172–190
  neighborhood of, 39–42
  restaurants, 108–124
  shopping, 218–219
Legrand Filles et Fils, 232
Les Berges, 8, 22, 196
  romantic itinerary, 32
  three-day itinerary, 29
Les Catacombes, 42, 189–190
Les Caves Populaires, 250
Les Domaines Qui Montent, 232
les grands magasins (department
  stores), 219–221
Les Halles, 145
  history of Paris, 12
  neighborhood of, 34
Les Invalides
  history of Paris, 15, 17
  neighborhood of, 41–42
Les Mots à la Bouche, 226
Les Souffleurs, 253
Les Trois Baudets, 242

LGBT bars and clubs, 252–253
LGBT travelers, 290
"Liberty Guiding the People," 141
Librairie La Hune, 226–227
Library of the History of the City
  of Paris, 213
Lido de Paris, 240
lingerie stores, 229
L'International, 245
live music, 243–247
L'Objet qui Parle, 223
lost and found, 290
"The Lost Generation," 225
Louis XIV, 15–16
Louis XV, 16
Louis XVI, 16
Louis XVIII, 17
Louvre and Ile de la Cité (1st
  arrondissement). See also
  Musée du Louvre
  accommodations, 46–47
  attractions, 129–146
  neighborhood of, 34
  restaurants, 82–90
  shopping, 215–216
Louxor, 243
lunches, prix-fixe, 91
Luxembourg Gardens, 9, 179–
  180. See also St-Germain-des-
  Prés and Luxembourg (6th
  arrondissement)
  family itinerary, 30
  kids' activities, 178
  picnicking, 7
  two-day itinerary, 28

M
Machine du Moulin Rouge, 251
"Madame Récamier," 141
magazines, 291
mail, 290
Maille, 230–231
Maison à l'Enseigne du Faucheur,
  209
Maison à l'Enseigne du Mouton,
  210
Maison de Balzac, 159
Maison de Radio France, 20
Maison de UNESCO, 20
Maison de Victor Hugo, 150, 214
Make Up Forever, 224
Mango, 228
Manufacture Nationale des
  Gobelins, 9, 173, 176
Marais, 8
  history of Paris, 12, 15, 16, 20
  two-day itinerary, 28
  walking tour, 206–214
Marais and nearby (3rd & 4th
  arrondissements)
  accommodations, 47, 50–52
  attractions, 148–155
  neighborhood of, 36
  restaurants, 90–93
  shopping, 216
Marché aux Puces de la Porte de
  Vanves, 222–223

Marché aux Puces de Paris
  St-Ouen–Clignancourt, 223
Marché Bastille, 221
Marché Batignolles, 221
Marché Cours de Vincennes, 221
Marché d'Aligre, 221
Marché Edgar Quinet, 221
Marché Grenelle, 221
Marché Monge, 222
Marché Raspail, 222
Marché Saxe-Breteuil, 222
marchés, 221–222
Marie Antoinette's cell, 134
Marie Antoinette's last letter, 211
Marie Puce, 229
Marionnaud, 223
Marly Horses, 164
Marmottan, neighborhood of, 37
Medici Fountain, 179
medieval glory of Paris, 13
Ménagerie, 31, 173
Ménilmontant, neighborhood of,
  39
Merovingian dynasty, 11–12
Métro, 281–282
Molière and La Fontaine, 168
"Mona Lisa," 139, 140, 142
Monet, Claude. See Giverny
money, saving. See saving money
Montagne St-Geneviève, 10, 11
Montmartre (18th
  arrondissement), 8
  accommodations, 58–61
  arcades, 218
  attractions, 164–166
  history of Paris, 11, 19
  neighborhood of, 38
  restaurants, 100–102
  shopping, 217
  three-day itinerary, 30
  walking tour, 200–206
Montmartrobus
  Montmartre walking tour, 203
  three-day itinerary, 30
Montparnasse (14th & 15th
  arrondissements)
  accommodations, 75–77
  attractions, 188–190
  history of Paris, 19
  neighborhood of, 42
  restaurants, 122–124
  shopping, 219
Morrison, Jim, 168
Mosquée de Paris, 9, 31
Moulin de la Galette, 202–203
Moulin du Radet, 202–203
Moulin Rouge, 241
movies, 242–243
Musée Bourdelle, 190
Musée Carnavalet, 150–151
Musée Cognacq-Jay, 152
  Marais walking tour, 212
  neighborhood of, 36
Musée d'Art et Histoire du
  Judaïsme, 152–153, 211
Musée d'Art Moderne de la Ville
  de Paris, 159–160

Musée de Cluny, 177
  neighborhood of, 40
  two-day itinerary, 28
Musée de la Chasse et de la Nature, 153
Musée de la Musique, 170–171
Musée de la Vie Romantique, 35, 148
Musée de l'Armée, 184
Musée de l'Homme, 160
Musée de l'Institut du Monde Arabe, 176
Musée de l'Orangerie, 136–137, 267
Musée de l'Ordre de la Libération, 185
Musée de Montmartre, 166
  Montmartre walking tour, 205
  three-day itinerary, 30
Musée des Archives Nationale, 211
Musée des Arts Décoratifs, 137–138
Musée des Arts et Métiers, 31, 154
Musée des Egouts de Paris, 185
Musée des Impressionismes, 267, 268
Musée des Plans et Reliefs, 184
Musée d'Orsay, 6, 185–187
  history of Paris, 21
  neighborhood of, 41
  three-day itinerary, 29
Musée du Louvre, 2, 6, 138–141
  history of Paris, 14, 15, 17
  map of, 139
  one-day itinerary, 27
  pyramid of, 21
  romantic itinerary, 31
  ticket lines, avoiding, 138
  two-day itinerary, 28
Musée du Luxembourg, 180
Musée du Quai Branly, 7, 187–188
  history of Paris, 21
  neighborhood of, 41
  three-day itinerary, 29
Musée Grévin, 146
Musée Guimet, neighborhood of, 37
Musée Jacquemart-André, 7, 160–161
  neighborhood of, 37
  romantic itinerary, 32
Musée Marmottan Monet, 161, 267
Musée Napoléon 1er, 274
Musée National d'Art Moderne, 149
Musée National des Arts Asiatiques Guimet, 161–162
Musée National du Moyen Age, 177
Musée National Eugène Delacroix, 180
Musée Nissim de Camondo, 37, 162
Musée Picasso Paris, 7, 36

Musée Rodin, 188
  neighborhood of, 41
  romantic itinerary, 32
Musée Zadkine, 30, 180–181
Muséum National d'Histoire Naturelle, 31, 176
museums
  best of, 6–7
  free admission, 152
  sightseeing packages, 135
  ticket lines, avoiding, 155
music
  chanson, 242
  in churches, 246
  free concerts, 7
  live music, 243–247
  opera and classical music, 238–239
  summer music festivals, 241

N
Napoleon Bonaparte, 17
Napoleon III, 18
Napoleon's Tomb, 184–185
neighborhoods, 34–42
  best of, 8
  Left Bank, 39–42
  Right Bank, 34–39
New Morning, 245
New Zealand Customs Service, 286
newspapers, 291
nightlife. See entertainment and nightlife
northeast Paris. See Belleville, Canal St-Martin, and La Villette (10th, 19th, 20th arrondissements)
Notre Dame de la Belle Verière, 264
Notre-Dame, 2, 3, 129, 132–134
  family itinerary, 31
  history of Paris, 12
  map of, 133
  neighborhood of, 34
  one-day itinerary, 27
  tower tours, 137
  two-day itinerary, 28
Nuit Blanche, 22

O
Odéon, Théâtre de l'Europe, 236
Olympia, 245
one-day itinerary, 23–27
Open Café, 253
Opéra and Grands Boulevards (2nd & 9th arrondissements)
  accommodations, 56–58
  attractions, 146–148
  neighborhood of, 34–35
  restaurants, 96–100
  shopping, 216
Opéra Bastille, 21, 238
Opéra Comique, 238
Opéra de Paris, 238–239
Opéra Garnier, 146–147
opera venues, 238–239

Orangerie. See Musée de l'Orangerie
Orcanta, 229
Orly airport, 278
outdoors, 9, 195–199

P
Palace hotels, 57
Palais Brogniart, neighborhood of, 35
Palais de Chaillot
  neighborhood of, 37
  one-day itinerary, 23
Palais de Tokyo, 162
  family itinerary, 31
  neighborhood of, 37
Palais du Luxembourg, 15
Palais Garnier, 4, 147, 238
  neighborhood of, 35
  romantic itinerary, 32
Palais Royal, 141, 143
  history of Paris, 15, 16
  romantic itinerary, 31
Panthéon, 3, 177–178
  family itinerary, 30
  history of Paris, 11
  neighborhood of, 40
  two-day itinerary, 28
Paradis Latin, 241–242
Parc de Bagatelle, 197
Parc de Belleville, 8
Parc de la Villette, 39, 171–172
Parc des Buttes Chaumont, 39, 172
Parc Floral, 7, 9, 198
Parc Monceau, 37, 163
Parc Zoologique de Paris, 9, 166–167, 198
Paris
  addresses, finding, 280
  arrival information, 277–280
  authentic experiences, best of, 2–3
  city layout, 33
  current situation, 21–22
  family itinerary, 30–31
  fast facts, 287–294
  free & cheap attractions, best of, 7–8
  history of, 10–21
  neighborhoods, 34–42
  neighborhoods, best of, 8
  one-day itinerary, 23–27
  public transportation, 281–283
  romantic itinerary, 31–32
  terminology, 295–301
  three-day itinerary, 29–30
  two-day itinerary, 27–29
  unexpected pleasures, best of, 8–9
Paris Commune of 1870, 18
Paris Passlib' cards, 135, 155
Paris Plage, 8, 22, 196
parks, 9, 197–199
Passage Choiseul, 218
Passage des Panoramas, 218
Passage du Grand Cerf, 218
Passage Jouffroy, 218

Passage Verdeau, 218
Passerelle Simone de Beauvoir, 151
passports, 291–292
pastry shops, best of, 124
Patrick Roger, 230
Père-Lachaise cemetery, 8, 167–170
  history of Paris, 17
  map of, 169
  neighborhood of, 39
perfume shopping, 223–224
Petit Palais, 19, 163
Petit Trianon, 262
Petits Appartements, 273, 274
pharmacies, 292
Philharmonie de Paris, 171, 239
Picasso Paris, 154–155
picnicking
  Luxembourg Gardens, 7
  terminology, 82
Piscine Josephine Baker, 199
place Billard, 266
Place Dalida, 203–204
Place Dauphine
  history of Paris, 14
  one-day itinerary, 26
Place de la Bastille, 167
  history of Paris, 18
  neighborhood of, 38
Place de la Concorde, 3, 163–164
  one-day itinerary, 27
  romantic itinerary, 32
  two-day itinerary, 29
Place de la République, 22
  history of Paris, 18
  neighborhood of, 38
Place des Abbesses
  Montmartre walking tour, 200–201
  neighborhood of, 38
  three-day itinerary, 30
Place des Victoires, 15
Place des Vosges, 155
  history of Paris, 14
  Marais walking tour, 214
  neighborhood of, 36
  two-day itinerary, 28
Place du Châtelet, neighborhood of, 34
Place du Marché Ste-Catherine, 213
Place du Tertre
  Montmartre walking tour, 205–206
  neighborhood of, 38
Place du Trocadéro
  history of Paris, 18
  neighborhood of, 37
Place St-Blaise, neighborhood of, 39
Place Vendôme, 143
  history of Paris, 15
  romantic itinerary, 32
Plastiques, 233
Pletzl, 210
Point Ephemere, 247
Point Zéro, 132
police, 292

Pont Alexandre III, 19, 151
Pont d'Austerlitz, 17
Pont des Arts, 151
  history of Paris, 17
  romantic itinerary, 32
Pont d'Iéna, 17
Pont Marie, 151
Pont Neuf, 2, 151
  history of Paris, 14
  one-day itinerary, 26
Pont St-Louis, 17
Porte St-Denis, 15
Porte St-Martin, 15
postwar Paris, 20–21
Pré Catelan, 197
prehistoric Paris, 10
Printemps, 220–221
prix-fixe lunches, 91
Promenade Plantée, 9
Promod, 228
public pools, 199
public transportation, 281–283
puppet shows, 195, 198

Q
Queen's Apartments, 260, 261

R
rampart of Philippe Auguste, 208–209
Ramses II statue, 141
Reflet Medecis, 242
refunds on taxes, 217, 293
Renaissance, 14
République, Bastille, and eastern Paris (11th & 12th arrondissements)
  accommodations, 61–63
  attractions, 166–167
  neighborhood of, 38–39
  restaurants, 102–104
  shopping, 217
RER, 282
reservations
  for hotels, 45
  for restaurants, 81–82
restaurants. See also Restaurants index
  after-hours dining, 93
  annual closings, 81
  Belleville, Canal St-Martin, and La Villette (10th, 19th, 20th arrondissements), 105–108
  best of, 4–5
  cafes, 126–128
  Champs-Élysées, Trocadéro, and western Paris (8th, 16th, 17th arrondissements), 93–96
  choosing, 82
  Eiffel Tower (7th arrondissement), 118–122
  hours, 81
  kids in, 98
  Latin Quarter (5th & 13th arrondissements), 108–114
  Louvre and Ile de la Cité (1st arrondissement), 82–90

Marais (3rd & 4th arrondissements), 90–93
  menu terminology, 299–301
  Montmartre (18th arrondissement), 100–102
  Montparnasse (14th & 15th arrondissements), 122–124
  Opéra and Grands Boulevards (2nd & 9th arrondissements), 96–100
  picnics from, 82
  République, Bastille, and eastern Paris (11th & 12th arrondissements), 102–104
  reservations, 81–82
  rude waiters, 88
  St-Germain-des-Prés and Luxembourg (6th arrondissement), 114–118
  tearooms, 125–126
  tipping, 86
  websites for foodies, 81
Revolution (French), 16–17
Rex Club, 251–252
Right Bank, 33
  accommodations, 46–64
  addresses, finding, 280
  attractions, 129–172
  neighborhoods, 34–39
  restaurants, 82–108
  shopping, 215–217
Rive Droite. See Right Bank
Rive Gauche. See Left Bank
Rives de Seine, 196
Roissy-Charles-de-Gaulle (CDG) airport, 277–278
Roman rule of Paris, 10–11
romantic itinerary, 31–32
Royal Apartments, 273
Royal Portal, 264
rude waiters, 88
rue Chantault, 266
rue Cler, neighborhood of, 42
rue de Menilmontant, 8
rue de Rivoli
  history of Paris, 17
  neighborhood of, 34
rue des Rosiers, 210
rue du Bourg, 266
rue du Temple, 210–211
rue Etienne Marcel, neighborhood of, 35
rue François Miron, 209–210
rue Montorgueil, neighborhood of, 35
rue Mouffetard, 8
rue Oberkampf, neighborhood of, 38
rue St-Jacques, 11
rue St-Rustique, 205
running, 199

S
Sacré Coeur, 2, 8, 164–165
  Montmartre walking tour, 206
  neighborhood of, 38
  three-day itinerary, 30

safety
in Louvre, 141
tips for, 292
Sainte-Chapelle, 3, 12, 134, 143–144
Saint-Marc, 218
sales (shopping), 231
Salle à Manger, 270
Salle de Bal, 273
Salle des Gens d'Arms, 134
Salle du Trône, 274
Salle Favart, 238
Salle Richelieu, 236
Salmon House, 266
Salon d'Apollon, 261
Salon de Guerre, 261
Salon de Paix, 261
Salon des Muses, 270
Salon d'Hercule, 261
Salon Louis XIII, 273
San Francisco Book Company, 225
sandwich bars, 92
saving money
free & cheap attractions, best of, 7–8
free museum admission, 152
hotel rates, 44
tickets, 235
typical costs, 290–291
walking up Eiffel Tower, 183
Seated Scribe statue, 141
Seine
addresses, finding, 280
Les Berges, 8, 22, 29, 32, 196
Paris Plage, 8
prior to origin of Paris, 10
walking at night, 2
senior travel, 292–293
Sephora, 223
Serment de Jeu de Paume, 211
Shakespeare and Company, 225, 225–226
shoe stores, 227–229
shopping, 215–234
antiques and collectibles, 223
antiques fairs, 222
arcades, 218
beauty and perfume, 223–224
bookstores, 224–227
clothing and shoes, 227–229
department stores, 219–221
flea markets, 222–223
food and drink, 229–232
food markets, 221–222
gifts and souvenirs, 232
hours, 220
housewares, 232–233
jewelry, 233
Left Bank, 218–219
Right Bank, 215–217
sales, 231
stationery, 234
taxes, 217
toys and games, 234
short-term rentals, 77–78
Showcase, 252
sightseeing packages, 135

smoking, 293
soccer (football), 253–254
Social Club, 252
SoGymnase, 240
Sorbonne
history of Paris, 13, 20
neighborhood of, 39
two-day itinerary, 28
souvenir stores, 232
specialty grocery stores, 230–231
spectator sports, 253–254
Square du Vert Gallant, 151
one-day itinerary, 26
romantic itinerary, 31
star system for hotels, 45
stationery stores, 234
St-Chapelle, neighborhood of, 34
St-Etienne-du-Mont, 3, 178
family itinerary, 30
history of Paris, 14
neighborhood of, 40
St-Eustache, 14, 144–145
St-Germain l'Auxerrois, 14, 145–146
St-Germain neighborhood
history of Paris, 15
two-day itinerary, 29
St-Germain-des-Prés, 181
family itinerary, 30
history of Paris, 11
one-day itinerary, 26
two-day itinerary, 29
St-Germain-des-Prés and Luxembourg (6th arrondissement)
accommodations, 70–73
attractions, 179–182
neighborhood of, 40–41
restaurants, 114–118
shopping, 218–219
St-Gervais–St-Protais, 12, 19
Stravinsky Fountain, 149
St-Sulpice, 181–182
family itinerary, 30
two-day itinerary, 29
student travel, 293
Studio 28, 243
Studio-Théâtre, 236
subway, 281–282
summer music festivals, 241
Supersonic, 246
swimming, 199
Synagogue de la rue Pavée, 210

T
taxes, refunds on, 217, 293
taxis, 285–287
tearooms, best of, 125–126
telephones, 293
tennis, 199, 254
terrorism, 293–294
theater, 236
Théâtre de la Ville, 237
Théâtre des 2 Anes, 242
Théâtre du Châtelet, 237
Théâtre du Vieux Colombier, 236
Théâtre National de Chaillot, 237–238

Thermes de Cluny. See Musée de Cluny
three-day itinerary, 29–30
ticket lines, avoiding, 138, 155
tickets
to Disneyland Paris, 275
to Giverny, 267
obtaining, 235
to Versailles, 256–257
Tikibou, 234
time, 294
tipping in restaurants, 86
toilets, 294
Tour Montparnasse, 2
history of Paris, 20
neighborhood of, 42
tours
bicycling, 191–192
boats, 190–191, 285
buses, 8, 191
Chartres cathedral, 264
guided, 192–193
hot-air balloons, 192
sightseeing packages, 135
tower tours (Notre-Dame), 137
walking, 192, 287
Tout S'arrange, 232
tower tours (Notre-Dame), 137
toy stores, 234
trains
for day trips, 255
into Paris, 279
trams, 283
Trocadéro. See Champs-Élysées, Trocadéro, and western Paris (8th, 16th, 17th arrondissements)
Tuileries Garden, 9, 135–136
neighborhood of, 34
one-day itinerary, 27
romantic itinerary, 32
two-day itinerary, 29
two-day itinerary, 27–29

U
U.S. Customs & Border Protection, 286

V
Variétés, 218
VAT (Value Added Tax), 217
Vaux-le-Vicomte day trip, 269–271
arrival information, 269–270
candlelight tours, 269
visitor information, 270
vegetarian restaurants, 90
Velib,' 3, 22, 32, 283–284
"Venus and the Three Graces Presenting Gifts to a Young Woman," 140
"Venus de Milo," 139, 140
Versailles day trip, 255–262
arrival information, 256
Château de Versailles, 258–260
daytime shows, 258
Domaine de Marie Antoinette, 262

evening shows, 257–258
gardens and park tours, 262
palace tours, 260–262
tickets, 256–257
visitor information, 257
Via Chocolat, 230
Viaduc des Arts, neighborhood of, 39
Vicxite.A, 228
Vieux Quartier (Old Town), 266
Village St-Paul, 208, 223
vintage clothing stores, 229
visas, 294
visitor information, 294

W

waiters, rudeness of, 88
walking tours, 192, 287
    Cinemacity app, 206
    Marais, 206–214
    Montmartre, 200–206
walking up Eiffel Tower, 183
water (drinking), 294
Water Garden, 268
websites
    for foodies, 81
    hotel rates, 44
"Wedding Feast at Cana," 140
western Paris. See Champs-Élysées, Trocadéro, and western Paris (8th, 16th, 17th arrondissements)
WH Smith, 226
White Bird, 233
"The White Horse," 187
Wi-Fi, availability of, 54, 290
Wilde, Oscar, 168
wine bars, 249–250
wine shopping, 231–232
"Winged Victory of Samothrace," 139, 140
World Wars, 19–20

Z

Zadig & Voltaire, 228
Zara, 228
Zénith, 171

Accommodations

Cosmos Hotel, 62–63
Eden Lodge, 6
Eden Lodge Paris, 61–62
Ermitage Sacré-Coeur, 60
Familia Hôtel, 69
Generator Paris, 64
Grand Hôtel des Balcons, 73
Hotel Aéro, 55
Hôtel Aiglon, 76
Hôtel Alison, 56
Hôtel Arvor St Georges, 57
Hôtel Balzac, 54
Hôtel Brighton, 5, 46
Hôtel Britannique, 46
Hôtel Caron de Beaumarchais, 6, 51
Hôtel Chopin, 58

Hôtel de la Porte Dorée, 5, 63
Hôtel de La Trémoille, 54
Hôtel de L'Empereur, 74
Hôtel de Varenne, 73
Hôtel des Arts Montmartre, 61
Hôtel des Bains, 77
Hôtel des Grandes Ecoles, 69
Hôtel des Jardins du Luxembourg, 68
Hôtel des Marronniers, 72
Hôtel Design Sorbonne, 68
Hôtel du Champ de Mars, 75
Hôtel du Cygne, 47
Hôtel du Petit Moulin, 50
Hôtel Eber Mars, 74
Hôtel Eldorado, 60–61
Hôtel Jeanne d'Arc le Marais, 6, 52
Hôtel Langlois, 57
Hôtel Le Clément, 73
Hôtel Le Vert Galant, 70
Hôtel Londres Eiffel, 75
Hôtel Louison, 76
Hôtel Marignan, 70
Hôtel Muguet, 75
Hôtel Paris Bastille Boutet, 62
Hôtel Saint-Jacque, 68–69
Hôtel Saint-Louis en l'Isle, 51
Hotel Seven, 64, 68
Hôtel Signature St-Germain-des-Prés, 74
Hôtel Thérèse, 47
Hôtel Tiquetonne, 58
Hôtel Verneuil, 72
Hôtel Vivienne, 58
Jules et Jim, 51–52
L'Apostrophe, 76
Le Bristol, 57
Le Citizen, 63
Le Fouquet's Barrière, 57
Le Pavillon des Lettres, 55
Le Relais Montmartre, 60
L'Hôtel Particulier, 59
MIJE Auberge de Jeunesse, 52
Millesime Hôtel, 72
Minerve Hôtel, 69
New Orient Hôtel, 56
OFF Paris Seine, 6, 69
Pavillon de la Reine, 50
The Plaza Athénée, 57
Relais St-Germain, 5, 71
Solar Hôtel, 77
Villa Madame, 71–72

Restaurants

Aki, 89
Aki Boulangerie, 89
Andy Wahloo, 247
Angelina, 125
Arpège, 4, 119
Astier, 101, 102
Au Bascou, 91
Au Folies, 248
Au Petit Bar, 89
Au Petit Marguery, 112
Au Petit Marguery Rive Droite, 112

Au Pied de Cochon, 93
Auberge Etchegorry, 70
Benoit, 90
Biglove Caffé, 92, 104
Bistrot des Dames, 61
Bistrot Paul Bert, 4, 102–103
Bob's Bake Shop, 107
Bob's Juice Bar, 106–107
Bob's Kitchen, 107
Boco, 92
Bonjour Vietnam, 113–114
Boulangerie Joséphine, 96
Boutique yam'Tcha, 89–90
Café Charbon, 248
Café Constant, 121
Café de Flore, 20, 26, 29, 40, 126, 179
Café de la Mairie, 128
Café de la Paix, 126
Café des Musées, 91
Café Jacquemart-André, 125
Café Lucy, 160
Café Zephyr, 97–98
Canard et Champagne, 97
Champeaux, 86
Chartier, 98
Chez Georges, 96
Chez Gladines, 114
Chez Michel, 4, 105
Clamato, 5, 102
Cobéa, 122
Coinstôt Vino, 99
Cojean, 92
Comptoir Marguery, 112
Coquelicot, 31
Crêperie Saint Malo, 98, 124
Dalloyau, 124
Dans Les Landes, 113
East Mamma, 104
Eté en Pente Douce, 128
Exki, 92
Experimental Cocktail Club, 248
Georgette, 99
Grand Marché Stalingrad, 248
Higuma, 89
Hôtel du Nord, 105–106
Huîtrerie Régis, 115
Imperial Choisy, 112
Institut Suédois, 213
Jardin des Pâtes, 114
Jeanne B, 101
La Bellevilloise, 32
La Brasserie de l'Ile Saint-Louis, 86
La Cerisaie, 123
La Coupole, 42, 127
La Ferme Saint Simon, 119
La Ferrandaise, 28, 116
La Fontaine de Mars, 120
La Palette, 248
La Régalade, 123
La Tour d'Argent, 4, 112
La Tour de Montlhéry–Chez Denise, 88, 93
La Truffière, 108
Ladurée, 32, 125
L'As du Fallafel, 92, 210
Lasserre, 93
L'Assiette, 122–123

L'Avant Comptoir, 117
Lazare, 94–95
Le Bar du Plaza Athénée, 249
Le Baratin, 106
Le Bistrot du Peintre, 128
Le Boudoir, 95
Le Café du Marché, 121
Le Casse Noix, 120
Le China, 249
Le Comptoir, 71
Le Comptoir du Relais, 114–115
Le Coq Rico, 100
Le Fumoir, 32, 88
Le Grand Restaurant, 94
Le Grand Véfour, 31, 83, 143
Le Malakoff, 95
Le Nemours, 29
Le Pantruche, 97
Le Perchoir, 8, 248
Le Petit Cler, 32, 122
Le Potager du Marais, 91
Le Pré Verre, 113
Le P'tit Fernand, 26, 116
Le Relais de l'Entrecôte, 4, 30,
    98, 116–117

Le Relais Louis XIII, 115
Le Rostand, 28, 128
Le Select, 42
Le Tambour, 93
Le Verre Volé, 106
Le Wilson, 95
Le Zeyer, 128
Le Zyriab, 176
L'Ebauchoir, 104
Les Charmilles, 269
Les Deux Magots, 20, 26, 29, 40,
    127, 179
Les Papilles, 5, 113
Les Petits Plats, 123
L'Escudella, 121
L'Excuse Mogador, 99
Likafo, 112
Mandragore, 59
Mangetout, 4, 117
Marché des Enfants Rouge, 92–93
Marché St-Germain, 26
Monsieur Bleu, 162
Mosquée de Paris, 9, 31, 125–126
Noglu, 5, 99–100
Ober Mamma, 104

Outland Bar, 248
Pâtisserie Viennoise, 117
Pierre Hermé, 124
Pinxo, 32
Poilâne, 116
Publicis Drugstore Brasserie,
    95–96
Restaurant Auguste, 119–120
Restaurant Baudy, 268
Restaurant Polidor, 98, 118
Rosa Bonheur, 4, 98, 107
Rosa Bonheur Sur Seine, 107
Saturne, 97
Septime, 5, 38, 102
Septime la Cave, 102
Spring, 83
Stohrer, 124
Taverne de la Forge, 124
Tondo, 103
Udon Jubey, 89
Virtus, 104
Wepler, 100
Willi's Wine Bar, 88
Zerda Café, 108

Map List

Paris Neighborhoods   24
Right Bank West Hotels   48
Right Bank East Hotels   53
Montmartre Hotels   59
Left Bank Hotels (Eiffel Tower Area)   65
Left Bank Hotels (Latin Quarter, St-Germain,
    Montparnasse)   66
Right Bank West Restaurants   84
Right Bank East Restaurants   87
Montmartre Restaurants   101
Left Bank Restaurants (Eiffel Tower Area)   109

Left Bank Restaurants (Latin Quarter,
    Saint Germain, Montparnasse)   110
Right Bank Attractions   130
Notre-Dame Cathedral   133
Louvre   139
Père-Lachaise Cemetery   169
Left Bank Attractions   174
Montmartre Walking Tour   201
The Marais Walking Tour   207
Ile-de-France   257
Versailles   259
Chartres Cathedral   265

Photo Credits

Frommer's EasyGuide to Paris 2018, 5th Edition

Published by

FROMMER MEDIA LLC

ISBN 978-1-62887-364-1 (paper), 978-1-62887-365-8 (e-book)

Editorial Director: Pauline Frommer
Editor: Pauline Frommer
Production Editor: Heather Wilcox
Cartographer: Elizabeth Puhl
Photo Editor: Meghan Lamb
Cover Design: Dave Riedy
Versailles map data © OpenStreetMap contributors

Front cover photo: ©Samot/shutterstock.com

For information on our other products or services, see www.frommers.com.

FrommerMedia LLC also publishes its books in a variety of electronic formats. Some content that appears
in print may not be available in electronic formats.

Manufactured in the United States of America

5 4 3 2 1

ABOUT THE AUTHORS

Anna E. Brooke relocated from her native Britain to Paris in 2000 and hasn't looked back since. She is now a full-fledged bohemian, juggling life between freelance travel writing (*Frommers, Sunday New York Times Travel, Time Out Paris*, and the *Financial Times*), children's fiction, acting, and songwriting for film.

Margie Rynn has been living and writing about France for more than 16 years. The author of *Pauline Frommer's Paris*, she has also written features for several travel magazines as well as *Time Out New York* and *Yoga Journal*. In a previous New York life, she acted in a Broadway play and performed her own one-woman show. Margie is married to a kind and understanding Frenchman, and they have a lovely 14-year-old son. She lives in Paris.

ABOUT THE FROMMER TRAVEL GUIDES

For most of the past 50 years, Frommer's has been the leading series of travel guides in North America, accounting for as many as 24% of all guidebooks sold. I think I know why.

Though we hope our books are entertaining, we nevertheless deal with travel in a serious fashion. Our guidebooks have never looked on such journeys as a mere recreation, but as a far more important human function, a time of learning and introspection, an essential part of a civilized life. We stress the culture, lifestyle, history, and beliefs of the destinations we cover, and urge our readers to seek out people and new ideas as the chief rewards of travel.

We have never shied from controversy. We have, from the beginning, encouraged our authors to be intensely judgmental, critical—both pro and con—in their comments, and wholly independent. Our only clients are our readers, and we have triggered the ire of countless prominent sorts, from a tourist newspaper we called "practically worthless" (it unsuccessfully sued us) to the many rip-offs we've condemned.

And because we believe that travel should be available to everyone regardless of their incomes, we have always been cost-conscious at every level of expenditure. Though we have broadened our recommendations beyond the budget category, we insist that every lodging we include be sensibly priced. We use every form of media to assist our readers, and are particularly proud of our feisty daily website, the award-winning Frommers.com.

I have high hopes for the future of Frommer's. May these guidebooks, in all the years ahead, continue to reflect the joy of travel and the freedom that travel represents. May they always pursue a cost-conscious path, so that people of all incomes can enjoy the rewards of travel. And may they create, for both the traveler and the persons among whom we travel, a community of friends, where all human beings live in harmony and peace.

Arthur Frommer